Fall Into Freedom

Fall Into Freedom

An Affair Inspires One Woman's Search for Truth

DIANA MARIE WEITZEL

WSOL
Publishing

WSOL Publishing
P.O. Box 1121
Cardiff by the Sea, CA 92007
www.fallintofreedom.com

Manufactured in the United States of America on acid free paper.

10 9 8 7 6 5 4 3 2 1

First Edition

Publisher's Cataloging-in-Publication
(Provided by Quality Books, Inc.)

Weitzel, Diana Marie.
    Fall into freedom : an affair inspires one woman's search for truth / Diana Marie Weitzel. -- 1st. ed.
    p. cm.
    LCCN: 2005939208
    ISBN-13: 9-7809-6714480-1
    ISBN-10: 0-9671448-0-9

    1. Weitzel, Diana Marie. 2. Mate selection--Psychological aspects. 3. Man-woman relationships. 4. Spiritual biography. I. Title.

CT275.W3756A3 2006   979.4'053'092
                                QBI06-600023

Is there a flower in the garden more precious
than you?
Is there a tree that stands taller, straighter, or has more green leaves
than you?
Is there a sky or a rainbow that paints the colors more brilliantly
than you?
Is there an ocean I would love to swim in more
than you?
Would I have chosen to spend my life with
anyone else?
Would I be alive if your hearts had not told me you
needed me?
We who speak of love dedicate this book to you,
my remarkable daughters.

THANK YOU

CHARLEY AND MARIE
FOR GIVING ME THIS MIRACULOUS EXPERIENCE
CALLED LIFE AND FOR GIVING ME SO MUCH
LOVE

CONTENTS

We came from paradise to make paradise on earth.

– US

Fall Into Freedom

1

My Driving Force

What is love?

It was the most terrifying time of my life. Into the tunnel of darkness I fell. Still, in the moments my mind found peace, an inner voice let me know that as long as I let love guide me, I would somehow survive. Living became a matter of survival. Trapped like an animal in the cage of my own mind, I had to fight for my life. If my existence represented life, then my life felt like an initiation into hell. The thought of any human being having to live in such a mental torture chamber destroyed my sense of what was real. The inhuman treatment of humankind toward humankind: How do we endure it? Why do we treat others that way?

I knew three weeks after my fall that I had to write my story, my feelings, my reactions. Like an adult instinctively knows to hug a child who is crying, the crying out of my inner world because of the fear I came to live in and my sudden burst of compassion for humanity told me I must write. I wrote because I wanted to tell the world the only way for me to survive *fear* depended on living my very existence through love. Otherwise, I would find myself trapped in a place I had seen all my life. A place where people were sad, tired, angry, bitter, hateful, lost, and finally destroyed. A place where *freedom existed no more.*

When I fell, the question in my mind became my answer . . . *to be . . . or not to be. . . .*

July 17, 1987 Friday

What a beautiful summer morning it was in southern California, USA. We were an all-American family of four living in an ideal house and neighborhood. John, the man of the house, was six-foot, three-inches tall with sandy-blond hair and baby-blue eyes. At 43, he still looked like the stereotypical California youth. I had been proud to marry such a handsome man on August 13, 1969. Now 40, my long brown hair, brown eyes, and trim five-foot, six-inch frame went well with my husband's boyish good looks.

On May 4, 1971, one year and nine months after our marriage, weighing in at a healthy eight pounds, Cherisse, our first child, was born. Entering the world on September 15, 1973, two years and four months after her sister, weighing in at an equally healthy eight pounds, eleven ounces was Tamara, our second perfectly planned daughter.

Not a cloud appeared in the brilliant blue sky. It looked like you could see forever. The rolling tree-covered hills surrounding our house encapsulated us in a virtual Garden of Eden. John mixed cement in the front of the house. Single-handedly, he had landscaped almost all of our 2.6 country acres. His newest project, a large circular driveway, was turning out better than any of his previous landscaping projects.

Inside the house, I worked doing everything necessary to maintain five thousand square feet, two teenage daughters, two dogs (Mickey and Suki), one horse (Telly), two birds, and miscellaneous goldfish. My duties were never done, but no one noticed, especially me. Woman's work, while considered necessary though unimportant, I performed gladly. After all, that was *the American way.*

Summer vacation had returned for Cherisse and Tamara. Busy in their rooms doing something important as teenagers always were, our fourteen and sixteen-year-old daughters were more traditionally clean-cut than their classmates of 1987. Times had changed drastically since I had grown up. Though untrue of their personal friends, most of their peers had given up on trying to be traditional or clean-cut. As their mother, I felt my daughters were perfect. Although perfection could be debated, their exceptional mental and physical health could not.

I believed health related directly to the way people were raised, so Cherisse and Tamara were given my unquestioned respect. They were my equals and my best friends from the day they were born. Watching each daughter lead her own parade gave me great joy. My job was to guide with wisdom and honesty and support their choices. What I felt to be the most important requirement of mothering, however, came to me easily. What I did naturally was to simply be there for my children and make sure they knew they were loved.

As morning progressed into midday, so did John's consumption of beer. In the past year or so, he had started drinking earlier in the morning and consumed more liquor daily. John lived in a world distant from mine, a mental world that over the years ran further and further away from my mental world. He worked five to six days a week, leaving the house at 5:00 in the morning and returning home as late as 11:30 at night. His days off were spent working on our property from dawn until he consumed enough beer to make it bearable for him to come back into the house where he knew I would be.

Something was causing John to appear more miserable every day. His suffering, so visibly obvious, had begun to give me the feeling he wanted to die. My concern for his state of mind made no difference to John. He refused to let me get close enough to his thinking process for me to *understand* why he lived in a world filled with so much *pain*. With the exception of our noontime breaks for making love or having sex as John called it, his relentless *words* reflected mostly disgust for me.

John's words of disgust were full of daggers aimed straight toward my heart. From the beginning of our marriage, I learned to emotionally suppress my husband's daggers. Suppression blocked the pain his words threatened from penetrating my conscious thoughts.

Suppressing my emotions enabled me to defend myself without anger. Allowing no anger protected the integrity his words attempted to steal. My lack of rage, however, did not stop John. It encouraged him. Whatever defense I came up with, John never stopped trying to break my spirit.

Because we were tired of living above our financial means, our house had been up for sale for more than a year. Although moving from house to house had been ongoing throughout our marriage, selling our unfinished dream home ended all hope that John would ever stop running away from me. Before we put our house on the market, I had made the silent decision I would not continue to live in a relationship full of hate. No longer did I want a man who gave me only two choices of how to communicate: fight him or ignore him. I wanted a kind, caring companion, a friendship based on mutual support, a lover who would talk with me before, during, and after sex. I wanted intimacy. I wanted trust. I wanted . . . I just wanted more. No, I wanted it all! I wanted true, unconditional love. . . . When our house sold, I would tell John I wanted a divorce.

I stared out the window watching John stir cement in his old corroded wheelbarrow. The cement-encrusted jeans hanging just below the crack of his buttocks looked as if they were going to fall down any second. Again, feelings that told me my husband wanted to die haunted me. Regardless of my intention to leave, I fell in love with John the night we met and loved him with all my heart every day since. Yet, from the day we became husband and wife, my inner voice repeatedly warned me that our relationship contained feelings of quiet desperation.

Desperation was no longer quiet. If John wanted to die, his death was his choice. Whether John wanted to die or had some secret alternative plan, the time had come to tell him I wanted out of our marriage. John and I were given one life on earth. Each of us had to make individual decisions about how to live that life. My driving force kept telling me to start being responsible for filling my world with love and stop feeling responsible for a man whose world was full of hate.

That's how it was that Friday afternoon, July 17, 1987. John quit working early because I had planned for us to take one of those timeshare tours. We owned one timeshare week and had not discussed buying a second week. John agreed to go because we would receive a free radio just for taking the tour. On the way home he suggested we stop for a drink at a neighborhood bar. Stingers was new, cute, and friendly. I was happy to stop at Stingers. Stopping would give us a chance to talk about our relationship.

As we sat on barstools at Stingers, the expression on John's face made it clear that he had things on his mind other than our troubled marriage. A dream-like state of mind made him look as though his thoughts were in some heavenly place, a place very distant from Stinger's bar and from the man I watched mixing cement earlier. I remembered seeing that glazed flush on John's face but could not remember when.

My husband's state of mind did not especially bother me, though. Whether his face had that outward appearance of inner suffering, a snickering sneer, or a grimace of disgust for me, even this unexpected dream-like gaze, none of his mental states bothered me that much. Nothing bothered me like it bothered other people.

You see, all my life I lived in a bubble. My bubble protected me from real pain and fear. It allowed me *to be free*. My bubble was filled with *love*, and I knew with love everything would be all right. Everything had always turned out all right and it always would. My bubble of love was my driving force. My driving force of love gave me the ability to look past our troubles. It gave me an iron will that made me fearless. Fearlessness allowed my spirit to fly free. It did not matter that our marriage was in shambles. When Diana went out, Diana always went out to have fun. No, nothing bothered Diana when Diana was having fun . . . nothing until today. . . .

2

Lowering The Boom

John and I sat on tall barstools at Stingers enjoying our beers. The faces surrounding us told me I looked good in my white leather miniskirt, black leather boots, and black wool-crepe jacket. In addition, the pile of cash sitting on the bar next to my husband's beer made it clear he provided well for his wife. My bubble flying high, Diana was having fun!

While we were discussing whether or not John wanted us to buy a second timeshare week, I pondered. *We're always short of money until John decides that we should buy something.*

I sat trying to calculate John's real income when these words popped out of his mouth. "Fate is just a girl. I know she's too young for me. She's only eight years older than Cherisse, but she loves me . . . and I love her."

The electricity of those words felt like a gunshot to my brain. My mind lost its clearness, and what felt like a grenade settled in my stomach.

In the past year, John had told me in so many words that he was attracted to a twenty-four-year-old girl with blond hair and large breasts. But this girl, who according to John never wore a bra, was not the first *other woman* he had teased me about. Therefore, I assumed no more would result from this flirtation than his history of flirtations. I suppressed the shock of his words and used my bubble for denial like I always had to convince myself that my husband was not having an affair.

I told myself, *John's attraction to Fate will fade away just like the others.*

But this was the first time my husband had ever said, "I love her." *Love?*

I set my beer on the bar and insisted, "Let's go home."

John did not argue.

At home, we sat next to each other by the fireplace in the family room and he repeated, "Diana, I love Fate. It's silly. She's 19 years younger than me." In heartfelt tones he added, "I love you, too."

Using my iron will to hold on tight to my protective bubble, I heard myself righteously protect my territory. "If you want her, you'll have to let me go. You can't have both of us."

John's face flushed pink and puffed up. His eyes stared at my mouth as if they were pleading. *Help me!*

Then he began to cry. It was the first time my husband had externally expressed a terrible inner sorrow. His heart-breaking tears made me feel closer to him emotionally than I had never felt before.

I watched impassioned tears fall from his glorious powder-blue eyes and run down his puffy, pink cheeks, realizing Fate was the reason it had appeared to me he wanted to die. My husband loved two women: one he had known for one year, the other he had been married to for nearly eighteen.

I attempted to ease his exhaustive pain by holding him in my arms. Warm shivers throughout his body physically expressed the seriousness of his feelings for a woman other than me.

The weekend following that July 17th Friday, I disassociated from John's proclamation of love for another woman by attaching my security to the sincerity with which he said, "Diana, I love you, too."

I hid from his love for another woman by having fun with Cherisse and Tamara and by using tunnel vision to assure myself, *Tears represent love for me. John's merely infatuated with this girl. Real love is a growing process. My eighteen years against her one? She doesn't stand a chance!*

Repeatedly interrupting my myopic safety net, however, were John's last words that previous Friday afternoon. "I haven't had sex with her *yet*."

July 20, 1987, 8:30 A.M. Monday

Up since dawn, John mixed cement in the front of the house in his old corroded wheelbarrow. Recently, I had begun to meditate in the mornings before getting out of bed. This particular morning, a ringing telephone interrupted my peaceful meditation. I reached toward the night stand next to my bed and picked up the receiver.

An unfamiliar female voice demanded in subtle, youthful tones, "This is Beth. Let me speak to John."

My thoughts raced back to John's words. "I love Fate! We haven't had sex *yet*."

Love. . . ? Fate. . . ? Sex. . . ? Yet. . . ?

This time, as if they actually were bullets, the same words John fired into my brain at Stingers exploded. Electrical impulses flooded my brain, discharging with such startling force, my ability to think normally collapsed. This chemical reaction in my brain coursed down my spine and into what felt like every cell of my body. The grenade that had settled in my stomach turned to stone. Propelled by my entire nervous system, my body flew out of bed and toward my closet!

I nearly ripped off my pajamas and then grabbed my pink-striped leotard and sweat-suit bottoms. Hurriedly, I stepped into the leotard and stretched it up and over my shoulders. I yanked up my sweat-suit bottoms, bolted out of the master bedroom into the entrance hall, and through the front door. As I rushed down the front steps, I spotted John standing up from his wet cement mixture holding his shovel in his right hand. He watched me walk toward him as if he had been forewarned of my presence.

Attempting to externally control the onslaught of internal panic, I stated as calmly as I could, "Beth's on the telephone for you in the master bedroom."

John stuck his shovel in the cement mixture and paced toward the house. I hurried behind watching him ascend the steps I had just descended. At the front door, he kicked off his shoes and proceeded, not into the master bedroom, but directly into his office.

I continued toward the master bedroom while listening to him pick up the receiver and give his typical greeting. "This is John."

From the master bedroom, I peered through the office door. Nervous energy abruptly pervaded John's demeanor. He lowered his voice to where his next sentence was indecipherable. I scurried into the master bedroom, instantly spotting the telephone off the hook. Instinctively, I went straight to the telephone and lifted the receiver to my ear. The youthful female voice had shed its demanding tone.

The now girlish voice spoke in a sweet hush. "John, this isn't Beth. This is Fate. I need your help with my divorce. How do I get my half of my husband's ten-thousand dollars?"

John broke in somewhat sternly. "I told you not to call me here," then gently added before hanging up the phone, "I'll call you back later."

As inconspicuously as possible, I set my receiver on the hook and then turned and watched John flee toward his thickening cement. Panic grew roots in my soul. Everything about my husband's reaction to Fate's telephone call caused a holy terror that ravaged a lifetime of the person I remembered as being me. My reality became a negative of the picture postcard it used to be. My light-filled free spirit faded into dark shades of panicky fear.

Fearless Diana evaporated into thin air. Fate's voice, so real, so young, so threatening, was eating me alive. One voice, one moment in time, blew away my mind, my control, my world. In the blink of an eye, the assured girl in a bubble intent on ending a hopeless marriage turned into a human massacre. My bubble burst and fell away, leaving me unprotected. *Into the tunnel of dark unknowingness I fell.*

My initiation had begun. . . .

An abhorrent need to have my husband near took charge of every conscious thought and feeling. Almost running, I raced out the front door, down the steps, and over to John. His cement mixture had not been touched. Stuck in thickening cement, the shovel was standing straight up of its own accord. John stood staring at the mysterious beyond, focused on nothing. His face stunned me! It contained that same dream-like gaze it had at Stingers three days earlier . . . a lifetime earlier.

Powerless to regain any inner control, I soundlessly begged John's mystical beyond. *Please don't let him notice this sudden change in me.*

Struggling to appear in control of my senses, I stared into my husband's eyes and pressed for an answer. "What was that telephone call about?"

Without a sign of his previous nervous energy, he replied, "Fate's getting a divorce. She needs my advice." Then he added matter-of-factly, "Diana, I'm not happy with you."

Sheer powerlessness had replaced sheer willpower. Fear that John might leave me to telephone Fate made me frantic.

Desperation took charge of my every thought. *He senses my terror. God help me!*

Fearing earth's gravitational pull might suck me down into a big black hole, I feebly retorted, "What do you want me to do?"

Compounding my fear of being sucked into never-never land, he demanded, "I want to have more sex."

How can he say that? I asked myself, confused in every way about how he expected me to respond.

The hypocrisy of the summons for more sex was evidenced by John's outburst months earlier. One day after our noontime sex break, he went outside to the backyard to stuff poisonous bait down gopher holes. Keenly aware of how hard he had worked to stop those cute little critters from reeking havoc on our property, I walked outside to ask if he would like me to make him lunch.

Yelling down at me, he broadcast for the entire neighborhood to hear, "No man can satisfy your sexual needs, Diana."

Now, I stood searching for every possible solution to his paradoxical brainteaser. There were no solutions. He had me nailed to the cross. No matter how much evidence I could come up with to defend my point-of-view, no matter how I chose to respond, stars in my husband's eyes were still going to proclaim, *I don't want an answer from you, Diana. I'm in love with another woman.*

The boom had been lowered.

John had used love for another woman to block my escape back to safety, then pushed me further down the shaft. "You always do what you want, Diana."

Nothing was new about John's relentless, belittling words, except this was the first time I heard them with my heart. Vanished was my ability to suppress the hurt feelings caused by his words. Words penetrated my naïve consciousness like an anchor in quicksand. Hurt feelings turned into a pain I had never felt before.

As always, John left no part of my life untouched with his uninterrupted criticisms. "I have to wait in line behind all the other things you do for my turn. I don't like the chair you bought. You cut the cucumbers up too thick."

Dropped powerless into a cruel, insane world, my heart and my mind reacted to his every uttered word with unanswered questions. *Does John really care about any of these things he is judging me for? Has he convinced himself nothing I do will ever please him? What does all this mean? I cut the cucumbers up too thick! Why did I never before notice his total absence of logical reasoning? Why do I so unexpectedly feel the cutting edge of his every word?*

As I listened, I began to recognize the familiarity of the disorderly assessment of my inadequacies. No, John's words were nothing new. Since the day we married, my husband had tried to break my spirit with words.

I stood like a frightened animal next to an old corroded wheelbarrow. Animal instinct told John of my sudden helplessness to defend myself. To John, I was not human. I was prey, and John knew his prey well. Debating human rights crossed neither of our minds.

My human rights vanished the moment I heard another woman say to the man I married, "I need your help."

If I fought to be treated humanely, John would know for sure he had finally broken my spirit. He would shout, *Victory!* then leave me sinking in panic's quicksand.

Groveling for time, I turned into all those other women I had seen all my life, the ones I had *judged* as weak. "John, I'll do things to make you happy. From now on, let's shop together. That way I'll be sure you like what I buy. I'll try my best to put you first." Like those other women, my muttering exemplifyed weakness. "You must know that I've always wanted more sex."

John stared at me, not saying a word. In the silence, my thoughts spun back in time . . . remembering . . . remembering . . . how we were before . . . before I was John's bride . . . the way he looked at me

. . . the way he sang to me, "Something in the way she moves . . . attracts me like no other lover . . . something in the way she moves me. . . ."

I remembered the way those words made me feel . . . the way I loved how John moved.

Silently, my heart cried out. *John, remember when our dreams were alive? Remember how we felt?*

I stared up at the same face, the face I fell in love with. I felt the same feelings I felt way back then . . . the ones that moved me . . . the ones that made me fly . . . the ones that made John fly.

More than anything else in the world I wanted to turn back the clock so we could fly together again.

My driving force of love talked to me, screamed at me, made me want to yell out loud. *John, we can fly together again! Remember when we were in love with each other and in love with life? Wasn't it wonderful? Didn't we have it all? Oh my darling, we can have it all again!*

Another memory from those days before we married flashed before my eyes. John and I were having cocktails in a restaurant with windows facing the Newport Beach harbor. Our table overlooked the dancing night lights mirroring off the harbor's rippling water. Reflected lights cast twinkling stars in our inseparable eyes.

John's words roared into the present. "Diana, you're one in a million!"

The appreciation I received that night in 1969 ignited a fire in my soul. My spirit soared in wondrous delight. "One in a million" told me everything I wanted to know about the way my future husband felt.

My mental clock pushed forward to 1971. John and I had been married less than two years. I was pregnant with Cherisse. It was a beautiful sunny afternoon. John was angry about something silly, but I was too happy to let his mood bother me. Without the whisper of a hint, I felt a fist punch me in the stomach. Being hit by my husband while pregnant was mentally and emotionally unacceptable. Like I did with his words, I pushed my hurt feelings into the far reaches of my mind where I had kept them hidden ever since.

Recalling that unthinkable horror sparked questions left

unanswered for sixteen years. *When was it that my husband's love for me turned into so much hate he would punch a pregnant wife? He knew when we met that I had a strong-willed, free-spirited character. He knew how deeply I loved our unborn baby. The depth of love that gave me my strength of character had to have been that one-in-a-million quality he fell in love with. When did he start wanting to destroy the very thing he loved most about me?*

In my mind, it was August 13th, 1969, our wedding day. I had just arrived with my mother and sister at *The Little Chapel of the Bells* in Las Vegas, Nevada. A perfect desert day, the sun was shining, yet it was not too hot. I felt radiant in my simple white skirt and blouse as I watched my tall, handsome fiancé walk toward me. His face glistened flushed tones. His eyes stared at everything about me.

When he got close enough for me to hear, he extended a complement. "Doesn't your sister look pretty!"

I did not understand then.

I did not understand now, as I stood staring intently into my husband's moonstruck eyes. *Our eighteenth wedding anniversary is in less than a month. After all those years, why do I feel myself falling . . . falling . . . falling . . . needing desperately to understand words that began the day I became his wife.*

Praying he could read my thoughts, I implored telepathically. *John, please say something to help me understand how your love for me could turn into a hate that would cause you to spend eighteen years trying to destroy the one thing that makes me who I am?*

After waiting for what felt like forever, John finally spoke. "Let's forget the past and start fresh at Christmas."

Yet again, words with no logic pushed my unknowingness further down the shaft of soundless questions with no hope for reasonable answers. *What's supposed to happen to our relationship between now and Christmas? Christmas is five months away. Just a few minutes of trying to survive my husband's infatuation with a younger woman who is openly out to steal him away feels unbearable. Enduring five months of this fear and panic will surely kill me.*

Rather than risk hearing John's ideas about those five months, I attempted a diplomatic reconciliation. "I only want you to be nice. Your yelling at me is hard, not only for me, but for Cherisse and

Tamara."

John's reaction confirmed that I had calculated correctly about not asking to be treated with human kindness. He said nothing. Nothing needed to be said. Starry-eyed, he looked past me toward his little yellow truck. Eyes I thought would always see me as "one in a million" sparkled for someone else.

Now my soul cried out. *John, please don't go to her. Please don't do this thing to us. Don't let a ruthless young woman destroy our chance to fly together again. Don't let a stranger steal Cherisse's and Tamara's chance to see how beautiful our love can be.*

In that moment of my mental pleading, John uttered the words I feared the most. "I have to go to the store to buy some rock salt before the cement dries."

He yanked up his cement-encrusted jeans as he walked away. A very old corroded wheelbarrow caught the corner of my eye. On the ground two feet from the wheelbarrow lay a fifty-pound bag of rock salt—nearly full.

I watched John scoot into his little yellow truck. I watched his truck bounce over every inch of our long, bumpy driveway. Cement mixture after cement mixture had built that driveway. It had been one of his first landscape projects. The bumps visibly exposed his inexperience. As the little yellow truck crossed over the last patch of cement and disappeared from view, for the first time in my life I felt completely abandoned. The man who had told me a thousand times he would love me forever and ever had turned his back on me to go to another woman.

I would have begged him to stay if I thought begging would do anything except make things worse. John respected strength. He spit on weakness. He left, stripping me of all my safe places. Fate should have been my perfect out, my way to finally escape John's hateful words. Instead, fear caged the free spirit who once lived in a bubble.

Man is born free and everywhere he is in chains.

– Jean-Jacques Rousseau

3

Partners In Crime

Every second John was gone felt like hours. I paced, stared out the window, and prayed continuously that I would see his little yellow truck light up the driveway

I kept thinking, *When John comes home, I'll be able to breathe and be free again.*

What felt like a never-ending wait ended when I heard the engine of a small truck and a bumpity-bump sound coming up the driveway. From the workout room next to the driveway where I was working out, I peeked out the wood-framed glass door and saw the little yellow truck. The sigh of relief I expected, however, did not come.

When the man of the house walked through the door, he announced, "I want us to try again."

The glowing look of love John had on his face when he left glowed brighter than before. The glow was not for me. At no time had John and I ever agreed to *try*, yet he wanted us to "try again."

I did not understand.

July 21, 1987, 4:20 A.M.

The alarm went off on John's side of the bed. Another beautiful new day had arisen on an ideal house and neighborhood in southern California. John reached up and pushed the snooze button.

The impossible had come to pass. The fear and panic that began the day before did not go away while I slept. I did not wake up from a bad dream. I awoke into a nightmare. Every move my husband made was one move closer to him leaving me to go to work. His every heartbeat threatened my safety. Every inch of my aching heart needed him to roll over and tell me that yesterday was a big mistake, a silly joke, that it really did not happen. My body lay in nervous panic while he appeared unaffected, capturing his usual five or ten minutes of extra sleep.

Staring at his dozing body as if I were seeing it for the first time, I asked myself, *Does John know that being emotionally controlled by the every move of another person feels like hell?*

The alarm went off again. John slid out of bed without saying a word. I lay very still. My bed had lost its capacity to make me feel safe. Nothing felt safe except my husband's love. I heard the shower water splashing over his body, the body to which I had grown accustomed to thinking of as mine. Never before did I understand that another person's actions could have the ability to cause a hurt so deep that all happiness is swept away, a hurt that leaves nothing in its wake except an inescapable mental prison.

Buried alive inside prison walls, I mourned, *Is it possible I'm feeling the same misery I saw on John's face when he looked as if he wanted to die? Is panic the prison I had judged to be weakness? Is fear the condition of human suffering for which fearless Diana had no understanding, therefore, no forgiveness and no compassion?*

The forgiveness and compassion for my husband's suffering, absent in me just one day earlier, flowed into and became part of my panicky fear. The extremes of emotion existing simultaneously was alarming.

Flooding my thoughts came an intense desire to tell him I cared and how much I wanted to understand why he was so sad. *When John gets out of the shower, I'll tell him I know how sad he's been. I'll ask him to please stay home so we can figure out what went wrong with us.*

After John stepped out of the shower, he did not give me the chance to utter one word. He dried off and dressed in his walk-in closet located directly off the bathroom. He walked around the corner into the bedroom on my side of the bed carrying a coat hanger with a clean change of clothes.

He sat down next to me on the bed and kissed me goodbye and then strolled across the bedroom, stood in the doorway between the master bedroom and the hall, and stated flatly, "I'm going to stay in a motel tonight."

A smile lit up his face as he turned to walk away; my thoughts crawled and my stomach convulsed with an indescribable sickness. *No, no, no, I can't stand it! He's leaving me to go to work and he's not coming home tonight. How will I survive this fear and panic until tomorrow night?*

I stayed glued to my bed paralyzed by an invisible enemy.

The Big G, where John worked as a golf-professional, was an hour-and-a-half drive from our house. He traveled three hours a day and stood on his feet all day long giving golf lessons. John stuck the tee in the ground for every single ball every student hit. He did this up-and-down routine for as many as 11 hours a day. That, plus the three-hour drive, meant he slept only four to five hours a night. Yet, never once in all our married years did he take an extra set of clean clothes and tell me he was going to stay in a motel.

John's story about how he met Fate clouded into my memory. She and her sister had captured his imagination the day the two of them blazed braless into The Big G asking about golf lessons. John's excitement over the blond bombshells had prompted him to tell me about his newest infatuation.

Both *femmes fatales* acted as an aphrodisiac, although John seemed to be mesmerized by Fate. It turned out she was serious about golf, even dreamed of going on the Ladies Professional Golf Tour. Over time, Fate began taking more and more golf lessons, all from John. He told me that her husband earned very little money, so I began to wonder how a twenty-four-year-old married woman could afford so many golf lessons.

When I asked John about this, he explained, "If she makes it on the LPGA Tour, I will get credit for being her teacher. That means more students and more money for us . . . I give her free lessons."

Fate? Fate? Fate? my mind shrieked, wishing the name would vanish from the face of the earth. *Will Fate be taking golf lessons today?*

Sunlight began to filter into the bedroom. I glanced toward the window. The big, scary world outside reached in and put a death grip around my neck. I jumped out of bed, rushed over to the window, and lowered the shade. I turned around and spotted the bedroom door opened to the rest of the house. I flew across the room and closed the door. That closing would be the first time in Cherisse's and Tamara's innocent lives that I did not come out of my room early in the morning to greet their new day with a happy heart. Shut behind a closed door would be the mother who had always been there for them with unconditional love.

Shutting out the entire world, nonetheless, did not make me feel safe. Safety walked away with my husband. I climbed into bed, pulled the covers over my head, and lay in fear . . . fear of leaving my bed . . . fear of losing my husband . . . fear of another woman . . . fear of who I was . . . fear of who I was not . . . fear of asking myself one question, *Why didn't I leave John before fear imprisoned my freedom?*

The long, lonely seconds of each minute tortured me. Lacerating tears streamed from endless rivers of punishing thoughts. Morning inched into day. Day crawled into night. Night lowered me deeper and deeper down the blackened shaft until, finally, *I entered the abyss, the black pit where lost souls go.*

My soul had been terrorized. . . .

In the pit, a fire began burning in my soul. It was the second time one man had ignited a fire in my soul. The first was a fire of love. The second was a fire of fear. Both love and fear burned with a pain that reached inward to the core of my humanity. I began to beg for the horrible nightmare to stop. It did not stop. I prayed for sleep to end the agony. Sleep did not come. I dozed only to be awakened by my shell-shocked hell hole. My hell hole was filled with one word. One word devoured any hope for relief. One word left traces of all the unanswered questions from all the years. The word had been uttered that fateful Friday July 17th afternoon. The word was John's. The word was "yet."

With nowhere else to go, I went to where souls burning alive in hell's fiery pit go, to God. *God help me, please! Please make this pain go away.*

I slid my torso down the side of the bed on to my knees, cupped my hands in prayer, and sobbed. *It hurts. God, it hurts so bad. Make the hurt stop. Please make it stop.*

It did not stop.

July 22, 1987, dawn

Muted light from the rising sun shone through the lowered shade.

Thank goodness the night is over. John must be getting ready for work in his motel room. I won't have to think about "yet" anymore, I resolved, talking myself into a more positive state of mind.

My comforting resolution was short lived. Remembering the pleased stare in John's eyes as he walked out the door the previous moring shoved me back down into the abyss.

Not one quiver of guilt was in his voice or on his face when he told me he was going to stay in a motel last night, I reflected back to the previous morning. *He looked confident, happy, beaming! Was the king of the castle ready to conquer a world other than mine?*

Years of naïveté bred from the bubble of love in which I dwelled all my life had been replaced by an obsession for answers. *Why was John so happy yesterday morning? Until Fate's phone call, he appeared as though he wanted to die. Is she his way of paying me back for my lack of sympathy toward his misery? Is she the biblical eye-for-an-eye he always joked about? Has the man who said "I do" to me freed himself from suffering by revealing his secret love for someone else?*

Then it hit me. *John plunged a knife into my heart when he told me he loved another woman. I didn't realize my heart was breaking until her telephone call. The brutality of her telephoning our home caused my panic. Fate's call was more than my nervous system could tolerate. John must have noticed the meteoric collapse of fearless Diana. After his long-suffering, was the change of clothes his way of congratulating himself? Has my husband escaped his emotional prison by causing my emotional prison? Did the look on his face mean he went to Fate gladly, anxious to end "yet?"*

The knife twisted and my heart bled when it recognized truth. Thoughts of the man I married happily having sex with a woman for whom he proclaimed to love were too much for me to bear.

With no previous experience in rising out of the depths of despair, again I kneeled, cupped my hands, and prayed, but this time I gave myself over to any God who would listen. *How am I going to survive this hell? What can I do? Please help me?*

Fight the affair! was the answer I heard.

Telepathic words, like a flying sword, cut through my heart to fence with my fear and panic.

Fight? I demanded, uncupping my hands and pounding my fists against the bed. *You answer my prayers by ordering me to fight? How can a loving God tell me to fight when I'm too petrified to even get out of bed? You insult the dignity of my pain! You attack the honorability of my suffering!*

Enraged and deflated by a God with impossible solutions, my thoughts lashed back. *How can I fight with no power, no self?*

There was no answer.

With no God to help my pain, no self to pick me up, no sleep to refresh my exhaustion, endless crying to compound my panic, and obsessive questions giving me answers I hated, at last, conscious thought and emotion released their stranglehold. Still on my knees, my body went limp and fell forward against the bed. My mind lapsed into a sea of mothingness, a *void*.

I did not understand the void. I did not care to understand the void. The pain stopped. Fear stopped. Panic stopped. Obsessive thinking stopped. The void felt simply like *being*. I yielded all conscious effort to wherever the void wanted to take my state of being.

I felt my body alone on the floor leaning against the bed. Then, I felt I was not alone. Companionship entered my state of being, spiritual companionship. Into the room, just above the floor, had floated an invisible being of light. This light being, that felt all loving and all knowing, stopped a little behind my right shoulder, lowered itself, then filtered into and became one with my being. A tremendous power existed in that force of spiritual energy. *Not only did the light being make me feel it was a part of me, it made me feel that I was a part of it, and it dwelled not only in my room, but everywhere.*

The light of spirit had broken throught the darkness of fear. . . .

Momentarily, I had a negative thought. In that instant of negativity, my spiritual companionship vanished. As instantly as it appeared, the spirit disappeared. Once more I felt myself kneeling on the floor alone. The fear that had incapacitated my visible reality returned. Fear returned. Panic returned. Obsessive thinking returned. Again, my mental prison burried alive.

The hours of my second day behind prison walls eeked by. Demons burned through prison walls. Every second became a new second to survive demons. *These ambassadors of Satan were ushered in by the dark side of my truth; demons were my initiatory companions.*

Satan's fiery emissaries had initiated my trial by fire. . . .

Satan's fire demanded that I seek my demons. My demons were all the unanswered questions from all the years. Demons were telling me that I would find the answer to why I didn't leave John before fear imprisoned my freedom by seeking the answers to one question, *Am I the person I want to be?*

My initiatory journey was to seek and find my truth. . . .

The sky fell dark. Day two in my burial room ended. The hour for John to return home had inched its way forward, then passed slowly into the depths of not knowing where he was or what he was doing. Contrary to all my assumptions, all those days I watched him mixing cement, John's desperation had never been quiet.

My unwillingness to understand the magnitude of pain lying beneath the surface of a man who would ask his fiancé on her wedding day, "Doesn't your sister look pretty?" rendered me, not John, the one who had been quietly desperate since the day we married.

As a result of my choosing not to seek deeper meanings all the years since my wedding day, my desperation was no longer quiet. I tried to think of anything except my husband making love with another woman, but my husband having sex with another woman was all I could think about. The flicker of my soul's driving force of love had shaken hands with the flames of Satan's driving force of fear.

July 22, 1987, later in the day

I do not know what time I dozed off, but I awoke to unrelenting panic. One more time I prayed. It did not matter to whom or what I prayed anymore because prayer purged my pain. Demons of unanswered questions poured into my thoughts and then released themselves in gushes of torrential, tearful outbursts.

When I could take the wounding prayer no longer, I attempted to meditate. Meditation failed to stop obsessions of John and Fate in bed together. I returned to prayer. I felt prayerful love, but even prayerful love did nothing to release me from thoughts of another woman stealing my husband from me forever.

I found myself on my knees, this time begging for answers. *Help me, help me, help me! Tell me why this is happening. Why can't I be the fearless person I used to be? Who is this pathetic stranger in my body?*

No answers came. Nothing was working. I was exhausted. Giving myself over to a sea of nothingness had been the only thing that stopped the pain. I pulled my body up off the floor, lay in bed on my back, closed my eyes, and let go of all thought. I entered the void.

A second time the void worked! This void felt like a spontaneous meditation, except conscious thinking and feeling separated from me to a greater degree than in any of my previous meditations. With my consciousness at rest, incessant, terrorized thinking flowed into another place. Fear and panic were gone, completely dispersed. The entirety of my demolished ego disassociated from me, an instantaneous rising out of the pit of darkness. Every painful emotion having to do with my attachment to matter ceased to exist.

Then, the veil between my visible world and the void's invisible world dissolved, and the core of my being ascended further into the void. Ascension expanded my consciousness until it merged with universal consciousness. The sea of nothingness in which my mind floated became a sea of intelligence and love in which my mind swam. We were one mind, a mind that felt both quiet and dynamic. From this sea of wisdom, the psychological and spiritual understandings my prayers sought came pouring forth:

Diana, John has been your tormentor for nearly eighteen years. From the day you were married, his words tore away at your being, intricately cutting up each and every detail of your life like a surgeon with a scalpel. He took every precaution to make sure that each word sounded like truth instead of the means to an end. When he finished degrading you, he cut away at your family and friends. John's words were convincing you that no one who had ever played a meaningful part in your life had any worth. To worthlessness, your husband added fear when he repeated over and over, "Diana, you will never be able to do anything in the real world. When I'm done with you, I'm going send you back to Santa Ana." Your belief that John's words were not affecting you in a negative way was an illusion. Over the years, you were slowly brainwashed into believing you were not worth anything without a man. Fear of living without your husband gradually rooted in your subconscious where your conscious mind kept it hidden. Your subconscious fears and who caused them were slowly eating away at you from the inside out.

My eyes were closed, but I felt more awake in this unseen universe than in my seen universe. The knowledge I had received felt profoundly correct. The information was a revelation. Revelations were awakening me to truths I had kept sleeping in the far reaches of my mind. The void felt as if I were viewing myself from the outside in. All my thoughts and feelings were an objective experience. I had been in complete denial of how John's words affected me. Because falling into the void stopped conscious thought and painful emotion, the need for denial vanished. With denial at rest, my repressions streamed forth from my subconscious mind and flowed directly into my conscious mind. *Forcing me out of denial by awakening my conscious mind to my truth, universal consciousness was making my subconscious conscious!*

Revelations were transforming me from the darkness of unknowing to the light of knowing. . . .

Suppressing my *hurt feelings* and pushing them into my subconscious allowed me to consciously deny my feelings had ever been deeply hurt. Denial of those dark feelings blocked my conscious thoughts from knowing I had a *dark side*. Staying in denial prevented hurt feelings from penetrating my light-filled bubble. The problem was the years of words that caused years of hurt feelings piled up into one huge subconscious dagger. Stockpiling relentless verbal violence and random acts of physical violence injured my sense of security so deeply that subconsciously I began to feel *fear*.

Over time, the piling up of fear conditioned my subconscious to think I would have no meaning in John's *real world*. Meaning came from Cherisse and Tamara, Mickey and Suke (our dogs), and everything I accomplished that involved our home and property. Above all, Cherisse's and Tamara's lives and their unconditional love gave my life both meaning and purpose. Nevertheless, by the time I consciously decided I would no longer tolerate a marriage full of hate, the courage to leave was buried beneath a stockpile of words that caused me to fear that in the real world I was *worthless*.

The sea of intelligence and love in which my mind swam had revealed that staying married had been testimony to my truth. *Not leaving John* was a *symptom* that fear was very much awake in my subconscious. Conscious *denial* of fear had *masked* the *truth* that, since the day we married, my free spirit was slowly being *conditioned* out of me by my husband's words. Denial that the love in my soul no longer felt completely free to guide my life, that my subconscious fear was blocking Diana's fearless love, was slowly eating away at me from the inside out. Deeply rooted in not leaving John was the accumulation of a fear that had gradually been imprisoning my driving force. *Fear, the symptom of my soul's loss of freedom, had been played out on the grand stage of not leaving John.*

The primal fire of my truth had been lit. . . .

Every detail of the amazing revelations streaming into my consciousness enveloped the totality of my being! Neither time nor space existed in my oneness with universal consciousness, nor did I care what time it was or what space I was in, I felt so psychologically and spiritually nourished. Answers were being handed to me on the silver platter of meditation, and I wanted nothing more than for the answers to continue.

Suddenly a story John told me about his childhood entered my state of spiritual being. Nearly every day when John's father came home from work, he would force John and his brother, Bobby, to box each other. John Sr. made his sons fight until one son defeated the other son. There always had to be a winner. Therefore, there was always a loser.

John's voice cracked as he described these boxing matches. "I won in the summer when Bobby and I boxed in the backyard because I could wear him down by outrunning him. In the winter, when it was too cold to box in the backyard, Dad made us box in the garage. In the garage, there wasn't enough room for me to outrun Bobby. Being one year older, my brother was bigger and stronger than I. He would trap me in the corner, overpower me, and beat me up."

The heart-wrenching cracking in John's voice brought his suffering to life. "On days when Dad did not make us box each other, he beat us up himself. I hurt more when I watched Bobby get hit than when my dad hit me."

John spent his childhood fighting his heart out to defeat and be defeated by the brother he loved, or get beaten up and watch his brother get beaten up by the father he loved.

Meditation's void of judgment made it easy to understand the underlying meaning of John's story. Every time John Sr. used *physical violence* against his sons, John's feelings were hurt. Because he was so young when the physical violence began, and the violence continued for so many years, John was unable to suppress his hurt feelings and hide them in his subconscious as I did when I denied how he hurt my feelings. Since children associate their parents with love, having his feelings hurt by his father *taught* John to associate hurt feelings with love. This early association conditioned John to think love and *pain* were emotionally inseparable.

The inseparability of love and pain caused John to *fear* that love was always going to beat up his feelings. But fear was unacceptable to the boy and not tolerated for males in American society. Though unable to deny hurt feelings, pressured by the world around him, John was able to suppress fear. His conscious mind pushed fear of love into his subconscious where those dark feelings had been buried ever since. Consequently, John's consciousness knew he was sad, but he lived in *denial* that he had a subconscious *dark side* filled with fear.

Trouble ensued! As the crack in John's voice had foretold when he recited his boxing story, his heart got in the way of denial. His heart starved to love and be loved without feeling fear. His heart loathed fighting. Moreover, it loathed seeing someone he loved getting hit. Although the love in his heart did battle with fear, love was buried under stockpiles of hurt feelings. That made the subconscious fear that he denied more powerful than the conscious love in his heart. In other words, fear had become more powerful than love. *The love in John's heart was imprisoned by the fear in John's heart.* The controlling power of fear took the form of a *false personality.* This false John was a soulless character called *ego.* John wore ego like a *mask.* Ego masked fear. John's mask of ego was fearless. Fearlessness hid fear behind this ego mask. Beneath John's fearless mask, the boy's fear of love enslaved the man's freedom to love fearlessly. When feelings of love got too close, ego pushed love away by doing what it was taught to do—fight.

Understanding that my husband's hostility was a mask that hid a boy's fear of love answered so many of my questions. I lay in bed enraptured by the information I was receiving. I did not attempt one thought that might interfere with what I was learning.

As a boy, years of hurt feelings broke John's heart into little pieces. Those pieces, having never been put back together, told the tale of a sad man. Hostility was testimony of a boy's unmet need for unconditional love, the unconditional love that gives a man freedom to retain his natural-born instinct to love and be loved, the depth of love that gives the soul a sense of value. The soul's sense of value that grows from being loved without condition had been beaten out of John.

Remarkably, hope had not! Not able to deny his heart's desire with every breath he took, John sought to love and be loved. He left home at seventeen and began to search for love without fear. He looked to the outside world to set him free from the battles within. What he found was a world fighting its own battles—bigger battles—Vietnam battles.

After enlisting in the Navy and being shipped to Vietnam, among other horrors John witnessed first hand was the death of Hendershot, his best friend. Positioned just off the Vietnam coast, John's battleship was waging a war at sea. Hendershot pulled an injured, screaming Vietnamese man up the side of the ship. When the Vietnamese was safely aboard, he pulled out a knife and slit Hendershot's face and throat. John was helpless to do anything but watch his best friend die. He told me this gentle soul had the most beautiful face he had ever seen on a man.

In the most vehement way, witnessing his friend's cold-blooded death by the hand of another human being did battle with John's search for love without the fear of having his feelings hurt. Like in his little world, in the bigger world, the fear of love took control of his heart's desire to love fearlessly.

No less orchestrated than his father's breaking his heart with boxing matches, and no less choreographed than John's beating up my heart with words, the *politics of war* had scripted *fear* into the theater of war. Staged political *drama* had taught John to think of other human beings as the *evil enemy*. Seeing his friend murdered by the enemy had set the stage to kill John's hope for fearless love. *Hate-and-kill-the-enemy ideology* had produced in John's mind the belief that human beings could be *born of evil nature*. *Born bad* escalated John's inner war between love and fear. War damned all the broken pieces of his heart by instilling *hate*, not love, as *the way* to fight fear. Serving his country in the Vietnam War convinced John's ego that to survive fear, hate was a much more powerful tool than love.

Incredibly, even after a four-and-one-half-year stint in the Navy, hate had not completely blackened the light of love in John's heart. Though a short failed marriage took place while John was on leave from the Navy, it ended after his honorable discharge. Starving for female companionship, once again, John's heart did battle with his ego. One starry night in a Newport Beach restaurant, I walked across a crowded room and straight up to one of the most beautiful men I had ever seen. Wearing a red alpaca sweater and white pants and shoes, John stood shouldered by two bleached-blond women. In that instant of our meeting, my future husband's heart recognized my bubble and the girl in the bubble. She was a person who, by some miracle, had retained that childlike freedom of spirit to fearlessly approach love. Diana possessed that one-in-a-million quality for which John's heart had forever searched, the freedom of her soul to be her driving force.

At first, the freedom with which Diana loved John made his heart fly. His heart thought Diana's driving force had set his heart free. As time passed, however, his heart realized that Diana's freedom to love fearlessly made John's ego feel fear. Recapturing love without fear was not to be found through Diana, and John was angry.

But alas! The fearless anger that came from John's ego made him fly higher than the fearless love that came from Diana's soul. To continue flying high, John did what his world had taught him to do: employ his fists and his voice as weapons to kill the soul he could not take for his own. He used his fists sparingly but created verbal boxing matches on a regular basis. As a reason to fight, he engaged the enemy with the *politics of war. Born of evil nature* was his warring strategy to *hate the enemy.* By thinking of Diana as *born bad,* he allowed himself to say violent words that devalued her humanity. His ego reasoned that dehumanizing a woman with words would easily break her spirit.

Oneness with universal consciousness was taking me more and more profoundly into meanings I had never before understood. John's hateful words were an external reflection of terrifying inner sorrows. Compounded by the Vietnam War, the roots of those verbal swords dug deep down into his boyhood conditioning to kill or be killed. By the time John met me and his heart felt love, the power of his conditioned subconscious made him incapable of feeling love without feeling fear. To deny fear, John's ego took control of his conscious way of reacting to his love for me. Ego knew that fighting would mask fear, so ego found reasons to be angry. *Anger, a symptom of fear conditioning,* gave John a reason to hate me. Hate justified fighting.

Again, trouble ensued; this time his troubles multiplied. At first, fighting the one he loved felt so familiar, so right. Fighting made his ego fly higher than his love for Diana. Nevertheless, when the relief achieved with one fight wore off, fear of love returned, making a fight-fix necessary. Inevitably, at the end of every fight, his heart had still been beaten up. Ego had failed to defeat either love or fear, so ego began to think it would die. If ego died, his subconscious would become conscious. That meant John would have to face, head-on, both fear and a lifetime of hurt feelings that caused his fear, and John would do anything not to come face to face with his truth. The impending death of ego made him desperate to beat up and defeat love.

Desperation waited until one hour before the man vowed "I do" in *The Little Chapel of The Bells* in Las Vegas, Nevada, for his driving force of fear to initiate a war with Diana's driving force of love. So, how was it possible that a person with a driving force of love could fall in love with a person with a driving force of fear? As it turned out, by employing challenging dialogue as a means to egg Diana into fiery conversation, John had married the right girl after all! Debate came naturally for his bride.

Whether it was my father's childhood as the son of a Naval Captain and French mother, or his experiences in World War II and The Korean War, Charles William Weitzel Jr., a USMC pilot for twenty-two years, loved challenging, upbeat dialogue. He saw every minute of life as an opportunity to seize the moment to do the things he loved, and Daddy loved to talk. To describe Daddy as an extravert would be an understatement. Beyond an inkling of a doubt, his maverick character forged a fun-filled life for the Weitzel family, especially me.

Daddy's personality sealed my life as one ongoing adventure. Absent in our home was the inertia present in other homes. Mundane did not exist. To add interest to adventure, the Marine Corps transferred Daddy every year or two, giving Daddy, Mother, my sister Susan, and me more than an abundance of new environments to keep life exciting. When my father was not on-duty at home or abroad, new environments proved to be one of Daddy's cues to initiate thrill-seeking conversation to fire me up, making me the person in the family designated to search my imagination for ideas.

Perpetually aimed at humor with farcical queries such as, "What's the most important thing about the bull fights?" or, "What makes the big ball roll?" our verbal exchanges were never boring or serious and nearly always made me feel valued. Invariably, both obvious and hidden solutions could be found to these oddly Zen-like queries.

Perhaps, because he raised me as the son he never had, while simultaneously protecting me from "the jungle," Daddy's eager participation in my life gave my personality qualities unlike other girls growing up in America.

The everyday adventure of lively discussions between Daddy and me taught me to have an assertive, confident character. From our challenging yet upbeat way of communicating, I learned the value and the fun of thought-provoking interaction. Not only did I love the comradery that grew from debate, I also loved debating an idea from opposing points of view to prove a point. Even if the point was just to have a good laugh, debating made me fly. By the time I met John, the take-a-bite-out-of-life intercourse I loved had become part of my learned instinct. Fearless verbal debate was part of my . . . *fun.*

While John courted me, our upbeat way of communicating felt so familiar, so right. I had found another comrade in the ongoing adventure of thought-provoking dialogue. In addition to his tireless, red-blooded instincts, John's style of talking contained a humorous twist similar to Daddy's. Being like Daddy made me fly and flying was . . . *fun.* True to my style, I had *fun* discussing any topic freely and fearlessly.

On our wedding day, John caught me off guard with his rhetorical question, "Doesn't your sister look pretty?"

Complimenting my sister left me speechless. It was neither a direct criticism of me nor a compliment to me. Indirectly, his question minimized my appearance. Masked devaluations had never taken place during our courtship. Incomprehensibly inappropriate, his question was decidedly not humorous, exciting, or adventurous. It was nothing remotely similar to any queries we shared while dating. Instead of looking for the underlying motive to his disarmingly offensive words, I pushed them out of my mind by defensively arming myself with the freedom of speech Daddy taught me to value.

After that first subtle humiliation, whatever hurtful words John threw at me, I would use the skill Daddy had taught me. I blocked his negative position by finding a positive point of view that defended my position. No matter what the cost, I asserted my ability to speak freely and fearlessly, value my position, and not quit until I felt I had proved my point.

True, on the surface John and I were a perfect study of opposites attracting. I entered the partnership of marriage with the obvious intention of having a fun-filled love affair, and John entered marriage with the hidden intention of having a fight-filled love affair. Underlying our polarity of objectives, nonetheless, my fun-filled propensity to debate until the end fit perfectly with John's fear-filled predisposition to fight to the end. His way of communicating was to attack using hateful reasons to start a fight. My way of communicating was to defend using loving reasons to prove a point. My learned love for debate fed right into the hideous deteriorating drama of a man searching for the pieces of his broken heart. Unknowingly, I was debating the pieces of a little boy who had fought his heart out to defeat the fear of love, as well as a man who believed there always had to be a winner. Therefore, there was always a loser.

After years of falling prey to his negative point of view by defending my positive point of view, John began saying, "Diana, you're too tough. You always win."

Being classified "winner" shocked unwitting Diana, so I justified having the last word by thinking, *Making a logical point represents the best solution to a problem, not winning a fight. The point is an exchange of ideas to reach a conclusion even if our conclusions differ. Anyway, he can't be serious. What does he think I've won?*

What I had won was denial. No matter what rational explanation I could come up with to convince myself that a positive attitude was better than a negative one, our debates did not solve any of our problems. Our debates compounded our problems. John was right. Our way of responding to each other set up competition, and competition was a fight. John attacked. I defended. Attack and defend meant, in John's mind, I had always been the winner. Therefore, he was always the loser.

In the end, however, it was not my superior debating skills that defeated my partner. Because I had a father who nurtured my natural born sense of value, and John had a father who beat up his natural born sence of value, what defeated my accomplice was that I valued myself and he did not value himself. When John started a fight, he was not expecting an *assertive, confident adversary*, especially while doing battle with a woman. That kind of strength in combat was reserved *for men only*. His inability to control my emotions drove his emotions out of control. At the end of every debate, my iron will intensified John's desperation a little more, making him feel he had been defeated. When his battle to ease his fear ended, because John did not feel valued, all those broken pieces of a boy's heart were what I had beaten up.

Again, John was right. I always won. But what I won was the denial that my childhood conditioning was just as powerful as John's childhood conditioning; I won the denial that I used my debating skill to defeat my partner; and I won the denial that winning made my ego fly just as high as fighting made John's ego fly. In the end, I did win, every single time. I won the denial that my character defeated my husband's character, and defeating his character threatened his ego. Because threatening his ego was a life or death issue of his false personality, defeating my husband turned his love for me into hate, and *hate was what went wrong with us.*

Yes, John and I were perfect partners . . . perfect partners in the crime of denial. Denial fed the illusion there was integrity in the fun of winning and nobility in the pain of losing. Denial fed the illusion that our way of communicating was not beating up each other's feelings. Denial fed the illusion that our way of attack and defend was not beating up our own feelings. Denial created an illusive drama that masked the truth. In our glorified ability to be perfect partners in the crime of denial, our way of communicating not only answered the question of what went wrong with us, it also answered the question of why I did not leave before fear chained my freedom. Fear chained my freedom because . . . *I was not the person I wanted to be.*

Behavior is shaped and maintained by its consequences.

– B. F. Skinner

4

Pieces To The Puzzle

July 23, 1987, just before dawn

What should have felt like the dark, tragic truth, instead felt like a bright light awakening me to the reasons why John and I fell in love and why his love for me turned into hate. How much longer my nervous system could have survived my crisis of fear and panic, I did not know. I did know that my descent into the primal fire of my breakdown was the prime mover of my ascent into the meditation that was breaking through my denials. My desire to seek the *understanding* that went with my sudden burst of *forgiveness and compassion* was instrumental in penetrating the veil of illusion that I had been the person I wanted to be.

By going into a spontaneous meditation, my mind transcended conscious reality. All conscious thought slipped into a dimension of pure intelligence and unconditional love. Every aspect of who I was became part of a sea of wisdom. My soul flowed with *universal soul,* my mind with *universal mind.* As one spirit, one mind, this sea of all-knowingness was piecing together the puzzle of my relationship with John and why I did not leave him before fear chained my freedom.

Given to me was the profound understanding that if I did not come face to face with the reasons my soul had been terrorized, I would never again feel free. The void had made it clear that recorded in radiant oneness was the history of everything that had ever happened to me. Every thought, word, and deed, every denied emotion, and every illusion awaited meditative review. *The dimensional shift had rendered a quantum leap in both the scholarship of my psychological knowledge and the evolution of my spiritual knowing.*

The union of human and divine was awakening my unenlightened consciousness to enlightened consciousness. . . .

I remembered hearing that every atom in the human body was the exact replica of the universe, a miniature solar system of electrons spiraling a nucleus like planets around the sun. Contained in each atom was all the information that had ever been. Quantum physics had found that everything in the known solar systems was made out of the same atoms, bodies of atomic energy differentiating themselves by frequency and pattern. Filled with *revelations*, meditation was showing me that my body confirmed scientific findings. For when my consciousness ascended into this dimension of higher frequency, dispersing the clutter of ego, both knowledge and knowingness were inescapable. Since the physical self and universal self were made out of the exact same atoms, discovery of truth was an eventual certainty, not only for me, but for everybody.

To my happy surprise, with truth came the solution to every mystery. The loving frequency of the union of human and divine made me feel so safe in the resolution of each mysterious behavior, I found myself a willing participant in seeking, finding, and understanding the thoughts, words, and deeds that made John and I partners in the crime of denial. By making my subconscious conscious, meditation was ripping away one denial at a time, helping me see how we had been struggling to hold on to past sorrows at the cost of present happiness. Unmasked were secret thoughts and feelings to which our marriage had become a slave, those repressed thoughts and feelings harvesting the ongoing drama of our marriage.

A higher consciousness was making my consciousness aware that *the seeking determined the finding of truth.* All the repressed thoughts and feelings that caused my fear had to be revealed to be healed. Revealing then purifying repressions with understanding, forgiveness, and compassion was the initiatory journey to becoming the person I wanted to be. I learned how John's subconscious had turned on the switch to his conditioning the day we married and started our cold war. The very day we became bride and groom, John's words jump-started my conditioning. Our marriage initiated a partnership in the mutual denial of hurt feelings. The win/lose battles making us both fly were really lose/lose battles. Attack and defend sowed the seeds of neither integrity nor nobility. Instead, it recreated and compounded the hurt feelings our egos were keeping secret. Responding to each other with *attack and defend* was a *symptom* of a giant *shadow* hovering over our marriage. Hurt feelings, or the *root cause* of those symptoms, were the *pieces to the puzzle* of our shadow. It was necessary for me to seek, find, and understand those roots for the symptoms to go away.

The roots of our mysterious shadow that had been ebbing and flowing into my consciousness in waves energized more questions. *How many pieces are there to the puzzle of John's and Diana's shadow? How many of those pieces were caused by our childhood conditioning, and how many resulted from the adult symptoms of that conditioning? Why did John's mother not rescue her sons from their father and save them from the beatings? How could she permit those acts of physical violence in her own backyard? Did she not know her children were crying out for her help?*

Immediately after I telepathically asked those questions, answers flowed into my consciousness from the annals of the history living in universal consciousness. Into my mind rushed a conversation between John's mother and myself not long after John and I were married.

While my mother-in-law and I were sitting on the sofa in her small, clean home, she casually mentioned, "When John was three-years-old, he took his older brother and walked in the snow four miles from home. His hyperactive energy always wore me out. Everyday when the boys' father came home from work, I gave them to him to punish."

The first time she told me that story, my thoughts were filled with esteem. *That's John, with his amazing energy!*

Revisiting my mother-in-law's memoir from a dimension of greater wisdom revolutionized my interpretation. John had led his older brother as far away from home as possible in hopes of escaping the beating ordeal to come. From her explicit remarks, every day John's mother sent a small child to a man she knew would beat him up. That particular day, John was beaten up for two of his most extraordinary gifts: enormous energy and instinctual initiative. John's parents judged his energy and individuality as something to be punished rather than applauded. Sadly, when John was only three-years-old, getting punished for being himself had already become a sure thing.

In my altered state of consciousness, I understood that the ordeal awaiting John when he returned home from the snow epitomized inhuman treatment. Rather than celebrate *yes* to their son's natural instincts by nurturing his search for the meaning and purpose of his life, John's parents saluted *no* by punishing those soul instincts. *Punishment* crucified the power of John's soul by nailing it to the cross of a power other than his own power. Over time, punishment would cause his learned instinct to kill or be killed by the enemy stronger than his soul instinct to love and be loved.

Stealing the power of their child's soul with punishment was something I did not understand until I was given the next piece to our puzzle. . . .

Being Catholic, both John's mother and father were raised according to standards set into place hundreds of years before they were born. Over the centuries, these standards became traditions. *Traditional standards* were religious rules rooted in doctrine invented by the patriarch. The patriarch was the orthodox Roman Catholic and Christian churches and the aristocracy (the government/military of the time). Traditional standards were based on a *hierarchical system* where all the power was concentrated at the top. An elite group of all male leaders held the power to control the masses.

Because the patriarchs were in *power*, they too were in the *money*. This tiny elite class had more money than the collective lower classes. Naturally, the number one most important mission of those at the top was to maintain the *status quo* of those at the bottom. Mortalizing the power of the many necessitated immortalizing the power of the few. Traditionalizing elitist power required religious rules that would produce, on a massive scale, a *system of control*. The goal of this system of control was to produce *mind dependence*. To institute mind dependence, the patriarch had to cover up individual meaning and purpose with *ignorance and fear*. Standardizing ignorance and fear was for the sole purpose of making permanent the wealth of the few. For buildings, positions, and privileges, it was the *politics of power*, not God, that drove these men to invent doctrine!

To lay the foundation of a new tradition of standards, the government sector commissioned the church sector to translate a spiritual book about love into a material book about fear. The book was titled *The Holy Bible*. The bishops cut, pasted, and translated the bible story until it voiced fear. But fearful traditional standards necessitated ignorance of the truth that the original nature of humanity is spiritual. Thus, missionaries were sent far and wide to spread their newly revised Catholic religion. Any individual who did not adopt this new doctrine as their faith was dangerous to the survival of the church. For disbelieving, thousands were tortured and/or killed. Tyranny and murder, however, were not enough to traditionalize the patriarchs' wealth and power. To ensure religious mind control, the church divorced itself from scholarly and spiritual systems gathered from millennia of initiatory experience. The church cut itself off from all knowledge of the ancient world by destroying great civilizations, traditions, artifacts, and scholarly works written throughout the ages. They continued their destruction until nothing was left to study except their revised bible.

The words in the bible were called scripture. Scripture was taught to be the one and only written word of God, and scripture was to be interpreted by church fathers and no one else. Not allowing individuals the power of *interpretation* gave rise to *psychological and spiritual powerlessness*. Powerlessness, in turn, gave rise to *psychological and spiritual dependence on church doctrine*. In other words, powerlessness produced dependence and dependence produced ignorance.

Over time, the loss of independent thinking literally embodied itself in Catholics and Christians far and wide. The evolution of mass dependence on the church to interpret the bible story fulfilled the patriarchs' mission. Doctrine gained control over the collective body of the church. Collective control was passed down from generation to generation, gradually universalizing the power *of* the patriarch, *by* the patriarch, and *for* the patriarch.

To universalize the power of religious politics by institutionalizing traditional standards, the fathers fathered scripture as follows: Scripture was written as one long continuing story. As the story goes, God was the Creator, the cause of all material existence. God, a masculine figure, created earth and called earth Paradise. In Paradise grew a garden. To live in the *Father's* garden, God created *man.*

God named man Adam. Adam soon grew lonely, so he sacrificed a rib. With Adam's sacrificial rib, God created woman. *He* called woman Eve. In the garden of Paradise grew a tree. On the tree grew fruit. Fruit contained God's *knowledge of good and evil.* God forbade Adam from eating the fruit because God lived in heaven and was made out of divine nature, and Adam lived on earth and was made out of human nature. Adam obeyed God.

One day a serpent came into the garden. The serpent seduced in Eve a passion for the forbidden fruit saying that if she ate the fruit she would be wise like God, knowing good from evil. Desiring to have God's knowledge, Eve partook of the forbidden fruit. By taking a bite out of a piece of fruit, Eve disobeyed God. After eating the fruit, Eve seduced in Adam a passion for forbidden knowledge. As a result of Eve's passionate seduction, Adam, too, ate forbidden fruit, disobeying God.

For the Roman Catholic Church to create fear and ignorance, this is how the garden story was interpreted: Eating forbidden fruit was *the first original sin.* Because Adam's sin was universalized to be humanity's sin, having *personal knowledge of God's truth about good and evil* ushered in the *fall of humanity.* Original sin turned the garden of Paradise into the garden of evil. The fall doomed humankind to be *born in sin,* and women's passion was to *blame.* Since the sin of Adam and the passion of Eve spoiled God's perfect garden, God judged and punished both sexual passion and the passion for personal knowledge of God's truth, plus any thought, word, or deed the church determined to be a sin.

*All words in *The Holy Bible* that refer to God as a male figure, such as "Father" were originally the word "One." The first bible, *The Old Testament,* written in 1850 B.C., was later translated to Aramaic, then Greek, then Latin, then English, plus numerous other languages. In each translation, thousands of words were mistranslated, obscuring the deeper meaning of scripture. For example, in many incidences the word "soul" was changed to the word "life," which materialized spiritual meanings. *The New Testament,* completed somewhere between 45 to 95 A.D., was first written in Greek. The fall into original sin was not *invented* until the 4th century by Saint Augustine, when he found his passion for the spoils of wealth and power over the masses too intoxicating to vanquish. The phrases "original sin" and "the fall" were not in St. Augustine's Greek bible. They were his personal interpretation of the meaning of the garden story, which demonstrates how one voice can change the world. St. Augustine lied for wealth and power. Over time, his lies became truth and truth became lies.*

A parlor game for a church and state elite who feared their fall from power, the fictitious fall into original sin destined the individual search for divine knowing, which comes from a direct flow of information between the mind and soul, to be judged and punished as a sin by a hateful, vengeful God. A judgmental God gave God evil qualities. Original sin gave the soul evil qualities. *The fall created both fear of God and fear of the soul.* St. Augustine's rendition of the garden story crucified the living soul of the Catholic and Christian multitude. A deeply spiritual story turned into a shallow materialistic story that taught all believers never to go deeper than surface thinking, for deeper thinking would wreak the wrath of God upon the soul's connection to the mind.

The fall into original sin fated the soul *not to be. . . .* Bringing about the true fall of humanity, the corruption and incompetence of patriarchal power passed *sinful predetermination* down through the generations. God-fearing men and women taught their children that they were born in sin. Ignorant that the soul was the incarnation of God's truth, generations of parents conditioned their children to fear God's punishment if they did not obey a spiritual power other than their own spiritual power. An outside voice taught millions of children to believe that listening to their inner voice would cause eternal torment. Brainwashed to have blind faith that the church alone held intermediary power to save them from a sin they could never escape, the faithful's ignorance and fear became the new *status quo.*

To see no evil, hear no evil, and speak no evil, millions of individuals paid what little money they could afford to the church to be saved from sin. The church, in turn, gave millions of dollars to the aristocracy to Christianize government policy. Conspiring together, churchmen and statesmen institutionalized the fall from original nature into original sin, dependence on doctrine closing the Christian mind to all other traditions, philosophies, and schools of thought. To further separate the mind from the soul, the church amassed manmade signs, symbols, and rituals, then made it law that church intermediaries were the only ones who could interpret the meaning of signs, symbols, and rituals. Since, in and of themselves, signs, symbols, and rituals had no meaning, the church told the faithful that signs, symbols, and rituals would save them from the inborn sin of succumbing to evil temptations. By having this temporary but always available fear fix, the church and its co-conspirator the state, partnered in conditioning Christian congregations to grow more and more dependent on signs, symbols, and rituals to think and feel for them. As was perfectly planned, ordered thinking and feeling universalized a new traditional standard: conformity to the "rule of faith."

This designed hypocrisy of the church and state succeeded brilliantly in its mission. The true fall, blind faith that soul nature was evil nature rather than divine nature, dis-empowered *en masse* the individual soul while it crystalized the power of the few. This fall into ignorance and fear universalized psychological and spiritual powerlessness. Ignorance of the soul's divinity and fear of punishment tyrannized the mind, which needs *psychological knowledge and soul knowing* for that spiritualizing process to take place.

When Paradise became evil, the spiritualizing process of the human mind fell into darkness. Personal responsibility to seek, find, and live the purpose of the individual soul gradually faded into obscurity, as did the church's and state's accountability for their inhumanity. *When Paradise became evil, psychological and spiritual freedom fell into fear.*

Ignorance and fear, the ambassadors of dependence, were the invisible chains that stole humanity's freedom. The fall into fear (the *why)*, the conditioning of fear (the *how)*, the 4th century (the *when)*, and the church and state (the *what)*, created invisible chains. Soulless doctrine that faith alone cleansed sin defined the inhumanity of traditional standards.

Traditionalizing the standard of conformity to the *rule of faith* was the church's and state's guarantee that *sin would flourish*. To encourage rebellion against the soul, the church laid down the law of *family values*. One family value was for the *father* to rule everyone else in the home. Given the religious right to judge good and evil, the man of the house determined what was evil and when to punish evil. For any behavior contrary to the rule of faith, doctrine dictated fathers should inflict punishment, corporal when necessary.

When John's mother allowed her husband to punish her sons by beating them up or by making them beat up each other, she was conforming to a family value by which she and her husband were raised. Neither John's mother nor father questioned whether the physical violence of corporal punishment had been formulated from ethical or moral principles nor if family welfare had ever been the goal of that standard. They did not ask themselves if the doctrine ordering that behavior had control over their lives in unethical or immoral ways or if the patriarch instituted those values to maintain their own economic lifestyle and political power. John's parents did not philosophize about the additional psychological and spiritual violence corporal punishment inflicted.

John's mother failed to take into consideration the absolute injustice, insanity, and irrationality of corporal punishment. Nor did she consider herself responsible or accountable for her participation in a psychologically, emotionally, and spiritually crippling ritual. Not educated by or even aware of scholarly philosophies, she had no conception that sending her sons to be beaten was doing them more harm than good. Ignorance of truth and fear of evil was the instrument of criminally protracted behavior on her part. By not investigating how sermonized values imposed the miscarriage of human rights upon her children, she could not conceive *why* elitist hypocrisy conspired for her to abandon her sons and *how* abandonment contributed to the decimation of the psychological and spiritual evolution of the next generation.

John's innocent mind must have cried out, *Is this how much you value us, Mother. To send us to be punished for being ourselves? Don't you care about our feelings?* His heart must have begged, *Please don't let Dad hit Bobby and me again.*

When John's childlike free spirit demanded protection to survive, his parents chose the family value of *physical violence* for what he was doing wrong rather than the family value of loving encouragement for what he was doing right. The *shame* of thinking neither his mother nor his father placed any value upon his suffering shaped in John feelings of not being valued. By unjustly persecuting John in such a manner over and over, the parents who lived by traditional standards systematically disintegrated their son's natural born instinct to value himself and replaced value with the fear. When original sin translated original nature into evil nature by way of corporal punishment, psychological and spiritual freedom was replaced with psychological and spiritual crisis.

Alleluia! Original sin had been designed for John's parents to kill his soul's freedom . . . *to be*. A grim separation between heaven and earth had been forged by his mother's and father's faith that their son's passionate energy was born of evil nature rather than divine nature. Unknowingly, the primitive way they violated their son's body and mind abandoned his feelings. When feelings of fear forsook feelings of love, God's eternal torment rooted in John's mind and his soul. Those roots halted the spiritualizing process before he was old enough to think for himself. So what was the result of the family value of corporal punishment? With every tragic punishment, with every step he took, John grew up to have faith that love was not only going to beat him up, love was also going to abandon him.

When John left home and went into the bigger world, new feelings were automatically translated to synchronize with the feelings created by his upbringing. Getting beaten up and abandoned were the consequences of his behavior as a child, therefore he sought situations that would cause him to get beaten up and abandoned as the consequences of his behavior as an adult. Joining the Navy was an excellent reason for original sin to continue doing battle with his original nature. As an instrument of good vs. evil, being sent to Vietnam was the lose/lose tragedy of choice. The external crisis of war mirrored John's internal crisis created by corporal punishment. War, the natural extension of *religious politics*, indoctrinated John on how to *project evil anywhere but here*, the perfect scheme for creating denial. *Over there*, the military's justification for not hearing, seeing, or speaking of evil at home taught John how to project evil onto anyone but himself.

When John married me, he systematically projected evil onto me. In partnership with the garden-of-evil hoax, projection proliferated a marital arena of his distrust of me. If he trusted that his bride's soul had never fallen into evil, that my thoughts, feelings, and sexual passions originated from good, then he would have been forced to feel the hurt feelings and face the fearful thoughts that had stilled the voice of his soul. Because he would have to suffer ego death to feel the tears his soul cried, and because corporal punishment separated his mind from his soul and replaced the love in his soul with fear, John found it impossible to trust me. *Our every tragic drama had been scripted by the evil garden and staged by the religious politics of war.*

Shadows of the time John beat me up stepped into meditation's passing parade of puzzle pieces. The corporal response took place in Darren's and Gina's kitchen. Gina and I had met in 1977 by way of our daughters' gymnastics. Following our meeting, John and I occasionally socialized with the couple. This particular night, John had been antagonizing me about some past, obscure event. Uncharacteristic of any of my previous behaviors, I retaliated by stepping on his sore toe. My retaliation gave him a window of opportunity to judge me as the evil enemy, then inflict punishment. He knocked me against the stove and continued punching me until he had beaten me down to the floor.

I picked myself up off the kitchen floor and bolted toward the back door. The need to flee the scene controlled my every desire. Fleeing resulted, not from fear but from feeling sick at heart. Darren and Gina tried to hold me back. Holding me back enraged my flight response. I yanked their arms off my body, ran out the back door into the back yard, tore an opening in their wood fence, and stepped through the opening and onto the street. Crying hysterically, I ran down the street until I saw a well lit, open garage. In the garage stood a young couple who were staring at me as if my hysterics made me the enemy. Whatever the reason for their fearful judgment, they did allow me the time to pull myself together, and then they drove me to my car.

Years later when Gina felt safe from John's retaliation against her,

Gina told me, "Darren thought John was going to kill you. Darren and I were horrified. You were losing consciousness when Darren pulled John off of you."

Subsequent to those deadly theatrics, John showed neither pity nor remorse for beating me up. One evening, several years later, I found out why. . . .

At home having one too many cocktails with an old friend, John jokingly romanticized hitting me, "Diana, you deserved it."

Rather than ask myself, *If it hurt John so much to watch his brother get hit, how could he humorously minimize hitting me?* I denied the possibility my husband would intentionally hurt me. If I were forced to think that the incredible trauma inflicted upon me was deliberate, I would have gone into a psychological and spiritual crisis so catastrophic, it would have devastated my sense of what was real.

The revelations flowing into my meditation were literally changing the earth upon which I once walked. Obvious were the devastating results of my consistently pushing away deeper meanings. Marrying a man who had been in psychological and spiritual crisis since childhood predetermined the eventual certainty of my psychological and spiritual crisis. Waves of information, followed by waves of understanding, were systematically piecing together a psychospiritual puzzle. Traumas to my consciousness stored in my subconscious were part of the history living in universal consciousness. By making my subconscious conscious, I was discovering how, why, where, and when I began to fall into a reality where the breath of my life no longer flowed freely.

The fall that chained my freedom chained it for many reasons. The puzzle of my relationship with John was a dualistic dilemma: his manufactured, institutionalized, and universalized by traditions his parents had championed; mine those same manufactured, institutionalized, and universalized by traditions my parents had shunned. From opposite poles came our parents' formulas for teaching us how to express our human nature. A magnetic force of polar opposites drew us together. The result was that John's driving force of fearful distrust locked horns with my driving force of loving trust. While I found it inconceivable to distrust, John found it unthinkable to trust. Immovable walls built with a lifetime of training made each of us unwilling to seek and find the meaning of one obvious truth. Neither total trust nor total distrust in human nature was appropriate for every situation.

While I lay pondering the issue of trust, an incident that took place when I was five or six touched off my next wave of revelations. Far less crippling than corporal punishment yet still categorically corporal [bodily], Daddy had just punished me with a spanking for some small mischievous deed (spankings he later told me he regretted for they hurt him more than they hurt me).

I lay over his lap, butt up, thinking, *When I grow up, I'm never going to cause my children to cry or feel sad.*

Rather than remain unhappy, I dreamed about being happy. The level of punishment far less and far frequent than John's, my spankings awakened in me dreams of raising happy children. I would raise happy children by giving them the best part of myself. Cherisse and Tamara were loved from the day my happy dreams awoke. The love that built those dreams strengthened my bubble and empowered my trust that all my dreams would come true.

As most beautifully planned, having trust in my dreams did make my dreams come true. When I grew up and gave birth to Cherisse and Tamara, their love for me was as pure as my love for them. Because they were born of happy dreams, encapsulating them in my bubble was not necessary. They were born in my bubble.

Cherisse, Tamara, and I discovered there was great power in our bubble. Our bubble was filled with love, and love empowered trust. Our bubble of love and trust gave us the ability to float above the troubles of the world surrounding us. Our bubble was like a circle of light that kept real pain and fear outside its boundaries. Our circle of light protected us from John's verbal attacks. The lightness of our trusting world repelled the darkness of John's real-world distrust. His distrust voiced a human condition to which our trust refused to participate. By unifying in a bubble of loving trust, the three of us made John an outsider in his own home. . . . By abandoning real-world distrust we had abandoned John.

Time sped forward in my revolving-door retrospective to October 1986, nine months before John told me he loved Fate. A friend had given me a book to read. From the moment I began reading *Dynamics for Living* by Charles Fillmore (who researched the realms of God Mind extensively), I felt my life had been forever changed.

Phrases such as "When [an individual] understands the laws of mind, [that individual] has solved the mysteries of the universe" filled me with a sense of warm inner wholeness, as if I had come home, not to the home of my family but to the home within myself.

The idea that the great mysteries could be solved gave me an infinite sense of peace. Peace armed me with a new way of responding to John. Behaviors of his I previously judged as weak were all at once tolerable.

Tolerance evaporated my well trained inclination to defend myself against his verbal attacks. No longer did I need to suppress his degrading words. No longer did I need to debate.

My new way of responding was not to respond. I remained peaceful and kept my silence. In my silence, I communicated in a more powerful way than I had ever communicated with self defense. In my silence, I defeated my partner. In my silence, I won every debate. In my glorified, effortless silence, once again, John had been beaten up and abandoned.

Puzzling over why my conscious mind was incapable of understanding, forgiving, or feeling compassion for how my winning every debate caused John to feel beaten up and abandoned, another insight stepped into the parade of puzzle pieces.

As with debate, Charley Weitzel had a knack for having *fun* in other arenas. Although learning how to have fun as a child instigated in me a natural ability to have fun as an adult, one of the ways Daddy had fun was drinking alcohol.

Mother told me, "Daddy taught me how to drink."

Alcohol, notwithstanding fun, caused Mother problems. Through the years of my growing up, I heard people talk about Mother's drinking. They talked in a tone of voice that made her sound *bad*. Daddy, on the other hand, adored mother under all circumstances. I never heard my father breathe one negative word about my mother or to my mother, nor did he ever let anyone else say anything bad about her or to her.

Regardless, Daddy's protection did not alleviate a growing mountain of problems surrounding Mother's drinking. Over time, she went to a few Alcoholics Anonymous meetings but chose not to quit drinking.

During one attempt to quit, she confessed, "Daddy wants me to drink with him."

Her eventual choice not to quit promised the inevitability of times when my life was not going to feel like fun. During those times, I lived by one of the mottos Daddy passed down to me. Daddy's "Live-and-let-live" motto allowed me to disappear into happy dreams. Many days and nights I sat alone, hour after hour, watching old happily-ever-after movies. I took the dreams I liked from those movies, added in the fun part of my home life, stirred it all up with the things I loved to do, and mentally formulated a happily-ever-after dream all my own.

Suddenly in my mind it was April 6, 1969. I was walking past the piano in a charming Newport Beach bay-front restaurant when I spotted a male figure standing at the other end of the long bar ahead of me. Tall and erect, a slender young man with sandy-blond hair and powder blue eyes stood like a beacon calling me. A magnetic force of energy drew me toward him. The inescapable pull of that powerful force caused me to walk straight across the room to introduce myself. From that moment on, John and I were inseparable.

Our romance brought my dreams to life. My future husband thrilled me with fun-filled nights, compliments, and an unceasing desire to satisfy me sexually. John acted like he loved having fun with me, and fun was something I had been raised to adore. From the first moment I set eyes on John, our mutual chemistry told me that I had found the man who would forever give life to my dreams. His every move assured me of my happily ever after. When our romance did not fit my dreams, I simply disappeared into my bubble and lived by my motto, "live and let live." By disappearing into my romanticized version of our relationship, I walked willingly into the fire. I married John.

Excerpts from my life were untangling the chaotic roots that predisposed both John and I to have a dark side. The missing pieces to our puzzle were being randomly filled by revelations that would normally have assaulted my sense of self. In meditation, however, I did not feel the paralyzing shadows of truth. As the experiences setting the stage for my fall unraveled, I felt more enlightened with each new understanding.

I married John believing our marriage would be exactly like our romance. Our marriage was nothing like our romance. The very day we married, the necessity of disappearing into my bubble took a quantum leap. Not only did he compliment my sister rather than me, he placed me, as a married woman, in a different category than I had been as a dating woman. The person it took me a lifetime to become was suddenly supposed to change. Overnight, he ordered me to transform from a free-spirited single girl into his version of a married lady. To my groom, becoming a wife symbolized that I should stop dressing like I wanted to have *fun*; moreover, I should stop wanting to have *fun*. . . .

Though our courtship meant always going out and having fun, our marriage meant never going out to have fun. As time passed, it became increasingly necessary for me to disappear into my bubble, making it harder and harder to live by my live-and-let-live motto. Not long after giving birth to Cherisse, John began going out to bars after work and having fun without me. I began asking myself why I should stay home alone. One lonely night when John did not come home after work, I decided to go out and have fun without John.

I drove to a familiar Newport peninsula restaurant. *Woody's Wharf* was packed with fun-loving people, music, food, and drink. I sat at the bar gazing through huge tinted windows at the yachts cruising up and down the serene harbor. Once in a while, one of the yachts anchored at the dock, and jovial people strolled up the plank into *Woody's* to have fun. It was just like old times, the kind of night I longed for.

Around midnight, in a happy mood and an alert state of mind, I left through Woody's two huge ancient mariner doors to go home. I walked across the small well lit parking lot. When I had almost reached my car, I heard two men calling me over to their car. Sitting in the front seat, they implored me to have a sip of the drink the driver held in his hand. Earlier in the evening, the men had offered to buy me a drink several times. Each time I said "no," feeling an intuitive sense of repulsion toward them both. In the parking lot, I repeated "no" several more times. Then thinking they would go away, I abandoned earlier instincts. I gave in and took a sip of the drink.

One sip and the next thing I knew I was walking through the front door of my house in a mental fog. I strolled around the stairs to the coat closet and hung up my bra as if it was something I would normally do. As I headed up the stairs, John headed down demanding to know where I had been. The next morning, I went on with my normal routine, not giving a second thought to the horrific outcome of placing my instinct to trust before my intuition to distrust.

A couple of days later John told me with his typical humorous sarcasm that he had chased the two men off our property with my father's military Colt 45. The incident was an isolated event, and I had no memory of anything other than taking one sip of the drink, then being home. As usual, I used "live and let" live to justify the bra incident and disassociated from its ominous implications.

Months later, with no explanation, John remarked, "Diana, you're just like your mother." After that, he irritated me by repetitiously repeating, "You're just like your mother." It would be years, however, until out of the blue, he finally told me what he meant by just like my mother. "Diana, I hate you for the night I had to chase those men off our property. You loved having sex with two men at the same time!"

His accusation was beyond my comprehension. I was a virgin until six months before we met. Participating in sexual behavior even remotely similar to what he was accusing me of had never crossed my mind. I had no history whatsoever for his remarks. Never once did I give my husband evidence for him to criminalize me in that manner. It was beyond belief that one circumstantial event would result in my husband judging me in the worst possible way.

I did not understand.

I was about to understand.

Not long after John and I met, I took him home to meet Daddy and Mother. John appeared to enjoy my parents and their partying fun, which, as I explained, included drinking alcohol. I began drinking alcohol during college, and John and I were both drinking the night we met. To me, partying with Daddy and Mother was a natural extension of everyone's lifestyle. But this was 1969, and American society held court upon women who drank, especially women like my mother whose behaviors became more sexual when they drank. Women's behaviors were held to a different standard than men's behaviors, a higher standard of morality. They phrased it the *double standard*. The double standard, based on traditional standards filtered into every aspect of life. Women who did not behave according to traditional feminine *roles* were judged to be bad. Frowning upon women who drank alcohol and behaved sexually was culturally popular. Popular opinion accounted for the voices I heard while growing up, *voices* who judged my mother's drinking to be *bad*.

Centuries after Eve's passions seduced Adam into eating forbidden fruit, the fall of the female principal was irreversibly ingrained in the collective consciousness. Women were judged so harshly, they were systematically stoned into a debilitating psychological and spiritual sickness. This sickness, bred from standardized belief systems, had been consummately arranged by a teensy-weensy group of rich men at the top of the patriarchal ladder. Through the centuries, beliefs about the female gender declined so drastically that all sorts of evil judgments had been placed upon anyone with female genitalia. Traditional standards every woman was held accountable for were so unachievably high, especially in the area of expected sexual repression, misogyny had become rampant. Because modernity failed to educate society about the inborn power of female sexuality, men grew to hate women simply because they were women. Irreconcilably rooted from generations of conditioned thought lay my husband's judgment of my mother's behavior as *bad*.

Universal wisdom had rendered impeccable truth. The night I went to *Woody's Wharf* alone, two men drugged and raped me. Though I had no conscious recollection of the rape nor did I figure out that I had been raped for years, my initial reaction was to mentally disappear from a real world so dehumanizing to the female gender that acknowledging the mortifying truth at that time in my life would have snuffed out the fire of my free spirit and broken my heart. My heart and soul chose to remain free rather than be victimized by the injustice running rampant in a fallen world.

John's reaction to my being drugged and raped was to further polarize our genders. He used the night I went out alone as a window of opportunity to prove his assumption that Diana was *bad* just like her mother. A single incident gave him the excuse he had been waiting for to incorporate the fall of the feminine principal into Diana's free-spirited nature.

Directly rooted in religious mind control was John's substitution of lies for truth. His dependence on fairy tales transgressed his ability to think for himself. Trance-like faith gave sexism the right to vilify my body rather than the villains who drugged and raped me. Primitive sexualization of feminine nature as evil nature had carved into granite our gender war. Gender roles divided our sexuality into two vastly unequal parts. The prostrated psychology of the female seductress of male passion had made John so fearful of my mother's powerful sexuality in me, the juvenile fantasy-land of Adam's rib had predetermined his invention of my fall into sexual sin. This I did not know or understand. Sexual predetermination made inevitable our battle between good and evil. The *Woody's Wharf* incident had set into motion our private armageddon.

Not once did John consider he might be wrong about his presumption that his wife enjoyed a salacious *menage a trois*. Being wrong never occurred to John because John saw what he was predisposed to see, and his predisposition did not know or understand the childhood my heart experienced. But then how could John know or understand my heart when I never told him about my heart? I never told John about my heart because I never told myself about that part of my heart.

My heart was about to be revealed to me.

Shut into the far reaches of my mind was a truth too painful to admit, even to myself, especially to myself. Though I felt that Mother's flurtatiousness with Daddy was *good*, if I had to admit to myself that when he was stationed in some far-away place some of her drinking behaviors *were* bad, if I had to admit the truth about her adulterous sex, then I would have been forced to feel *bad* in my heart. If I felt her shame in my heart, my heart would have felt too sad for me to bear. As not to feel sad feelings, I disappeared into my bubble's happily-ever-after dreams.

Because I had a bubble of dreams to escape sad feelings, my mother's shame remained impacted in the far reaches of my subconscious when I married John. Denial kept Mother's sexual perils a secret, not only from my conscious mind, but also from the mind of the man I married. My happily-ever-after dreams had been so shamed by my mother's sexual behavior, those dreams imagined that if John knew the truth, that Mother's sexual behavior made me feel so sick at heart that I had to repress my own feelings, he would stop loving me.

The consequences of keeping my heartache a secret turned out to be far worse than John not loving me. After he met Mother and Daddy, he judged Mother's drinking behaviors as bad but never told me. Years later, one misbegotten night proved to John all his assumptions were true. The man who was supposed to love me had judged me as he had judged my mother. He hated me because he thought I was just like the kind of behavior that sickened me more than anything else in the world. As a result of keeping my feelings of shame a secret, the man I married raped me with his judgment to a far greater degree than two morally impoverished strangers who raped me with their bodies.

The pieces to our puzzle were falling into place. Exposed by revelations was a vast web that John and I wove. Our shadowy web disguised the parts of ourselves we both refused to admit. Each of us used the other to nurture our repressions. John *projected* his *shadow* into me. His projection helped me hide from my shadow. Through the years, the weaknesses I recognized in John, I failed to recognize in myself. Our shared tendency to point the finger of *blame* at each other grew into a mountain of reciprocal, emotional abandonment.

Flames of reciprocity burned. Each of us armed ourselves against the other's shame with our own shame. John attacked. Diana disappeared. The cold war we fought, we fought with ignorance and want. The understanding, forgiveness, and compassion we each wanted, we both refused to give. Each of us created the habit of denying our secret feelings by violating the feelings of the other. Our reciprocal, emotional abandonment epitomized an ignorant refusal to face the underlying meaning of why our marriage was in shambles.

That underlying meaning was a defining piece to our puzzle. It was the *lynchpin* that held together all the other pieces of our partnership in crime. One puzzle piece would solve the mystery of *how* a person with a driving force of love could fall in love with a person with a driving force of fear. I could feel the power of the repressed meaning reaching up from the far reaches of my subconscious. *It reached into my consciousness with a spiritual force that made me feel so loved, I could not deny its coming.*

The truth revealed itself in a huge spiritual roar. . . .

All my life, I gave myself credit for loving without condition. My positive attitude had no limits; when anyone asked me about my mother's drinking behavior, I would rekindle live and let live by proclaiming, "Mother's behavior didn't bother me."

In truth, the *lynchpin meaning* in the furthermost reaches of my mind had nothing to do with anyone else. But this meaning had a lot to do with my lack of understanding, forgiveness, and compassion for my husband. Of all my repressed feelings, my most sacred secret feeling was *fear*, a very different kind of fear than my husband's fear. I had placed judgment upon every single person who called my mother bad. Above all, I too had judged my mother's behavior as bad. Bad as a judgment created feelings of fear that I was not the person I wanted to be. For years, I disappeared from the fear of my own judgment. The growing demon of fear stored in my subconscious talked to my heart every day of every year in endless chatter.

Fear said, *Diana, you are not who you proclaim yourself to be. You are guilty of judgment. Therefore you do not love unconditionally.*

The voice of fear spoke truth. My most sacred repressed feeling was born from the truth that I had judged my mother the same way my husband had judged my mother. I had judged her sexual behavior as bad, and my judgment meant I did not love her unconditionally. My subconscious fear of not being the person I wanted to be spoke silently to my conscious mind.

Fear said, *Diana, you must be punished for not living up to your dream of unconditional love. Your dreams will be persecuted until your judgments are revealed and vanquished.*

Then I knew! I knew our marriage was in shambles for the same reason I lost my freedom. It was the same reason I married John. Though opposite in nature, I married John because my soul knew that the shadow of his fear mirrored the shadow of my fear. John played upon my fear with harmonic precision. He gave me the exact amount of punishment for which my fear cried. Each time I did not say "stop" to his punishing words, I gave the go ahead for more. Each time John stirred my shadow a little more by judging me, he untangled my web a little more. Each time he nurtured my fear of my judgment, he brought me one step closer to my truth.

In truth, I did not understand, forgive, or have compassion for John's fear because I did not understand, forgive, or have compassion for my fear . . . of my mother in myself.

All at once my revelations stopped and my eyes popped open. What I had experienced in meditation was unbelievable! Utterly spellbound by one revelation after the next, countless insights had flowed like angel's dust from my subconscious into my consciousness. My fear of the judgments I had carried in my heart since childhood had been revealed and set free from its secret hiding place.

I was made to see that John's inhuman behavior toward me originated from his being treated inhumanely, first by his parents, then by religion, then by war. I had been made aware of how we aggravated each other's fears and hid from our own. Above all, my revelations helped me understand *why* I fell. I fell because my soul told me the time had come for me to seek, find, and understand my truth. For only when I knew the whole truth could I be the person of unconditional love I wanted to be.

In the void, miraculous discoveries both wonderful and awful contained no judgment about the truths they revealed. Oneness with the universe demonstrated that a humanity void of fear, judgment, and blame and full of understanding, forgiveness, and compassion would reveal win/lose battles to be archaic blunders. A humanity who understood that the darkness of war, personal or global, had no chance of driving out the darkness of fear. A humanity who understood that only love could drive out the darkness of fear would change the world.

My heart spilled forth prayers of thanksgiving for the knowledge and the love. Joyous tears flooded my eyes. I prayed for and thanked my husband. By being the relentless antagonist, he had made my night of transcendence into those realms of the universe possible.

Lovingly, I forgave my mother for hurting me. After asking her forgiveness for my judgments of her, Mother's love and forgiveness generated back to me from her heavenly resting place. I felt my mother had always led with her heart, and that had not changed. As my forgiveness of my mother completed itself, I was able to forgive myself. Self forgiveness felt like climbing out of a dark, mysterious cave. How many of my feelings came from Mother's weaknesses and how many from my judgment of her I had yet to learn. Shown to me was that true forgiveness did not judge between the two. It came by being a living example of non-judgment and unconditional love.

My father's love for my mother had been a living example of non-judgment and unconditional love. Because he loved Mother for her weaknesses as well as her strengths, for Daddy no forgiveness was necessary. In addition, I had always felt that they both loved me without condition. If life's greatest tragedy is not being loved and life's greatest gift is being loved, then my parents gave me life's greatest gift. As a result of the way I was loved as a child, I did not have to spend the rest of my life searching for how love felt.

In those predawn hours of July 23, 1987, my psychological and spiritual awakenings gave birth to understanding, forgiveness, and compassion for humanity. Upon the exorcism of my denial of fear, judgement, and blame was written the indelible manuscript of their human destruction. Being shown the dark side as well as the light side of reality helped me to understand the initiatory journey upon which I had embarked.

Through the trees of denial of my dark side, my revelations had awakened me to the forest of humanity's magnificence! Glory lived in the spirit of each person's heroic participation in the human struggle. Humanity's willingness to struggle against invisible chains that caused a dark side unavailable to the conscious mind took a kind of courage to which I had just become aware. Understanding, forgiveness, and compassion for humanity's unmet need for unconditional love lifted me up and discarded invisible chains of self-deprivation.

From within rushed an urgent desire to wake people up, kiss them on the cheek, and whisper, *There's a better way to live!* I wanted to scream to the world, *Stop wasting love!* With that urgency my thoughts rushed to John. *What I have learned will change our lives!*

July 23, 1987, dawn

Nature's playful quality sang to the new dawn from behind my lowered shade. I sprang from my bed, flew to the window, and pulled down the cord. Up went the shade! My lungs breathed in the freshness of my awakening. With a thousand pounds of suffocating denials lifted off my shoulders, I loved the world and everything in it.

John, John, John, I thought in jubilant elation. *Everything I learned last night can help you just as it is helping me. We can make up for hurting each other. With understanding, forgiveness, and compassion, together we can amend our every mistake. By working in oneness to live a life of unconditional love, we can learn to live our happily ever after.*

I jumped back in bed and let my revelations take me on a different kind of magic carpet ride. With my eyes wide open, I let my spirit free-fly in timeless, weightless, heavenly space.

Across the room, a vision of John appeared. His body looked youthful, slim, and agile. It illuminated a magnificent energy. The pure goodness of that energy radiated out and connected with the elevated energy I felt. The connection united our souls in a rapturous loving oneness. The vision wore the same red alpaca sweater, white pants, and shoes John had worn the night we met. The wisdom contained in the vision made me feel that all our years of spinning each other's web had actually expanded our souls' love. The love the vision and I exchanged was eternal, untouched by sorrow, and limitless.

Two understandings came to me from the vision: Nothing earthly could ever change the truth that John and I loved each other on a soul level, and soul love is possible on earth.

The vision dispelled, leaving me with feelings of love greater than I imagined possible. As with my mother, my forgiveness of my husband completed itself, and he became my heart's desire all over again.

July 23, 1987, 7:00 A.M.

Enchanted and serenely happy, I waited for the time when John would arrive at The Big G from his motel room. Bubbling from within was the urge to repeat the whole meditation story and how my love for him had expanded. Humbled, yet joyous, I wanted to tell him how and why our marriage was in shambles and how we could work together to heal ourselves and our relationship. My fingers turned the rotary of my bedside telephone every five minutes. When John answered, I enthusiastically paraphrased my revelations, wondering if he might be thinking I had lost my mind.

He remained silent until I finished, then responded in a voice that sounded sweet, cheerful, and patient. "Let's talk about it tonight."

Words spoken so sweetly caused me to reconsider the conclusion I reached before my meditation began. *Maybe John wasn't with Fate the last two nights.*

I hung up the telephone with hopes for new beginnings. Great expectations took flight!

Excited to share the happiness I felt with the rest of my bubble of love, I bounced out of bed, opened the door, and called out, "Cherisse! Tamara!"

Cherisse and Tamara entered my room slowly with cautious, curious faces. In my elation, I had forgotten to consider that I had been shut up in my bedroom for three days. My daughters did not know why, and by the look on their faces, not knowing frightened them.

The three of us sat on my king-sized bed in a small intimate circle. I began my story, not leaving out one detail. They both concentrated intently on my every syllable. Tears flowed freely from all three of us as I stepped once more into the trajedy and the beauty of events that so affected their lives. No judgment showed on either of my daughter's faces. Each daughter expressed an understanding and depth of loving acceptance that made my heart leap. The love they gave without condition was the embodiment of all my happily-ever-after dreams. The individuals two young women were showing themselves to be clearly defined that neither Cherisse nor Tamara would have to spend the rest of her life searching for the meaning of life. Their unconditional understanding of their mother's revelations revealed the magnificence of the light in their souls, reminding me of a saying I had heard: *How much of your soul that is expressed in your life is shown in your children's eyes.*

The appreciation I felt for who my daughters were was what exalted me that morning. Nothing existed in my room to prostitute the enormity of our experience. Our circle of love united our minds, our hearts, and our souls in eternal oneness.

The soft morning sun filtered through my bedroom window adorning Cherisse's and Tamara's tear-stained cheeks. I hugged each daughter and glorified in watching them hug each other. Without telling me in words, I knew two miraculous young women had forgiven their mother for disappearing into her room. Forgiveness set me free to go forward in seeking my truth in the light of day.

After Cherisse and Tamara left my room, I sat in bed thinking about my vision of John. I felt my vision represented the real John, the John who longed to give and receive love without fighting. The spiritual love I felt for my vision of John intertwined with the physical love I wished to share with the real John. Thoughts about the sexual manifestation of the spiritual vision impassioned my desire for us to be as one. The earth shook from my longing for my husband's passionate touch. At that moment, more than anything else on earth, I wanted to make love with the man I married.

Awake, O north wind; and come, thou south; blow upon my garden,
that the spices thereof may flow out. Let my beloved come
into his garden, and eat his pleasant fruits.
— The Song of Solomon 4:16, *The Good Samaritan Bible*

5

A Night To Remember

July 23, 1987, 11:30 P.M.

John came into the house quietly. I was standing in the kitchen waiting to step into my new world, a world driven by understanding, forgiveness, and compassion. Filling the room was the scent of warm, freshly baked pork chops. He entered the kitchen glancing at me in my negligee and breathing in the aroma of the home cooking I had prepared for the soul I had recognized in my vision. A sober, relaxed air articulated his every step. The down-turned lips that had become so familiar had been replaced by sensitive appreciation.

Why John was in such an unusually peaceful mood, I did not know or care. At that moment, even the fantastic revelations I had planned to tell him about took second stage. I was standing on the edge of all my tomorrows. From my husband's body alone I would learn what his heart felt.

I walked across the kitchen and put my arms around the tomorrows with which my dreams were consumed. The touch of his skin felt soft, warm, and velvety, not a way it had ever felt before my night of spiritual transcendence.

John reciprocated my gentle seduction as he asked, "Are those pork chops I smell?"

I released myself from our embrace, walked over to the oven, and opened it. Scented heat rushed out to brush my face. Pork chops, potatoes, and carrots sizzled an enthusiastic wish to please. I carried the hot food to the counter, carefully arranged it on my husband's plate, then watched him eat. As he devoured every tender morsel, he glanced up at me, then down at his dinner, then back up at me. Faster and faster, he looked up then down, mentally evaluating the changed woman he saw before him.

John must have learned to inhale food during his four-and-one-half-year stint in the Navy. Before I knew it, nothing remained on his plate except tiny bones. I carried the bone-filled plate to the sink, returned, and took his hand. Anticipating what was to come next, he stood up and followed as I led him, hand in hand, to our bed. With my negligee still on, I slipped under the covers and watched my husband undress and climb in bed. Typically, he dozed off with supernatural speed. His sleeping wizardry did not faze me. From eighteen years of our sleeping in the same bed, I knew he would awake with the same spellbinding speed.

The reciprocal love I shared with my spiritual vision seemed to have ballooned my capacity to feel love for the physical man. My most heavenly desire was to duplicate the soul connection with the man. Although intercourse would not bridge the separateness human flesh mandated, it would make us as physically close as was humanly possible.

The moon filtered a dim light across the length of John's dozing body. His ability to fall into and out of an easy sleep fitted my mood to perfection that night. In our moonlit, king size bed I felt a quickening. The mystical elation I had felt during my night of transcendent revelations remained. Because of one night, a divine power was operating in me.

I moved closer to John. His skin and profile reflected the moon's light, making him look radiant. The same glowing essence of my vision emanated from his physicality.

Mesmerized by what I was seeing, I thought, *I can feel love vibrating from every cell in this sleeping body. Love shines from every pore.* The new way in which I saw a man who only a few days earlier had filled me with disdain, moved me to question what I felt. *Is the love pulsating from within my husband his soul connecting with my soul? Or is it the quickening of my energy that allows me to witness the loving soul of another? Will the soul light of the man I am seeing make any difference in the way he sees me in the light of day?*

Our bedroom flowered with a marvelous life all its own. It felt as if the earth and every beautiful garden that grew was in bed with the two of us.

My mind searched for a way to distinguish the present from the past. *Is John different? Or is it only me who has changed? He must have noticed the remarkable difference in me tonight. What I feel is too big, too overpowering, too wonderful not to recognize!*

I gazed adoringly at every inch of John's body. Something more exalted than human nature exuded from each and every atom of that body. The change in me was not my imagination. *Meditation had done far more than enlighten my mind. It had spiritualized the totality of my being.*

The quickening of my energy frequency had begun. . . .

The love beaming from my soul called forth a physical desire that had been burning since morning. Botanical treasures hidden deep within my female chambers had been arising to capture my soul, captivate my heart, and lodge in my conscious awareness. I could think of no other rational way to explain the sudden pleasurable response my body felt from simply looking at the body of another.

For the second night in a row a miracle was occurring. Something in me was preparing to set itself free. That something was an inhibition that I did not know I had until I experienced what was to come next.

The inhibitions ready to be set free were born from the understandings I gained from my revelations. What I had learned about the fall of humanity had been represented in my life experiences. By charging women as having evil sexual organs, scriptural interpretations elevated the male kingdom to a position higher than the female kingdom. Men played God by idolizing their bodies and subjugating women's bodies. Statues of mortal men were glorified as immortal gods, while those of women were reduced to virgins or whores. Male strength and sexual organs were prized, while female spirituality and sexual organs were criminalized. Temples were erected to ritualize the higher status of men. Women were denied even the right to occupy a religious position where they could serve God.

When male nature infected female nature with evil nature, the dastardly deed crippled the world. When woman was sentenced by the Catholic church as guilty of commiting the first original sin, then sentensed a second time as guilty of the commiting fall of man, those lethal interpretations of the garden story created a religious separation between men and women. Woman as twice-guilty, man as victimized by a woman's passion, made half of the souls on earth less than the superior other half because of gender. In devaluing one-half of all souls, the narcissistic nonsense stole the divinity of all souls. In extracting divinity from the soul, making female passion to blame, and giving God the judgmental, punishing qualities of man, the church sentenced humanity to be doomed to fall into fear.

The church's sacred oath to keep the divinity of every soul a secret compounded the mystery of the meaning of life. By giving God the qualities of man, the translations endowed all men with the religious right to treat all women as if they were less human than men. The less guilty gender took the more guilty gender as captive entertainment. And what entertainment! Into slavery one-half of the human race fell. Anyone with male genitalia was given the authority to violently persecute anyone with female genitalia. Men used their God-given right to enslave and slaughter women. Women's slaughterhouse of enslavement making real original sin in the mind of man, *the fall of all souls was complete.*

When woman's passion for *truth became sin* in the eyes of man, both the female principal and male principal fell into darkness. The male principal descended into dense matter in which light could no longer penetrate. This gross, sex-driven energy went to work defining rules that would terrorize the human soul for centuries. Gender-driven standards were passed down generation to generation as the word of God, punishable by a God's hateful judgments.

This dark, unforgiving God created women solely to serve man, with much of that servitude being sexual. A woman was given two choices: she could be either a virgin or a whore. Both were life sentences. Virgins were created by this male creator solely for procreation, to service boy babies. Once a virgin's birthing years were over, she was placed on a pedestal and honored as a Mother Mary figure. Since husbands did not sexually desire the Mother Mary figure, the mother of his children should not expect to have a satisfying sexual relationship with him from then on.

Forevermore he would have sex with mistresses or whores. Mistresses, the higher standard of whore, were created solely to service man's sexual appetites. Mistresses were the only women who consciously chose to be paid for sexual service. If a man could not afford a mistress, he would pay prostitutes for sex. Prostitutes, the lower standard of whore, were created to service male genitals. They were used and abused, then disposed of like garbage. In reality, prostitutes were poverty-stricken girls who had no alternative other than to sell their bodies to survive. If a virgin had sex with anyone other than her husband, she was immediately judged to be a whore. Whatever the title, women's sexual service to men exemplified the slavery of inequality.

The philosophy of woman as less human than man sailed from the old world to the new world, the United States of America. As in the generations following the creation of forbidden fruit, gender inequality was handed down to each succeeding generation, the unquestioned standard separating men and women. During the Victorian Age of the 1800s, sexual feelings were severed from a female baby's brain at birth. From the moment baby's genitals were determined to be female, "down there" became dirty. As she grew into childhood, denied to her was the natural instinct to touch herself. Female masturbation was sinful, the mere thought of sex strictly forbidden, condemned. Foremost, when the child grew into an unmarried adolescent, intercourse was fatal to the female's reputation. Hence, hellfire and damnation would reign down upon a woman of any age caught enjoying any kind of sexual behavior. Any status short of virginal, thought, word, or deed, which included incest and rape, was a social and financial death sentence.

In the early 1900s, Sigmund Freud stood guard on behalf of Victorian mercilessness toward women. He reared his at first brilliant but later cowardly head by coining the expression "biology is destiny." Freud's biological destiny deified the penis as the superior expression of preference and subordinated the clitoris as the inferior expression of undesirability.

Freud aggrandized the ever-enlarging penis by theorizing that the vaginal orgasm was more mature than the clitoral orgasm. A female unable to orgasm by intercourse alone did not embody the required transformation from girl to woman. Freud concluded that if she could not orgasm in and of the penis, there was something mentally, physically, or emotionally *wrong* with her. Freud's dilly-dallying with a subject in which he could not possibly have had experience turned out to be as effective as surgically removing the clitoris from the social consciousness. Freud's most effective cowardice, nonetheless, was his theory that human nature originated in sexual nature, not soul nature. As with forbidden fruit, the human capacity to gain knowledge of the history of humankind, i.e., of good and evil, was not factored into Freud's equation. Original nature theorized to be sexual nature was a fundamental error of the human ability to learn. Rather than speak to a higher-minded standard which would have antagonized the church and state, plus risk his career, reputation, and wealth, Freud convinced himself he was speaking truth, even standing his ground with Carl Jung and losing his friendship, and chose to reinforce the lower-minded standard of original sin. Original nature as sexual nature rather than spiritual nature atrophied the psychological and spiritual evolution of the world. This human-animal philosophy once again annihilated human-divine philosophy and added the *scientific right* to be penis driven to the *religious right* and the *political right*.

Sexual nature as original nature exposed Freud as just another whore for corrupt political and religious institutions. His sex theory not only raped the evolution of the reasoning mind, it raped the evolution of the spiritual mind. By supporting the secrecy of the truth that the original nature of human nature is spiritual, Freud robbed the mass consciousness of a potential spiritual evolution. His scientific sexual takeover of the soul further widened the separation between the body and the soul in the mind of humanity.

When original sin severed the soul from the thinking mind and replaced it with sexual sin, mind became lazy and reverted to animalistic thinking. When the mind started focusing its awareness on biological urges, mindless, soulless animalism sowed the seeds of object sex as preferred above spiritual love. The mind of the collective became confused and began to think object sex represented spiritual love. In reverting to sex as original nature, Freud contributed to the evolution of the short-term relationship. By scientifically institutionalizing biology as a power greater than the power of the soul, Freud helped the church and state thrust the postwar western world into the dark age of the soul.

And so, the pulsating beat of biology as destiny moved on. The armistice of the Second World "War to end all wars" brought an incredible level of *man-as-animal, woman-as-less* thinking to modern America. Inequility of biological destiny opened the door for a staggering machismo addiction to biological urges. What Freud's dim-witted penis superiority helped the religious and political machines to sow, the land freed by war was about to reap.

The religious politics of the double standard was no more than the systematic extension of the religious politics of war. As such, the *land of the free had nothing to do with female sexuality.* The spoils of war guaranteed to all men were guaranteed to no women. Sex as human nature was *for men only. Father knows best* gave a new name to the severe limitations reaped from a long history of gender falsehoods.

The reaping of pleasurable sex by men was the reaping of dirty sex for women. Blind obedience to fossilized biological standards predetermined the biography of every modern woman and every modern man. Father knows best was simply a modernized translation of politics as usual, politics perpetually being the offspring of religion. Brainwashed into becoming no less fallen than Eve, millions of women literally began living their lives as mind; body; and soul-impoverished imitations of eating forbidden fruit.

Those postwar years were the years in which I grew up. Following World War II, when the boys came home from overseas as *winners*, women were forced into the magical thinking that would define their modern role as *losers*. The spoils for women demanded they return from the workforce, mutate backwards into full-time homemakers, and shape their children into cookie cutters of the dark ages of the patriarch's double standard.

Opposite and opposing roles defined modern America's *gender-gap*. While boys were not so secretly masturbating their sexual needs away in bathrooms across America, girls were warned to ignore and repress their constant cravings. Freud's penis as superior, clitoris as inferior pitted male against female. A new enemy at home replaced the old enemy abroad. Biology as destiny championed gender wars in a time of peace. The battle of the sexes was the peacetime offspring of wars' good vs. evil ideology.

Primitive ethics thrived in modern America. A girl was disciplined with "no" conditioning to close the door on self-gratification until she married. On the bride's wedding day, she would finally *win* the dream of saying, "yes" and become as-one with the *other half.* On that magical day, her knight in shining armor would romantically ride up on a white horse and lift her up with him. Together they would gallop into the sunset where he would satisfy her every sexual (and financial) desire forevermore, and they would live happily ever after.

The chances of this fairy tale taking place in reality were slim. Forced to disassociate from her sexual organs until marriage, brides across America developed an incapacitating lack of orgasmic understanding. Deeply imbedded in cultural judgment was "down there" is dirty. The forbidden fruit of the virgin psyche, masturbation would continue to be personally evaluated in the light of prior *no* conditioning. After marriage, in the back of the bride's mind, the voice of *whore* refused to shut up. Unless the groom was a magician, his chances of freeing his bride from her role as orgasmic gatekeeper were dismal. No less trapped inside her body than before marriage, neither the bride nor the groom had the remotest understanding of sexual happily ever after.

The freefall of shared spiritual love was the world I witnessed as I grew up. More and more often I watched girls using their bodies as objects of boys' animalistic entertainment. Object seeking of men, object being of women was hurrying to dominate the contemporary scene. In one unified mass, young women learned to use the temple of their souls as seductresses of materialistic rewards. Seduction was the meal ticket. Look pretty, be passively permissive, get married, and have babies.

Little did this naïve population know, after babies supplanted the role of seductress with the role of maid/mother, sexual happily ever after was pretty much thrown out with the dishwater. From seductress, to maid, to mother, once dishwasher hands were a permanent fixture, if a married woman still knew nothing about her own orgasm, chances were she was never going to experience the emotional balancing effects of sexual relief.

As time would tell, the priesthood could throw out a woman's sexual needs with threats of eternal hell and damnation, but sexual needs would rear their ugly heads again and again. Sooner or later the damage caused by repressed sexual energies would implode, resulting in an explosion of mind, body, and spiritual symptoms. There lies the tragic irony. Psychological, physiological, and spiritual symptoms of exploded implosion would prove, yet again, the fall of the female principle. Modernity's enslavement of women would prove that the *meaning of the soul* would remain the *secret of the ages*.

Remarkably, new information regarding male and female sexuality was about to rock the western world! Published in 1966, *Human Sexual Response* contained the results of experiments conducted during the 1950s. Dr. William H. Masters and his assistant, Virginia E. Johnson, by direct observation in a laboratory setting, performed studies on the physiological response to sexual stimulation. To measure changes during and after sexual arousal, they used a penile strain gauge on male volunteer subjects and a vaginal photophethysmograph (no joke) on female volunteer subjects. Their findings were based on 10,000 completed sexual response cycles.

Taking into consideration natural variations, Masters's and Johnson's research found that male volunteers did not have the capacity for repeated orgasms. Individual biology as the control, male subjects had a refractory (recovery) period between ejaculations. The refractory period was a temporary inability to reach orgasm. Conditioned in bathrooms across America to get it over with quick, the average male's sexual response cycle lasted three to four minutes, and the conditioned tendency was to stop after one ejaculation.

Again taking into consideration natural variations, female volunteers were found to be capable of multiple orgasms. Individual biology as the control, the female sexual response cycle did not contain a refractory period. Female subjects had an orgasmic platform. This platform gave volunteers the capability of repeated orgasms with no refractory period. It was not necessary for female subjects to recharge their sexual battery, as it was for their male counterpart. The legendary weaker sex had the capacity to go on and on and on—five, six, seven orgasms before satiation. Additionally, the average female sexual response cycle lasted fifteen to twenty minutes.

Thanks to Masters and Johnson, scientific investigation had shown there did exist a biological gender gap. Stunningly, the sexual gap heavily favored female orgasmic capacity and endurance. Male orgasmic capacity and endurance shrank when compared to female orgasmic capacity. These results turned every published theory pertaining to human sexuality upside down. By virtue of two courageous individuals, gender inequality had been shown to be a scientific fact. In the case of orgasmic capacity, women were by far the *stronger sex*!

As if the stark contradiction between belief and biology were not enough, further findings showed that the clitoris was the female counterpart to the male penis. Equal in status, women achieved orgasm from clitoral stimulation in the same way men achieved orgasm from penile stimulation (masturbation). These findings exposed Freud's speculation that a clitoral orgasm was sexually immature as trumpery. The penis was not the magic wand hailed as preferable and indispensable after all. A woman did not *need* a man to orgasm any more than a man *needed* a woman.

One further finding added one more sad commentary on the tyranny oppressing women for hundreds, even thousands of years. Sexual arousal produced a condition called vasocongestion (swelling of the sexual organs) in female subjects as it did in male subjects. This swelling was caused by engorgement of blood flow. In this case, however, there was a significant difference between genders. Male sexual organs swelled outside the body, making the swelling visible to the naked eye. Female sexual organs swelled inside the body, making the swelling invisible to the naked eye. If male or female subjects did not achieve orgasm after arousal, the abatement of engorgement slowed. Continuous arousal with no orgasm in female volunteers caused a condition called chronic pelvic congestion. Since swelling, the symptom of chronic pelvic congestion, was not visible to the naked eye, the ailment had never been diagnosed or treated correctly. To add insult to injury, unabated swelling led to physiological and psychological problems whose abatement was the orgasm women were chronically denied.

Masters's and Johnson's avant-garde discoveries did blow the roof off the world, the scientific world whose livelihood depended upon patriarchal wealth. So, scientists used patriotism to justify calling Masters's and Johnson's studies unscientific due to populations studied. As if the biology of the human body was significantly different in different populations because scientists said so, a preponderance of Americans chose the way of the religious right and bowed down to the hypocrisy of scientists. The moral majority dusted off truth, again turned their heads backwards in time, and clung to the dark gravitational pull of crystallized standards. In doing so, they placed a huge sexual shadow over their lives and the lives of future generations. Demonstrating that the power of denial should never be underestimated, populations collected in mass and suppressed biological truths that might have sourced the evolution of sexual, psychological, and spiritual truths.

Capitalizing on the will of the people, *politics as usual* kicked up secret-keeping a notch with the power of conglomerated money, the money that was won when the church and state conglomerated into one huge monopoly and then upped the ante on a struggling humanity. The obvious result? Rich men got richer, poor girls got raped, women got blamed. Rape 'em, call 'em whores, rehabilitate 'em. Needless to say, as long as the controlling few could bolster their pocketbooks with this *blame the victim* holocaust, Americans were not going to get the rehabilitation they needed to go anywhere but backwards sexually, psychologically, and spiritually.

When female nature fell out of God's grace, truth fell under a shroud of secrecy. To cover up the oath of secrecy, conglomerated wealth championed a new god called capitalism. Capitalism clearly defined the corporate world's carefully directed upheaval of materialistic standards. Trading one (win/lose) materialistic master for another, capitalism idealized competition by labeling it *free* enterprise. This new American *freedom* glamorized individual wealth at the cost of the greater good. Who cared if this freedom was guaranteed to suck dry the less fortunate multitudes as long as every American had a chance to get rich quick!

Stirred in with the ever-widening psychological gap between men and women, the patriarchy's materialistic standards kicked up the financial gap between the rich and the poor. The few at the top retained the spoils at home as they had at war by romanticizing the freedoms of those at the bottom. And those at the bottom were jumping on the materialistic bandwagon in droves. "We're in the money" was the theme song for a population at war with their bodies, their souls, and . . . their pocketbooks.

In spite of secret-keeping, by September 1961 when I entered high school, many girls were becoming aware that traditional standards were insidiously keeping them sexually and financially oppressed. While my generation searched for the meaning of love, nonsensical *biology as destiny* drafted us into one long ongoing battle between sexual aggressor and sexual gatekeeper. S/he relationships turning into adversarial cold wars. If the boy *won*, the girl *lost*. He got to be called macho. She got to be called whore. Sexual secrecy as normal produced a contest of wills. Whoever best upheld the mysterious sex-role stereotype won.

Sexual freedom for young women was the freedom to participate in the battle of the sexes. Looking was sex. Dating was sex. Touching was sex. Sexual status quo was the extension of nothing new about politics. Politics was personal. Personal was political. Politics was about making money off of a new generation of struggling youth. We were given no choice. The system manufactured and marketed the opposite sex as the enemy. We all had to play the game to some degree. Girls were marketed to view their bodies *not* as temples of their souls but through the eyes of boys. Truckloads of magazine advertisements showed girls how they should look . . . how they could never look . . . how they could lose all self-esteem if they did not wear the right makeup and maintain prepubescent bodies with breasts. Boys, too, played into the system. They loved judging girls' bodies. Judgment gave them the illusion of power. Power gave them the illusion of meaning.

Contrary to boys, the imposed disconnect between a girl's sexual needs and her thinking mind caused a normal girl to fear her search for meaning. A lifetime of being told her sexual needs were dirty had taught her to think that neither her body nor her soul had meaning in the real world. Her thinking was not far off base. In the material world her meaning did come from her cover-girl ability to seduce a boy. Since she had spent so much time identifying with her outer appearance rather than her inner meaning, boys were literally her meal ticket.

This commercial-laden, soulless lifestyle was the reason many of the girls and boys of my generation began to sink into a senseless psychological and spiritual poverty. The mind/soul connection for which my peers searched, from which the meaning of love sprung, was falling fast into delusional win/lose sex games.

Sex games were the heart and soul of high school gender wars. Romance bought high drama. The drama centered around erotic performances that gave the illusion of love. The illusion was enacted by commercialism. Commercialism sold sex as war games. In the theater of commercialized war, who won or who lost the meal ticket became a *life* or *death* game. Sex games climaxed with deadly feelings that perpetuated the money trickling up to the top. The heart of these erotic performances was the family jewels (penis). The boy's role was to ask a girl for a date, then spend all night working to get *it* in (or have her help him blow it out). If the penis lost the battle, the boy would ask the girl for another date. Doing double duty, the girl's role was to say "yes" to a date, then spend all night saying "no" to his sexual advances plus her sexual needs. The entire youth of America was hypnotized by this flesh-eating entertainment!

If the boy won the battle of wills, one quick ejaculation and it was all over but the shouting . . . of his friends. Never would he return to petting again, with that dirty girl anyway. Unless she did not mind being called whore, even if the girl lost the battle, she would perform her passive duty and stop when he stopped. Win or lose, the girl would go home and lay in physiological and psychological pain on a package full of miracles never realized, unaware that an unexpressed sexual powerhouse remained literally trapped inside her . . . believing she needed a boyfriend . . . when all she really needed was an orgasm or two or three. . . .

Relentlessly, the system held sexual truth captive. Budding romances were the misinformed leading the uninformed. Splendor in the grass was about the loss of the splendor of innocence, not the gaining of the splendor of paradise. Why should a girl or a boy not grieve for what they left behind? How in hell could the voice of lost innocence find strength in soul poverty?

In the 1960s, commercialized sexual freedom was the springboard for the boom of Hollywood illusion. Whether the agony or the ecstasy, Hollywood romanticized sex as the ultimate freedom. In the real world, however, the mismatch between the inner and outer condition of young women was colliding in mammoth proportions. The gap between sexual capacity and sexual relief made psychological and sexual freedom impossible. Natural feelings mutated into unnatural feelings. What resulted was a nauseating kind of energy pattern fabricated by the fear of the life-altering cost of the word *whore*.

I watched the incredible waste of energy it took for the girls of my generation to focus their attention away from their true nature and toward the nature of their relationships with boys. Abhorrent traumas over the perceived life or death of a romance set up endless tragic dramas. Life-and-death entertainment energized a stream of budding relationships that never blossomed. The energy it took to *just say no* produced *emotional chaos*. Girls were not getting the balancing energies of the orgasms they believed were supposed to be produced by a boy. Because sex education had been withheld from them, boys had no more insight into a girl's orgasm than girls themselves did. When reality and biology collided in the minds of the girls and boys in my high school, the *symptom* of emotional chaos took the form of *quiet desperation*. The *symptom* of quiet desperation was the *unexpressed anger* I witnessed in the world in which I moved from girl to woman.

As naive as I was about the bigger world during my high school years, my smaller world had taught me to see the symptoms of unexpressed anger. The world that had taught me *to be* was very unlike the one that taught much of my generation *not to be*. I was born a Marine Corps "brat." As such, I found myself living in a constant stream of different neighborhoods. Always the new kid on the block, I was considered an outsider by the established groups. Outsiders were not allowed inside until they were known. Until high school I never lived anywhere long enough to be known. Therefore, I had never been deluged by peer pressure to *act* my gender's stereotypical role.

Not performing was fine with me. My life, though small in numbers, had been packed full of untraditional experiences. Mother loved me dearly and ever so sweetly, but she let my father take the lead when I was born. Daddy and Mother knew they were not going to have any more children, and Daddy wanted a son. So, he raised me as if I was his son. Consequently, I did not learn to feel like a girl or a boy. Not associating myself to either gender gave me an unusual freedom. I felt free to be me without judgment or restraint. Climbing trees, swimming, playing in nature and with animals, and being with my family: those were the things that freed the tomboy in me *to be* happy, and those things were everywhere we moved.

When we moved to new neighborhoods, we traveled by car. While we drove, we played games and sang songs. When it came my turn to pick a song, I would ask to sing *The Sino Song*. From trip to trip, it took Daddy, Mother, and my sister, Susan, a long time before they figured out that I wanted to sing the song I learned in Sunday school, titled, "Jesus loves me, *this I know*." From my days in Sunday school, the unconditional love I felt from those words was what I wanted to sing about.

Unconditional love was what I felt coming from Mother and Daddy. They never preached hell and damnation. I cannot remember one suggestion that I should fear anything I could not see. I knew people did bad things in the world outside my house, but since the world inside my body felt only good intentions, instinct told me everything was going to be okay. My simple "okay" philosophy seemed to be okay with Mother and Daddy. Not once did they tell me that I should not believe in my instincts. Rather, they seemed to have a special appreciation for how my inner world responded to the outer world.

Once Daddy asked me, "Diana, you think life is a bowl of cherries don't you?"

Those cherries originated from my mother's and father's love for me and my love for them. Love was my driving force, and my driving force told me that Mother's and Daddy's romance was an epic love story. The love they openly demonstrated exemplified the soul to soul connection missing in the homes of other children I met. The romance that kept my parents' love alive seemed to be taboo in other homes. Other children learned love restrictions in their homes that I did not learn in mine. If my parents missed the mark with behaviors that were destined to cause me problems, the tremendous love they felt for each other taught me that love was the original feeling I was born having, and sexuality was a human feeling I was going to acquire. Their example of love and sexuality showed me that human nature had both a light and a dark side. More importantly, it was the interpretation, in other words, the judgment of human nature that colored it. The feelings the dark side of my parents' behavior gave me was why I decided I wanted to emulate the light side.

Letting my loving instincts guide me led me into nature. Nature, even in its seeming turbulence, felt like the right place for me to be. By the time I reached high school, the voice of nature was so strong inside of me, I was not blind-sighted by the outer voices that had my peers hypnotized by blind adherence to the social masquerade. My openness made me *different* from my peers and they knew it. They saw me as *different*. Conditioned by a lifetime of being seen as *different*, I knew everything would turn out *okay*.

Because the nature inside of me had not been conditioned to be encumbered by social restrictions, my energy was free to see the symptoms of the unexpressed anger the girls felt for the masquerade. I watched the way they interacted with their parents. Their parents communicated to them with the same quilt-infested, old-fashioned rules that had failed from generation to generation. Suffocating standards of behavior caused my friends to be emotionally and verbally guarded in their own homes. While growing up, they learned to pretend to be who their parents told them they had to be. Because girls were not given the human right to express what they really thought and felt, a *tragic family drama* was endlessly waiting to happen.

The sad hearts that were the root cause of all those needless dramas were absent in me. Since I had been allowed to follow my instincts and those instincts sought only happiness, I wished I had the power to make the *sad eyes* I saw happy. Because my inner being felt happy, I was not searching for any outer force to make me happy. Diana was searching for fun!

To compound my being different, my father/daughter experiences had been so much fun, my personality took on a more typically masculine than feminine flair. My search for a fun boy was decidedly not passive. To me, there was not one rational explanation for passive/aggressive sex games. Game playing wasted energy and was a sure-fire way for the speedy death of a romance. It seemed to me a natural outcome that a failed relationship was the indirect expression of a failed parent/child relationship. I looked for solutions, not problems, and plain as day, gender war games were no long-term solution for short-term relationships. My simple solution was to stop playing games and be real. Therein lie the fun!

During the latter part of my freshman year of high school, my search for a fun boyfriend settled on Tim, a senior boy. Tim was truly a good human being. When we began going steady, my will power made it easy for me to physically express "no" to Tim's sexual advances. At fifteen I had yet to acquire a biological need for sex, so after about six months, Tim stopped trying to slip it in. Although I did date other boys after our first few years together, our relationship lasted seven years. More and more with each passing year, my feelings told me that Tim's love protected me as Daddy's and Mother's love had protected me. What all that protection made me safe from, I had no clue.

It was not until my sophomore year in college that my forthcoming sex drive kicked in. Well practiced in the strong arm of *no,* it was not a challenge to remain a virgin. It was a challenge to remain biologically unaffected. One weekend while Daddy and Mother were driving me home from college, I was feeling the uncomfortable ache of sexual frustration. With no remedy at hand, I told Mother about my frustration. Without a doubt, a sexually actualized creature, she suggested I try a vibrator.

Mother knew best; a vibrator was the magic cure. Quickly, multiple orgasms became easy to produce. Orgasms, nonetheless, were not part of my experience in my twenty-first year when, at long last, I made the decision to have intercourse with Tim. My long habit of being the vagina/penis gatekeeper had closed the door on my ability to orgasm with a partner during intercourse. Six years of heavy petting without climaxing took on new meaning. Losing my virginity changed nothing about my orgasm. After about one year of intercourse with Tim, I did climax, but the climax was a product of oral clitoral stimulation, not intercourse.

That same year I met John. Through oral stimulation, John too found the magic button to my capacity for multiple orgasms. Regardless, after eighteen years of marriage my long habit of being a gatekeeper before we met still inhibited my sexual response. I had not released one orgasm by intercourse in and of itself with my husband. Although at forty years old, I neither knew nor cared that a very important part of my sexual nature remained imprisoned by the patriarchal standards that had kept truth secret.

By letting go of the me I thought I was when I entered the void, I fell into the hands of the universe. One magical night of revelations had lifted my consciousness out of the physical kingdom into the spiritual kingdom. The kingdom of heaven gave me truths held secret through the ages. Truth closed the gap between spirit and flesh, spiritualizing my biology.

Oneness of spirit and flesh had set me free. Freed was an inhibition I did not know I had! Merely looking at the body lying next to my body switched on a heavenly light. Spiritualized desire compelled me with the understanding that the royal road to heaven on earth resided in the mind's connection to the soul. Spiritualized flesh felt like a heavenly mansion, dwarfing the importance of mansions built of stone.

That's it! I thought as I stared at John's glistening body. *Oneness with universal truths has freed my inhibitions by connecting me with my soul in the light of day. I can see John's soul shining because my soul is shining.*

Until that night I did not understand that sex was relative to every other aspect of life. Because of all the outer voices I heard while growing up, the ones that said female sexuality was bad, my love for a physical aspect of my humanity had fallen into negativity. The rigid separation between intercourse and orgasm had been no less rigid than the learned separation between my mind and my body. That separation was a figment of conventional imagination, not the imagination I was born having. When meditation lifted me into the spirit of the nonjudgment I was born with, learned judgments were purified.

Purifying those internalized outer voices felt like heaven meeting earth. Heaven washed away my sexual inhibitions. The inner glory that had been hidden for so many years was exposed for my eyes to see. Suddenly, my outer world mirrored my inner glory, transforming all those voices that had said, "Sex is bad."

Inner glory said, *Sex is good!*

My soul had given my sexuality permission *to be*. Good feelings took the place of bad feelings. Every part of me felt sensual without the mere touch of my husband's body. Because my body had been reborn in the image of my soul, it was falling in love with the man my heart fell in love with almost two decades earlier. The man of my dreams was born again in my heart, and that man lay no further from me than one rollover of my body.

My human body and my spiritual body moved as one, imploring me to physically express what my soul desired. Natural impulses lifted my hand to stroke John's skin. He awoke, reached for me, and pulled the entire length of my body next to his. As human and spiritual energies commingled, the totality of my life's experience was consumed with an upward spiral of heartfelt gaiety. Simple touching was the aphrodisiac. Skin alone filled me with pure rapture.

The familiar texture of my lover's skin treated my every longing as he returned my touch. His fingers grasped the tiny straps of my negligee and moved them one by one over my shoulders. The rapid pulsations of his beating heart reminded me that we shared the same human need to touch and be touched. Fireworks exploded in every inch of the skin his fingers brushed as he lowered my negligee, flung it over the side of the bed, and anxiously watched as the satiny material glided downward toward the floor.

As if it had a mind of its own, my naked body began to express itself. Because my natural impulses did not judge themselves, they were free to explore. With my lover effortlessly following my lead, the two of us found positions I had never envisioned before. Past sex paled in the reflection of present sex. Our old pattern of clitorial stimulation to the point of orgasm became merely one aspect of a diverse sensual universe. I played with what came naturally and felt no limitations about telling my lover every lovely word that came to mind. It was all so happy, all so fun!

Orgasmic sensations came and went. I was not sure if they were orgasms at first. They were nothing like the familiar volcanic eruptions of the past. Present orgasms came easily, abundantly, and from any position. All kinds of free little releases sprung from all kinds of positions. Not only that, for the very first time I was having orgasms during intercourse in and of itself. One peak after the next took me to untroubled levels of satisfaction. Heaven met earth in the unity of our two bodies.

I do not know how long we made love. I do know that we did not stop until every earthly desire had been most beautifully expressed. My soul vision and the physical man melded together into one human-divine encounter. Nothing was missing between the two of us that night. The union of heart, mind, and soul had manifested in my body.

When our night of fireworks concluded, my experience told me that I had begun my journey home. By journeying my way back to myself, I had begun to *fight the affair.*

In becoming full people,
everyone must embrace his or her shadow.

– Carl Gustav Jung

6

The Music Stopped

July 24, 1987, 6:30 A.M.

I awoke enfolded by big, strong arms. John and I had met mind, body, and soul in a night of passionate love. A window to my heart had opened and my soul flew through it causing a different kind of dimensional shift. My body had been reborn in the image of my soul.

My soul flowered within physical matter. Every cell, every atom, every molecule had spiraled into a higher vibration, a quickening. Neither time nor space held any power over my heart's desire. Divine consciousness had manifested in my consciousness a fuller realization of the spiritual possibilities of human nature. With all previous emotional boundaries lifted from me, I experienced an elevated level of pleasure with another human being that I did not know was possible.

Positive our night of physical, psychological, and spiritual sex proved I was not the same woman my husband left three days earlier, I felt sure John would want to know why.

I spoke without hesitation. "I want to tell you about my meditation and my vision of you."

The disarranged revelations began to unveil themselves through the story's passageway, my beaming heart. Listening impatiently, John's eyes rolled up at the ceiling then down at me. He smiled proudly when I described my vision of him and how beautiful and youthful he looked. Nevertheless, his patience quickly wore thin. He broke into my miraculous story by brushing it off lightly.

"Let's talk about it later at Stingers," he said.

Without articulating another word, John scooted out of bed and rounded the corner into the bathroom. He returned yanking up his cement-encrusted jeans and headed directly toward the front door and outside to his old corroded wheelbarrow.

July 24, 1987, 12:15 P.M.

A noontime sun streaked through corner windows onto small tables to our left as John and I entered Stingers. The room gave me the feeling we were in a quaint café rather than a bar serving no food. Except for the bartender, two men wearing cowboy hats were the only people in the room. The cowboys sat at the farthest end of the bar. John chose a stool for himself three to the right of the men and pulled out the stool to his left for me. He gave the cowboys a knowing nod then ordered two beers.

After we settled on our barstools, I noticed that when John and I looked at each other, he faced the cowboys and me simultaneously, yet I faced only John. For me to greet the men as John had, I was obligated to deliberately turn my head away from John. In his mind, turning away to be friendly with men would justify my flirtatiousness. The alternative was for me to be passively unfriendly. Uncomfortable with ignoring anyone in such close proximity, man or woman, I chose a brief greeting.

The bartender placed two bottles of beer on the bar, looked me in the eye, and asked, "Would you like a glass?"

"Please," I replied.

While he retrieved a glass, poured in a portion of the beer, I contemplated the man I witnessed in our bed the night before. *Will my seeing this man's soul radiating from his body make any difference in the way he sees me today? Our lovemaking was too phenomenal not to have changed everything about the way he will react to what I'm about to tell him.*

Anxious to hear my husband's response to our night of great love-making and to explain how learning to live our lives with understanding, forgiveness, and compassion could unmask our love for each other, I watched him guzzle his beer, then set the bottle on the bar.

Emerging from a puzzling silence was the semblance of a man

under the influence of an enchanted spell, raving in wondrous delight. "Fate is a wonderful, kind person, and she loves me!"

Struck dumb, I felt a cold shiver slither through my body. *It is only me who's transformed!* I realized in disbelief. *The metamorphosis that has forever altered the way I understand life has done nothing to mend the way this man sees me. He identifies with the body, caring nothing for the soul. He humiliated my humanity by having sex with Fate, then came home and let me give him not only my body but my heart, mind, and soul. Does he think the price I pay for loving him is to rave about her?*

Bewildered, I sat waiting for my lover's next epiphany; he gave it to me freely and without conscience. "I know you love me too, Diana. Since you and Fate both love me, I'm going to have to choose one of you and kill the other."

Suspended in disbelief, falling hard and fast was the spiritual lifting of emotional boundaries that had literally connected my soul with the soul of another. While reacquainting my nervous system to the insanity of psychological and emotional violence, I entered a *chamber*.

In the chamber dwelled every denial exposed in my revelations. Unlike my meditative sanctuary, this chamber required that I feel the burning flesh of the feelings my mind denied. This earthly tunnel-shaped *tomb* mandated that I go beneath physical reality and uncoil, in the light of day, all my *denied feelings*. Rendering subconscious truths into conscious thought required me to *feel* the *primal fire* of all my entombed *fears*, the fears that were becoming the death of my life's driving force. The primal fire would process and *purify* my denials. From the *pit* of my heart, this part of my *initiatory journey* required me to mentally ascend a counter-clockwise *spiral* in the tunnel of my fearful judgments. Ascending the spiral of denied emotions would purify every atom of my biology from the untruths that embodied my fall. Only at the top of this spiraling tunnel-shaped tomb, when all my denials were purified and I saw the light of truth, would the chamber set me free.

My every revelation had come to life. My biographical shadow was now my biological shadow. The *consequences* of denying my hurt feelings, my fearful feelings, and my judgmental feelings—feeling all my denied feelings and all the behaviors that resulted from those denied feelings—was the *ordeal in the chamber of my shadow*. The humanity in me that yesterday lit up heaven, today burned in hell. As I had judged my mother for her weaknesses, so I had judged my husband for his weaknesses. Now, he was using my weaknesses to wage a kill-or-be-killed war between me and a younger lover.

The outward ugliness of his monstrous gender war mirrored the inward terror of my beastly dependence. The denied feelings that created my insecurity built my dependence upon my husband. Insecurity and dependence were my enemy, not my husband. He was merely the messenger of who I had become. The kill-or-be-killed ordeal he chose to test my endurance in the chamber's fiery pit was my fear of my mother in myself. My ordeal was my fear that I had judged myself to be . . . *less*.

The fire in the middle of my soul raged as I sat on my barstool staring at John. Mooning over Fate, each utterance energized his spirit a little more, each innuendo found humorous the woman I had become. The power and control he had won by breaking my spirit had already begun to corrupt him, heart, mind, and soul. He believed winning gave him the right to kill whomever he did not choose. My newfound vulnerability encouraged monstrous behavior in my husband, and all I could do was sit and wish I had never been intrigued by his drama.

No, I was not the same woman my husband left three days earlier. Every syllable he regurgitated agitated the insecure nature of my hard-won dependence. Every exclamation called back the life or death fear of losing his love. Every adjective describing his other lover lacerated every debate I had ever won. My ability to disappear into my bubble and fearlessly defend my integrity had exploded in my face. The chamber of my shadow had stripped me of the choice to use live and let live to disassociate from my feelings. John could play with me all he wanted. It was my job not to be killed. . . .

As I sat on a barstool at Stingers with all the odds against me, a voice from the far reaches of my mind called out.

All for one and one for all!

It was the voice of my father's spirit. All my life I believed Daddy's words. Now, my husband was telling me my father had lied to me.

Again, Daddy's voice roared into my mind.

Don't give up the ship!

Daddy was trying to tell me something. Not giving up was the way he lived his life. By watching my father step up to that ideal, I learned to live my life by that ideal.

No, no, no! my heart screamed. *John is wrong. Daddy didn't lie to me.*

I reached into my heart so I could feel truth.

From my heart and into my thoughts came the wisdom of what Daddy's words had conveyed. *My husband never learned to live by my father's creed. Naturally he thinks an all-for-one and one-for-all philosophy is a lie. Even though Cherisse and Tamara are the only people aboard my ship with me, those two people are all for me not giving up on not being killed. Daddy has made it clear. If I am not going to be killed, it is essential that I conquer my enemy. To vanquish my fear of being less, I must open my heart to unconditional love. To open my heart, I am required to walk through the consequences of not being the person I wanted to be by seeking to undo the ways I have wronged my husband. By seeking, finding, and purifying the denied feelings that injured the man I chose to marry, I can learn to love unconditionally. If I am ever going to know if unconditional love is what he truly wanted from me, I have to show unconditional love. Whomever he decides to chose, if my children and I are going to survive, as Daddy said, I cannot give up the ship.*

I stared through John's eyes into his sensibilities and began the battle for my life and the lives of my children. "John, you know Fate is too young for you. When you're sixty, she'll be only forty-one. How will you feel when her infatuation with you is over and she begins to look at younger men?"

John nodded in agreement.

Hoping I had found a course for my tiny three-person vessel, I pressed on. "You must at least guess that Fate is after your money?"

He responded with half-truths. "Fate is too young for me. I don't know what she sees in me. I'll probably end up with you."

My foe had thrown me some rope tied in the shape of a noose; he gulped down his second beer, chuckled, and continued, "If I were a

Mormon, I could have you both for wives."

He's using a sick sense of humor to jerk the noose around my neck, I thought, preparing my emotions for his next hysterical remark.

Once again, comic relief took on new meaning. "Diana, you haven't changed. You were faking it last night."

It was then I witnessed first-hand how the man I married used ignorance as a defense and hid his strategy behind a chuckle. My meditative review had given me the ability to interpret the symptoms of my husband's denial. For the first time I understood how his chuckling insult afforded him the necessary amount of self-deception to believe his own "faking it" lie.

The trials ahead would be for me to face my self-deceptions by recognizing self-deception in John. No matter how displeasing, if I failed the test of enduring this ordeal, it would be impossible for me to ever return to that moment when my soul shined so brightly that it connected with the soul of another. I had begun the process of finding and feeling my repressed feelings. If I wanted to wake up to the whole truth of the person I had become, it was vital for me, this time around, to feel John's every dagger. Walking through the tunnel of painful feelings would awaken each of my self-deceptions, one by one.

Fighting my husband's war of lies would have been the death of hope for either of us to ever reunite the breach between our souls. Debating "faking it" would add just one more degree of separation between us. At last I understood why. The ultimate downfall of past debates was that John never felt that I heard what he was saying. Feeling that he never felt heard afforded him the anger he needed to initiate a new war. War had to end. Our partnership in crime had to be terminated. Learning to communicate in a way that my partner felt heard was the road to peace. Regardless of John's contemptuous behavior toward me, my meditative life review had taught me that my fall had given me an opportunity. Extending understanding to a person who was unmistakably crying out for help would be one small step toward healing the disconnect between our hearts and souls.

The new knowledge he had just given me helped me summon the courage to wave the proverbial white flag. "John, I know I have hurt you by not acknowledging your pain. I'm truly sorry. But I have been there for you in other ways. Our house is always clean. You come home to a hot dinner every night. You've never questioned my being a good mother to Cherisse and Tamara. And you know I've always given you as much sex as you wanted. Every duty a wife and mother is supposed to do, I've done gladly. You said I take care of myself. Isn't that taking care of you, too? "

By giving away a small part of myself, my words struck an honest chord in John.

He humbly retorted. "I've been hurt by a lot of the things you've done, Diana."

I matched his honestly. "Never once did I hurt you on purpose."

Truthful communication turned out to be the tiny step I hoped for.

John's tone changed. "Diana, I've always loved you."

Words told me my ship's hull had found a course. Words also reminded me that language was only half of the way to fight the affair. Action went hand in hand with words.

I squeezed John's hand and affectionately suggested, "Let's go home."

The understanding, forgiveness, and compassion I sought to live my life were meaningless if they were practiced only when convenient. Offering a helping hand to another at a time of extreme inconvenience turned out to be my salvation that day. In seeking the deeper meaning of what appeared on the surface, I found the man I loved one degree closer to me.

We drove the curvy, tree-lined road home, went into the master bedroom, and made love. Another mythical sexual experience transformed our bed into fantasy-land. It was not something anyone could fake. From the impassioned love we shared, I hoped John would soon figure out one truth I had always known. Infatuation was not in the same league with real love. Sexually, it could not even get into the ballpark!

July 25, 1987, 4:30 A.M.

John pushed the snooze button on the alarm clock, rolled over, hugged me sweetly, and whispered, "I'm going to end it with Fate. We can try again."

John and I clung to one another, filling the needs we had both neglected for so long, after which he showered, dressed for work, and returned to my bedside. He sat on the edge of the bed the way he had a thousand times, hugged and kissed me goodbye, then stood up and walked over to the door. A change of clothes was draped over his arm.

In the center of the doorway he stood majestically stating, "I love you."

The change of clothes made it impossible for me to return my husband's profession of love. Without asking me why, he turned and walked away. With John's change of clothes went the security I had gained from one night of miraculous revelations followed by two nights of love-making. Nothing I had ever learned or experienced had any power over the threat of my husband going to another woman.

The magnetic force of polar opposites that attracted me to John nearly eighteen years earlier had calculated my present position. My unforeseen vulnerability to his every move had affected more than one metamorphosis. It transformed my husband into a man who wore "who shall I choose, who shall I kill," like a king's ransom. He was using another woman to play sex games with my life. As long as I stayed stuck in fear, his desire for her would be my flesh burning in my initiation's fiery chamber.

After the engine of John's little yellow truck faded from my ears, I did not even try to fight the inevitable. I dragged myself out of bed, trudged over to the window, lowered the shade, and trudged back to bed.

At bedside, I kneeled and pleaded, "Please make this nightmare stop."

The nightmare did not stop.

The now familiar demons raged forth through an ocean of tears. I purged painful prayers until I could not take the punishment a second longer; then I pulled myself back in bed and stared at the ceiling.

I was angry. For the first time in my life, I was able to feel the deep profound anger unraveled by revelations of denied truths. I was angry at John's every hateful word and deed. I was angry that he pushed me away by forcing me to disappear into a love triangle with Cherisse and Tamara. I was angry because now that I was in serious emotional trouble, he made it easy on his emotions by capitalizing on another lover. And I was angry because he was using my renewed love to wage a kill-or-be-killed war I could not fight with anger. His kill game was like bait in a trap. Expressing the anger I had never expressed in any of our debates would be the be-killed trap John would use not to choose me.

Personifying the irony of my fall were the needs I denied myself from day one of our marriage. The comic tragedy of present neediness lay in past projection. The insecurity I projected onto my husband by convincing myself he was dependent upon my love mirrored the insecure part of me that was actually dependent upon his love. My unenlightened assumption that I did not need my husband's love jack-knifed while being enlightened psychologically and spiritually. If my life review had taught me anything about my truth, it taught me that what really angered me was my stubborn, fearful refusal to tell my husband what I needed before it was too late.

July 27, 1987, 11:30 A.M.

John had not come home since he left with a clean change of clothes three days earlier. Endlessly, I waited by the telephone for him to call and tell me he had ended his affair. Endlessly, the telephone remained silent. The anger I felt for the first time in my life had come too late. All the years I was unwilling to give up a little bit of my fearless self-concept to make John feel important had come back to haunt me.

Not giving up on fearless Diana explained why John repeatedly accused me of being stubborn. By stubbornly withholding the truth that I needed his love, I denied both of us the feelings I began repressing in childhood. By my own undoing, the anger I was forced to feel now hurt only me. It had come to my attention that there was more than one school of thought on not giving up. . . .

For three days I lay in bed crippled by an overload of unmasked feelings. There was nothing for me to do except bear the demons; one by one, I felt every hurt I had ever caused my husband by ignoring the needs he now ignored in me. Remorse, guilt, and amazement over my stupidity ripped away at the Diana I had been praying so desperately to recover.

I lay in the blackness of hell on earth when I heard a faint tap on my bedroom door.

Knowing it had to be either Cherisse or Tamara, I answered, "It's all right to come in."

The door opened slowly.

Tamara tiptoed in and announced timidly, "My dance class starts at 1:30."

I lifted my head, looked at Tamara's humbled face, and replied instantly, "Okay, I'll get ready."

As I started to get up, Tamara turned and stepped quietly out the door. After she closed the door, I discovered that there was one truth more powerful than all the other miserable truths reality could throw at me. Truth was spelled out on the expression on Tamara's face.

Written all over my daughter's disparaging face was, "Mom, where have you gone? I feel scared and alone without you."

Without warning, the loving, supportive mother Tamara counted on all her life to be there for her had disappeared behind a closed door into a darkened room. Except for the few moments my daughters sat on my bed listening to my revelations, Cherisse and Tamara felt abandoned by my closed door.

If I could not find the courage to enter the world outside my door for my daughter, not only would my room be a living hell for the rest of my life, the desolate look on Tamara's face would be my eternal, infernal purgatory.

Leaving the safety of my bed threatened my thinking with unimaginable monsters. In an attempt to ease the meteoric onslaught of anxiety, I turned on the radio. A sad love song was playing. The tune exchanged anxiety for paranoia. Hurriedly, I twisted the radio's OFF button. The music stopped.

I scanned the room for help, saw the television, walked over and turned it on with a wish. *Maybe one of my old happily-ever-after movies will be on.*

An old-maid, lonely hearts club TV series slashed my hopes for comfort.

I questioned hope. *Is the entire world sad?*

My fingers switched off the television. I finished dressing in panic-stricken silence. Attempting not to think about anything except my goal of taking Tamara to dance class, I paced out of the house and joined her where she sat on the front seat of the car waiting for me. I slipped the key into the ignition and turned it, detonating the rumbling diesel engine. I backed the car out of the garage and drove down our long bumpy driveway. As we exited the driveway, Tamara turned on the radio.

Words vaulted melodically from the speakers. "Alone, just my lonely heart knows why, I want to be wanted."

More than my nervous system could tolerate, when I heard those words all emotional control released itself from me, and I heard a stranger with my voice scream, "What's wrong with you? Don't you care how I feel? What kind of a daughter are you?"

I punched at the OFF button, not believing that music could cause me to take complete leave of my senses. Again the music stopped. Only the thunder of the car's diesel engine remained. The unimaginable demonic beast had slithered out of my mouth and hurt my daughter with untrue accusations. Regret consumed my every emotion.

I looked at Tamara. What I saw was a face stricken with pain, imploding purple tones. She was crying the deepest, most heart-wrenching tears I had ever seen. My soul heaved forth shame. I would have walked through the eternal infernos of hell and damnation to save my daughter from the suffering I myself inflicted.

What have I done? I agonized to myself.

At 14 years-old, my daughter could not have possibly understood the fear controlling her mother's every waking moment. All their lives Tamara and Cherisse effortlessly filled the needs John had failed to fill. It had never been necessary for me to ask my children to meet my needs. Now, the only thing I needed was for Tamara to reach over and hold my hand. But the needs I sought and found were stuck in past habits. The past habit of not asking for what I needed held power over the present wish to ask to have those needs met. The small comfort that may have saved both of us was overridden by my fear of Tamara thinking of her mother as being needy.

"I'm sorry. I don't know what to do," she cried, trying to tell me that she could not read my mind.

Since childhood, live and let live justified suppressing my hurt feelings. I disassociated from my needs, first because of my mother's weaknesses, then because of my fear of my mother's weaknesses in myself. By creating the habit of using happily-ever-after dreams to hold in unmet needs, I built a mountain of the fear of feeling needy that I could not tear down with the brush of a magic wand.

My daughter was reaping the heartache her mother's denial had sown. And the only thing my guilt-ridden self could do was keep my anguish silent and steer the car for the remainder of the drive.

After I parked the car, Tamara braved, "Are you going to come in and watch me?"

"I'll wait in the car," I answered, digesting the price we were both paying for the needs I could not to ask to be filled.

A sweltering July sun pounded through the car windows onto black seats as I watched Tamara tread alone across the gravel parking lot. The sun-baked soil beneath the tiny pebbles upon which she stepped imitated the desolation I felt for not *being there* for my daughter. Everything outside the car immobilized my ability to deal with the real world. Neither a thousand degrees of heat nor Tamara's aloneness had a chance of forcing me from the safety of the car. Still, the car did not feel safe.

I climbed into the back seat, laid down, closed my eyes, and prayed. Remorse lunged at my heart. I felt remorse for hurting John. I felt remorse for Fate's involvement in miseries that should have been dealt with long before she entered our lives. I felt unbearable remorse for lashing out at Tamara. And I felt remorse for Cherisse, whose abandonment was a cross I had yet to bear.

Every part of me prayed prayers that longed for forgiveness. My entire being immersed itself in a catharsis of remorsefulness. My body trembled and my eyes heaved tears in an attempt to vanquish guilt. The unearthed passion to be forgiven was rearranging the very energy of my emotions. I sunk deeper and deeper into the seat of the car until inner and outer space became indistinguishable. All of a sudden, I was in the void. This time I recognized the spontaneous meditation. Guilt vanished! Pain vanished! Fear vanished!

Then something astonishing happened. A magnificent stream of electricity bolted straight through the top of my head and down the center of my body. An electrical charge of exhilarating spiritual consciousness had entered my human consciousness. I felt so loved, so forgiven, so ingratiated with this loving force, tears of gratitude were pouring from my eyes and running down the sides of my cheeks. As suddenly as before, my tears stopped. I lay in a wondrous silence. Then, as if my prophetic soul knew what was about to happen, a message entered my consciousness with perfect clarity:

> *John is being taken care of, as your daughters are being taken care of, as Fate is being taken care of. All people are being guided in loving directions. You and John have always been a part of each other and you will be a part of each other eternally. Do not be afraid, Diana. You are much more than the trials you are experiencing. All your judgment and fear can be washed away. Both John and you have the ability to be healed. When you end fear and live in pure goodness of thought, word, and deed, you will have the opportunity to create the paradise on earth available to you!*

My eyes popped open! A message of boundless wisdom had been given to me, reminding me that unconditional love was the universal truth I should never doubt. Truth so inspired me, a stirring peace replaced every little bit of remorse. With peace came a remembrance of an emotion. In the far reaches of my mind lived the memory of a feeling. I did not know where or when, but I remembered paradise.

As the energies of love grow stronger,
the shadows of fear become more visible than before.
— Ken Carey, *The Return of the Bird Tribes*

7

Walking Through Fear

July 27, 1987, 1:55 P.M.

Exhilarated, I sat up, looked out the car's windows, and viewed the world surrounding me! In a few short minutes, the way my mind's eye beheld the earth had been transformed. I was transported into the beholder of awesome beauty. Baked soil had become magnificent earth! The sun's heat warmed me affectionately. Telepathic words had astonished, honored, and elevated my consciousness. My experience in the back seat of the car fashioned everything in my environment to feel magical.

The eminent immediacy of recording the message propelled me out of the car and into the driver's seat. I opened the glove compartment, grabbed a scrap of paper, and wrote down each word exactly as I remembered hearing it.

Doused in splendiferous joy, I breathed in the euphoria of lingering ethereal energies and aspired to mentally articulate what I had just experienced. *The universe plugged into me an elevated level of energy that felt like a force of electricity. An electric field of energy higher than mine descended straight through the top of my head and down the center of my body, raising the vibrations of my energy field. My very breathing, my every heartbeat, my thinking mind embodied my soul and its interconnectedness with a spiritually advanced universe. Heart-wrenching prayers for forgiveness thrust my human mind of suffering into unity with a spiritual mind of wisdom. The instant quickening amplified my soul to a level where it could be a microphone through which this higher universe could speak, one on one, to my mind. Bestowed upon the river of my life force was a message so sweet, so caring, so overflowing with equality of love for every human being that this bearer of good news has written in stone the most important thing I have learned since my fall. A second spontaneous meditation had cemented my philosophy that seeking the soul determines the finding of the garden of paradise!*

Tamara's image caught the corner of my eye. I could hardly wait to tell her what had happened and read the message to her.

She had no sooner opened the car door when I blurted out, "Tamara, you won't believe what just happened!"

As soon as she closed the door, I simplified the story of how I had laid down in the back seat, closed my eyes, and meditated. I explained how I heard healing words from a spiritual source who told me I should not be afraid, that every single person was being taken care of and led toward a life of love. I told her that since I was interconnected with this spiritual love, every other person had to be interconnected with its love too. That meant all people were interconnected by spiritual love, so we should always treat others the way we would like to be treated. Then I read out loud the words on my scrap of paper. As I read, I repeatedly glanced at Tamara's face. Worry gradually faded away, and her sad eyes were replaced with a peaceful glow. When I finished reading, I told her that the lack of separation between spirit and me felt blissful.

Tamara radiated hope as she responded, "Mom, I want to do that too!"

My daughter's animated appreciation and desire to be a part of my experience helped heal the tears in my heart for yelling at her. Regardless, neither the good nor the bad nor the ugly of what took place that day was going to simply disappear. Neither of us attempted to turn on the car radio during our drive home. Although nothing would ever bring back the simplicity of the world we once shared, a gentle serenity and a new world we both wanted to get to know better flowed between the two of us, interconnecting our hearts with a deep, profound love.

When we returned home, Tamara entered the house ahead of me

and went straight to her bedroom. I stared down our long, narrow hallway.

With no forewarning, the walls closed in on me as if they were literally vibrating, *Did I miss a telephone call from John?*

A different kind of electric shock shattered lingering euphoria. The thought of missing a call from John instantly threatened the safety I had received from a far more loving universe. I scrambled toward the master bedroom to escape visibly frightening walls. Once in my room, I hurried to the closet, changed into comfortable clothes, traipsed over, jumped into bed, and pulled the covers over me. Haunted by the suspicion that John phoned while we were gone, I fixated my stupefied emotions on the telephone.

July 27, 1987, 10:30 P.M.

For the eight hours since Tamara and I had returned home, I lay in bed staring up at the plastered ceiling, questioning why castle walls caved in on me the second I stepped into the house. In the ceiling's plaster, like an ink blot, I saw shapes that took the form of faces: laughing faces, crying faces, beautiful faces, ugly faces, young faces, old faces, rich faces, poor faces, female faces, male faces. A multitude of faces imitated the conflicts shadowing my life.

For years, I had looked in every nook and cranny for answers to why John was so angry at the world and angry with me. I was a housewife dusting, vacuuming, scrubbing her heart out in search of reasons for her husband's negativity, hostility, and sad state of mind. The harder I searched, the angrier John became.

Rather than look at my growing negativity toward my husband, I looked at my husband's growing negativity toward me. While I avoided facing the truth about how I was internalizing his sorrow (shaping in me a negative mindset), that misbegotten negativity was stripping away my childlike freedom to feel joy.

"It's a jungle out there," Daddy used to tease.

My father's slang was funny to naïve Diana. All Daddy's slang expressions were funny because I believed Daddy would always be there to protect me from the jungle.

"They're all bad out there in the real world," John often chuckled.

Childlike Diana laughed at her husband's common judgments

because he told her he would be there forever and ever to protect her from the bad world.

All my life men protected me. All that changed. It took fifty years, but the jungle finally succeeded in killing my father. And John was out there in the bad world protecting another woman. In a matter of one telephone call from a young female voice who intended to steal the security of my castle walls, being protected by a man mutated into a monumental handicap. A lifetime of protection from the jungle, combined with no preparedness for a bad world, produced a fear that ran away with fearless Diana.

My fall into fear was a rude awakening that I had been spoon fed a lie. No matter how hard Daddy had tried, he could never have protected me from the jungle of John's real world. It was beyond human capacity for me to forever disappear from the traditional warring standards that had trickled down into nearly every household on planet Earth.

A global war dead set on good murdering evil had created an inescapable human dilemma: Who's the jungle? Where's the bad? What's the point of separation between the good and the bad? Judgment of evil by popular opinion was doomed to terrorize the soul of individuals like me whose beliefs were different, even if different meant *all for one and one for all.* Cultural agreement concluded that anyone who disagreed with the will of the moral majority should be targeted as evil. Consensus that ordinary individuals were flawed justified the lack of responsible behavior. Self interest at the cost of the greater good was applauded by victims of retarded psychological development who drove around with spiritually retarded bumper stickers, such as *the one who has the most toys wins.*

Short-term gain closed its eyes and ears to long-term loss. The method of winning freedom was to kill the enemy and be done with it. Don't let your left hand know what your right hand is doing. When all the votes were counted, unveiled were the results: It did not occur to the average citizen that short-term violence begat long-term violence. Getting what he wanted at the expense of his family was John's socially acceptable goal, his short-term materialistic morality that reflected long-term results upon Cherisse, Tamara, and me.

Knowing all that, John's mission was a mission for which I was required to have understanding, forgiveness, and compassion. If I failed to manifest those qualities in my *heart*, the weaknesses I had projected onto the man I *loved* would haunt me for the rest of my life. To free myself from bondage to the man I married, I was required to bear the burden of his sins until they were vanquished from within myself. Until then, I would be crawling between heaven and earth.

When Tamara and I returned from her dance class, what should have felt like the security of a long hall that represented my material reality instead reminded me that my fallen emotions were dependent upon a psychologically and spiritually handicapped man who romanticized the cheating that had broken my spirit. The jackpot question was could I survive and then live up to the higher psychological and spiritual standard I had set for myself?

I continued staring at the plaster on the ceiling and counseled myself. *I've been split down the middle, alternating between two separate and distinct states of being. I'm bouncing between heaven and hell on the battlefield of earth. A huge emotional gap has been forged between my physical reality and my spiritual reality. The vulnerability of my human nature is doing battle with the invulnerability of my spiritual nature. In the back seat of my car, in a very black hole, a loving light shown through and lifted me out of my dark emotions. No separation existed between my human consciousness and my spiritual consciousness. The direct experience with divine forces has convinced me that if judgment is the lynchpin that holds the web of fear together, then love is the lynchpin that will untangle judgment's web of fear. The message told me if I end all fear and live in a state of pure goodness of purpose, the energies of heaven and earth will fuse together and become one. If that is true, then the separation is an illusion, and earth is a paradise waiting to happen. I have been instructed to forever study my soul. By studying my soul, my mind will develop the pure, loving feelings that dwell in my soul. Spiritualizing my mind will make it possible for me to survive my fall. Understanding, forgiveness, compassion, and connecting with my soul are the way for me to bridge the gap between my spiritual and material states of being!*

July 27, 1987, 11:15 P.M.

The mystery man walked into the master bedroom wearing the clean clothes he took with him when he left. This time draped over his arm were his dirty clothes. He went directly into his closet, undressed, and tossed both sets of clothes into the hamper for me to wash. He returned wearing only boxer shorts and ended the mystery of where he had been for the past two nights.

"You haven't changed, Diana. You're faking it. Fate agrees with me. No one changes overnight," he scolded.

"Fate agrees with me" envenomed the quickening of my love for my husband. Thanks to the herculean leap in my ability to feel my feelings, John's gruesome version of *all's fair in love and war* magnified the shadows of my fear. My change of attitude toward my husband was as pure as the untouched snow after a winter storm, as sweet as a baby's dreams, as colorful as a rose when the sun turns a bud into a valentine surprise. My lovemaking transcended human passion. It originated in my soul's desire to love unconditionally. "Fate agrees with me" had to originate in the partnering of two people whose thoughts and feelings were so dark that light was unable to penetrate.

Silently, I processed the anger I knew would do battle with the man I was walking through fire to make peace with. *My passion to live by the light in my soul seems to have brought the darkness out of my husband. He legitimizes "faking it" with the endorsement of an adulteress who is trying to steal the husband of another woman and the father of two children. My husband has informed me that he has chosen to join forces with a twin avenger. John and Fate have teamed up for the sport of killing Diana, never once feeling responsible for the harm killing Diana is doing to Cherisse and Tamara.*

When John left my bed carrying an extra set of clothes, intuition told me he would not end it with Fate. But it never crossed my mind that she might have a power over my husband that was so strong, even his common sense would fall prey to her control. Despite Fate's power to intensify John's unrelenting determination to get his eye for an eye with me, he made an uncalculated error. When he returned from Fate's bed to my bed, he inadvertently gave me the secret of how she won her power. His brawn-over-brain mindset made him susceptible to Fate's feminine wiles, and she knew it. She would triumph over Diana by using her youth and beauty to make John's ego her mission in life. Encouraging his self-interest mindset would amputate his emotions for me by manipulating his emotions in her favor. Fate had chosen a teammate with her same goal. They were both working hard for his money. . . .

John went straight to bed, fell asleep, and began to snore. The snoring hammered away at the dark side of human nature. Trusting my husband's humanity had gotten me into serious trouble. John gave Fate all the information she needed to reinforce his belief that I was bad just like my mother. Neither Fate nor John cared how much of Cherisse, Tamara, and me they obliterated with their adulterous affair. Their team sport luxuriated in our loss. Adultery thrived in a jungle that rewarded a winner-take-all ideal. Controlling Diana's thoughts and feelings was sporting entertainment. The political and religious ideology of stamping out evil afforded each of them the excitement of imagining they were the ones on the side of good, and good gave each of them the illusion they were the one with the power. But Alas! Their brand of power had an Achilles heal. Controlling another person's life in negative ways corrupted the soul of the controller. The interconnectedness of humanity made it impossible for John and Fate to kill me without killing themselves.

No, John's affair had nothing to do with the way I cut up cucumbers. But "you haven't changed" had everything to do with elitist conspiracy to decimate his natural-born instinct to value pure goodness. Pure goodness of thought, word, and deed had lost value for John. The exhilaration his ego gained from fighting till the end was what John had learned to prize. The feelings my spiritual love stirred in him could not compete with his sexual infatuation with her. Fate had her finger on the control button. She manipulated John's emotions by acting as his alter ego. She confirmed for him that Diana's sex, rather than her adulteress sex, represented the seductress's forbidden fruit. Fate was winning their control game by using me to reinforce John's garden-of-evil standard.

The dynamic duo of John and Fate ate, drank, and breathed jungle standards. Every single battle in their crusade to champion animal sports manifested directly upon my ongoing struggle to live by a higher standard. Fighting the affair was turning out to be more than a skirmish in the Pacific. If my todays were not going to be Cherisse's and Tamara's tomorrows, I had to survive a *different* way of doing battle with the monstrous political and religious machines that lived in the hearts and minds of the man and woman who stole my freedom.

8

D-Day: The Art Of War

The headline of the newspaper read, "Opponents Prepare Plan B for The Big G." An offer to buy the lease on The Big G, where John had taught golf for sixteen years, was made by a development firm who planned to tear it down and build a shopping center. John had talked for years about the probable sale because commercial development would force him to change job locations.

During his sixteen years of teaching golf at The Big G's driving range, John amassed an enormous number of golf students. The trouble was, there were no other driving ranges within miles. Being forced to teach at a distant facility would cost him a loss of golf students and therefore a loss of income we could not afford.

Building a commercial center on recreational land required a zone change. Since The Big G—a nine-hole, three-and-four-par golf course—was one of precious few recreational facilities left in an overcrowded city, the people opposed a zone change. But the City Council, not the people, retained the power to vote for zone change, and the City Council's bottom line was money. A shopping center's projected tax proceeds of $300,000 annually far outweighed the annual $8,000 tax money obtained from The Big G. Therefore, all five City Council members favored the financial gain of a "yes" vote. The people and the city were at odds. Therefore, the fate of The Big G had become a political dispute.

As the date for the sale of the lease approached, John made a discovery. Although the council members had zone voting power, the people had council voting power. If enough people signed petitions against zone change, the council members would be forced by the threat of job loss to vote "no." *The people's power was in numbers.*

Giving golf lessons enabled him to meet so many people in the community, John's discovery evolved into a means to save The Big G's recreational zoning status. In a self-appointed effort to fight the City Council's profiteering mindset, John organized a people's protest. With the help of his students, he made connections with local organizations, clubs, businesses, etc., who were in favor of saving The Big G. He organized a coalition to go door to door with petitions against zone change.

In the process of trying to save his income and lifestyle, John had stumbled upon an opportunity to do a nice thing for others. He became the leader of the People's Committee, a group that fought to save a place in its community where people could have fun. When the day came for the City Council vote, if the people won, John would be a hero.

July 30, 1987, noon

Voting day had arrived. For the first time in all our years together, I watched John reach out to others and give of himself in an effort to protect their quality of life. He had my genuine good wishes. With all my heart, I hoped he truly cared about a social situation that previously meant nothing more than the rewards that came with the money in his pocket. Along with my fondest wishes that the People's Committee would pressure the council members to vote according to the peoples' desires were dreams of humanitarian opportunities for John. In view of the fact he had little more than a high school degree, a City Council vote in favor of the people might open doors not available to him in the past. Winning could turn his life in the direction of aiding others while simultaneously helping him understand the benefits of having his wife by his side.

In the days since Fate became John's accomplice in the game of my "faking it," he refused to make a choice between us by playing musical chairs with our beds. The emotional holocausts of his bed hopping kept me in the custody of my cave when he was not home. As far as I knew, John did not know I had been shut up in my room because when he was home, the safety of his presence enabled me to go about what appeared to be a fairly normal routine. Though my subservience to his every earthly desire had replaced my strong-willed independent personality, I never felt sure if he knew I lived in a nearly constant state of trauma.

Despite the insanity of our relationship, this was voting day! John was far too distracted to concern himself with anything except the possibility of becoming a hero. Early that morning, he quit working on the driveway, took a shower, and dressed for a celebration. He planned for us to spend the day waiting for a call from The Big G with the vote results. High-spirited anticipation had the master of the castle floating on cloud nine. He suggested we go into his office, where he immediately popped the cork of a bottle of champagne. Smiling, he handed me the newspaper article and asked me to read out loud the excerpt quoting him.

With pleasure I read, "We feel that people should have a choice, not just the five council members. We're not going to give one inch. We're going through with this all the way . . . file suit if we have to. We just want to keep our facility."

It did not matter that I was skeptical that my husband's intentions were completely pure. The admiration I felt for his fighting on behalf of people's relief from concrete aided me in focusing my attention away from the battles going on inside me. He handed me a glass of champagne, and we toasted to the assurance that he would be a hero. His jubilation seemed to fill particles of the air we breathed. Just by breathing in the elation of the occasion, everything started to feel sweet. I permitted my elevating energy to continue to rise and flow with the cloud upon which he floated. Inner visions drifted back in time to a day I had never told him about, a day that altered the course of my life. . . .

It began several months earlier as a coincidence. When I was almost finished reading *Dynamics for Living*, I wished for another book that would give me those same feelings of cozy inner peace. Never in my life had I been a reader. Thus I possessed very limited ideas about where to begin my search. Soon after I made my wish, Mickey, our black standard poodle, and I were playing ball in our massive master bedroom. With his nose, he pushed his ball under our king size bed for me to retrieve. While on the floor looking under the bed for Mickey's ball, I spotted a small paperback book. I pushed the ball out from under the bed and then clutched the book.

On the cover I read these words, *"A Search For The Truth* by Ruth Montgomery."

I scanned my memory as to where the book had come from. I would forever be clueless as to how the book found its way under the bed, but I did recall buying it on sale for ten cents at a community college where I had been studying art for the past four years. If the coincidence had not taken place, my reading may have ended. It delighted me that a little book had unexpectedly presented itself so soon after I wished for it. To add to my delightful surprise, *truth* had always inspired my curiosity. With that, my initiation into reading information I did not know existed took flight.

I remembered that when I was a little girl attending Sunday school, I learned that life was without end. Yet in my forty years, discussions about the possibility of life after life was as far as my spiritual curiosity had taken me. Spiritual enlightenment remained an abstract term in philosophy books I had not read. I had no idea that *A Search For The Truth* was a spiritual book until I began reading. Almost instantly the words on the pages inspired and amazed me. I felt a heightened sense of pleasure with each reading. I would later learn that a book I found to be miraculous was merely one of hundreds of published texts on the subject of before and after a person "shuffles off the mortal coil."

Among the many "miracles" described in the book was Montgomery's "automatic writing." She simply closed her eyes, set the tip of a pencil on paper, meditated by silencing her mind, and allowed what she termed "Spirit Guides" to speak through her. Her hands automatically wrote (later typed) "philosophical dissertations" telepathically dictated by the Guides.

Automatic writing intrigued me to no end. Leaving me elated were dissertations such as these: "The person who aids another is setting off a chain reaction that never dies," and "Why is it so difficult for us to believe in communication between two phases of life when we accept without question . . . the splitting of the atom." The Spirit Guides quoted the bible on this subject. Ezekiel in Exodus 14:25 said, "Spirit entered into me when he spake unto me?"

Though spiritual and biblical information was new to me, the automatic writings made complete sense. Even as a child, I felt intuitively that if life was truly without end, then seen and unseen reality had to be interconnecting, a self-organizing whole with each little life fitting in perfectly. If there was no divine plan, no guiding force of intelligence and love, then the world would be an out of control, chaotic mess that would have self-destructed billions of years before my tiny self came into being.

Montgomery's communication with Spirit Guides sounded like common sense to me. Ezekiel became one with and heard the voice of spirit. Yet hundreds of years later in the evolution of the human mind, because of controlling biblical interpretations, it was socially unacceptable for an individual to communicate with two worlds simultaneously. In my unstudied view, it made no sense for the clergy of the modern world to discount, even warn against, communication with spirits. Their warnings had to be for another reason. It was later I learned that individuals who knew they could directly communication with God were a threat to the survival of the church and its wealth. One billion Catholic contributors of money to the church looked to me to be more the reason for priestly intermediaries between wo/man and God.

Even before I read the excerpt about how the spirit world is all around us and in us, making direct communication available at all times, a joyful warmth permeated around me and in me at every reading. One beautiful sunny day while tanning by our pool with Mickey by my side, I read this quote by the Montgomery's Spirit Guides. "Anyone with an open mind who is willing to put psychic phenomena to the test can do it." The words "open mind" flew off the page straight into the realms of my curiosity. Open-minded Diana did not take long to reach the conclusion that she would give automatic writing, as Daddy used to say, "that old college try."

With the easy-going feeling of having nothing to lose, I followed the Guide's instructions. I located a pad of paper and a pencil (with an eraser just in case I did not like what I wrote), sat down at my desk, rested the led gently on the paper, and closed my eyes. I silenced my mind (which at the time was not difficult) and sat waiting. The pencil did not move.

I laughed to myself at my silly endeavor, *Thank goodness no one can see me,* then I stood up and strolled around the house.

Good vibrations strolled with me urging me back to my desk. *Why not?* I queried myself. *Might as well try it again.*

So it was, on June 17, 1987, exactly one month before John told me he loved Fate that I sat in a chair, set a pencil in my left hand, rested the tip on a pad of paper, stopped thinking, and opened my mind to the spirit world. My pencil moved of its own accord! The following was my very first automatic writing.

> *Share yourself with others. Come with us on a journey up there, somewhere. Hear, see, believe, stand tall. We speak of love. Trust in humanity . . . yours to have if you will lovingly give of yourself every day. Forgive, love, hate no more . . . Call your sister!*

Stunned by "call your sister," which had a different tone than the rest of the writing, I dropped my pencil. My eyes burst open! I read the words, rose to my feet, and pranced lightly around the house. My mind spun mysterious delight!

I did it! I thought in absolute amazement. *But the knowledge I received was unlike Ruth Montgomery's dissertations. Spirit Guides did not introduce themselves by name, nor was I given philosophies about the past, present, or future of humankind. My short writing had a simple theme: we speak of love.*

Loving words flowed through a loving woman's soul onto a small pad of paper. Though it was my first spiritual experience, I did not even guess how the words bypassed my brain and caused my hand to move. At no time did fear of the words or the source of the words enter my thoughts. The only thing important to me was that the message contained nothing except good advice, and the bearer of the message felt like pure intelligence and love.

Not until my deep meditation after my fall did I begin to comprehend the concept that all knowledge since the beginning of time was on the other side of the veil of human consciousness. I was learning that every individual body was truly a temple for universal consciousness, and purifying learned feelings was the key to making that knowledge a part of physical reality. Before my revelations, my intuition was much too innocent for me to have known why life was a precious gift. I was far too simple minded to understand that in every single living person dwells a soul consciousness waiting to actualize that knowledge in everyday life.

My soul instincts were what taught me about cause and effect. By responding to human behavior intuitively, I came to the conclusion that every act had an effect. Therefore, any action that was not caused by a loving search for truth was not only a waste of time, the effect of that action would return to the one who caused it. For better or for worse, like attracted like. The laws of energy made attraction an absolute certainty. In search of who I was, however, I did not have the wisdom to understand that my soul was the intuition I followed and the voice I sought. I did not know that by responding to my soul instincts, I had been studying my soul my whole life.

In that first automatic writing experience, I did not doubt the truth *"We speak of love"* wrote on my little pad. I was a childlike woman seeking to open a door to another world, not knowing what I would find. What I found was radiant consciousness speaking through human consciousness. It was my miracle! Instead of questioning, *Why me?* after that day, I set my pencil on my little pad every day.

Footsteps transported me back to the present. I looked up from the sofa where I sat. John walked on thin air. Champagne dreams of being a hero had elevated his mood so high, he appeared buoyant. The illumination I witnessed in my vision was exuding from the man contagiously. He was sharing his cloud with me.

In that high-spirited moment, a thought radiated into my mind. *John knows nothing about my automatic writing. If our marriage is going to survive, there can be no more secrets between us. His mood makes this the perfect time to tell him about my automatic writings.*

I walked out of the den and retrieved my little pad from under my side of the bed. I rejoined John on the office sofa where he sat popping the cork of another bottle of champagne. Delicately, I explained automatic writing, and then I flipped through the pages until I found a few passages in which he might relate.

> *Your everlasting love lasts a lifetime and beyond. Go to the place where love is, on the hill, beside the still waters. . . . Still waters are found in the heart. The heart is where peace comes first. Face the sun. Sing of love and be happy. . . . Begin each day with prayer and meditation. Power forth with love. You will continue to grow in happiness, as there is peace on earth for those who desire to strive for it. . . . We always speak of love for love is the most important thing there is on earth and in heaven. . . . Love is heaven on earth.*

John responded passionately. "The writings are beautiful! If you are capable of writing like that, you're brilliant!"

The sentimental look on my husband's face combined with his words of praise further elevated my mood. I was not convinced he understood that my writings were exalted mind flowing through mortal mind, but my gratitude for his appreciation of what I had accomplished was enormous. We floated on air together.

My eyes returned to my automatic writings. Inserted between the pages at the appropriate date was the message I wrote in the car. Speculating if I should risk reading it to John, I settled on taking a chance.

After I read the part about Fate being taken care of, John interrupted, his enthusiasm blatant. "You shouldn't be writing about Fate. She's the person who's going to call me later with the results of the City Council vote." Pouring more champagne, he bragged, "Fate is loyal and honest. She did the secretarial work for the People's Committee. She typed the letters I dictated and sent them out. She even fought with me! She did whatever I wanted."

My thoughts were falling apart and coming together simultaneously. "Whatever I wanted" rung a bell. John had warned me for years that a zone change would destroy his income. One day as the date for termination of the lease approached, he urged me to let Cherisse and Tamara go to The Big G with him to help gather signatures on petitions. Naturally, I agreed and convinced them that they would be helping their father save his job.

Although they were distinctly not excited about the idea, Cherisse and Tamara decided to go. As long as they were going to be at The Big G, I requested that John give each of them a golf lesson. Asking, in this case, did not mean receiving. At no time did John acquire a passion for his daughters' golfing ability. His attitude never ceased to baffle me, especially since he bragged from their very first golf lesson that they were both "naturals."

Later that day when Cherisse and Tamara returned home, Cherisse recalled her experience for me. "Tamara and I went door to door. Getting petitions signed is lot of work, but we had fun with Fate. She's cute and has a lot of energy. She did whatever Dad wanted."

"Did Daddy give you and Tamara a golf lesson?" I inquired, ignoring the queasy feeling that Cherisse and Tamara had spent the day with Fate.

"No. He was too busy." Cherisse replied with a look of resignation that had become more frequent over the years.

Bouncing around in his champagne-filled hero's bubble, John frolicked out of the den and into the kitchen to open a third bottle of champagne. My thoughts fought off repercussions of Fate calling our house a second time, this time with John's permission. I could not imagine surviving a second time the emotions that befell me the first time she called. Needless to say, I was no longer floating on any cloud.

John frolicked back through the door, champagne in hand, and continued where he left off. "Fate used to be a legal secretary. Her experience helped our cause tremendously. At the City Council meeting where the zoning debate took place, Fate amazed me! She stood up and bawled out one of the council members for not wanting to keep some recreational land for the people."

I speculated whether Fate's experience as a legal secretary afforded her political experience or if she fought for John's sake alone. Either way, John's story clarified for me that Fate was not afraid to assert her power to procure an affair with another woman's husband.

The hours passed. The telephone did not ring. John drank champagne and wasted no words on any subject other than his mistress and their heroic endeavors. Each time he spoke her name, he defiled our marriage vows a little more. Every time he reiterated the name Fate, he pounded another nail into the body of my crucifixion.

When John had drunk enough champagne that he could not wait one more second for Fate's call, he announced, "I'm going to phone The Big G and find out what happened."

The ever-present champagne glass in hand, John paced toward the master bedroom hollering back at me. "Let me call in private. Don't bother me."

By shutting me out of our bedroom to call Fate on my telephone, my husband may as well have taken a gun, pointed it at my head, and fired. Into the underworld I returned. As before, the physiology of my descent had an immediate effect upon my nervous system. It paralyzed all emotional controls. The flight response snatched my ability to reason my actions. I hurried toward the bedroom door, pressed my ear hard against it, and listened.

John was inquiring ever so gently. "Why did Fate go home crying?"

I beseeched myself. *How could I be hearing sincere compassion in my husband's voice for Fate when I am the broken one?*

The thousand shocks attached to his concern accelerated my flight pattern. The receiver clicked down.

To the kitchen I scrambled, my conscience questioning the virtue of my actions. *If John catches me eavesdropping, what will he do?*

The master bedroom door swung open and the commander of my wayward ship stomped out, broadcasting, "Fate went home crying. Since she filed for divorce, she's been living with her parents. I'm going to call her there and find out what's wrong."

He filled his glass, then swaggered headstrong back through the bedroom door and ordered, "Stay out!"

After disappearing behind a closed door to call his younger lover a second time, I realized that not one word had been mentioned about the results of the City Council's vote.

Stricken with terror by his angry command, I questioned my sanity. *When did Fate start mattering more to John than saving his job? What was the reason for all those years of trying to make me worry about not being able to pay the bills that ceaselessly piled up on his desk? If The Big G is that unimportant, why did he constantly encouraged my fear? How much of this adulterated emotional violence does he think I am supposed to tolerate?*

Again, I scrambled to the master bedroom door, flushed my ear against it, and suffered the consequences of my flight toward truth. Truth possessed evil spirits.

Evil spirits took the form of John's sugary sweet voice asking, "What's wrong, Fate? Joe said you went home crying."

I did not resist the two evil spirits permeating my ring of fire. The primal fire of twin Satans danced in inexhaustible circles, burning with the malignancy I had sought. My cremating soul embraced the cancerous "hate-your-wife-so-you-can-love-your-mistress" ritual with impassioned mania.

My flight to Cherisse's room was swift. When I got there, she stared at the crazed woman entering her room. Mania erased any possibility of compassion for Cherisse's need to flee.

Evil spirits, now my own, whispered to Cherisse. "Daddy's on the phone with Fate. I must hear what they're saying. Be very quiet."

I sat down on the floor next to Cherisse's nightstand. With extreme caution, my left hand lifted the receiver. My right hand covered the voice box. I held my breath. My ear hugged the receiver. Cherisse held vigilance over the cursed naïveté that had taken control of her mother's heart.

Fate's voice resonated from the other end of the line. "I can't stand sneaking around anymore."

Her words escaped all imaginable possibilities. One of John's favorite accusations was to call me a "sneak." At long last, I understood what he meant by "sneak." None other than the woman he was sneaking around with had delivered it to me.

The tone of Fate's voice sounded like she had been crying for hours. Her sorrow penetrated my sorrow. My sorrow was Fate's sorrow. She and I wore the same translucent slippers women down through the ages had been forced to wear. We were one woman lost in one man who was playing a gender game with both of our lives.

I entered her cave by emotionally sympathizing, *It must feel terrible to be hidden away, forced to keep love a secret.*

Fate's next words tore at my heartstrings. "How is Diana doing?"

Her question advised me that I was right. We were comrades. We shared the sisterhood of being controlled by the love we both felt for the same man.

Fate thinks no one sees when everyone sees, it dawned on me, my gut feelings bursting forth. *Everyone sees this woman having an affair with the man wedded to me.*

My inner voice ripped out my heart. It made comradeship instantly chilling and forbidding. Feelings of oneness with Fate disintegrated.

I questioned myself. *Does John believe this seductress of violence against his wife is actually concerned about my feelings? While Fate is having sex with my husband, does he believe their sex is anything less than a murderer of my soul and the souls of my children? After he hears her profiteering cliché, "No one changes that fast," does he believe her tears are caused by anything other than the possibility of losing his money?*

Deliberating on how Fate's opportunistic manipulations were controlling the man controlling me, I heard him reply to her question. "About the same as you."

His response brought my search for solutions to a sane halt.

Oh my God! I realized. *He sees my wretched state of mind just as clearly as everyone at The Big G sees his affair. "You haven't changed" was an out and out lie! He knows I'm in crisis. He telephoned Fate to intensify his terrorist attack upon my life force!*

My frenzied pursuit had detonated the two-headed beast I embraced when I picked up the receiver of Cherisse's telephone.

John yielded the irreversible mortal wound. "Fate, you know I love you."

Poor, sobbing Fate on the other end of the line took the ball and ran with it. "I know you love me, but I can't stand sneaking around anymore."

Pronouncing not one syllable about the City Council's vote, John promised the mistress of my chamber of horrors, "We can talk about it tomorrow."

The telephone went dead.

I sat consulting my memory as to how long I had been an imbecile. *How could I, even for one second, have believed this lost soul and I were comrades. All I have ever sought in my life is to find a way to keep my little world a happy place to live. Fate seeks her greedy goal no matter how much unhappiness she brings to the world.*

Sitting a few feet from me, Cherisse was the recipient of my dimwittedness. "Daddy told Fate he loves her."

She strained for a response, but found none.

Unable to tolerate the sincerity in John's voice when he said to Fate, "You know I love you," I stood up and wept out loud, "I can't stand it."

I bolted down the hall, arriving in front of the closed master bedroom door just in time for John to open it. He strutted out arrogantly, noticed my presence, and gave me a dirty look.

"What happened to Fate?" I petitioned, my nervous system devouring the speed with which John's demeanor had shifted from loving Fate to hating me.

"Nothing. Leave me alone!" the drunken headsman commandeered, waving me aside as he stomped toward the kitchen.

Our eighteen-year marriage-hoax had at long last disintegrated. *He intends to leave me hanging. How long has he been steering my ship behind my back, pointing my life in the direction of his fancy? Has he imposed his will upon me by keeping truth a secret from the very beginning? My goody-two-shoes attitude must have been silly amusement. Pointing evil in my direction intoxicates his feelings of power over me. Projection gives him the right to punish my misery. He sits on our bed and tells another woman he loves her, intentionally choosing in the most sadistic way to be entertained by my pain!*

The lid was off the hoax, and I refused to close it.

I admitted to John that the fool he was looking at had caught on to his trickery. "I heard you tell Fate you love her."

Hell-bound to tantalize demonic spirits were John's bestial roars. "You sneak! You haven't changed. You never loved me. You're just a bitch, a witch. Fuck you . . . you cunt . . . I hate you, you fucking. . . ."

The degree of loathing in John's ranting was more than my flesh could endure. Back to Cherisse's room I fled.

I stood in her doorway and exhausted my last chance to stop the demonic inferno from cremating what was left of my hope. "Please tell Daddy I've always loved him even though he's mean to me when he drinks."

A mountain of love poured out of Cherisse's face. Nonetheless, the helplessness she felt was indelible.

She uttered the simple truth my heart was unwilling to feel. "Mom, it won't matter what I say to Dad. It won't do any good."

In my spinning-out-of-control flight to feel once more the safety of my husband's love, I used my daughter. "Please, please, help me. Talk to Daddy for me."

Cherisse confirmed her stance. "Mom, I don't want to do this."

Driven to believe Cherisse was my last hope, I pushed, "Daddy must hear that I love him from you."

She gave in and walked out the door. I caught up. Together we paced to the master bedroom where John sat in bed calmly sipping champagne and looking pleased with himself.

Cherisse went straight to the point. "Dad, Mom has always loved you . . . but you yell at her. You say bad things about her all the time."

My cowardly exploitation of my daughter peaked John's hate.

"Cherisse, go back to your room!" he ordered sternly.

Convinced that ordering stole integrity and discussion heightened integrity, I had never allowed my husband to order our children to do anything. Now I watched him ordering, fearing only one thing. By using my first-born child to do a job I should have done years before, I had greatly worsened my situation.

Cherisse turned to leave. Her wounded face mirrored the virulence of the battle she had just fought in the name of love.

John looked at me as if I were trash. "You're a horrible witch for bringing my daughter into this. Fuck you . . . you snake. . . ."

My hideous guilt told me that John was right, and Cherisse was right. I had used my daughter as my last hope when there was no hope. I wasted both of our hearts.

Racked and torn by too many lose-lose battles, I stopped fighting. John's and Fate's little hunting expedition could celebrate "victory." The absolute pettiness of the partnership they forged to steal my power had depleted all my resources. Bringing their despised love into my home had infused their sickness into my veins. Inoculated by their selfish pursuit, I trudged outside, sat on the front steps, and bowed my head.

The clear, warm July night contrasted sharply with my foggy haze. My tears fell aimlessly onto cement steps that had dried only a few months earlier. My head felt like it was going to burst. I pushed my hands hard against my temples to stop the explosion. No impulse to hate or retaliate entered my weariness. All that was left of the carcass was the soul. The art of the war Fate and John waged against my free spirit had prepared my ego for the sarcophagus from which it would never return.

I pictured Fate at home surrounded by the protection of her parents, crying her heart out, painstakingly oblivious to the truth about what happens to a family when a woman decides to have an affair with a married man. I sat defenseless, stripped emotionally naked by the realization that I could never trust my husband again, and distrusting was a way of living of which I had no experience.

The remorse that fell with each tear spoke of lost trust. *The deception my husband has brought into our home to mask the truth about himself has caused a needless tragedy. How could I have remained so gullible for so many years, meanwhile growing more insecure and dependent with each passing day?*

Discovering that John had an inexhaustible affinity to ravage the lives of the three people who loved him the most had stripped me of my last hope. Because my fall made it vividly clear that my every thought, word, and deed was coming back to me, it was an eventual certainty that my husband too would someday be held accountable.

Cherisse walked out the front door, sat down next to me, and put her arm around my waist. My body slumped against her body.

Words came to my lips, but my soul spoke. "Cherisse, I believe in the golden rule. It says to me that we should give others the love we would like to receive from them. Daddy receives our love and returns it with hate. Someday he will feel the feelings his hate has caused us. I can't bear to think of him suffering the way I'm suffering."

"I know, Mom. I agree." Cherisse said compassionately. "The hurt he has caused us will come back to him. There's nothing more you can do. Please stop torturing yourself."

Cherisse and I sat side by side. Neither one of us spoke another word. Her arm around my waist and our tears said everything that needed to be said.

For a time, my sixteen-year-old daughter willingly carried the weight of her mother's burden. As was true with Tamara, the world we shared had ended. The end of the simple joy with which we lived our lives was so utterly unnecessary, such a needless waste. After Cherisse went to bed, I sat alone on the porch exhausted by bottomless whirlpools of manmade hells. Under a star-filled night sky, my soul had guided me to the understanding that *all for one and one for all* had been terrorized by the popular opinion that convinced my husband and his mistress their affair was acceptable.

Slowly, my numb body picked itself up and made its way into the master bedroom. The odor of John's drunken breath and the sound of his intoxicated snoring nauseated me. I sat on the edge of my side of the bed. John's hideous deteriorating drama had depleted all my emotional guards. Another wall around the far reaches of my mind crumbled. A shadow from years past stepped across the rubble of my denials.

The year was 1967. I was a sophomore at the University of Southern California. My father had called to invite me over to the apartment where he and my mother were staying. He had retired from the Marine Corps when I was a junior in high school and was working for National Helicopters, a company that assigned him temporary international helicopter jobs. Mother was not there that night.

When I arrived, Daddy poured two cups of sake and requested, "Don't tell Mother we used these glasses. They're special to her."

I could not figure out why Daddy would go behind Mother's back. It was not something he had ever done before, and I felt bad for her. Then, my father asked me to make love with him. He knew I was a virgin and explained that he thought it would be a good first experience.

My answer was swift and firm, though it embodied my easygoing spirit. "Daddy, you were the one who taught me to save myself for my husband. Remember, you always said, 'Do as I say, not as I do.'"

One of my father's slang expressions was what I reiterated for him that night. That particular slang, however, was anything but true for our relationship. Because Daddy gave me the attention reserved for a boy child, he spent more time with me than he did my older sister, Susan. He taught me to swim, to swing dance, to play tennis, to body surf, and so much more. Countless sunny days, I surfed the waves of the Pacific Ocean on Daddy's back. Countless afternoons we danced to Big Band records. My easygoing spirit learned from his easygoing spirit. My world mirrored the world he gave to me. I took on a great deal of Daddy's personality because Daddy was how I learned to view the world.

That night in 1967, it did not take me long to convince Daddy that "no" was my answer. He reacted like a gentleman, appearing to take no as easily as he would yes. I, too, took the proposition lightly. I drove back to school and never thought about it again.

Twenty years later, I found myself sitting on the edge of my bed reliving Daddy's request. The toxicity of the wound his proposition inflicted upon my humanity seeped through the wall it had built around my heart. After twenty years, the toxic wound penetrated my conscious thinking. By asking me to make love with him, my father sexualized the relationship I held most dear. In sexualizing our father/daughter relationship, he diminished my human value and shamed both of us. After that night, my love for a portion of my sexuality and my humanity closed a door.

I turned my head and glanced backward at John's sleeping body. I felt the sorrow I did not allow myself to feel two decades earlier. The exposure of the lost part of my human nature ached for comfort.

My heart cried, *John please hold me. Help me ease the wound out of my heart by giving me any tiny bit of love you have for me.*

He opened his eyes and looked at me as if he heard my thoughts. Grief lacerated my open wound as I recalled out loud an experience I wanted to keep secret forever. When I finished, I sat waiting for a kind word.

"I've heard all this before," John's vengeful voice retorted as if the rape of my feminine nature was old news.

He closed his eyes and went back to sleep.

My wretched soul, annihilated by the virulence of the day's events, fell dead. The tunnel of darkness puzzled my will to survive increasingly severe trials. I failed to understand how I could have been so near to spirit and so fallen from spirit at the same time. The chamber of my shadow had enveloped me. Only blackness remained. The dark side heaved the demonic beast who had taken possession of my soul.

There's a satanic beast lying in bed next to you, the demons warned.

My eyes monitored John's body. Its slime began mutating from man to monster. The freakish surreal creature squirmed around the bed, coiling and uncoiling, spewing venom from its slimy outer covering. My body reacted with giant shivers alternating with dry-heaves. I doubled over with spasmodic stomach pains. The serpent slithered around my bed, growing more and more grotesque as it alternated from man to monster, monster to man.

Cherisse, Tamara, and my tiny boat was swirling on the edge of the earth preparing to be sucked down its spiraling black vortex, this time to disappear forever. Fear of disappearing into a mental penitentiary overpowered fear of beasts.

My conscious mind forced itself to focus on reality. *No, I will not cross that fine line between sanity and insanity. I refuse to give in and end up incarcerated in a mental institution where no one will understand why I am there, where I will be blamed for this craziness. I will not be a victim of the drugs they will pump into my veins to keep my brain anesthetized. Losing my life to the institutionalized victimization that would maintain my insanity will not be my fate.*

Fear of the drug-induced asphyxiation typical of an insane asylum convinced me to turn away from John, curl up in the fetal position, and concentrate on letting go of monsters. The spasms in my stomach slowly eased, then stopped. My body heat calmed my shivering. All emotion drifted out of my body, and I fell asleep.

July 30, 1987, 11:45 P.M.

The ringing of the telephone woke me up. John lifted the receiver.

Sounding sober, he answered, "This is John."

He listened for a short while, then replied, "Thanks for calling, Joe. We'll celebrate our victory tomorrow night."

He hung up the phone, then saluted his heroic status. "We won the vote!"

I felt nothing. I said nothing.

John said it all for me. "They are giving a party in my honor tomorrow night at The Big G. Fate did so much work on this project, she has to be there. If you go, it will upset her."

He laid his head peacefully on his pillow with his back facing me. Within seconds he began to snore.

July 31, 1987, 4:30 A.M.

The alarm went off. I looked at the repulsive stranger pushing the snooze button.

"Who is he?" I asked, my feelings deadened by the uselessness of dues paid to show a man I loved him.

The stranger turned over and hugged me. I felt nothing except two bodies moving like shadows of the life they should have been living.

John slithered out of bed, slumped toward the toilet, sat down, bowed his head in a hungover stupor, and regurgitated, "Diana, I'm all yours. I'm going to tell Fate today."

July 31, 1987, dawn

When John left for work, he left nobody. No emotions remained to be protected or saved. When I forged the beast out of my body, I also forged out my soul. Life without soul felt meaningless. My decision to die was no decision. John's artful war between good and evil had readied me for my sarcophagus coffin.

I had not eaten more than a few bites of soft food for eleven days. Sure my shrunken body would take no time to decay, I made the decision to stop eating and drinking completely. For the first time in my life, I pictured the world without me in it.

Sometime around midmorning, John telephoned and said, "I told Fate I'm going to stay with you."

Why does he play games with a dead woman? I brooded, questioning what motives he had left to achieve.

My body remained facing the shadowy wall.

July 31, 1987, 1:00 P.M.

Something grabbed my attention. I rolled over and stared at the window. The sun filtering through the lowered shade was so strong, for a second the warmth of its light pervaded the blackness of my chamber. I did not want to feel light. I did not want to feel anything while I died. I wanted everything in the pit to go completely black so I would never have to feel again. I rolled over again, turning my back to the light. I lay facing the wall, except now, the cold darkness of the wall contrasted sharply with the warm brightness of the light. I gave in, turned my head toward the window, and looked at the light. From the light came these words:

> *Feel the joy in nature. Summer is upon us and nature is alive with spirit. The loving spirit of nature calls you to rise up and seek life. Come unite with the beauty of the love that awaits you. Get up. Get dressed. Go to the celebration party. Face your tormenter and stand tall.*

No, I won't, I stubbornly retorted.

With that retort, an initiate turned her back to the light of the earth. Without hesitation, I climbed into my coffin, lay down on the bottom of the pit of life, and shook hands with death.

9

Initiatory Rights

July 31, 1987, 1:15 P.M.

Why should I rise up and seek life? I challenged the voice of nature as I stared at the wall. *Why should I live when I feel empty inside? My husband is a monster whose cruel affair has broken my spirit. He has stolen my reason for living. There's nothing left of me to save. In this room I will stay until I die.*

Willing my rendezvous with death, I refused to face the light. Along with eating and drinking, I stopped praying, meditating, and doing my automatic writings. The courage to treasure the harmonious feelings of mother nature that heretofore breathed life into my soul had left my body. The initiatory trials in the tunnel had been too severe, the primal fires too terrible for my soul to endure. I had failed the test of endurance necessary to get past the monster.

Twenty years of suppressed feelings had grown into multitudes of parasites feeding off the synapses of my brain. For eleven days, the dense shadows in my subconscious mind had been transgressing my conscious mind. The speed with which those initiatory companions were stripping away my old identity by bringing my insecurities, dependencies, judgments, and projections to my attention was compounded by my husband's lust to devour every last bit of my soul's free will. The apocalyptic fire that cremated the person I had grown accustomed to thinking of as me left nobody in its place. It was the end of the world as I knew it.

Being sucked down by one black hole after the next had caused in me the catastrophe of hopelessness. Awakening to the art of John's *war of lies* had set off an emotional nuclear reaction. The spell of the material conditioning that had taught my husband to fill his carnal appetites by having secret affairs behind my back had swallowed up my last hope for new beginnings. The breach of trust had infiltrated my mind with a psychic infection that deadened my driving force. I could not reconcile John's real-world exploitation for selfish pleasures with the selfless world of spiritual love I sought to make real. With or without John, my heart saw no light at the end of a long, dark biological tunnel of slavery to a planetary underworld hypnotized by greed and lust.

The cataclysm of my fall was one infinitesimal symptom of the political and religious ax-men who conditioned John to kill true freedom. Through nearly two decades of labored effort by the man who took my hand in marriage, the darkness of kill-or-be-killed forces had gathered together to fire up my ordeal in the chamber. Reaping humanity's shadow ended life as I knew it and defeated my will to live. It took forty years, but the fall of the mother in the mind of the father had taken what gave my life meaning: the innocent love that made my soul fly.

Even the sun that shown upon mother earth could not lighten the darkness in my heart. Without the freedom to let the driving force of my soul guide me, I was *dead wo/man walking.* The emptiness in my heart chose the suicide of physical death rather than the suicide of John's material life.

I had insisted on learning the truth even if it killed me. My discovery that the man I wedded chose the self-deception of believing his own lies resulted in my passage into psychological and spiritual death. Buried alive under the covers of my king-sized casket, I believed the empty spaces left by his deception gave me the right to end my life. Gaping holes filled with the fusing together of dark forces held a death grip on the wounds inscribed on the ceremonious tombstone of stubborn self-pity that still held me in bondage to my past.

Walled behind my heart had been a part of my humanity that closed a door twenty years earlier. The meteoric collapse of my ego identity demolished that wall. Over the rubble of the far reaches of my mind hobbled an injury so damaging, it was exposed as a monstrous beast squirming around my bed, spewing toxic waist. By envenoming what was the last spark of the force that drove Diana, the creature had opened a door to my lost humanity. From my youth had slithered a dark side of truth that had a flesh-eating effect in shaping my personality.

Because my father spent the time with me he would have saved for a son, I grew up idolizing him, seeking in myself what I interpreted as his way of thinking, feeling, and acting. What I saw as Daddy's strength of character was the character I decided I wanted to have. As I grew into a woman, however, the delicate, sensitive parts of my mother in myself could not be denied. No matter how hard I tried to separate my character development from her vulnerable heart, the arising of my repressed feminine nature had become the bud of a flower ready to blossom. By the time I was in college, the unification of my masculine and feminine natures was within my grasp.

My father's proposition nipped my opportunity for wholeness at the bud by forcing me to choose between my mother and father in myself. Because he went behind my mother's back to make my body an object of sexual desire, I had to either unite with my father's strengths and once again abandon my mother's vulnerabilities or acknowledge that my father had weaknesses that were no less severe than my mother's weaknesses.

At twenty, as I always had before, I welcomed Daddy's world view as my own. Rather than face the truth that worshiping my father's image would deepen my aching fear of my mother's image, I suppressed the underlying oppression and continued to shape my identity around Daddy's ideals. Developing my character in the image of male values amputated my passage into womanhood. I hid the bud of an ebbing tide in the far reaches of my mind and further separated my identity from my mother in myself. I embarked upon my voyage into maturity with both a masculine and a feminine sense of worth that abandoned and sexualized my feminine worth.

In the process of losing the desire to seek the ebb of my soul force, I lost the courage to find my own dream. Getting caught in the devil's snare chained my dreams to patriarchal thoughts, feelings, and behaviors. After that, my feminine universe grew much more a slave to my masculine universe.

Regardless of a huge percentage of outstanding fathering, Daddy's sexualization of my humanity was the toxic wound that held my dreams a captive of the archaic gender roles my self-deception believed I had escaped. As the political and religious ideology of the Garden of Eden had erected a sarcophagus tombstone for my soul's creative purpose, my father's proposition carved in that stone the ideological rape of my childhood dreams. The deflowering prostrated the half of my soul embodied in my womanhood. Womanhood's prostituted myth crippled the creativity born of the harmonious balance of the ebb and flow of my life force.

The fall of my mother in myself had been scripted by my father. That fall made masculine my identity while poisoning my feminine identity. On D-Day, when the walls I built around the weaknesses of my masculine identity broke down, my worst truth broke through. Though John's, "You're just like your mother" haunted me, it was not the fall of my mother in myself I feared feeling the most. It was feeling the fall of my father . . . in myself.

Now, I lay like a corpse remembering the inescapable pull I felt the night I spotted John across a crowded room. When his father beat him up and his mother deserted him, the masculine side of his life force was forced to suppress the feminine side of his life force. One half of his soul was cut off in a very different but no less crippling manner than mine. He suppressed his aching fear of the feminine creature within him by constantly rushing headlong into acts of hostility. Sheepishly led by the influence of political and religious macho-machines, John's fear of his sensitive feelings punched gaping holes into the ebbtide of his soul force.

Both John and I carried an imbalance of masculine and feminine energy in our bodies. Consequently, we attracted that male-dominated imbalance wherever we went. On the surface, John and I were polar opposites. I was full of positive energy. He was full of negative energy. Underneath, our mutual admiration for masculine values and fear of feminine values were mirror images. It was the way our personalities communicated that underworld as positive versus negative energy that charged the magnetism. The instant we met, our souls recognized the electrical charge of the toxic aspects of each other. That soul recognition was responsible for our inescapable chemistry.

The partnering of two strong-willed personalities resulted in one never-ending battle. Our gender war was each soul's effort to subdue the other's masculinity long enough to expose her/his femininity. When John and I verbally boxed each other's shadows, the boxing matches were subconscious impulses meant to lay bare those underworlds for what they really were: the lost half of our human potential our souls sought to recapture through another person. Our ability to make each other fly was our souls servicing each other's wholeness.

On the morning of July 20, 1987, one telephone call from the "other woman" blew my masculine identity into smithereens. Following a revealing but painless meditation, one subconscious wound after the next transgressed my consciousness. My whole body interpreted those apocalyptic feelings as my initiation into fear and panic. While fear and panic's purifying flames burned away at the gross aspects of my male-driven energy, from the far reaches of my mind my female energy was rising. Childlike in its newness, the lost half of my human potential longed to be valued.

A window of opportunity to recapture the wholeness our souls sought from the first moment John and I laid eyes on one another was at-hand in me. But since his mistress chose to make it her mission in life to make his masculine ego fly, John refused to witness the rebirth of my feminine nature. Rather than see in me what he had yet to find in himself, he used Fate to mutilate the childlike vulnerability of my beaming heart.

John's rejection of my chance for wholeness was the cutting edge of the possibilities I rejected the day my father asked me to make love with him. By choosing not to witness the imperfections of my father, I chose not to see the weaknesses of the father I internalized in myself. After that, I denied my masculine weaknesses by building a chamber. That chamber not only entombed my father's weaknesses, it also buried alive my mother's strengths.

The consequence of the fall of my mother's power was for me to stop feeling safe and start feeling dependent upon men for power. My husband's punishment for my sin of dependence was to go behind my back to have affairs, just as my father had gone behind my mother's back with me. When John's affair broke down chamber walls and my heart broke through, released were my mother, my father, my husband, and my misbegotten truths. Feeling those long-entombed truths fired up flames that burned alive my masculine identity. Remarkably, it was those same revelations that helped me understand the *devil's snare* that set my feminine power free. But as that underdeveloped power gave John the fullness of its love, he did what he had learned to do by the time he was three years old: kill love before love killed him.

The man for whom I offered the sweetest blossom of my feminine rebirth rejected it, just as I had been rejecting the fullest bloom of my love for myself since the day my father's proposition beat my possibilities into submission. By allowing a wound that took twenty years to feel to be wounded again, my twice-mutilated heart turned into a serpent writhing around my bed, spewing toxic waste. To Lucifer's joy, I understood that the repulsive demon was not my husband. His behavior had not changed. The demon was the awakened feelings that had separated my body from half of my soul for twenty years. Because truth was something for which I had always been curious, I had willed myself to battle the devil. As a result, I had come face to face with that liberator of the woman in my mirror.

With the help of my husband and his other lover, setting free my *insecurities, dependencies, judgments, and projections* mutated into a grotesque monster I did not have the courage to get past. By willing my passage into death rather than standing tall and recognizing that the twisted *four-headed beast* masked a spiritual creature of luminous beauty, my mind witnessed the dark night of my soul.

July 31, 1987, late afternoon

Unrelentingly, I turned my back on nature's healing force. Two decades of blocked feelings had crystallized, turning the potential evolution of my mind and soul into the stone wall I had interpreted as strength of character. Fate's telephone call had terminated my double-digit struggle to hold on to the heroes of my past and sent me spiraling down the dark gravitational pull of the weaknesses of my character. My eleven-day initiatory rites revealing what was not working in my life climaxed with the unblocking of the feelings bred by my deepest, most repressed fear: because of my gender, my father, my hero, had set me up to be sexually oppressed by my husband.

Falling into history's forbidden forest of bestial gods ignited fiery revelations that penetrated an army of accumulated, repressed hurt feelings. That penetration caused a great upheaval of those masked feelings. The upheaval thrust the mask off denied truths that had walled up my chances for wholeness. As understandings heaved forth, demons were exorcized from my body with excruciating speed. The dying of the masculinated superiority I thought was my friend, combined with the birthing of the feminine luminosity I thought was my enemy, resulted in the passing away of something I never expected: the mask of ignorance my denials flaunted, a mask that had turned the evolution of my mind and my soul into granite.

I lay in bed thinking the death of my old identity left nobody in its place. In truth, *my soul had compelled my mind to traverse the tunnel of mirrors to test my courage to overcome the passing away of the mask of denial: my ego.*

If I passed the test, I would be awarded initiatory rites to the next level of my initiatory travels back to my true nature. . . .

Despite all those hours of unmovable self-pity, I had passed the test of endurance. Through the window covered by a lowered shade in a darkened room, the voice of nature had, after all, lit an involuntary candle in my nature. The evolutionary candle flickered a delicate, feathery hopefulness that flowed gently into my emptiness, easing the pain of the end of the world as I knew it.

On the other side of the end times of my ego lay an understanding but frightened little girl. The girl was frightened because in the palm of her hand she held a mirror that reflected dark shadows. She did not know it yet, but those shadows were of a world that had passed away. When the walls of ignorance crumbled, the forgotten dreams in the far reaches of Diana's mind fell into remembrance. Because she braved the initiatory journey awarded her not by conscious choice but by her soul force, Diana's courage had transformed her mirror into magic. *The scared child's magic mirror now reflected the understanding that had taught her that forgiveness opened the passageway to the next level of her initiation: a new world full of hope, the hope that what she thought was her enemy had always been her friend.*

The awakening of my feminine nature was at hand. . . .

Femininity's nakedness took a breath, then spoke of hopefulness. *Maybe Cherisse and Tamara will knock on my door and ask me how I'm doing. Oh, I hope they will ask me if I would like some soup and crackers so I can feel better.*

Though the candle of hope flickered, I resolved to look at the light only when I could see the faces of my precious daughters. For hours I stared at the wall, eager to hear the sweet tapping on my door, confused as to why the children for whom my life had been dedicated could not read my mind and feel my hope.

At dusk, the telephone rang.

Silently, I wished, *Please let it be John calling to invite me to the party! Boy, would I love for Fate to see me in one of my little mix-and-match outfits! I'll let Cherisse or Tamara answer the phone. Then they'll have to come and find out why I'm in my room.*

Hours passed. The knock on my door did not come. Still, it was too late to turn back. My human nature had felt the light and heard the voice of earth's nature. Death had lost its power over me. I turned my head and looked at the window. There was no light! Night had fallen! The window was as dark as the wall.

Oh, no! I thought, not wanting to trust my memory, the reverberations of John's morning call blasting out in my mind, "I told Fate I'm going to stay with you."

Choosing me was everything I wanted, I agonized, my love for my husband falling backwards into the burning ring-of-fire. *He gave me what I wanted and I threw it away. My God! Could the second call have been John calling to invite me to the party after all?*

My eyes darted toward the clock. It said 10:03 P.M.

Reality set in. *No! No! No! The party's probably over.*

Swept to my feet by the realization of my stupid death wish, I jumped out of bed, charged toward the door, flung it open, and rushed down the hall toward Cherisse's room. On her window seat, Cherisse sat quietly gazing out the window.

How could she be just sitting there? I queried myself. *All those hours I waited in my room, how could she have been doing nothing?*

Cherisse remained calm when she saw me.

"Did Daddy call?" I asked, my tone making plain my fear of her answer.

She hesitated for a moment, then responded, "He called around seven thirty asking where you were."

"What did you tell him?" I asked, my mental reaction to her behavior growing more jumbled.

"I told him you were in your room." She answered as if I should not be the least bit confused, then went on, "He said he didn't like you spending all that time in your room."

"Why didn't you tell me?" I implored. "Daddy's call was all I wanted in the world. Didn't you notice that I was in my room all day? I waited and waited for you come and ask me what was wrong. I wanted to die. I didn't want to live anymore!"

Tamara walked in looking petrified. She stopped next to her sister. They both stood silently staring at their mother with sorrowful, questioning faces.

Tamara pleaded, "No, Mom, no! What would we do without you?"

Side by side, my daughters stared at a sobbing stranger.

The phantom of buried heroes had arisen from the dead, this time dancing the dance of surrender. Back down the hall I scampered, arriving at my bedside table to dial the telephone number of The Big G. The line rang and rang and rang. My worst fears had been confirmed.

The party's over and I missed it! I mourned, giving in to the humble needs I had not expressed since I was a child.

Feminine needs, once awoken, refused to sleep. Driven to be near the husband I now had confused with a vision, my latent needs longed for the sensitive lover who once filled a starry-eyed girl's dreams. Into my husband's closet I stumbled, falling onto my hands and knees, kissing and hugging shoes worn by a man I romanticized as my happily ever after. Still childlike in its experience, feminine nature found me clinging to shoes as if they held the magic. That sweet inner child spotted a flower-covered comforter in the corner. She grabbed it and flung it around her shoulders.

That's better, I thought, my hope restored. *The party's over and that means John will soon come home to me.*

Comforter surrounding me, I exited the closet, wove through the master bedroom, into the entry hall, and tripped out the front door. Down the steps I hurled my body, plummeting onto the cement driveway. All curled up in my flowered covered comforter I lay waiting for the sound of a small truck.

An evening breeze began to stir. Though the breeze was not cold, I began to shiver. My shivering came from the primal birth of a long awaited stranger. The stranger was in-between two worlds. In this unfamiliar passageway I could not stop the flow of the breeze from blowing through me. This time I found it impossible to turn my back on nature's healing spirit. The tender night air comforted the little girl in me, relaxing all dark thoughts caused by history's habitual pull.

My shivering stopped. My thoughts cleared. Confusion synchronized into order. The spell of matter had been broken. Nature had freed me from the entrancement of my past. I became aware of my body. It was all curled up in a flower-covered comforter lying on cement that led to a circular driveway built from cement mixture after cement mixture.

What am I doing out here lying on this driveway? I puzzled, suddenly conscious of the infantile nature of my waiting.

In the blink of an eye, Cinderella illusions had been swept away. Nature had done its finest work. The intelligence inherent in nature's breeze had graced my life. By blowing calmness into my body, the breeze gave my mind the initiatory rite to step over dead heroes and find my way home. From the innermost part of my heart, I heard my children crying. I visualized the look on their faces when I left them standing in the middle of Cherisse's bedroom.

Comforter in tow, I stood up, and together we waddled back into the house. I passed Cherisse's room, unable to face the maturity of her sorrow, and continued on to Tamara's room. On her bed, in the fetal position, Tamara was crying uncontrollably. Her face showed a grief beyond human tolerance, deep purpled skin swollen to such a degree that her eyes were barely visible. It was not her fetal position, swollen face, or purple skin that transformed the naïve girl in me into a *compassionate* woman. It was the look in Tamara's eyes.

Her eyes were crying, *Mom, where have you gone? I'm so scared without you.*

I sat down next to Tamara well aware that nothing either one of us ever did was going to change the results of my fall. My unwillingness to be a witness to my father's imperfections took from my daughter what I spent all her life trying to protect. Because she experienced the violent emotional death of the mother she loved, the sorrow in Tamara's eyes revealed her regret. The wisdom of her regret echoed . . . the loss of innocence.

Cherisse came into Tamara's room and joined us on Tamara's bed. Her eyes beheld the profound knowing of her sister's loss. The three of us huddled together, crying for the innocence we had all left behind. It was no more necessary for me to tell Cherisse and Tamara what I was suffering than for me to ask them what they were suffering.

We stayed together on Tamara's bed staring into each other's tear-swollen eyes until every available feeling had been shared. Our oneness of emotion expressed what we all knew. Our little bubble of love had been forever changed.

Through a dark tunnel birthed by the loss of innocence, Cherisse, Tamara, and I had been illuminated. By sharing the lowliest place on earth, the three of us were able to walk through the passageway toward the height of mature love in true oneness. In the agony of what we lost lay the ecstasy of what we gained. Our lack of emotional separation divinely graced our rite of passage. Through our tears, light marched forth carrying multitudes of angels singing about the new world ahead. No possibility existed for our oneness of love to remain in that tunnel.

The force of nature that drove me to live again spoke. *One love, born of three souls, is our light at the end of the tunnel.*

But thy eternal summer shall not fade,
Nor lose possession of that fair thou owest;
Nor shall death brag thou wander'st in its shade,
When in eternal lines to time thou growest.

– Francis Bacon, *Sonnets XVIII*

10

Get Up, You Fool

August 1, 1987, dawn

I awoke to sensations left by a midsummer's night breeze. Nature's amazing grace blew away my tragic wound and blew new life into me. Every atom of my physiology had been miraculously transformed. When a tender breeze broke the spell of fear, the very essence of who I was crossed over into a new way of being, and I arose reborn.

My eleven-day fall into fear's bottomless abyss ended at the pit where I lay in my mental coffin. During my trials in the chamber of humanity's shadow, I purged feelings sucked down by the invention of hell in the minds of man. The beast who translated my garden of paradise into a garden of evil brought into the light of day the corruption of my flesh, the devil's snare of patriarchal sin. The religious role of my journey through those hells was to separate my mind from my soul. Ironically, the exact opposite came to pass. My supersonic fall into the acute deliverance of my denied pain purified the internalized sins of those who introduced to the world that soul separation.

My revelations about the consequences of my fear conditioning and the realization that I had not grown up to be the person of unconditional love I wanted to be were the severe tests of my initiation, the initiatory rites reconciling the gap between my mind and my soul. Just how many fiery wakes it would take to purify fear I did not know.

I did know that my initiation was a journey through a tunnel of mirrors leading me to my truth. In the core of my being was a primordial fire burning a path to the person of unconditional love I knew I could be. The ceremonious passing away of the parochial narrow-mindedness that taught me to fear that I was less had been waking me up to the hidden river of divine light that flowed through my soul into my mind, then down through my body. That radiant consciousness had reached through my bedroom window to prove the impossible possible. Earth's sun had united with me in oneness and sparked life into my entire body, tip to toe. Catching the sparks of nature gave me the courage to step out of my sarcophagus coffin. The empty sarcophagus meant that I had traversed the impossible ordeal. I survived the death of the masculine identity that taught me to feel so comfortable in a man's world.

As I lay on our cement driveway, the primal birth of my feminine nature all cuddled up in a flower-covered comforter, a midsummer's night breeze awarded the dark night of my soul with an early dawn. No, even Satan could not stop the dawn. When the angel of air blew life into my body, my heart arose newborn. Earth's sun and a tender breeze had calmed the beast of lost innocence. By channeling divine consciousness into me, nature cleared my way home . . . home to my heart's desire . . . home to the magic mirror of love I had found . . . in the eyes of my children.

I recalled my death on Cherisse's and Tamara's faces. Their eyes mirrored my eyes. Cherisse and Tamara shared my tragedy as if it were their tragedy. Our shared grief gifted us by connecting our souls in everlasting oneness. Oneness forced darkness to yield its shadow to a flicker of light. I felt that light burning brightly as my eyes opened to greet the dawning of our new world. I felt, once more, the pain Cherisse, Tamara, and I shared. The sharing felt like the earth rising to meet heaven. Heaven and earth had met in a oneness of emotion that made us feel nothing less than the eternal glow of pure love.

In those early morning hours, the revelations that led to the death of my prostituted self remained. Their remains were necessary. My revelations were the behavioral symptoms of the pieces of me cut out in my youth. Fate demanded I seek, find, and reunite with those missing pieces. Burgeoning wholeness required that I understand, forgive, and learn compassion for my symptomatic behaviors.

Every wound life thrust upon me, I in turn thrust upon life. Since I chose to live with gaping holes in myself, my road to wholeness had to be back through those same open cavities. To live by the higher standard offered to me by my initiatory rites, I had to get out of bed, stand in front of the mirror, look face to face at myself, and take responsibility for my every transgression.

Taking responsibility meant becoming accountable for the monster I judged to be John. Regardless of my husband's monstrous behavior toward me, many of my behaviors wounded him. My father's weaknesses had been revealed in my husband. Accountability meant I had to separate the weaknesses of my father that I had internalized in myself and then projected onto my husband from the weaknesses that were uniquely John's. Everything that happened since my fall showed me how I pointed the finger of blame for our troubled relationship toward him. I had to accept the outcome of that blame: the husband I created.

The consequence of the husband I created was *atonement*. Atonement required I pay penance for the beastly feelings I projected onto my husband. No matter what the *sacrifice*, the next trial of my initiation was to choose to walk into another fire. To pass my next test, I had to slay the beast with unconditional love. To free my husband from the sins of my father in me, my task was to *reenter the crucible*.

Choosing to stay in my marriage at such a critical juncture in my life was sure to be the choice of ordeal. The ordeal ahead was not as easy as doing the right thing. Nor was it as simple as learning to live my truth. *The crucible was my choosing to nail myself to the cross to give the devil his due.*

After all, was it not John's monstrous behavior that sent me spiraling down the darkness of my shadowy denials? Was he not the archetype of the serpent who liberated me from ignorance? Was it not falling into death that set that inner demon free? Even as Satan himself sealed my coffin shut, was it not satanic behavior that gave me the golden opportunity to raise myself from the dead? Who else but the devil himself had a chance of waking me up to the light of my soul?

I lay in bed evaluating accountability. *I must face the stupidity of my foolish deeds. I will journey that less-traveled path because the vision of who I know I can be is more powerful than my fear of who I have been. If, while in pursuit of atonement, I find more darkness, I will walk through that darkness. If it is demanded of me, I will stoop to progress up the tunnel I have fallen into. Only by following the path of pure goodness of action will I be able to live the enlightenment awakened in me. I have seen their pure love for me light my children's eyes. Their love burns with sorrow for my sorrow. Only when they see me heal my sorrow and learn to be fully alive will they learn to be fully alive. To heal my sorrow, I must find the sorrow I inflicted upon my husband. I must give all I have to give to amend every hurt I caused.*

Get up, you fool! I ordered my body. *Get out of this bed! Get out of this bedroom!*

I sat up and lifted my body out of bed. I dressed and walked out of the master bedroom, through the dining room, and into the kitchen.

As I passed through the kitchen and headed toward the family room my mind was spinning. *I feel a powerful need to move, to find solutions, to fight for my life, to fight for the lives of my children, and to fight to heal the wounds I created in my husband.* I reiterated to myself.

Determination in every step, I walked straight over to the vacuum closet, pulled out the vacuum, plugged it into the wall, and began my mental journey in search of real-life answers. *I will find a cure for the malignancies that devoured my chances to be whole.*

The vacuum advanced under the power of sheer will, as did my mental exploration. *After Fate's call, reality became empty and miserable. Except for yesterday, spirit alone lifted me toward wholeness and peace.*

What exactly happened yesterday? I asked myself, then answered my own question. *After I made the decision to die, the voice of nature reached through my window and called for me to rise up and seek life. I felt the warmth and joy of nature's call, yet I turned a cold shoulder. Even my cold shoulder could not stop earth's healing power from scaring away the serpent of death. Then last night, a peaceful breeze cleared the cobwebs out of my brain, bringing my consciousness back to reality. All at once, my feelings told me my children needed me.*

Then it dawned on me. *Earth is a soul and that soul lives in perfect harmony and balance. As I lay on the driveway, earth's soul force connected with my soul force and harmonized the imbalance in my body. That balancing of my energy caused a sudden shift in my conscious way of thinking. My unhealthy need for my husband evaporated and was replaced by a healthy need for my children. Natural forces had cleared my way home to Cherisse and Tamara.*

The vacuum dug into corners as I refocused my thoughts on the trial confronting me. *The pedestal I placed John on the night we met has, at long last, crumbled. I can't count on him to be my happily ever after any longer. Because I visualized the man I married as my dream for far too long, the wounds I brought into our marriage broke open and bled all over the place. Now, I must pay the price for causing them to bleed. How am I going to survive the ordeal to come?*

I unplugged the vacuum in the family room and carried it toward the dining room. As I passed back through the kitchen, I glanced out the window to the backyard. Reflections of the water in our pool captured my attention. Turquoise ripples replicated miniature images of the sun as they frolicked like twinkling stars.

Thousands of tiny stars cast into my mind the spirit of the water. *Diana, water has always graced your life. You have loved water all your life because you learned to swim before you learned to walk. Swimming taught you to trust yourself in water. You loved the honesty of water before you had a chance to fear the honesty of water. How does swimming make you feel?*

Good! I answered. *I feel good! Swimming makes me feel fluid and strong, safe and alive. Swimming feels. . . ?*

I felt myself swimming. *Water and I move in perfect harmony. No separation exists between water and me when I swim. I feel . . . I feel. . . ? Nothing is missing when I swim . . . I feel whole!*

In that moment of my reminiscing, standing in the kitchen with a vacuum in my hand, I understood that the thousands of laps I swam all the years of my life were like food for my soul. My lifelong relationship with water personified the bubble in which I once lived.

Water whispered how I would solve the mystery of surviving penitence. *Your love for and knowledge of water is the secret, Diana. The places in nature that come naturally to you are the places you feel whole. You will survive penitence by seeking and finding those places.*

Experiencing the birth of the forbidden fruit of my feminine nature seemed to have given me the ability to connect with nature in a way I never imagined possible. Body and soul, I had always found union with nature. Now, my mind was connecting with the wisdom of nature. Earth nature to human nature, I was able to hear knowledge about myself in which I was completely unaware. I carried the vacuum into the dining room knowing that my most private thoughts were not private at all. The natural forces I loved so much had heard my every thought, every second of my life. Earth knew me better than I knew myself. It knew there was nothing missing in me that I could not find in nature because I trusted nature.

Understanding that nature could teach me everything I needed to know about trusting myself if I would just listen, I entered and then vacuumed the dining room, stood up, and straightened my back. From my new vantage point, on the other side of the window, before me stood a tree. I stopped my thoughts, focused on the tree, and listened.

The tree spoke to me of the wisdom of sacrifice. *Find earth's nature and you will find your nature. Find your nature and you will find divine nature. Find divine nature in yourself and you will find divine nature in humanity.*

I walked toward the master bedroom understanding that the tree was the virtual tree of life. Its sacred wisdom had solved the mystery of enduring sacrifice. By sacrificing myself for the man I loved, I would gain the knowledge of how he sacrificed himself for me and how his sacrifice mirrored the sacrifice of humanity.

At the bedroom entrance, I stopped and looked in. The room that had been my refuge looked dark and dismal. The vacuum slipped from my hands and fell to the floor. My legs moved toward the window. I pulled down the cord. Up went the shade. In rushed light so bright, it felt electric! My eyes peered through the magic window at a sight I could hardly believe!

Color burst from nature with phenomenal clarity. Harmony within diversity stimulated emotional holocausts throughout my body. I could not get enough of the sight I beheld. Trees stood stately and proud, whimsical and gay. Leaves dipped in shades of green played symphonic melodies as they fluttered on dancing branches that reached to touch fluffy clouds swimming in the bright blue sky. Tree trunks led my eyes downward toward the browns of the earth. Roots grew deep into the soil as treetops grew high toward the heavens. Suspended between heaven and earth, every part of the paradise outside my window was the real-world Garden of Eden!

Again, I reached to move forward with my life by going back in time. *Everyday of my childhood I looked forward to going outside to play. I loved to play with dirt. I loved to climb trees. I loved earth and all its creatures. For me, heaven had always been firmly grounded on the earth. On rainy days, I would sit staring out the window dreaming of when I could, once again, go outside and play in heaven.*

That's it! I congratulated myself. *The child in me did not want to remain dead. She wanted to live again. She wanted to play in the natural surroundings that made her feel whole. She wanted to grow old and teach her grandchildren to swim as she had taught her children to swim. She knew that if she could teach them to love water as much as their grandmother loved water, they would be learning to live in the divine state of consciousness that was their true nature!*

And she will! I decided firmly. *The child in me will live again. But this time, the child will have knowledge of and learn to love all that she is and all that she can give to the world!*

I marched back into the family room, placed the vacuum back in the closet, marched into the den, and sat down. My battle toward wholeness through the passageway of contrition was about to begin. For my adversary, this war would be different from any of his past wars. John would be fighting an armegeddon against the understanding, forgiveness, and compassion that would breed my unconditional love. His foe would be the air, water, earth, and trees that were my apocalyptic allies. If, as the wisdom of my vision convinced me, John and I loved each other on a soul level, then soul love was as possible on earth as it was in heaven. And if earth was heaven, then the earthly sacrifice I was about to make was for the purpose of delivering both of our souls to the heaven right in front of our eyes!

The feminine creature birthed in me was right after all. My husband's shoes did hold magic. They held the magic mirror of the girl in me who lost and found her soul because of the man who wore those shoes. To repay that man and earn initiatory rites of passage, I was required to lend him the soul he helped me find. Only then would I be truly free from the debt I owed my husband. At this critical juncture, the crucible of contrition was solely in my hands. I opened John's desk drawer, found a pencil and paper, and wrote the following:

> My darling John,
> I finally know what is meant by love to die for. I love you more than I ever thought possible. If you could forgive my stupidity for being the biggest fool in the world, I would be grateful.
> Your love forever, past eternity,
> Diana

It delighted me that my husband would never fully understand my experience of "love to die for." Even though the man I married and the man in my vision were different in almost every way, they were alike in one way. They were both the man I married. And with that man, I would do what came naturally. The man coming home that night, devil or angel, was going to have the opportunity to experience the earth rising to meet heaven in the feminine creature alive in me. In my body he would experience my soul.

I placed the letter upright on John's desk so he could not miss seeing it. Then, I went to the master bedroom, took off my clothes, and took a shower. I washed and dried my hair, powdered my body, and put on my sexiest negligee. I was going to make sure eternal summers existed in places other than trees!

Biology is truly a land of unlimited possibilities.
We may expect it to give us the most surprising information.

– Sigmund Freud

11

The Tree Of Life In Eden

August 1, 1987, 11:30 P.M.

My body was responding naturally long before John got home from work. Deep within my female chambers had begun a yearning. As I powdered the curves and crevices where I anticipated perspiration would soon form, I felt the excitement of spiritual energies tingling light-heartedly as they commingled with sexual energies. The pleasure of my clean, perfumed body dressed for my soul's exploration of my erotic nature honored the wisdom of my passage into a different kind of contrition. The man who made me aware of how I had separated myself from my soul was about to reap the rewards of the wife he helped create!

Yes, my life had taken another startling turn since the last time I saw the man I intended to make love with. And no, he did not need to know I had shut myself in my room with the serious intention of dying. The husband I created caused foolish behavior on my part that punished my children as severely as it punished me. Despite that fact, his war against evil women birthed in me a feminine creature ready to eat from the tree of penitence. This night my pentecostal obligation was to play the serpent in the garden of paradise. In the gardens of my sensual nature, I would joyously consume the holy fruit of redemption.

When I heard the door close behind John as he entered the house from the garage, I could feel every beat of my pounding heart. I stood waiting in the kitchen, listening to the quick, light footsteps that told me a proud man had just returned from a noble cause. John stood tall and staight as he strutted through the family room, ready for a hero's welcome. Stopping at the other side of the kitchen counter, his eyes went directly to my breasts. He was visibly surprised and curious about what he saw. My apprearance did not fit comfortably into his memory of our last meeting. The black negligee I lovingly put on a few hours earlier was cut in a low V down the middle of my chest. A ribbon that began at my navel had been strung all the way up to the point where the V ended and then was tied loosely, so that the upper portion of my breasts protruded buoyantly. Firm nipples displayed themselves demurely under the transparency of the negligee's silky material.

My eyes were consumed by the man standing before me in animated self-adulation. John won his zoning fight with the City Council, and his every move made it evident that he reveled in heroic grandiosity. Piping hot roast beef filled the kitchen with the fragrance John loved the most. A dinner plate, knife, fork, and napkin were neatly placed on the sink in anticipation of his perpetually healthy appetite.

"Congratulations," I offered sincerely, then picked up the plate, walked over to the oven, and sliced off large portions of beef.

"We did it. We saved The Big G," he began. "You should have seen all the people lined up to meet me. Everyone wanted to buy me a beer. That's why I didn't make it home last night."

I felt proud too and wanted John to enjoy his special moment. Hoping my attitude and actions would show how much I cared about his success, I reinforced his victorious mood. "I'm proud of you, John. And just think, you won't have to worry anymore about losing your job!"

I opened the refrigerator door, spied the ever-present stock of beer, and asked, "Would you like a beer?"

John nodded a *yes*.

I lifted out the beer, popped the pop-top, rounded the kitchen's center island, and placed it directly in his hand. His face flushed pink. Able to see my legs and black silk loose-fitting panties barely below my negligee's hem, John's focus of interest shifted from the celebration to me. He relaxed onto a kitchen stool as if a bit of the wind had been knocked out of him and took a long sip of beer. Studying every inch of my appearance, his left hand twitched as his right hand lowered the beer from his lips.

Watching and waiting, I tried to determine what the personality sitting before me was going to reveal about the man. It did not take me long to figure out that the character bulldozing his dinner anticipated only a supporting role in the drama to come. After he emptied his plate, he stood up and stepped over to me. I took his hand and intertwined my fingers with his. Hand in hand we wasted no precious moments getting to the master bedroom.

I rolled back the covers and slipped into bed. John's clothes fell to the floor with spectacular speed. Watching his little strip tease instantly tantalized earlier instincts. The nude male body with its ready, erect penis decidedly intensified instinctual yearnings. Remaining dressed to entice sensory excitement, I shifted to a position that let John know exactly what was going to happen next. He lowered himself onto the bed, smiling in a cute sort of knowing way. Not once in all our years together did John have an erection problem. Although his bragging usually endeared the size of his phallus rather than the capacity of his manhood, his endurance and enthusiastic oral adeptness held greater value for me. Our night to remember was the first time I ever climaxed during intercourse, in and of itself. Prior to that, John's tongue had been the one part of his physicality that stimulated me all the way to orgasm.

I used to joke, "They can cut off your penis, but we'll be in trouble if they cut off your tongue!"

Although my teasing told a reasonable truth, John's negative reactions were an attempt to show me that those kinds of remarks embittered his sexual-esteem and fondness to satisfy my every desire. Not until my revelations did I at last understand that communicating in less than compassionate terms was one of the reasons our sexual relationship dwindled over the years to three times a week. It did not matter to me what the national average was for making love. My sexual needs required satisfaction every day. My husband's desire to have sex less often than I proved that my telling all, without experiencing all, was not the most successful way to promote future possibilities.

The responsibility for our sexual relationship becoming a pattern, however, fell into both of our hands. Habits formed and time-honored problems hindered our inspiration to change stagnant cycles of behavior. Status quo held a certain comfort factor that inhibited the growing and deepening intimacy that would have inspired grander biological horizons.

Regardless of the limitations of our sex life, from the first time we made love, John physically expressed the importance of my climaxing. In the months before we married, when he could not get enough of me, he learned that oral stimulation resulted in a sure-fire orgasm. Since it mattered to me that I orgasm, not how I achieved orgasm, I thought it should not matter to him. I was wrong. After he began his affair with Fate, he informed me of the importance he placed on my climaxing during intercourse without the assistance of a vibrator.

For seventeen years, he left me in the dark by neglecting to mention an important psychological need. Not being a mind reader, I could not possibly have known how consequential one aspect of our sex life was to my husband. His cold indictment of what I had not given him was one more nail in the coffin of great sex. All of that changed on the night to remember. Spiritual intervention kicked in, and grander biological horizons were no longer future possibilities. Tonight, affirming actualized possibilities was my itinerary for atonement!

John maneuvered his body next to mine. As if our two bodies were one, our four feet thrust the covers off the end of our king-sized bed. He raised my negligee over my head and slipped my panties down over my feet. I flung them off my side of the bed and pushed the pillows off with them. Nothing remained on the mattress except our naked bodies.

Being naked felt good that warm August night. Lying bare-skinned next to the man with whom I was about to share my most intimate self gave me a sense of the miracle of being human. To be able to physically experience the awesome nature of the omnipresent force that gives life was truly miraculous. On my mind that particular moment, notwithstanding the ubiquitous universe, was more than the opportunity for a soul to soul connection. The firm manliness between John's legs was far more distracting than I could have ever imagined.

There was no doubt about it. That part of his torso held a splendid renewal of my interest! Discovering that my husband's penis incorporated special capabilities changed my attitude dramatically.

Phallic limitations on behalf of my thinking were no longer marooned in the past. The spell of those subconscious liabilities had been broken, and the chance to explore capabilities was only an arm's length away.

I reached down to touch soft penile skin. The texture of the object heralding unmatched historical acclaim felt like nothing else on earth. The sensory pleasure it extended was absolutely a trance breaker. The hypnosis of past habits had definitely passed. As my fingers surveyed the spaces of the velvety kingdom they beheld, my heart soared with adulation for the exhilaration the commingling of two people was capable of producing.

Earth had met heaven, and it grew more heavenly when I looked down and spotted the stiff organ growing red. I could literally feel a neurochemical pleasure-response taking place in my brain as it worked in harmonious delight with my hands. They gently caressed the fleshy instrument of good tidings, then each testicle individually. My fingers moved down the inner side of each of my lover's thighs, savoring his mounting muscle tension. I smiled as he showed off, exercising the main event by bouncing it up and down, up and down. The art of carnal knowledge danced jovially in the form of a man's phallus.

Spontaneous responses to my husband's phallic dance surged, transcending me further into his seductions. Those instinctual urges were screaming at me to get closer to the fantastic organ oozing the juice of passion fruit from its head. John's hands brushed over my breasts, down my back, and over my buttocks, inviting every corpuscle of my body into paradise. I mounted my lover with intended purpose. My left leg wrapped around John's right leg, which resulted in my straddling him calf high. Sitting up and looking down, my eyes observed the universe of manliness beneath me. His face, neck, and forehead were developing a sexual flush, while his shoulders and forearms were taking on a pink measle-like rash. Tense stomach muscles elevated his pelvis as he looked up at me, waiting, watching, and thrilling to the sight, sound, and weight of hormonal turbulence. Because my spiritual experience originated inside me, I could not know if John was feeling the same holistic union of body, mind, and soul that I was feeling.

His eyes belied only one remark. *Anything you do is all right with me.*

Those amazing powder-blue eyes told me that my husband was, at the very least, honoring his wife's interpretation of her sexual self. Eighteen years of sharing the same bed with one man had reified my belief that sex was as intrinsic as breathing. Sex, as a root physiological need, refused to be ignored. The necessity of sexual relief was a biological certainty, a profound function of human nature. Blocking those intrinsic needs with negative religious and political attitudes was a sure-fired method of producing a plethora of ways to go crazy.

The most important sex organ, albeit, I had found to be the brain. John was not required to say a word. His physical responses were enough to enlighten my brain about the husband I created. At that moment, the male body my husband gave was blessing my mind as an instrument of communication, the bounty from which I hungered only for more. If this was contrition, *well hot damn!*

John tried to wiggle his legs, but my legs were too tight. Tension in his thigh and buttock muscles contracted, further elevating his pelvis. I had the control of his torso that I needed to allow motion for my own arousal. The position solved the mystery of conjugal redemption. I was free to grace my passion with the satisfaction that would not only grace my husbands psychological needs but also his soul needs.

I continued lowering my body. My hands stroked the entire range of John's penile shaft, then lifted it gently up toward my lips. My mouth enclosed the tip as my tongue massaged the protruding corolla. Slowly, my mouth and tongue meandered, exploring the remainder of maleness that aroused John the most. The appreciation I demonstrated had rooted the night I fell in love with the man I married. My heart ached to free itself from the toil of all the intervening years of John and me spinning each other's web. This night, my choice to set my heart free would be by permitting the multiplication of that love.

And oh! what multiplicity reaped! John's hands tugged aimlessly at my shoulders and arms with mounting aggression, causing libidinal euphoria to elevate to a degree beyond all expectation. The free flowing orgasmic experience on the night to remember had deepened and matured, actualizing limitless potentialities. Unheard of frequencies of spiritual energy had arrived sexually to surprise and delight. Divine grace, unleashing higher and higher levels of nirvana, John and I were playing rhythms created by powerful musical instruments.

Body, mind, and soul, I entertained unprecedented elation. My consciousness escaped to a spiritual world where no goal existed other than getting to the utopia the spasmodic impulses of our bodies were taking me. Engulfed in this new Shangri-La, nothing mattered except lingering in the white light of a soulful experience that seemed to have no lid on the bliss it offered.

Becoming ravenous to go further into the land of Oz, I let go of sexual containment. My body rushed headlong into insatiable fervor. Hormonal charges were demanding I turn loose the massive turbulence. Inflamed mania was driving me to exonerate the bestial chemistry now trapped in fiery frustration. Without thinking, analyzing, or planning, I lifted my torso and lowered my hips over John's penis. His long, thick masculinity penetrated my vagina. Its fullness touched every inch of that marvelous canal. My magic carpet had arrived to liberate the tunneled beast.

The intimate interconnectedness of two bodies created a springboard for synchronized movement. Synchronicity unleashed powerful, pulsating vaginal sensations. A volcano prepared to erupt as the ravenous aching intensified. The serpent demanded escalated motion to dispel guttural explosions. I drove my pelvis up toward John's upper body, then down toward his feet in a rowing motion. The rowing action caused my spine to lower its position until my clitoris rubbed against John's stomach. My pelvis pumped faster and stronger, stimulating clitoral excitement.

By lifting my pelvis up and leaning my body back toward his legs, John's penis rotated upwards inside my vagina. A new form of creature comforts resulted from the penile prodding. My pumping slowed into a steadier tempo. Tunnel walls thrilled to the motion of the exquisite instrument created specifically to massage the caverns of that life-giving passageway. Spectacular peaks flung me into yet another dimension of reality, the melding of the male and female body into oneness with cosmic forces. Ecstatic hands were around me as far as they could reach, sometimes pulling and pushing, sometimes holding on tight.

John stared at my face with a look of intense curiosity that told me I appeared to be lit on fire. My erratic frenzy was something neither one of us had experienced before. Once again, my mind's unity with cosmic forces had transformed the very atoms of my body. Realms of soul-revived sexual energy had me captured in conjugal mating. My head began to turn from side to side. The motion set free any tension that might have interfered with the exorcism of forbidden fruits. The pace of my body shifted again, moving in-tune with the pressure of my lover's masculine organ. In return, his pelvis matched the changing tempo of mine. The perfection of unplanned interchangeable harmonic movement felt sublime. Sensitive nerve endings exploded like firecrackers. They eased forward in gaiety and boom! The serpent's tongue heaved forth full-bodied orgasmic spasms, relieving me—body, mind, and soul—of the monstrous frustration never before released. At long last, I knew what all the shouting was about. As far as sex was concerned, grander biological horizons were a thing of the past!

Immediately following the crest of my climax, John ejaculated, the pulsations from which added the finishing touches to the wonder we shared. One orgasm had unearthed and exterminated the female biological dilemma. The all-consuming Grafenberg orgasm had been exquisitely purged. Its exoneration embodied the release of a tension I had carried in my body all of my adult life.

I could not nor would not ignore a truth so pleasing; it unlocked eternal summers no less than divine. I had prepared to redeem myself by surrendering my body, my heart, and my soul to my husband. That meant completely letting go of our past and our future. Still, the ecstasy I felt was filled with a greater wisdom than I could have imagined. This bliss included benevolence, joy, and the reconciliation of opposites. By outwardly manifesting my inner driving force of love without judging it good or bad, I had given John what he wanted since we began our romance. His psychological need had finally been met.

The event heralded for me a sublime religious adventure. The sacred feminine reborn in my body had made it possible for me to sexually express the desires of my soul. Through the tunnel of the vaginal caves where darkness had been scripted unto the world, I found the light of God. By taking the ultimate trip to heaven on earth, inadvertently I solved the mystery of great sex. Although my soul's union with my mind allowed me to experience the divine perfection of my body, it was the unity of two bodies that had opened the gates to the tree of life in Eden!

*Healing . . . must be first the correct choice for the spiritual
import held as the ideal of the individual.*

– Edgar Cayce 2528-2

12

Small Miracles

August 2, 1987, 6:00 A.M.

Birds singing songs about paradise found awakened me from a
sound sleep: great sex cascaded into my thoughts. *Last night a sexual
part of me that had never before been released gushed forth. I was
free-flying in a heavenly paradise where bliss alone mattered. My
consciousness felt euphorically suspended in Eden. Rivers of rapture
ebbed and flowed effortlessly into eternally expanding rivers of rapture
until complete contentment had been reached.*

Feminine nature, yet again, had taken on new meaning. Unleashed
was a sanctified inner power whose sheer strength made gender-driven
standards punishable by God's sinful judgments more sinister than
small-mindedness. The minds who dictated that passion had brought
sin and death into the world were the minds of a dark underworld
who subjugated humankind's natural born instincts, exploiting one of
its most sacred pleasures. Spiritualized sex mutated original sin into
a crime against humanity.

Eden's rebirthing spirit was what I found in the gardens of my
sexual chambers, the feelings of which involved every good sensation
of rightness in every sense of the word. The balancing of opposites,
the harmony of biological instincts, and the release of a tension that
paroled a source of unlimited energy: those were just the tips of the
fruits I picked in the garden of human sexuality.

Enlightened sex was another initiatory rite, one more biological unification of human consciousness and soul consciousness. Experiencing the light of my soul while making love with my husband was a *savior-faire*, a unity of two bodies that was certainly one of the almighty whoop-de-do's of incarnation. Fig-leaf mentality was out of the closet of my subconscious. Merely thinking about what a man's body could do for my body excited me all over again. Grander biological horizons had a smashing bon voyage party! Now, she wanted to enjoy the ride.

Silently, I indulged my good feelings. *I want to stay in bed all day long making love.*

The entire length of my body snuggled against my husband's body. Another door to the universe had been opened, liberating us from our habitual way of making love. I assumed my lover would also be ready for more. He snuggled me back for a few minutes, then got out of bed, pulled on his cement-encrusted jeans, and headed outside toward his old corroded wheelbarrow and a new cement mixture.

August 2, 1987, noon

John strutted through the front door announcing in his jokester style, "Get dressed. We're going to Stingers."

Familiar barstools awaited at Stingers. Everyone there seemed to beam with the same delightful afterglow exuding from every particle of my body. Never before did I feel more grateful to be alive. Even the over-the-hill cowboys looked good!

By then, John and I knew Terry, the bartender and owner of Stingers, on a first-name basis.

"How are you two today?" Terry asked, as he placed two beers and one glass on the bar in front of us.

John smiled and nodded a positive response. I did not set in motion any conversation with Terry because I could hardly wait to hear what John had to say about our sexual fireworks.

He skipped our usual toast and went directly to the point. "I didn't mean it when I said I'm yours. I felt sorry for you because you were crying. I'm ashamed of you for staying in your room all day. I don't like that kind of thing."

Like a gargantuan wasp, John stung me again. Imminent danger permeated his words. They were a caustic response to the greatest sex on earth. I had eaten the fruits of redemption. Now, the husband I created was blackening those fruits, turning them into a burnt offering. "I'm ashamed of you" was the valley he chose to begin the ordeal of my penitence.

"Ashamed" rendered my pursuit of redemption—by being a living example of my ideal of understanding, forgiveness, and compassion—a journey of pure faith. Ever since I began my automatic writings, my every spiritual experience assured me that purifying the shadowy part of my subconscious mind would free my conscious mind to hear my soul. It had been my choice to serve that truth by way of the magic mirror of the man I married. My initiation delivered me responsible to know the belief-programmed part of myself that I projected into my husband, no matter how many perils I encountered. I could right the ways I had wronged us both only if I could find those wrongs. However excruciating the birthing pains of *unifying my human consciousness and my soul consciousness*, there was no turning back. A *unified consciousness* was my goal and that was that. I sat straight up on my barstool and patiently waited it out.

John held the tickets to the show. "Let's go to the country club. This place is dead."

Large tinted windows at the far end of the clubhouse displayed the golf course beyond. Sand traps intermingled with rough grass and well-tended greens. A small lake cast the early afternoon sun back through the windows, lighting up the entire length of the long bar to the right as we entered. To our left, golfers sat at tables agonizing over eighteen holes of sheer delight.

We were barely through the door when John, in his prankster custom of capturing my attention, jested, "Guess who's here?"

At the farthest end of the bar a man who appeared to be around sixty sat alone with a copper-colored cocktail in front of him. His eyes were cast glumly down toward his glass. John took off, darting straight toward the aging man. I followed at John's pace, my posture erect. The closer we got, the more familiar the man looked.

When we arrived at his barstool, John greeted the man eagerly. "Hi, Dutch! Guess who's here? Charlie's daughter, Diana!"

The words "Charlie's daughter" prompted a memory. In the wee-small-hours of the morning after coming home from one of the numerous saloons he frequented, John woke me up exclaiming, "You'll never guess who I met tonight . . . Dutch! He told me he was an old friend of your father's."

The man looked up at me. Mirth was suddenly and unexpectedly written all over his face. A giant burst of loving energy exuded from him that compelled me to feel immediately comfortable. John was right. I recalled the name "Dutch" spring affectionately from my father's lips countless times.

Dutch wasted no time in his zest to relive those times; his happy sentiment and obvious worship of my father carried me back in time. "I bounced you and your sister, Susan, on my knee when you were little. I used to babysit while Chuck and Marie went out to party!" Dutch generated such a unique wit in bringing my parents to life, I could feel Daddy's charismatic personality while Dutch reminisced, "Remember, Diana, one of Charley's favorite gibes. 'What makes the big ball roll?'"

John and I laughed and laughed as Dutch, tossing in here and there a quote from the bible, told hilarious stories about the antics Daddy got him into. Dutch respected my father's talent for creating his own live-action, fun-filled adventures. He went on and on about Daddy's rare gift for treating every individual equally and his unquenchable curiosity about people, places, and environments. While memories poured from his lips, Dutch made it evident that he had the time of his life with the man who showed me how *to be*. Daddy took a bigger bite out of life than anyone either of us had ever known.

I loved Dutch a little more with his each and every anecdote. He was giving me back the fun part of my roots critical for me to recover at that moment. As far as our father/daughter relationship was concerned, my father had taken a few poor strokes in a lifetime of dynamic races. The tales Dutch told expressed what my heart felt. Daddy would always be a hero to me.

Dutch and I sat side by side nurturing each other's need to feel in our hearts happier times, when out of the blue he changed the subject. We had more in common than Charley and Marie.

Dutch did not mince words. "I have a gun in my car. Before you came in here today, I was going to use it on myself."

"Why?" I requested empathetically, grateful for the words "before you came."

He answered, "Today is the anniversary of my daughter's death. I miss her more than I can bare. I've been married six times. None of the marriages worked out. My second wife, the one I loved, left me. She didn't do anything wrong. I let her leave because I wouldn't let go of my anger. If I could go back and do it over. . . ."

As though he were deaf, dumb, and blind to Dutch's heart-wrenching catharsis, John interrupted, "I'm involved with a twenty-four year old girl I met at work. Since I told her about Fate, Diana says she's changed. Fate agrees with me that no one changes that fast." After a slight hesitation, he added mischievously, "I'm having sex with Fate."

My body leaned against Dutch for support. My mind needed time. It had to digest the fact that I was going to need all the endurance I could muster to journey the lights and shadows of the husband I never had the courage to leave. John's tone had resonated no guilt-conscience about ambushing a long-time family friend for the barbaric proclamation intended for his wife. His seemingly unquenchable appetite for vicious reciprocity was scrounging around to see if his booby-trap would send Dutch and/or me heading for the hills. John underestimated a man my father called *friend*.

Dutch rescued both himself and me. "John, I can't believe you're having an affair when you have this beautiful woman you're married to. These affairs with young women seldom work out. You're going through middle-age crisis. You've lost objectivity. Where's your sense of proportion? No couple lives together for eighteen years without problems. Don't you know that?"

"Look at all these bad marks Diana has against her," John rebuffed by pulling another fast one on Dutch's solid reasoning.

A cocktail napkin sat on the bar in front of John. While Dutch was making his case, John had drawn a line through the center of the napkin, dividing it in two halves. Scribbled on the upper half were two wind-swept rows of short dashes representing bad marks against me. On the lower section two-and-one-half long, straight, vertical dashes were neatly drawn for Fate.

Dutch examined John's slay-of-hand earnestly. Disappointment scribbled lines all over Dutch's face as he resumed his confrontation on behalf of a beloved friend's daughter. "It says in the bible, thou shall not worship false idols. Your infatuation is making you think this young girl is your savior. To you she is nearly divine. I'm sure you're overlooking her flaws and magnifying her strengths. You're narrowly focused on a flashy romance while dismissing the permanence of your marriage. What do you think all of this is doing to your wife?"

John chuckled from head to foot.

Beginning to show anger, Dutch concluded his reprehensible assault. "John, you're a fool."

John laughed out loud as he turned his back on us and sauntered in the direction of the bathroom. His cartoon-constructed celebration of feeling as if he were the prince of deception admitted no boundaries. By way of an old family friend, John had used adulterous sex to deliver himself from an evil wife.

Notwithstanding John's determination to re-entrap me, the devil's snare had been warded off. By standing up for me, Dutch made me feel as tall as a mountain. I sat straight up on my barstool, this time knowing Dutch's presence saved me that day as surely as my presence saved him.

As soon as John was out of earshot, Dutch's strong, warm hand surrounded mine, and he proceeded gently. "Matt: 6:24 says that a man cannot serve two masters. That man is going to leave you for this other woman. In John's mind, the odds are stacked against you. The girl will keep fighting for him. She has nothing to lose. Kick him out of the house before he has a chance to hurt you anymore. You are too much of a person to waste yourself on this situation."

I listened lovingly to an angel who delivered me from the devil knowing I would not take his advice. My opportunity to open the door of communication between my mind and my soul through purging and atoning refused to step aside for John's childish romantic fantasy. Besides, there was a clue neither John nor Dutch detected. All those wind-swept, free-spirited "bad" marks against Diana . . . were on top!

August 5, 1987

To help me understand the concept of "two masters" in the days following our meeting with Dutch, I looked up Matt: 6:24 in my *Holy Bible*. The quote came from Jesus Christ's Sermon on the Mount as remembered by Matthew. "No man can serve two masters: for either he will hate one and love the other; or else he will hold to the one, and despise the other. Ye cannot serve God and mammon."

Dutch's choice of reference was no understatement in spelling out the disparity between how John showed himself to love Fate and hate me. It turned out, however, that Matthew's two masters were not both material. His two masters were God (spiritual) and mammon (material). John trading me in for Fate was merely trading in one materialistic master (i.e., carnal pleasure) for another materialistic master, a sort of Darwinistic survival of the most seductive.

In his heart, John knew I had changed, that I could no longer be subjugated by the dark ocean of suffering fools, born and bread by fig-leaf conditioning. My choice to be ruled by my soul's connectedness to universal soul meant that I had, in Matthew's words, chosen God as my master. My service was to my husband's soul, not his materialistic mindset. No longer did I compete to win, and John knew it. My transformation was why he told me he was ashamed of me. John was ashamed of his wife for choosing to serve a master other than her husband. Moreover, he was scared to death of my transformation (into a higher energy vibration). My less-traveled road to redeem my soul was the walking, talking Satan on his over-crowded, money-paved road to perdition.

Dutch's words of advice, "She has nothing to lose," hit the bull's eye. John and I were not alone in our marriage bed. Fate's provocative actions proved her materialistic mindset. She would stop at nothing to get my husband's money, even fight to win. Fate personified the greed that my husband believed was his savior. John was not choosing between Fate and me. He was choosing, in Diana's words, between Universal Spirit and the spirit of materialism. For as much as his money-paved, carnal-lined highway appeared to be the straight and narrow path on John's paper napkin, free-spirited truth was still on top. . . .

Time was of the essence for me to step in between John and the materialistic affliction he got himself involved with. Goodness of action certainly went hand in hand with assisting a woman in taking responsibility for having a sexual relationship with another woman's husband. Confronting Fate meant leaving all my safe places and driving one-and-one-half hour on the most dangerous freeway in the world. No obstacle, even if it threatened my life, had the ferocity to stop me. I wrote down every word of responsibility I could think of, stacked a pile of scrapbooks in the back seat of the car, and left for The Big G.

For one-and-one-half hours I avoided fear and panic by focusing every bit of my attention on my car's ability to stay in my lane of the freeway. The consistent roar of the Mercedes diesel engine kept panic at bay by reminding me my message and I were one mile closer to the pestilence fighting to win my husband.

I pulled into The Big G's parking lot. Every neuron in my brain anticipated meeting Fate for the first time. Out of nowhere, John appeared blocking my way. I managed composure as I watched a man, who always seemed to have eyes in the back of his head, march staunchly toward me.

"What are you doing here?" he extorted, without a sign of his typical chuckle.

John's thinly veiled threat is dangerous only if I give him the power to control my emotions. I silently determined.

Intuition was telling me to push him out of my way, but he was too big to push, so I held my ground by firmly rebutting. "I came here to talk with Fate."

"Fate isn't here," he lashed out, then hastily backed down. "She's painting her bedroom."

"Where does she live?" I prodded, feeling empowered by the return of my will. "I'll go there. It doesn't matter where I tell her what I have to say."

"Let's go to a restaurant. I'll call Fate and ask her if she wants to talk to you," he said hurriedly, glaring with uneasiness to get me away from The Big G.

My car stayed behind John's little yellow truck until we arrived at a nearby restaurant. Though I had never seen the restaurant, to John it seemed quite familiar. His truck had barely pulled into a parking space when John jumped out, slammed shut the car door, then paced casually, yet hurriedly, toward the restaurant entrance.

"Wait here. I'll go in and call Fate on the pay phone." he shouted back, as my car came to a stop, making sure I did not tag along.

I slid out of the driver's seat and stood on the black pavement. John disappeared behind the solid wood restaurant door. While I gazed at the closed door, visualizing John dialing Fate's telephone number, a sense of inner peace and love came over me. A light that felt heavenly encircled my body like a protective halo. The world outside my halo appeared dreamlike. Wide-awake, in the middle of a black tar parking lot, I was standing in the void! This void was filled with a white light of extraordinary love.

The outcome of the telephone call stopped mattering. It did not even matter that Fate was most likely at The Big G, or that the prince of deception I married was really no more than a crass trickster. What mattered to me was having the courage to live my truth. By simply feeling the goodness of being true to myself, everything had become brighter. I watched John stroll, easy mannered, out of the restaurant and advance toward me. No matter what his intentions, as he approached I felt only a deep appreciation for what he had just done.

Oddly, he stopped very close to me and dutifully reported, "Fate won't see you. She said she is insulted you would even ask."

John stood staring down into my eyes as if he were truly curious to hear my reaction to Fate's attitude.

"Fate is insulted?" I puzzled out loud at her audacity. "She's doing everything she can to steal my husband and the father of my children and she thinks she has the right to be insulted!"

Without another thought, my head turned and my eyes looked down. In the back seat of my car sat a pile of scrapbooks. They were carefully stacked, one on top of the other, in the order I thought Fate would be most touched. John's eyes following the direction of my eyes.

After seeing the scrapbooks he sheepishly asked, "What were you going to say to Fate?"

As though my heart were singing a song of my everlasting love for the hopes and dreams those pictures contained, one family's truth guided my words. "I wanted to help Fate understand that no family lives together for a long period of time without troubles. It can be those very troubles that bond their love. I came here today to coax Fate into feeling responsibility for the outcome of her actions. There will be consequences for everyone if she succeeds in taking you away from your family. I planned to say, Fate, if you really love John, you must at least consider that you might not be the best person for his welfare or the welfare of his family."

When I finished speaking, I realized John was standing in my halo. His eyes were full of love. Light was emanating from his body. Like before, intuition guided my actions. My arms reached down to pick up the scrapbooks. My fingers pointed out each and every picture I had hoped would help Fate in seeing for herself that there was more at stake in attaining her goal than money (in Matthew's terms: mammon).

"See all the good times the four of us have had." I beamed, pointing to John's smiling face. "Look how happy you were."

Warm sentiment glazed over the love in his eyes as John analyzed himself in each picture. He looked happy and peaceful standing in my halo. Then, as plain as the nose on his face, he censored the photo as if the story they told was a lie. They were evidence which did not fit neatly into all those "bad" marks against me. Abruptly, he stepped back. The face of love returned to nonchalance.

"I have to go back to work now. I'll see you Thursday night," he said, standing his ground and reminding both of us that he was not coming home that night; then he sashayed away.

I watched my husband drive out of the parking lot until every inch of his little yellow truck had disappeared from sight. The change in plans was beyond anything I had the ability to control. I could not have forced Fate to talk with me nor to be accountable for her behavior. Regardless, I was not at all disheartened. Fate's resistance offered me the good fortune to stand in the light of my truth with my husband watching. It meant so much more for John to hear what I had to say than Fate. Because love guided me, spirit intervened to transform my plan and paint a huge protective halo around that transformation.

The way I had communicated with my husband was the person of unconditional love I always wanted to be. Because my heart had been willing, my mind unified with my soul and painted a huge white halo around my body. Standing in that bubble of radiant consciousness, I remembered that my ordeal was not merely a journey through the valley of my shadow. My ordeal was also a journey to the mountaintop of my soul. No, divine intervention was not a coincidence the day I drove to The Big G. Divine intervention was spirit bringing me an everyday small miracle!

Before enlightenment, chop wood and carry water.
After enlightenment, chop wood and carry water.

– Zen saying

13
Delusions Of Granduer

August 5, 1987, 4:40 P.M.

I did not need to drive my car home. It floated home with me, my halo, and my wanderlust. Wide-awake! In the light of day! When unconditional love guided my truth, fear dispersed. My material consciousness and spiritual consciousness became one.

This means opportunities for oneness between spirit and matter are unlimited. Oneness can happen anywhere, anytime I feel unconditional love! I concluded joyfully.

The maze of traffic on the southern California freeway surrounding my car felt as dreamlike as had the black tar parking lot. Physically, I was driving my car. Mentally, I was far removed from freeway realities. I was still standing next to my husband, both of us encircled by a halo of white light. What I once thought to be a simple-minded girl's bubble, I found that day to be the aura of my own soul. While standing in the light of my soul, the man I married stepped into that bubble of love and for a few brief moments we were divinely graced with the oneness of two souls. In those blissful moments, I experienced the reason for *atonement: at-ONE-ment.*

When penitence spiraled me up into *at-ONE-ment*, everything became brighter. With that rising of my human nature to wed my spiritual nature, I looked into John's eyes and knew beyond a shadow of a doubt that we both had the same earthly meaning. The day I drove to The Big G a heavenly host surrounded my halo. That legion of light shielded me from the dark side of the man I married, protecting me from fear so in the light of day I could experience what I knew in my fearless heart before my bubble burst.

I glorified in my enlightening thoughts, *The meaning of my life is for my mind to co-create with my soul. In those few glorious moments, I was a walking, talking example of the living soul!*

My halo lit every mile of the drive home, but the instant I walked into my house the hypnotic spell of walls returned. My halo took its turn dispersing, fear returned, and I knew why.

Ruth and I had been friends for fifteen years before she made me aware of her dark secret. That awareness happened one day while we were shopping. After getting separated, I looked around the store and saw Ruth standing in line about thirty-five feet from me, ashen. She spotted me and waved me over. I hurried to her. Stricken with anxiety, her hands were shaking, and she said she could not breath.

Ruth implored frantically, "Diana, I'm having a panic attack. I feel dizzy and nauseated. Standing in line to buy these things makes my heart pound so fast I feel like I'm going to die. Please don't leave me again. I need you to be near me to feel safe."

Later at home my dear friend explained, "I have agoraphobia. Agoraphobia is an intense fear of something unknown. The fear causes panic attacks. I've been having panic attacks for years. They began without warning and for no reason. They have become habitual. When I'm having an attack, I feel as if I'm going crazy. I live in fear of having an attack in places where I can't escape embarrassment. I meet with a group of agoraphobics. They say the fear of having panic attacks in public can become so addictive, some women, even some men, can't leave their houses for decades. No one knows how many, but a percentage of agoraphobics literally wind up living in their closets."

I knew the reason I hid in bed was the fear of losing John. With the exception of meditation, automatic writing, and prayer, none of which unfailingly came to my aid, my panicky fear was not an attack but one long ongoing event. To exonerate the unrelenting terror, I fought to end John's affair. I presumed when I got my husband away from Fate's control, my panic would end.

On the surface, my symptoms appeared to be different from Ruth's. She did not know the reason for her panic attacks nor how to stop them. I thought I knew both. Gradually, as I gained the psychological and spiritual insights that were cutting through my self-deception, I admitted to myself I had agoraphobia. Intuitively, I knew there had to be a reason for Ruth's agoraphobic *disease* just as surely as there was a reason for mine. The reason went far deeper than Ruth's fear of being embarrassed by a panic attack or my fear of losing John. Our symptomatic *dis-ease* had its roots in the fear of discovering how far we had both strayed from the meaning of our lives.

As heightened awareness continued showing me more of the light of spiritual reality, each higher level of light was making clearer the dark side of human reality. My experiences with automatic writing, meditation, nature, and sex were spiraling my consciousness up toward the light while removing obstructions from the dark side of my subconscious. That shadowy part of my mind had spilled forth corrupted feelings. My corrupted feelings were birthed by the minds of the powerful few who had control over the minds of the multitudes.

Born knowing that precious time was wasted on the fear cultivated by a few greedy men who sold original sin to make people think they were *born bad*, the ebb and flow of my uncorrupted mind moved as naturally as night and day. Because I believed people were *born good*, my feelings told me time ought to be spent cultivating good feelings. In the natural flow of life, there should be a time for work, a time for play, a time for rest, but most of all a time for seeking knowledge of truth. I had fallen into the false knowledge that previously talked to me of energy wasted on feeling bad. My fall was teaching me how original sin controlled the human mind.

Living in a bubble for forty years had externalized my internal belief that the origin of human nature was good. I lived in the light of a free spirit because the love in my soul drove my every thought, word, and deed. Since that direct connection from my soul into my mind was my driving force, my heart was void of anything but happy intentions. Because after my fall into fear my ability to love expanded exponentially, confirmed was my belief that the original nature of human nature was the goodness of love, which originated in the soul.

Synchronistically, even as my mind dwelled in the bottomless abyss of fear, every word of the automatic writings that began one month earlier flowed unfailingly with unconditional love.

It was not until my meditative revelations, however, when my mind swam with my soul as one with Universal Spirit, did it dawn on me that Universal Spirit and its offspring, the soul, contained more than love. It contained knowledge, therefore mind. That meant the original nature of human nature, which was love was also mind. My soul contained the same beautiful, wonderful ocean of mind as Universal Spirit. It contained both love and knowledge, the very definition of wisdom! As I continued wandering my initiatory path, I gradually came to understand that since the love and knowledge in the soul was the original nature of human nature, the dark side had to grow from the separation between human nature and original nature. When human nature separated from soul nature, it separated from Universal Spirit, the origin of all souls. Still, not until I learned about original sin did I begin to understand how *original sin caused fear and ignorance of the soul, thus ignorance of Universal Spirit*. The effect of fear and ignorance *was separation between the mind and the soul.* The following is my simplified version of how separation between the mind and the soul develops:

The human mind is made up of two parts: the conscious mind and the subconscious mind. The conscious mind is born pure, void of human knowledge. The subconscious mind is the soul mind, filled with love and knowledge. At birth, the soul mind flows freely, but silently, into the conscious mind. This direct connection between subconscious mind and conscious mind is inborn, innately human. Therefore, at birth the conscious mind (void) and subconscious mind (soul) work as one indivisible guiding force to co-create life.

The instant after birth, a baby's conscious mind hears everything in its environment. A baby also feels the behaviors of those in its environment. This people-filled environment means the soul mind loses some of its power to guide the conscious mind once the first breath of life is taken. The soul can no longer fully co-create with the conscious mind. The process of separation of the soul mind from the human mind has already begun.

To distance this gap, the subconscious soul mind is abruptly split into two parts: *soul mind* and *learned mind*. This is how the split takes place. A baby's conscious mind learns from words and behaviors in its environment, but because a newborn's conscious mind has not yet learned to understand words, words in the baby's environment go straight from the conscious mind into the subconscious mind, where they are stored. Storage of words is the *learned mind*. Behaviors, however, determine how the words are felt. For instance, a harsh voice feels bad and a tender voice feels good. Good and bad feelings are stored as learned feelings. Learned feelings become the learned mind. Therefore, *in the beginning of life, words are learned as good and bad feelings.*

The conscious mind does not remember these early words and feelings, but since they are all stored in the subconscious mind, the subconscious mind remembers every word and feeling. As love and knowledge in the soul flow into the conscious mind, so do the learned good and bad feelings. However, since bad feelings are inconsistent with soul feelings, and since the learned mind now shares space in the subconscious mind with the soul mind, the love and knowledge in the soul flows less and less freely from the subconscious into the consciousness.

As the baby becomes a toddler, the words s/he learns enter the conscious mind loud and clear. Then the words are stored in the subconscious mind, where they are silent. As the toddler begins to understand the meaning of words, those meanings co-exist with stored good and bad feelings and the love and knowledge in the soul. When words and behaviors in the toddler's environment speak of original sin, because original sin is inconsistent with original nature, words are remembered and felt as bad thoughts and feelings. Except now, the toddler is old enough to feel fear, and bad thoughts and feelings produce fear. Therefore, original sin words are felt and remembered in the conscious mind as fear, and then they are stored the subconscious mind as fear.

As the toddler grows into childhood, if there are more words and behaviors in the environment that speak of original sin (fear) than of original good (love), then more fear than love goes from the conscious mind into the subconscious mind, which in turn flows back into the conscious mind as automatic thoughts and feelings. If this cycle continues, as the child grows from an adolescent to an adult, eventually the learned mind will take up more space in the subconscious mind than the soul mind. As such, mostly fear will flow from the subconscious mind back into the conscious mind, a thickening downward spiral of fearful thoughts and feelings called the dark side (also called the shadow). Without healing the subconscious mind from fear, the conscious mind has no escape from the (learned) dark side. No matter how much the individual wants to love, if there is more fearful thoughts and feelings than loving thoughts and feelings flowing from the subconscious into the consciousness, fear will corrupt every attempt to love.

From birth to adulthood, the sheer number of original sin words has built a mountain of stored fear in the subconscious mind. This mountain of fear has built a wall around the soul mind, imprisoning the soul in the far reaches of the subconscious mind. Original sin imprisoning original good has blocked the love and knowledge in the soul from flowing into the conscious mind. With the soul's power to guide the person diminished to negligible, the soul has been subjugated to what is known as the *still small silent inner voice*. Even when the loving voice of the knowledge in the soul succeeds in breaking through the wall, which it does in everyone, the conscious mind is much too busy listening to all the loud and clear voices flowing from the environment to pay attention to it.

Original bad (sin) has taught the human mind, both conscious and subconscious, to fear original good (soul). The learned mind and the conscious mind have imprisoned the soul mind. Not only has the individual learned to fear the soul, s/he can no longer remember the soul and therefore is ignorant of the love and knowledge that once flowed directly into the conscious mind. Now, there is nothing to get in the way of the individual feeling and thinking that original sin is truth.

Fear and ignorance of the soul and its origin, Universal Spirit, is what is meant by *the condition of human suffering*. The classic battle of good versus bad (evil) rages in both the conscious and subconscious mind. Original soul nature has fallen into original sin nature, learned mind the separator of the conscious mind and the soul mind. Learned thoughts and feelings speak more of fear than of love. Fear flows into the conscious mind saying, *I am bad. . . . Love is . . . **not to be.***

What was once a co-creation between the soul mind and the conscious mind is nearly complete separation. *The soul voice has fallen into silence, the true fall of humanity.* Summarily, that is how the corrupted minds of the powerful few control the mind of the multitudes. Original sin maintains separation between the mind and the soul. Moreover, sin has closed the mind to Universal Spirit and the oneness of all souls.

Initiatory journeys are for breaking down walls between the mind and the soul built by ignorance and fear. As each fear falls, a little more of the soul mind breaks through into the conscious mind. Journeying the tunnel of fearful thoughts and feelings stored in the subconscious (chamber of the shadowy dark side) is making the subconscious conscious. Feeling and understanding repressed fear is the process of purifying the false learning of original sin words. An initiatory rite takes place each time an *I am bad* thought and/or feeling is purified. Initiatory rites gradually set the soul mind free to once again flow into the conscious mind.

Inscribed on the inner walls of the great Pyramid of Giza, the initiation is a metaphor for the process of enlightenment. Initiations are extraordinary crises divinely scripted in each person's life to fall from original sin back into original soul, from bad back into good, from fear back into love. Initiatory journeys are journeys of salvation. They end separation by building a bridge between the mind and the soul. *Fall Into Freedom* is the journey of the soul back into co-creating with the mind. . . . And the voice of the soul says, *I AM good. . . . Love is . . . to be!*

The feelings I learned from my parent's words and behaviors spoke mostly of love. That is why my mind did not fully separate from my soul. I do not know if Daddy and/or Mother believed in original sin because sin words were not spoken in our home. I do know the reason my mother left the Catholic church was because she did not believe Catholic laws, and she never found another church or spiritual philosophy to help her to heal her sorrows. Nevertheless, the way she loved me was without condition. True, Mother and Daddy had their heartaches and their failures, but they almost never projected them onto me by making me feel bad about myself. So, my mind did not learn to think or feel fearfully about who I was. Though they made some serious mistakes, my parents graced my life with unconditional love. Protected from the "jungle" or not, while other children's souls were being separated out of their minds, Charley and Marie made it possible for my mind to stay connected with my soul mind. All my life my original nature spoke to my thoughts and feelings, saying, *I AM free . . . to be!*

After I married, John pounded original sin words into my mind. So that my conscious mind would not be corrupted, I suppressed his words and the bad feelings they threatened by storing them in my subconscious mind. When I fell, in a matter of seconds eighteen years of stored fearful thoughts and feelings flooded from my subconscious mind into my conscious mind. Fear of all those "bad" thoughts and feelings burst my protective bubble of love. Original sin broke down the original love that was the home inside myself. What bled all over the place were those fearful thoughts and feelings that for eighteen years had been slowly taking control of my mind, the control I later came to understand as the devil's snare.

Regardless of getting ensnared by the corrupted mind of one man conditioned to fear his own soul, my mind had lived in a protective bubble of love far too long. Down but not out, the voice I heard in meditation, the one with nature and during sex, was the same voice that made me want to scream to the world, *Stop wasting love!* The bubble that remained floating for so long and then had been blown into pieces was my original nature. Yes! That uncorrupted voice of pure soul mind born unto me was the voice who, after my fall, relentlessly shouted, *Get up and stand tall!*

Determined to fight my fear, pay penitence to John, and live my truth, I faced the grand slam head on. Driving to The Big G turned out to be a dazzling breakthrough. What I considered a huge success, nonetheless, vanished the instant I walked through the doorway of my house. My walls heaved me back into fear and panic. An overwhelming need to get to the safety of my bedroom came over me. With all that, my knowledge of Ruth's ongoing battle with panic attacks stopped me cold. Her habitual fear reminded me that if I got into the habit of returning to a darkened room, agoraphobia had the power to cage me forever. To regain my power, I had to intentionally welcome the underlying reason for my fear of losing John: the wife my husband's words created.

I recalled the old Diana, the one who laughed when her husband unyieldingly snickered, "Diana, you'll never be able to do anything in the real world. When I'm done with you, I'm going to send you back to Santa Ana."

Every time John hammered words into my brain about a poverty-stricken city he would send me to, he did more than brainwash me into feeling bad about myself. Every time I suppressed his words by laughing, I internalized the prejudice his words taught. Every time I laughed, my husband taught me that poverty was a weakness and weakness was unforgivable. And every time I laughed, I learned to be less understanding, less forgiving, less compassionate of human suffering, and more scared of poverty.

Every single time I laughed, the walls of my house became more symbolic of how my husband's sin standard had corrupted my mind. Invisible chains created by the wealth inherent in castle walls had been eating away at my driving force of love from the inside out. My husband's money standard had become my money standard to the degree that I feared miserably ever after more than I loved happily ever after.

The wife John's words created was a woman whose walls were a constant reminder of, "You'll never be able to make it in the real world because you're bad." Her secret fear of "When I'm done with you" had caught fire and was whirling inside chamber walls; flaming wheels of uncovered secrets represented a comfortable world that bad Diana was scared to death of losing.

To take the power out of the hands of bad and put it back into the hands of good, I would be required to uncreate the wife my husband's words created. I had to take my safety away from the temple of fear and put it back into the temple of soul. There was no way of knowing how many secret walls were waiting to be broken down, but if the thousands of laps I swam represented how many breakthroughs I needed to experience to fill the gaping holes created by eighteen years of "You'll never be able to make it in the real world," my driving force told me *I better dive in and start experiencing.*

August 8, 1987, 11:30 A.M.

To conquer fear, I continued facing fear head-on. I stayed out of bed, kept the door to my bedroom open, and focused my attention on Cherisse, Tamara, and the household routine. To reinforce my faith in good, I prayed, meditated, read, and kept up with my automatic writing. Leaving the house, nevertheless, remained an effort of sheer will.

While I was making sure the kitchen looked picture-perfect, Tamara walked in and asked, "Mom, can you take me to the store? I need some jazz shoes for my dance class."

"Okay. Get ready and we'll go right away." I replied without hesitation, knowing that leaving the house for my daughter's sake was now or never.

I backed the car out of the garage. Tamara did not attempt to turn on the radio. I felt she was giving me a second chance while simultaneously trying very hard to keep peace between us. Throughout the entire drive, I paced my breathing and thought about how much I loved my daughter.

When we arrived at the outdoor mall, certain I needed to meditate, I handed Tamara enough money for her shoes and asked affectionately, "Do you mind if I wait here?"

She replied in earnest, "No, I know what shoes I want."

Tamara forged her way out of the car and across the cement walkway toward the shoe store. I looked around. A variety of stores made a horseshoe around my car. People strolled past, peering into fancifully decorated windows. Their eyes dazzled with hopes and dreams of buying some new object of their affection. Both the beauty and ugliness of what money could and could not afford passed before me as if I were viewing a theatrical production produced specifically for me. For the first time in my life, I felt with my eyes the power money had over human emotion.

It was easy to see how populations could be programmed to worship the almighty dollar. After all, printed on every dollar in the United States was "IN GOD WE TRUST." The materialistic aspect of the dollar, for God's sake was what the collective mind had been marketed to have faith in. While speculating how much control money had over the happiness and unhappiness of humanity as a whole, I heard laughing voices. The celebration of life expressed so humorously by a hand-holding young couple transported my mood. My spirits were immediately lifted by my adoration for the romantic vision my eyes beheld!

I wanted to point cupid's arrow at their hearts with the inscription, *Fly with the joy you share, young lovers. How blessed you are that love is what brings you laughter. Hold on to each other and don't ever let love go. Don't let anything or anyone come between the two of you and love everlasting.*

Tamara opened the car door. Her cheerful face drew my attention away from my daydream. Before getting in, she pulled her dancing shoes out of a large plastic bag and examined her shopping achievement proudly. Tamara's unfailing desire to view the object of her affection as soon as possible made my heart sing!

August 8, 1987, 2:30 P.M.

From the backyard, I heard the telephone ring. By the time I made my way into the house, Cherisse had answered the telephone in her room and was talking with Brittany, her close friend since kindergarten.

When they finished their lively conversation, Cherisse handed me the receiver saying, "Kassy wants to talk with you."

Kassy, Brittany's mother, and I had been casual friends since our daughters met. Not only was Kassy strikingly attractive, she was also a published author and successful businesswoman who traveled internationally, orating success seminars.

When she greeted me with, "Hi, Diana! How are you?" her energetic tone reflected her strong yet giving personality.

My emotions instantly succumbed to Kassy's ability to make me feel cared for. My story about how John's affair had affected me spilled forth without interruption, after which Kassy reacted with alarm.

Her call to arms offered neither pity nor condescension. "As things stand Diana, John has you where he wants you, *trapped*. He never really felt he had you."

"What?" I questioned, not believing my ears.

"He never felt he had you," she repeated.

It was not so much Kassy's words that puzzled me as how easily she spelled out what took me eighteen years and one long, quintessential panic attack to figure out.

From the day we married, John used words relentlessly to break my spirit because he wanted to get me trapped. To feel he "had" me, John needed me trapped like he was trapped . . . trapped by the beatings that punished him for being himself . . . trapped by the institutionalized violence of a warring world from which he tried to free himself . . . trapped by the sin his religion heralded that would forever deny him spiritual freedom . . . and trapped by a sea of learned thoughts and feelings so deeply rooted in his subconscious that he feared who he was underneath his trapped self.

Kassy's sharp-witted worldliness snapped into place another piece to our puzzle. No, John never doubted my love for him. To John, having me never meant me loving him. Having me meant having me trapped . . . trapped by a tyrannical system of mind control that would someday make my life an inescapable mental prison . . . trapped by verbal beatings that would cause a sea of fear to be so deeply rooted in my subconscious that all happiness would get swept away . . . and trapped by castle walls that protected me from being sent to a place where poverty would forever have me trapped. John thought if he trapped me just like he had been trapped, he would never feel lonely again.

Kassy's straightforward, uncluttered approach to stating the facts forced me to face my situation head on. In John's real world I was no less trapped than the day Fate called to attack my comfort ability. Kassy easily solved the mystery of agoraphobia. My dis-ease was merely a symptom of being trapped. I had gotten trapped by the tradition of female economic servitude that trickled from my husband's lips into my bubble of love.

What surfaced with one telephone call was a fear so violent to the core of who I was, those feelings involved every "bad" sensation of "wrong" in every sense of the word. My fear that Diana was worthless in a world of wealth did not surface with one telephone call. My fear of Santa Ana's walls took eighteen years of degrading words spoken by the man who told me I was one in a million.

Ironically, because it took John so long to burst my bubble, getting caught in the devil's trap changed nothing about what my mind knew the instant I fell. Diana could not remain in that mental torture chamber called human suffering or she would find herself living in a place she had seen all her life: a place where people were sad, tired, bitter, angry, hateful, lost, and finally destroyed, a place where life existed no more. The only way for me to free myself from the devil's trap depended on living my life through the eyes of love which was not going to begin to happen until Fate stopped blowing smoke up my husband's ego. Until then, one too many tricksters would have me trapped.

Fate ran from me once. She's not going to run from me again, I resolved, knowing her affair with my husband would do me in if I did not do it in.

I left Cherisse's room, walked into the den, and sat down at John's desk. I picked up a pencil and paper. What I intended to write on that paper was ruled not only by my compassion for the sanctity of two other human beings, my intention was also ruled by my passion to salvage my own sanctity. To state my point, I used words I guessed would fit into Fate's religious beliefs:

Fate

When I came to The Big G, you refused to see me. I don't think you are aware of how you are hurting John by continuing to pull at him. It is God's beautiful plan for the families of the world to be the center, the glue that holds the earth together. By trying to break up a family, break the hearts of two, sweet, young girls and destroy another woman, you are going against God's plan. You cannot do this, then wander off into the sunset happily ever after. The joy of falling in love with my husband a second time and having an explosive sex life is a true blessing. People do change! I am going to spend my time proving to my husband that my love is true. Please do not go against your responsibility to be a good person by continuing your affair with another woman's husband. Face the reality of what you are doing. With true sincerity, I do not want your life to be injured.

Diana

Satisfied with my choice of words, I stood up and went back to Cherisse's room. Tamara had joined Cherisse on her window seat where they sat quietly talking. After asking their permission, I read the letter out loud and then asked for a critique.

Cherisse offered her critical evaluation, "It's caring and to the point."

Tamara added with assurance, "You should definitely send it."

With the affirmation of the two people whose opinions I respected most highly, I mailed the letter to Fate, in care of The Big G. Telling my story to Kassy and writing the letter to Fate had lifted the burden of keeping John's affair behind closed doors. The human connection felt great! Connecting with the world outside my home empowered me so much, I decided to connect again.

It was 1977 when Darlene and I met. We were both enrolled in a typing class at a local community college. Ten years younger than I, petite, energetic, and with the thickest naturally curly blond mane imaginable, Darlene's physical appearance hinted at a lion on the lurch. Her rambunctious manner of filling every opportunity for silence with small talk left no leaf in her jungle untouched. One day after class, Darlene proudly produced a picture of Don, her new boyfriend. A detailed description of what was evident in the photograph followed. Don was a tall, broad-shouldered, narrow-hipped, dark-haired young man with a relaxed demeanor.

As time passed, Darlene fell in love with Don, and Don fell in love with Darlene. Their first child, a girl, was born out of wedlock. Nevertheless, a year later, Darlene and Don were married in my living room and went on to have two more healthy children, both boys. Don provided a beautiful home and sperm to produce their babies. Darlene birthed beautiful babies and took care of their home. Of Christian heritage, the five of them went to church every Sunday and spoke frequently of their "Lord and master, Jesus Christ." I dialed the telephone number of a couple I cherished and felt I knew well.

Don answered and replied to my greeting in his mellow manner, "Hi, Diana."

After asking to speak with Darlene, Don answered, "Darlene isn't home."

Don's comfortable, low-key voice cut through the possibility for small talk. Its warm familiarity opened the door for my story to release itself as it had with Kassy. A second time, the response I received surprised me.

"Darlene is running all over town with another man," Don lamented in what I suddenly heard as a depressed tone. "She's using my credit cards for the two of them to party every night."

Don's humiliating story came all too close to my predicament with John. Don and I were in the same boat, each of us trying to put together a fornication survival kit. I wondered if the commandment, "Thou shall not commit adultery" had been stripped from church rules and people everywhere had jumped on the "can-do" bandwagon. If Darlene believed Jesus Christ was going to save her from the consequences of the feelings she was crusading in her husband, it might have been more a saving grace if she would have opened her bible and read the words I found while reading Christ's Sermon on the Mount.

My husband's cheating had been a deliberate crucifixion of my feelings, a measured murder of the childlike way my heart trusted him. Though John was raised Catholic, he did not read the bible. After our meeting with Dutch, I read Christ's words in Matt: 18:18: "For whatsoever ye shall bind on earth shall be bound in heaven: and whatsoever ye shall loose on earth shall be loosed in heaven," made John hurting me and my children and Darlene hurting Don and his children, food for fetter!

I voiced my concern for Don's suffering. "Don, what are you doing about you wife's affair?"

"Nothing," he replied.

"Who's taking care of your children?" I asked.

"Our kids are here with me," he answered, this time an undercurrent of anger apparent.

John ought to take lessons from Don's fathering skills, I thought, remembering years of watching him raise three children. *But Don sounds like Darlene's affair is a common occurrence and he's not going to do anything about it.*

I knew that nothing I could say would make Don's anguish go away. I had showed I cared by simply listening and hearing his feelings. Alarmingly, what I heard was a man who planned on doing nothing to save his family from being torn apart.

Once I watched love bloom and grow a plentiful garden. Now I watched love whither and fall onto parched earth. Families were being torn apart because conscience had lost value. Apparently, while Cherisse, Tamara, and I floated around in our protected little bubble, in the real world, distinguishing between right and wrong had gone out of style. I hoped my being there for Don had aided his distress. Regardless, hearing his story turned out to be the best medicine for my trapped condition. Don's refusal to confront Darlene about her affair opened my eyes to the necessity of confronting John about his affair.

I put down the receiver, then picked it up again, and dialed The Big G. John answered.

Rather than give him time to say anything, I spoke quickly, choosing words he would use if he were talking to me. "I'm not happy with what has been going on between you and Fate. I want to talk to you tomorrow about our relationship. Think about it between now and then."

He replied cautiously, "Okay."

I ended our short conversation with, "Goodbye," then clicked down the receiver.

August 9, 1987, 7:20 A.M.

John stayed in bed longer than usual, snuggling with me. I took advantage of the romantic mood I had created with one telephone call by lying silently in his arms and soaking up the love he was willing to share.

He offered a sweet query. "Would you like to go out to lunch today? We can talk things over then."

"I'd love to," I answered, reaping the teensy reward of walking through fiery hells for the man I loved.

I spent the entire morning beautifying, after which I walked, my head held high, onto the front porch. John looked up from his cement mixture.

He stuck his shovel in the wet cement, headed up the steps, and ordered, "Open some champagne. I'll get ready!"

John drove the car with one arm around me and one arm on the wheel.

"Where would you like to eat?" he said in a dreamy manner.

"Let's go to the country club," I suggested, catching on to the fact

I had a changed man on my hands.

After parking the car, John opened my door, escorted me through the country club's entrance, and walked behind me to our table. In his most gentlemanly style, he pulled out my chair. After I was seated, he asked me to choose the wine. We talked about everything except Fate. The stars of love in my husband's eyes were for me. Stars told me the best way to break up the dynamic duo of John and Fate was to let John experience the way he loved me.

When we finished eating, he took my hand and we strolled hand in hand into the clubhouse. While seating ourselves upon tall mahogany barstools, he ordered two glasses of champagne. Even in the beginning when we made each other fly, I could not remember a time when John did what he did next. He leaned his head against mine and kept it there. I did not move. Never before had both John and I forsaken our public persona so completely to demonstrate our love for each other.

John took my hand tenderly, turned it over, and kissed my palm. He stared at it as if one palm held a great treasure. He drew my arm up and pressed my hand against his face. With his eyes he affirmed how understanding, forgiveness, and compassion had changed both of our lives. The underlying reason for my unconditional love was not to get my husband back. Above and beyond all the fiery hells I had to walk through to fight his affair, my unconditional love was for the purpose of helping him stand in the light of his soul as he had helped me stand in the light of mine.

Experiencing the unconditional love of his soul would change his life with or without me. As we sat on barstools at the country club that day, for a second time my unconditional love for my husband made it possible for our two souls to unite. Two-as-one, after all, did embody our marriage vows. John was laying bare the possibility for us to be a living example of the reason two people promise in the name of God to be one. The love for me I felt in my husband's eyes as my hand caressed his cheek washed away all the years of punishing each other for what we ourselves lacked.

Just as little angels were whispering in my ear, "It doesn't get any better than this," my lover said, "Let's go home."

Arm in arm, we scaled the walls of heaven. Like young romantics, we rushed home to make love.

"I love you," John murmured, as he unbuttoned my top.

My top fell to the floor. My heart was too full of appreciation for me to speak. With the experienced wisdom that I had entered Eden's garden of treasured fruits, I looked at my lover. He looked like a man in paradise.

August 10, 1987, 8:35 P.M.

The entire day I floated on air. I had just kissed Cherisse and Tamara goodnight and was heading to my bedroom by way of the kitchen when the telephone rang. I picked up the receiver.

John's voice fumed hostility. "Why did you write this horrible letter to Fate? What are you trying to do to this poor girl? You have ruined everything for us."

"John, you're wrong," I asserted honestly. "The letter is good. Did you read it?"

The phone went dead.

My thoughts raced for a lifeline. *What have I done? How many times must right intentions pave my road to infernal regions?*

The fight or flight response tugged at me. I sought to think of any way to fight off panic.

Cherisse and Tamara know what the letter said, I remembered. *They put their stamp of approval on it.*

I hurried to their rooms and made them my allies by reiterating their father's hostile remarks.

Cherisse extended her offended sensibilities. "He must be crazy!"

Tamara nodded her head up and down in frightened agreement. Whether or not I had considered that Fate might show the letter to John, Cherisse's and Tamara's support felt right. Their support was the lifeline I needed to fend off extramarital behavior I knew was wrong. It was crucial that I find a psychological resolution to short-circuit panic's repeated knocking.

"We have to call Daddy and tell him he's wrong about the letter," I warned.

I hurried to the kitchen. Cherisse and Tamara followed close behind me. I picked up the telephone's receiver and dialed The Big G. Two buzzes buzzed.

"This is Fate. May I help you?" Fate's sugary-sweet voice rang out as if it had been artificially inseminated.

In the "poor girl's" voice, I heard no sign of fear or panic. I heard a jubilant shrew who reveled in devouring her competition.

"This is Diana. May I please speak with John?" I requested calmly.

"I'll call him." The lollipop coating had vanished; snide strength had detailed every syllable snarling from a woman who felt she had a right to be my husband's next wife.

John's voice sounded on the line demanding harshly, "What do you want?"

Fate mumbled demurely in the background. Her candy coating had returned. Masked was the manipulative vixen beneath a thinly veiled shell. I could have cared less if Fate turned into a gigantic candy cane. Even in her Barnum-Bailey world she knew right from wrong. Her helium filled circus balloon was all about John showing her the money. I was not deterred. Not even Pandora's molecule could stop me from completing my mission.

I handed Cherisse the phone insisting, "Tell Daddy how you feel."

Cherisse tried truth. "Dad, why are you playing this horrible game with Mom?"

Tamara grabbed the receiver and took her turn with her father. "Mom has done nothing wrong." Then she lowered the receiver from her ear, looked at me strangely, and said, "Dad hung up on me!"

Cherisse's and Tamara's courageous, unfaltering stance had given all three of us a gift. By ignoring his daughters' plea, John's true colors were revealed. He, too, knew right from wrong, yet his delusions of grandeur were not about to let conscience stand in the way of being trapped. With his silence, John had given his daughters their father's truth. His candy-coated armor did not protect a gallant man. John's candy cane weapon protected a coward. Cherisse knew it. . . . Tamara knew it. . . . I knew it. . . .

O researcher of things, do not praise yourself for knowing
the things that nature ordinarily determines by itself,
but rejoice in knowing the purpose of those things
which are designed by your own mind.

– Leonardo Da Vinci

14

Write Your Book!

August 10, 1987, 8:45 P.M.

My eyes drifted away from Tamara and toward Cherisse. She, too, was taken aback by what she had to report.

"Dad told me he's going to make his choice, you or Fate. He's going to tell us when he gets home tonight," Cherisse announced dumfounded.

The outright childishness of John's romance inscribed every curve of Cherisse's and Tamara's faces. Their voices were inflicted with affections stained by the wisdom inherent in children, their heartaches symbols of cultural traditions that prostituted all women. The man they called "Dad" had chosen to arm himself with carnal daggers, but his daughters understood his game long before their mother wrote a letter to his newest playmate. John's yellow-bellied choice to play kill-or-be-killed sex games with the three hearts who loved him the most was the color of the stripe he wore straight down the center of his back.

Because of my willingness to stay in an abusive marriage until I was trapped, my daughters were also trapped . . . trapped by their father's all-for-me system of soul-extermination that trickled down from his lips into our bubble of love . . . trapped by an adulterous affair that burst their mother's all-for-one, one-for-all system of extermination-avoidance, then pushed it into a big black gravitational hole . . . and trapped by the hideous deteriorating drama their father used to tighten the control he had over their mother's already trapped condition.

On the outside, it looked like Cherisse and Tamara were living examples of the American dream: a big house on a big piece of property, a Mercedes for Mom, a truck for Dad, closets full of clothes, a big dog, a little dog, a horse for Tamara to train, gymnastics lessons for Cherisse to compete, and a full time mother and bill-paying father who were still married and living under the same roof.

On the inside, however, their Disneyland lifestyle cut like a double-edged sword. Before they were old enough to understand that their family had more money to spend than most families, they knew that their father was constantly saying mean things to their mother. By the time they realized their father was not coming home several nights a week, they had stopped wanting him to come home. When he did come home, he would drink until he became drunk enough to express his hate for their mother. Not wanting to witness what was to come next, Cherisse and Tamara would go into their bedrooms and sit helplessly, forced to hear humiliating words about their mother that inevitably came and lasted for hours.

Verbally abusing their mother was only one edge of the blade that cut illusions of American dreams in half: if either of John's daughters asked for anything other than what he believed a father should provide, "a roof over their heads and food on the table," he would retaliate with, "What have you ever done for me? All you ever want is money."

John's retaliation cut through Cherisse's and Tamara's developing minds into their loving hearts. His backlash ruled out what his children's hearts and minds needed more than a roof over their heads, more than food on the table, more than all the earthly riches money could afford. His backlash ruled out communication. It ruled out closeness. It ruled out *his* love. . . .

Now, I looked at the two miracles whose love had made it possible for me to remain protected by a rainbow-filled bubble and recognized the nightmare the weaknesses of their father was causing them.

I recalled Cherisse's and Tamara's warnings, "Mom, we don't like the way Dad treats you. He is never going to change. We think you should divorce him."

I gave myself credit for hearing their warnings. I planned to divorce John. But did I do anything about ending our marriage? I neither contacted an attorney nor made any concrete plans for a divorce. In reality, my daughters were willing to risk a loss I had been unwilling to risk. Their intentions were rock-solid. My intentions were built on sand.

Sand castles had crumbled, leaving me with the non-escapable sight of the internal damage done to my children long before their mother disappeared into a darkened room and long before their father was seduced by the pleasures of a woman young enough to be their sister. Because I had refused to recognize the weaknesses of my father in myself before Cherisse and Tamara recognized the weaknesses of their father, more than innocence had slipped away from my two most precious jewels.

Of course, John did not come home as he had told Cherisse, and of course, I cried myself to sleep. But this time my tears were not because of John not coming home. My tears were for children who reaped their father's abandonment long before their mother reaped his abandonment.

No, my tears were not for a man who learned family values from a patriarch who prospered by making violence against women and children normal behavior, nor were my tears for the weaknesses in myself for which there was evidently more dues to be paid. My tears were for the price Cherisse and Tamara were paying because their mother once lived in a for-better-or-for-worse bubble that had zero chance of remaining afloat.

Over time, stains of a world at war with the soul of humanity had conspired from their father's lips to create an atom bomb destined to blow gaping holes in the magic kingdom where the three of us lived. By using my free spirit as tunnel vision to hide from an impending doomsday, I had allowed Cherisse and Tamara to lose more than their innocence. Because their father lived in an all-for-me reality that scared their mother to death, Cherisse and Tamara lost the all-for-one, one-for-all mother who's protective bubble had made it possible for her to always be there for them with love.

The malignancies eating away John's soul, written upon Cherisse's and Tamara's faces, tore away the veil of the all-loving mother for which I had given myself credit. Their warnings had been cries for me to wake up and hear what their father's words were doing to all three of us. With the shock of awakening to Cherisse's and Tamara's ability to see their father's true colors before I did came the realization that by disappearing into a darkened room, I too had abandoned my daughters. With the catastrophic blow to my heart that their mother was no less guilty of abandoning her children than their father, the great mother fell. The end of that illusionary giant unearthed another torrential wretchedness to rain down upon my soul.

I had hurt the two angels whose love made my life the promised land for so long. I lay in bed agonizing over the guilt tormenting my already trapped condition. My nervous system was falling backwards into the pit. Sure the pit's crematory fire had been too excruciating for me to ever survive again, for my children I had to find a way to stand tall and never disappear into a darkened room again.

I rolled off the bed, kneeled, and prayed to enter the void, the place where unconditional love poured down like Niagara Falls cascading into great lakes of pure serenity. Immersing myself in that ocean of intelligence and love was my only chance of being saved from further abandoning my two reasons for living. While on my knees, once again the essence of a spirit appeared on my right side. Vibrating power and wisdom, the soft white light lingered a little higher and slightly behind me. I felt a gentle touch on my right shoulder and then heard words in my mind as dreams sometimes do while we sleep. The message was void of sin and full of love:

> *Diana, allow the seeing, hearing, and feeling of your children's truth to exterminate your guilt. Go forth and live your life according to the knowledge you have gained. Know that your heart is pure and has always driven you. Your heart was merely unwilling to live in a world where evil exists. Forgive yourself, stand tall, and speak only of love.*

Spirit vanished. Apparently I had been too hard on myself. I climbed back in bed infused with information I would not have learned if I had studied a thousand books. Described by an energy more enlightened than mine was an unseen reality where the only sin was a mind closed off from the soul. Among their many wonders, my automatic writings were making me aware that I had discovered the ability to live in two realities simultaneously: a reality of conditioned sin and a reality of unconditional love.

With one foot in heaven and one foot in hell, I had to free my heart from a humanity at war with its own soul. Consequently, even with the revelatory wisdom contained in the message, magical self-forgiveness was not to be mine. For me to free myself from guilt, my heart told me it would be necessary for me to someday see my children's pain washed away. Until I saw with my own eyes the return of innocence in the faces that made my heart sing, my soul would not be completely free.

With the profound conclusion that my freedom was a spiritual event I wanted to share with the two souls who graced my life with their unconditional love, I made a vow I prayed spirit would understand. *I don't know how, where, or when, but I will find a way to get back what my husband's fantasies about sinful nature has taken from Cherisse and Tamara. I will set our bubble afloat once again. But this time it will be filled with more than love. Our bubble will contain the intelligence gained from seeking and finding truth. A bubble of love set afloat by the wisdom of three souls will be ours. I don't care how long it takes.*

August 11, 1987, 9:15 A.M.

The sound of John's little yellow truck driving up the driveway sounded in my ears. Cherisse and Tamara came scurrying into the kitchen and stood next to me. John entered the house from the garage. His slept-in clothes reeked with the odor of smoke. Stale-liquor breath accompanied a pale face and down-turned lips.

"You have all made my life miserable. I hate you," he bestowed upon us. "I'm mad about the letter. I didn't decide. It might take me six months to choose."

Cherisse took action. "Dad, you're carrying on this game too far!"

One more time, Tamara backed up her sister. "You're hurting Mom."

A multitude of emotions ran through me, all scrambling for their position of importance. From my core came the most esteemed feeling possible for a mother: admiration for her children's integrity.

Risking emotional holocausts, Cherisse and Tamara had made a stand. Each daughter stood up to a man who had the ability to intimidate the biggest of men with his braggadocios bullying about his superiority. That morning, my daughters stood tall and faced Goliath to defend their mother.

No doubt existed in Cherisse's, Tamara's, or my mind. John had made his choice. In my fallen condition, I had summoned the courage to love the man who provoked that fall. Yet he had been weakened by theological conflicts so deeply rooted in his subconscious that he rebelled with hate. By projecting a symptom of his internal hostilities with his accusation, "You have all made my life miserable," John confirmed his choice not to change. Blaming the victims of his miserable attitude was the lowest form of defending himself against change. Running from his crime of hate by terrorizing us made him appear small. Smallness dissolved the power his words had over our emotions. The compassion we were feeling did not include the miseries of a man who chose blame over change.

Needless to say, nothing about Cherisse's or Tamara's ethical challenge had any effect on the man whose blood they carried in their veins.

He disregarded his daughters' wisdom and fixated on single-mindedness. "Your mother should not have sent the letter. I'm mad. I will not make a decision until I'm ready."

Kindergarten dissertation over, he slouched toward mental and emotional paralysis and went to bed. It had been a long night of hard drinking.

August 11, 1987, 2:30 P.M.

After sleeping all day, John ambulated into the family room and appealed in a depressed tone, "Let's go to Stingers."

"Okay," I replied soberly after scrutinizing his erratic mood swing.

As soon as we were seated on barstools at Stingers, John answered a question that had never crossed my mind. "Fate is like a child in bed. I'm yours."

No happiness existed in his torrid admission. Cheerless eyes spoke louder than bedeviled words. The love potion the "other reality" injected into my heart had liberated me from the fear of the "other woman." My understanding, forgiveness, and compassion had finally snapped the latch on Fate's trap. John ending the mystery of Fate's sex made his chamber of secrets a secret no more. The sexual door he opened for me to walk through was a penitence I had already paid.

August 12, 1987, 4:50 A.M.

A sigh of relief could be felt throughout the entire house when John left for work. Offering himself up because his mistress was a "child in bed" would have been laughable if it were not for the price my children and I had paid for the master of the castle to have childish sex.

John's prophetic confession defied the absence of comic relief, solving more than one problem. Obsessing about his other lover ceased to be an affliction levitating above my bed. His naked confession graced my freedom from being trapped. Whatever the outcome of Fate's presence in our lives, never again would she be a threat to the sex I shared with the man I had vowed to love for better or worse. With Fate no longer the ever-present curse upon my life, my affair with a never-ending panic attack was laid to rest.

The kiss of the death of Fate's control over my life lifted many demons up and out of me, including agoraphobia. At least in my case, I had been right after all. Defeating the *myth* of sex greater than my own eased my agoraphobic fear dramatically! With the confidence that John could never again use sex to kill my spirit, my need to be near him came to a halt. The comfort I gained from knowing Fate failed to be the creature of carnal passion my husband imagined truly inspired me! I felt driven to turn my thoughts to the spiritual events taking place in my life and my desire to be the person I had always wanted to be. Going forward with my search for truth was the number one key to enlightening Cherisse and Tamara to truth. With them off to summer school, the automatic writings whose steady wisdom saved my sanity in my time of crisis took center stage.

With my feet firmly planted on the earth, by way of automatic writing I reached for the stars. More than curious to know the identity of the allies without whom I could not have survived my fall, I asked,

"Who are you?"

> *We are the multitudes, but we are also you. You contribute*
> *only good or this would not be so. Now is the time to hold on.*
> *Don't give up the ship. Your love will solidify. Try, try, try,*
> *hold on. We are your love and inner strength shining through.*
> *Those things made it possible for us to come into your being.*
> *You made it possible. We would come into anyone's life who*
> *willed it so. Your love is great for humankind and is growing*
> *daily. This is the key to plateau climbing.*
> *Love, US*

This message, the first automatic writing with a signature, caught me off-guard. Giving up on waiting for John to come aboard ship with Cherisse, Tamara, and me was true. If my interpretation of the message was correct, *US* was advising me to "try, try, try" with John. Trying sounded foolish. It seemed to me I had paid more than enough dues to the incorrigible adolescent I married. It seemed I was wrong. More important than my being right or wrong was the answer to my question, "Who are you?"

Doubting my penmanship, I questioned the writing before me. *Could the authors of my automatic writings be the multitudes? When I sat down at my desk that fateful day and put pencil to paper, could the unseen group with whom I sought to make a direct connection possibly be the multitudes?* Then it dawned on me. *US stands for Universal Spirit! The multitudes are Universal Spirit, a oneness of all spirits. But the multitudes said they are also me or my soul, which includes all souls. The multitudes on earth and the multitudes in heaven must be one voice indivisible, an unseen indivisible universe. Weather unseen spirit or unseen soul, we are one universe indivisible. All for one and one for all!*

Although I did not like the advice about trying with John, Universal Spirit was far ahead of me in emulating Daddy's motto. His motto felt right in meditation, prayer, automatic writing and with Cherisse and Tamara. But it no longer felt right with John. Ergo, with some difficulty I rearranged my mind in favor of allowing my love for John to shine through. I pictured him as a gigantic spoon stirring my psychological and spiritual awakening.

August 12, 1987, 11:00 A.M.

    With the end of fear's never-ending entrapment, spiritual forces continued to do their magic. On this particular day, magic was, once again, about to dramatically change my life. While sitting on my bed with the sun's indirect rays making me feel warm and full of love, from out of nowhere came a thunderous telepathic voice:

WRITE YOUR BOOK!

Oh my! That was loud and clear, I thought, blinking my eyes in happy remembrance. *That's right. That's what I'm supposed to do. Okay, I guess it's time to write my book.*

    From out of the blue, there came a voice. From out of the blue, I felt I spent my entire life waiting for the moment when the purpose of my life would present itself. It felt as natural for me to be told to write a book as to remember to brush my teeth. It made no difference that I knew nothing about writing a book or that I had never in my life read one book from beginning to end. It only mattered that it felt one-hundred percent right for me to write a book.

    Wasting no time, I picked up my calendar and began recalling and recording each day's events since the whole affair began, the day John told me he loved Fate. My book was going to start there.

If you walk the footsteps of a stranger,
you'll learn things you never knew, you never knew.
See how high the Sycamore grows. If you cut it down,
you will never paint the colors of the wind.

– Native American Poets

15

The Wisdom Of A Foolish Heart

August 12, 1987, 11:05 A.M.

One voice, one moment in time, saying *Write your book* made an instant connection with a forgotten longing. In the far reaches of my mind, behind all the repressed voices of others, lay a sleeping voice all my own.

That slumbering voice awakened to remind me that a passion had been screaming to reach up from its resting place to tell me, *Your dream has just begun!*

Not once in my life did anyone suggest I should look within myself to find my life's purpose, that I should fulfill a dream all my own. Never was I encouraged to openly admit that my mind dreamt of being something in addition to being a wife and mother. Because they would not surrender some of their outdated ideals, with their silence and by their example, outer voices told me that because I was a girl, an individual dream was not to be mine. Not taught to listen to that passionate inner voice, the one that flowed into my mind as loving feelings that spoke of dreams coming true, with the passage of time I stopped admitting even to myself, especially to myself, I ever wanted to be more.

As I grew up, I watched the voice of America. America was created to be a democracy, a government of the people, by the people, and for the people. The fathers of democracy wrote a document on behalf of the people they named the Constitution. The Constitution includes a Bill of Rights stating that men and women are given the unalienable right to be treated as equals. Growing up, I watched the voices of men and women who were not treated equally. Inequality taught men to have careers and women to have babies. To prove men and women were significantly different, scientific experiments were performed, only on men. I watched the voice of my father who willingly went off to fight wars and came home with ribbons. I watched the voice of my mother who waited at home fighting her own wars, except she was awarded no ribbons.

Because I watched year after year and saw how girls were required to be less than boys, my passionate inner dream was steadfastly silenced. And because I was able to feel loving feelings, but no longer able to hear the voice of my dream, John's words confused me. Since I could not *remember* wanting to be more than a wife and mother, when John's words told me we were different, that I was less than him, I had no dream on which to fall back. If while growing up I had been encouraged to express an individual purpose for my life, inspired to believe in my purpose, and given the opportunity to work on it, then when words started that were so contradictory to my belief that we were equal, perhaps I would have had the courage to leave.

No, not until the voracious voice of spiritual multitudes reached beneath the internalized voice of human multitudes to fuse with the sleeping voice of my soul did I *remember* my dream to write. That fusion turned a subconscious passion into a conscious flame!

August 13, 1987, 8:00 A.M.

During my morning meditation, a suggestion popped into my mind. *Keep a journal.*

What a fine idea, I decided instantly. *A journal will be the perfect way to keep track of the events taking place in my life as they happen. When I write my book, my journal will prevent me from writing anything other than truth.*

I got out of bed, walked into the den, and located some lined paper. I returned to my bed, sat down, placed the paper on my lap, then began searching for my feelings beginning July 17, 1987, the day John told me he loved Fate. As I wrote, something happened. My goal to tell only truth drove me to take very seriously the responsibility of writing about the behavior of other people. How could I write about those I loved without knowing their inner truth. My passion to know the whole truth obligated me to learn to view life through the eyes of others, as if their hearts were my heart, their minds my mind, their souls my soul.

After I heard the voice, never once did I look back. I wrote in my journal every day. *Write your book* had reminded me of a dream I had that was all my own. I recorded my feelings while making every effort to understand the feelings of others. Every single human being had his or her individual set of outer voices, the voices that infiltrated their subconscious mind, separating their conscious mind from their soul mind. As I recounted each day's events, feeling accountable for my interpretation of the individual uniqueness of others as well as my own uniqueness, intense emotions ran through me. After every writing I restored my sense of peace with prayer, meditation, and automatic writing.

On August 13, 1987, after my very first journal entry, my automatic writing turned out to be a prophetic spiritual event:

> *This is the time to begin with us for the souls of the world who are in need of our help. We must be the universe's instrument. This is our purpose for now. Teach love at every turn in your book. Remember your lessons and begin to understand life at a different level. Open your eyes to all the beautiful things of the earth. Here there is only love. No competition, no games, as you on earth play, unnecessarily wasting precious time when love is the paradise each soul seeks. There is a solution to every problem. If one searches the soul, the answer will always be there. Love, US*

After opening my eyes and reading the message, I celebrated in mental jubilation. *Universal Spirit (US) and I are going to be partners in writing my book. The lessons I learn will be tools to aid humanity. Learning my lessons will teach me the universe's solution to the problems I encounter. Seeing outwardly with the love in my soul will help me be one with the love in the soul of all people!*

My husband's affair had activated fears that triggered emotional holocausts. Those holocausts were the extraordinary crises divinely scripted for my mind to remember a dream in my soul. To gain my soul I had been required to lose my mind, for in losing my mind, nothing remained in the way of my dream to write.

I had learned many lessons after my fall. Nonetheless, my automatic writing that day had made it clear there were many lessons yet for me to learn. Though grueling, those initiatory lessons were teaching me a psychological and spiritual philosophy: *understanding, forgiveness, and compassion (UFC) was the psychology of the mind as the builder of the soul, and directly connecting with Universal Spirit (US) was the spirituality of the mind as the builder of the soul. With UFC+US, as my psychospiritual philosophy, a bridge could be built that closes the separation between the human mind and the soul mind.*

One voice saying *Write your book* was the final piece to the mystery of why I fell. In seeking to regain the truth in my soul, I was given my individual purpose. By way of writing a book, Diana could reach over the rainbow to co-create a psychospiritual philosophy with Universal Spirit. As one voice, *UFC+US* was going to speak through my writing. A rainbow-bridge linking heaven and earth was to be my voice!

August 13, 1987, 11:30 P.M.

By thinking of him as the benefactor of lessons, I succeeded in rearranging my emotions in favor of loving John. The timing was impeccable because this day was our eighteenth wedding anniversary. Forgiving the man I married for having an affair would be my way of showing my loyalty to our wedding vows.

I began the day by having an anniversary bouquet sent to The Big G. The rest of the day was spent preparing for that night's dinner and the next day's celebration. By evening, a soft fire flickered light on a table full of presents, all for John. In the center of the candle-lit table, a silver champagne bucket displayed a chilled bottle of Korbel. A thick, juicy New York steak, ready to be thrown on the barbeque, awaited the anniversary boy. With excited expectations about the gifts I was about to surprise my husband with, I stood by the fire waiting.

I heard his little yellow truck coming up the driveway, then the door to the garage open and close. Into the family room John stomped carrying the anniversary flowers in his right hand. Barely glancing at the table or me, he passed directly in front of me aimed toward the kitchen.

He tossed the flowers in the sink while lashing out, "You sent these flowers to annoy Fate!"

My heart settled in my throat.

"The flowers were sent lovingly to make you happy," I explained, in an earnest attempt to soften his mood.

He opened the refrigerator door while proceeding to lay claim to his interpretation of my anniversary surprise. "Fate said you haven't changed. She didn't see the flowers. She left for a week's cruise this morning before the flowers were delivered. I put them in the refrigerator at work and left them there all day."

He glared anxiously back and forth between the table and me. All day long I visualized the sweet-smelling yellow and white petals displayed on the counter at The Big G where every person coming and going could delight in their lighthearted delicacy and delicious perfume. The thought of the life's breath of the bouquet stuffed in a dark cold icebox saddened my hopeful heart.

I might have been mad at John's obstinate backlash if the reason for his anger was not exhaustingly transparent. Fate left to take a week's cruise at a crucial juncture in his *who-shall-I-choose, who-shall-I-kill* drama. His devious plot, a power device to control both Fate's and my feelings, had fallen into a big black hole. By abandoning John to have fun that particular day, again, Fate stole his power.

I also might have felt pity for John's projection of his anger at Fate onto me if it were not for her huge error in judgment. By leaving for an entire week, she fortuitously left the door wide open for me. My unexpected but fruitful plans did not include pity.

I forked the steak and laid it over the fire, very much aware that I had seven days to pound some sense into a man hell-bent on staying in an affair with "a child in bed."

"You must be upset about Fate's going away?" I inquired, handing John a plate covered with a charred-rare piece of beef.

"You're going back to your old ways," he growled, chewing and threatening at the same time.

Wondering if the juicy steak prepared and served at his beck-and-call had anything to do with "your old ways," I politely engaged in friendly conversation until the man of the house finished eating. Then

I went to bed. Once under the covers, my sleepy prayers gave thanks for my planning to celebrate our anniversary the next day.

August 14, 1987, 7:30 A.M.

As expected, I went to bed with an angry man and woke up with a happy one. Certain the happy one was our chance for a meaningful anniversary, I took advantage of the opportunity. By early-evening music rang out, candles flickered, roast beef simmered, and the champagne cork had been popped. Cherisse, Tamara, and I gathered around the table to watch John open his presents.

Every gift he unwrapped blew renewed life into his ego. He even complimented me for the anniversary flowers I had arranged on the center of the table. When all the presents were opened, discussed for better or worse, and then placed decoratively around the flowers, I picked up the card John had placed flat on the table earlier.

No name was written on the envelope, so I asked John, "Is this for me?"

John nodded his head up and down, cock-sure of his motive.

As Cherisse, Tamara, and John watched, I pulled the card out of the envelope and read the front:

Bless You On Your Anniversary

Blind-sighted by every word except anniversary, I opened the card apprehensively and read the verse:

Joys that mean the most to you, very special dreams come true, fond memories. May you be blessed with all of these contentments, peace of mind and love that holds you close together. May God bless you with these forever.

Each word slapped me in the face harder than the one before it. I handed Cherisse the card wishing she would tell her father what I felt. She read it and then granted my wish.

"Dad! This is a religious card you give another couple on their anniversary," she declared, outraged by the insult to her mother.

Untouched by his eldest daughter's sentiment, John stood up and strutted into the kitchen to get a beer. Strutting, the head-to-foot cue for them to exit to their bedrooms, Cherisse and Tamara made a speedy get-a-way. John's strut, uninterrupted by the hasty departure of his daughters, led him into the family room to play pool and get drunk. As it was time for them to go to bed anyway, I accompanied Cherisse and Tamara into their bedrooms, individually tucked each daughter in bed, chatted a bit, kissed them goodnight, and then joined John.

Confounded about *try, try, try, hold on*, I watched John practice pool shots from different angles. That was when they started . . . the words . . . words Cherisse and Tamara knew were inevitable . . . words that after eighteen years had trapped me in a mental cage that felt like hell . . . switchblade words that once begun, became a river of no return.

"Diana, you dumb shit. You can't make shit in the sky. You ain't done shit without me. You've got a big mouth and say nothing. I'm a lion in a cage. I'd of cashed you in a long time ago if it weren't for Cherisse and Tamara. You know why I drink? Because of you. The easiest way out for me is just to hit skid row."

Caught off guard a second time in one night, I felt as if the words were a sharpened knife cutting me up piece by piece. Cutting Diana into little pieces gave John's ego nothing but joy. He left no space between words for me to rest from the cutting.

"You're a fucking whore, you bitch. You've screwed up my life because of all your boyfriends. Nobody likes you. You don't know anything about anything. I listen to a ration of shit people say about you. They can't figure out why I stay with you. You're just like all women, a witch with no brains who sits on her ass all day. When I'm done with you, I'm going to send you back to Santa Ana. I'm the best. I can do it all. If it weren't for you, I'd be a lot farther by now. I hate all women. I'm unhappy and you are to blame. I don't want to be married. You were the reason I didn't make it on the golf tour. Let me tell you how bad you are. You didn't know anything when I married you. I learn more in one day than you've learned your whole life. You have used me for 18 years. You fucking women don't know anything. I can't stand the sound of your voice. You don't deserve to be on this planet. You have me boxed in. I can't stand to be boxed in. You fucking cunt."

Deeper and deeper the words carved away at my humanity until the drunken sailor could not enunciate another syllable. He ambulated toward the sofa, lowered his body by balancing his swaying torso with his arms, and plopped down. Somewhat settled, his head fell backwards, and he passed out on the way down. His head lying backwards against the sofa, his mouth open, loud snoring replaced the romantic music I had long since stopped hearing.

Snores blasted into my ears, every snore thundering through my brain like a freight train. I wished I had not drunk the champagne. Unlike old Diana with her ability to have fun and her willpower to not feel her husband's words, alcohol heightened the feeling that the new Diana had been beaten up by those identical words. Endeavoring to flee the scene of the crime against me, I aimed my body in the direction of the kitchen. As I rounded the fireplace, before my eyes stood a table full of opened presents, dirty dishes, an empty bottle of Korbel, and a bright little bouquet of yellow and white flowers. My anniversary card loomed forbiddingly as it stood casting a shadow on the flowers.

I picked it up, read it again, then slammed it face down. Just when I had been set free from Fate's sex, a new lesson awaited.

Does John pity me? I recoiled, feeling as if a rope with an anchor at the end if it had been draped around my neck and tied with a seaman's knot. *What kind of victor adds pity to hate and hides it under religious righteousness?*

Wrought with uncontrolled grief, I surrendered to the repulsion of witnessing my own defeat. Too delirious to run from the sight, sound, smell, and feel of being eaten alive, I stumbled to my closet, grabbed my terrycloth robe and my car keys, exited the house, and drove away.

Tears blurred my vision as I pointed my car down the narrow, curved country road leading away from transgressions toward my soul. In my despondency, the car swerved, crisscrossing the middle of the two lanes, heading nowhere, anywhere to flee intentional infliction of evil I still did not want to believe existed.

No, John's drunken words had not changed. Far more terrifying, infiltrated into every syllable of my anniversary card was the religious justification that blatantly illustrated John's sober thoughts, the true revilement which bore my grief. Over the years, John's learned hatred for "all women" molded him into a pitiful prototype of *screw the womb*. Helpless against the sheer weight and mass of historical opinion, the programming of "you fucking whore" had become about as changeable as the pyramids.

Those staggering implications made *try, try, try* feel like wickedness unredeemable by any philosophy. The religious fanaticism of institutionalizing women's sexual organs as evil was the real "ass" who stole my husband. The "cunt" who had my husband "boxed in" was his learned helplessness to fight off humanity's underworld matrix of conditioned sin. That world-wide-web separating human mind from soul mind characterized the real *chamber of the shadow*, the real-world *cave*. The obsolete chronology of that institutionalized *beast* had computerized John to mentally kill the very organ that incarnated his soul. Deeming "all women" the evil destroyer of man rather than the sacred giver of life had dropped an atom bomb on my anniversary surprise.

The road sped by, racing in the opposite direction. Trees on either side reached out their arms as I rounded each curve. It all felt unreal. I did not know if my blurred vision came from tears or rain. An old movie flashed before my eyes—a heartbroken woman driving recklessly down a dark road. It was raining in the movie, and the windshield wipers were going back and forth, back and forth. Her husband, too, had proved his cowardice by having an affair. I remembered wondering what it would feel like to be that unhappy.

The hood ornament and the centerline were all that were visible. The dizzying maze of my thoughts worsened. Feeling contemptible humiliation for my masterful loss of self-control, I could not fathom the lesson I was supposed to be learning by *holding on.*

Emotional exhaustion caused me to pull the car off the road. It ended up in a dirt area immersed in thick foliage. Too weary to be scared of the eery darkness, the lost, forsaken child in me climbed into the back seat, curled up, and cried herself to sleep.

August 15, 1987

I woke up in the back seat of the car. Barely able to raise my puffed-up eyelids, I struggled to see the car clock. It said 4:04 A.M. I remembered driving to the desolate spot like one remembers a nightmare. Mortified by my reckless behavior, I felt more than grateful no one else was on the dangerous road the night before.

Ashamed, appalled, and wanting it all to disappear, I quickly assessed my situation. *Everyone will still be sleeping. No one needs to know what happened to me.*

I drove home, tip-toed into the master bedroom, took off my robe, and snuck quietly into bed. My heart was still racing when, as usual, at 4:30 A.M. the alarm went off. John turned over and cuddled me.

He doesn't know what I did, I realized, relieved.

After snuggling, he showered, dressed for work, then stepped around the corner, filling the air with a crisp, clean smell.

He sat down on my side of the bed, leaned down to kiss me goodbye, and announced with an anticipatory flair, "I'll see you tonight."

I watched his hearty stroll out the door, questioning what my unsuspecting mind had never conceptualized before. *John doesn't remember the last part of last night. All those hateful words, all those years, how many does he not remember? Have we spent years abandoning each other for words he doesn't remember saying?*

Around noon, John called from The Big G to say he bought me another anniversary card. At 8:30 P.M., he promenaded into the master bedroom where I sat reading and tossed an envelope on the bed. On the front in John's handwriting was printed, "Diana."

I picked up the envelope and opened it. As I slid the card out, a fifty-dollar-bill floated down onto my lap. I gazed uncomfortably at the fifty. The year before it had been a hundred-dollar-bill. Even so, my sentimental heart grew tender when I read the inscription:

With All My Love,
On Our Anniversary. When I think of all the wonderful times that you and I have known, the joys that you made happen, just by being you, I fall in love with you all over again. When I think of the life we're sharing, trusting one another, through both good and trying times, I fall in love with you all over again. When I think of all the days and years ahead, all that we have yet to learn about one another, my heart is filled with happiness so complete, I fall in love with you again.
Love forever and ever, John

Asking myself if the words reflected John's true feelings, I looked up. He looked like a little boy, proud of the gifts he gave. The feelings I received from that "look" resolved all my doubts about *try, try, try, hold on.*

True, John was a man who wore many masks. But those many masks contained many lessons. Although choosing to walk through penitence was an ordeal, I had to keep walking through that fiery pit. If I gave up on my husband by shoving the huge love I felt into the far reaches of my mind, my love for him would eventually turn into hate, and my hate would not destroy my husband. It would destroy me.

By not giving up on love, my heart and mind had been gifted with knowledge. The most fearful thing for John to discover would be to find within himself the thing he despised the most. The words "happiness so complete," were the anniversary boy's silent cry, "please help me . . . me . . . me . . . this stupid cunt I have become."

If I could not find within myself mercy for the judgments cursing John's soul, then I could not find within myself mercy for the fall that saved my soul. Each time a lesson came full circle in the cyclical journey of my initiation, my mind had spiraled upward to a higher level of understanding. Each understanding made me more forgiving, and given enough time, merciful forgiveness of the many masks my husband wore would season both of our lives with compassion.

Knowing in my heart our time together was growing short, I made love with the man I loved that night. In the morning, I made love with him again. Afterwards, I lay in bed watching my lover pull up his cement-encrusted jeans and head toward the old corroded wheelbarrow waiting for him next to the driveway.

True, by *holding on* to my love for my husband I played the fool, but I learned that each time I played the fool, my love transcended his cruelty, his hate, even his fear of losing "happiness so complete." In my willingness to give in to human suffering, I learned to see life through the eyes of all the fools who had been strangers before my fall.

By walking in the footsteps of strangers, I found that the unknown feelings I supposed were my enemies were actually my friends. Experiencing humanity's sorrows expanded the colors of the life I lived within myself.

Playing the fool taught me the sweetest lesson that I should not be afraid of my feelings even if they were foolish because my feelings were my truth. If I cut myself off from my truth, I might never learn how how high my spirit could soar.

*How salty is the taste of foreign bread
and how hard a path it is to climb
and then descend the foreign stairs.*

– Dante

16

Goodbye To All That?

– Charles William Weitzel, Jr.

August 18, 1987, 6:45 A.M.

John and I made love all week long. In the mornings, he left our bed to go to The Big G or to his old corroded wheelbarrow, a fresh cement mixture, and the driveway. My days were content knowing that I had done everything in my power to right the wrongs of past mistakes with my husband, and I had come full circle in my determination to atone. The cycle of atonement had been steep and thorny, beset with perils of every kind, but my choice to feel love for the man I married led me to a feeling of oneness with the feelings of the multitudes. Passing through human nature into eternal nature, I could almost reach out and touch the beautiful new world I invisioned.

By walking through the ordeal of the fiery pit to own my shadow, I had lifted many of my denials up and out of me. A purifying fire had burned in my soul *eating away* the veils that protected reality's *illusions*, obscuring my enlightenment. With each unveiled illusion, life became a little more the outward expression of my inner connection to truth. The power of truth's flame burned with the realization that the awakened inner voice was my soul speaking to me. My soul was my channel to Universal Spirit, and Universal Spirit was the divine spiritual nature of my soul that was the light at the end of the tunnel.

Clearing the passageway for the voice of my soul effected a

spiritual shift in my mind. The awakening of my divine spiritual nature dramatically transformed my attitude about reality. Without ego's illusions disguising truth, life all around seemed to be awakening with me as the sun's arising filtered through the window into the master bedroom. Droplets of morning light reached in to touch every object in the room. I felt like a charmed spectator of the dance of sun angels. I closed my eyes and breathed in air that expanded the tremendous love I already felt.

When I opened my eyes, opened to me was the soul of nature. A cut piece of crystal reflected sparkling sunlight in an array of colors more electric and diversified than I had ever seen. Everything in the room had a halo encircling it. Lit from within, visible angel-rays illuminated out.

If my lessons are about experiencing the agony of an ugly world to learn how to experience the ecstasy of a beautiful world, why the dichotomy of extremes? I questioned the mesmerizing light. *With Fate temporarily out of our lives, John suddenly transcended from devil to angel. When Fate returns, will the devil in John return with her? I have looked death straight in the eye and saw no evil. Nor did I see in death the opportunities for salvation to be found on earth.*

Having learned that life was a soul journey filled with possibilities for magical progressions, but also frightening regressions, I picked up my little writing pad, hoping my automatic writing would clarify the evil lurking around every corner:

Fear no evil Diana, for only when you walk through the valley do you experience enlightenment. Valleys are not lowly places. They are journeys teaching appreciation. Valleys educate humanity on how to see, feel, and know the diverse majesty of the sea of life. Like ocean floors, valleys are detailed with the intricacies of life that cannot be fathomed on mountaintops. You will fear valleys until you recognize the magnificence of what is learned there. When you get to the top of the mountain, you will know freedom only if you have experienced the beauty below. Until you have walked through the valley of lessons learned, you cannot dance upon mountaintops. Love, US!

After reading this early morning message, I knew that every single object in my bedroom had been by my side as I walked through my valleys. That morning every single object danced with me on mountaintops. Once a fiery tomb, now my room was an illuminated temple. I had walked through the valley of the shadow of death, through at-ONE-ment with my husband, into oneness with nature. Detailed in every object in my room, earth's diverse majesty had been rooted in that cycle of my life. Passing through nature into everlasting life, oneness resurrected my divinity from the ashes of my funeral pyre.

Though feeling the majesty of life while walking though valleys sounded more angelic than human, I understood that my automatic writings were my connection to angelic forces within myself, and only if I walked hand in hand with those eternal powers would I survive future valleys leading to higher mountaintops. If I could stay true to my divine self, someday in a magnificent valley, once again my driving force would dance with me on mountaintops.

August 18, 1987, 1:00 P.M.

I drove the quarter-mile to the mailbox room attached to the guard station of our guarded-gate community. In our box sat a letter from my sister Susan. The seven-year gap since Susan and I had seen one another was a valley I had only recently acknowledged. Not seeing my sister was a choice I made.

Because while growing up we were Marine Corps "brats" and thus moved every year or two, our homes and our peers were invariably changing. Not given enough time to bond with any particular peer group, we clung to one another in a very profound way. The older of two siblings, Susan watched over me, shielding her little sister from the impediments outside our home and the obstacles within our home. Being two years and three months younger, I watched her learn by trial and error from our particular homespun hurdles. Watching had advantages. Learning not to make Susan's errors saved me from the tremendous price she paid by witnessing first-hand many of Mother's and Daddy's poor choices.

By protecting me from many of my parents' personal battles, Susan aided me in disappearing into my bubble. Disappearing saved my strength and my innocence. Living inside nature's bubble allowed me to shield my sister in a very different way than she shielded me. Whenever life became more than Susan could bare, Diana waited in the wings armed with what came naturally.

"Everything's going to be okay," I would say to Susan when she needed my support.

"Okay" did help. Without being aware of it, my innocence and my strength saved my sister time after time. As sure as the *natural law* of cause and effect is unchangeable, Susan grew to count on my *natural inclination* to be there for her. Inevitably our very different cause=effect lives as children manifested into two very different cause=effect lifestyles as adults. The price Susan paid for our parents' imperfections as a child, she continued to pay as an adult.

In judging how to react to their behavior, Susan told me later, "I could either fight or join Mother's and Daddy's drama. I decided it was easier to join."

As the years passed, I found it increasingly difficult to experience the sting of my sister's "easier" choices. Gradually I disappeared from what I judged to be unacceptable character flaws. Disappearing did not erase Susan's well-nurtured cause=effect inclination to count on me to be there for her. When I was not waiting in the wings to tell Susan everything was going to be okay, at first she felt abandoned. Inescapably, with time disappointment *caused* abandonment to *effect* anger.

Then, on June 17, 1987, the *Call your sister* tagged on the end of my first automatic writing called to account my judgment of Susan's character. Three short words felt so forceful, they had to have come from a different source than the rest of the writing. I dropped my pencil and reared back. It took me several hours to settle down from the euphoria of my automatic writing miracle and ground myself in the meaning of *Call your sister.*

Meaning arrived by way of the truth incorporated into every word of that first evidence of spiritual forces at work in my life. The message had gently prompted me to rethink my reason for walking out of Susan's life. The truth written in the words *hate no more* required I think about my judgment of my sister as a manifestation of hate. It was not my older sister for whom the bells toll. Standing tall mandated that I hate no more, in other words, judge no more. The enormous love and forgiveness three little words called forth convinced me that *Call your sister* had to be of pure heart. In a few short hours after my very first automatic writing, inner knowingness told me that pure love and unconditional forgiveness were mainly for the giver and had very little to do with the receiver.

With the knowledge that the seven-year gap since we last saw each other was caused by my judgment, I dialed Susan's telephone number. She answered, and forty-five minutes into our conversation the love I gave without condition resulted in my sister's voice going from bitter to affectionate. Telling her how my automatic writing had inspired me to seek and find the meaning of life in turn inspired the return of the Susan I knew as a child. She sounded ready and willing to protect her little sister, this time knowing the special bond we shared was what really protected both of us.

As soon as our telephone conversation ended, I wrote Susan a letter explaining more about the change in me and, more importantly, how much I loved her. A lifetime of sentiment passed through me as I opened and read Susan's letter:

> My Darling Sister,
> Sorry it's been so long getting back in a letter. My heart and thoughts are always with you and family. Your letter is so beautiful. I can feel how the light glows inside you. It shows. I understand! Inner peace brings so much beauty into life. Aren't you happy we're sisters!!!
> Heart filled love, Susan

I drove home, sat down at my desk, and placed Susan's letter in front of me. I retrieved some stationary from the drawer, picked up a pencil, and began to write her another letter. After seven years, I wanted to see my sister again. I wanted to invite her to see my beautiful daughters, to share the home John and I built. I just wanted my sister back in my life. Most of all, I felt grateful to have a sister. Yes, I was happy we were sisters!!!

August 20, 1987, 11:30 P.M.

As soon as John walked through the door, he joined me in bed and responded to every movement of my body with sensitivity and passion. For seven days Fate had been gone. For seven days John could not have been more good natured or sexy.

Something happened during those seven days, though, that contradicted the love-making we shared. With each new day, the expression on John's face grew increasingly tired and depressed. In the middle of the night, I awakened to the sound of crying. This was not John's first crying spell in the past seven days.

"Why are you crying?" I asked, sympathizing with the sadness in the tears he shed.

"Was I crying?" he answered my question with a question.

I held my teary-eyed husband close, hoping to ease the pain he declined to release verbally. He replied sexually, letting me know exactly what kind of release he wanted from me.

August 21, 1987, early afternoon

The driveway looked spectacular! Nearly completed, John drove to town several times to buy last-minute supplies. Each time he returned, he returned more intoxicated. An hour or so after his final departure, the telephone rang. I answered.

In low, serious tones, John explained, "I'm at Ed's bar. Fate is back from her cruise. We need to talk. Get dressed and meet me here."

Ed's was one large open space with a bar reaching from one end of the room to the other. No one played at either of the two pool tables as I entered. A jukebox hummed an old song I remembered well, making me feel a pleasant sense of *déjà vu*. Ten or so people were sitting and standing in various parts of the room, most of them smoking. The smoke was not thick because an open door at either end of the bar provided good ventilation. It was that time of the day when hangovers were gone and drinkers began to feel a new high. The light-hearted atmosphere welcomed me as I walked over to the bar where John sat, drinking a beer.

As always, he spotted me with the eyes in the back of his head. He stood up, pulled out the stool to his left and, when I got close enough, introduced me to a couple of the guys standing nearby.

Glee streaming from his face, one of the men staring half at me and half at days gone by remarked to John, "Remember the times you bought rounds of drinks for the whole room? Boy, that was something!"

Eager to share his happy recollection, John's bar-buddy answered one of my longstanding speculations. It seemed John always had a wad of hundred-dollar bills in his wallet. Yet for years, an ever-enlarging stack of unpaid bills sat on his desk as an ominous reminder that I should scrimp and save. At Ed's bar, John was a generous man.

Two cheerful fellows walked off to play pool, leaving John and me alone. John looked pensive and cavalier as he stared straight across the bar toward rows of bottles of hard liquor. A prideful task came into his eyes. Pride spoke of the long-endured challenge that made him fly.

After careful deliberation, John addressed me with his verdict on cavalier. "Fate is worse than you." He hesitated then pushed more buttons from our past. "Diana, you know you have always been bad. Why do you write letters? I don't like your letters."

As I sat on a barstool at Ed's bar reminiscing the history the two of us shared, my heart wept for the "bad" part of our history John refused to let go. The buttons my husband pushed no longer worked.

He tried again. "I love Fate more than I love you."

Oh help him sweet heavens. I did not marry a wise man, I reminded myself with the compassion of a women who understood she had married a very sad man.

No longer afraid of the death of our relationship, no need arose to fight *bad*. Nor did John's loving Fate produce the familiar fight-or-flight syndrome. Our grand debates, me on the side of good, John on the side of evil, were the judgments that toxified our marriage. John's garden of evil genealogy that defied all hope for intimacy between us had stopped making me fly. His soul's divinity birthed him with a face of love he covered up with a mask of hate. Flesh as the extension of his divinity, John had painted it over with the sins of the flesh. The weeping in my heart was for a man who that very moment told me he intended to spend the rest of his life bowing to an evil force for whom he had no understanding.

- - - Wherefore they are no more twain but one flesh - - -

John said he would have to "choose one of you and kill the other." He succeeded, but his affair killed in me what John's ego needed the most. It killed the part of me that was just like him. John's affair killed the denial that caused me to abandon both him and me. The exhilarating temptation *worse* seduced in him explained why the sexual fireworks and romantic love we shared did not supersede what Fate took away.

When Fate left on her cruise, she took John's sparring partner. She took the fights that made his ego fly. With no battle to lift masculinity's illusions of grandeur in flight, John had no defense against Diana's love. And the truth in Diana's love contradicted every evil word he had ever been taught. Inconsistent with his assumptions about the nature of women, my love confused John. Confusion caused him to feel tired and depressed. Heading toward the apocalyptic turning point of ego-death, with Fate's return John concluded Fate was worse than Diana.

John did not understand why when Fate was gone he had been heading toward the precipice of no-ego or that an armageddon between his ego and his spirit was an eventual certainty. He just knew Fate's being worse filled his desperation for a reality consistent with his basic assumptions. Saved by worse, Fate's feisty-fights gave John permission to stay in denial of Diana's love. His ego flying on the wings of denial, John's cavalier expectations about Fate prepared themselves to take on new levels of *bad*.

My waking up from the sleep of my illusions about John meant that he could no longer fly worn out patterns with me. If he wanted me, he would have to take off his ego-mask and come face to face with his illusions of grandeur. He would have to release his grip on the "Diana, you know you've always been bad" he used to project into me what he did not want to see in himself. He would have to trust his experience of my love.

The truth in John's soul waged a gigantic battle against a lifetime of false evil. For the love in his soul to win the battle against the demons in his mind, John would have to surrender narcissism's prideful task, enter the void of no-self, walk through the ordeal of the chamber of the shadow, and atone for how he had wronged others. Only by entering the initiation's trial by fire would John be given the opportunity to re-experience both the horrific and the remarkable experiences of his past. Only then could he learn to make love with the agonies of his shadow and ecstasies of his soul.

No, John did not understand that losing oneself was finding oneself. He knew only that his decision that Fate was worse than Diana made him fly higher than he had ever flown before. The look on John's face told me Fate serviced the denials I once held as my own. Fate being worse made it too easy for him to still the silent inner voice of his soul and persist in fighting his war. "Worse" would assist him in clinging to the familiar presumptions that controlled his fear of the unknown. No, John and I no longer functioned on the same wavelength.

I sat on a tall barstool listening to John determine the degree to which Fate was worse than me. I could feel his shadow thickening. His fear of facing the beast within helped me understand why, for centuries, poor men devoutly fought rich men's wars. Both John and I were consumed with roaring flames. Our flames, flying higher than ever before, came from opposing forces. The passionate flames burning in me told me it was time to go.

I gazed into the eyes of a man who had lost the dream I had found and said, "I'll see you at home," and then I left.

At home in bed that night, I cried the warmest tears. *How am I going to leave a man I have loved for eighteen years? The man I fell in love with the first second I set my eyes on him and have loved every second since. How can I watch him walk into the arms of a woman who will discourage every spiritual possibility and encourage every hostile probability?*

I looked out the window at the night sky. Stars were twinkling.

August 23, 1987, 1:15 P.M.

In the days following my Ed's bar experience I began to emotionally adjust to the reality that John and I were not going to spend the rest of our lives together. He had not initiated any conversation about divorce, so I got the hint that the move toward separation would be my job. This was not a good day to begin goodbyes, however, because it was John's forty-fourth birthday.

Cherisse and I were in the car on the way home from shopping for last-minute birthday goodies when Cherisse turned on the car radio. It was the first time I had heard music since the music stopped. No paranoia or anxiety came over me, nor did the need to make the music stop. Music sounded good!

While listening to the words from the movie *Tootsie*, "I've been saving love songs and lullabies and so much more, no one's ever heard before. So many quiet walks to take, so many dreams to make . . . and so much love to make. I think it's going to take some time. All we need is time. Something's telling me it must be you . . . for all of my life, " I laughed out loud.

Cherisse asked, "What are you laughing about?"

"My stupidity," I exclaimed. "This song is singing words that describe my dreams about love. Since the day I married Daddy, I've been playing a stupid joke on myself. My dreams included his happiness, but his dreams did not include my happiness. "

Cherisse retorted, "Mom, you finally figured it out."

August 23, 1987, 9:30 P.M.

For hours, Cherisse, Tamara, and I had been waiting to surprise the birthday boy. Patience for our long-overdue guest of honor had grown into impatience. Just as I noticed how the candles on the table were melting down, the phone rang.

I picked up the receiver and heard John on the other end of the line slur, "I got stuck in traffic, so I stopped at a bar to call you. I'm leaving now."

"How long will it take you to get home," I inquired.

"Twenty minutes," he replied.

Sensing disappointment in my voice, the happy facade faded from Cherisse's and Tamara's faces. We ignored our dashed hopes and continued to wait another hour, when finally we heard John's truck.

Summoning smiles, we paraded to the front door prepared to yell, "Happy Birthday."

Just as we opened the front door, we heard John entering through the back door in an unapologetic, intoxicated condition. Three "good girls" sat politely while the king of the castle opened his birthday presents. Then, three "good girls" politely watched that same king stumble into the family room, sit down on the sofa, pass out, then snore in his typical freight train style. The apple pie Cherisse and Tamara spent all afternoon making sat on the table uneaten.

Following what could not have been termed a celebration, I did something I had never done before. I helped John stumble to bed. I did it because I wanted him to be next to me in the morning. For his birthday, I had put off what John spent eighteen years preparing me for.

The time had come to say, "Goodbye to all that!"

*This chapter is dedicated to my father Charles William Weitzel Jr., who as a 1ˢᵗLeiutenant in the United States Marine Corps wrote a book about his World War II experiences as a Corsair pilot in the Battle of Okinawa. Written more like a journal than a memoir, *Goodbye To All That?* describes in vivid detail, how from January to October 1945 my father won the Air Medal, the DFC, the Presidential Citation, and the Blue Cross in the last and most deadly battle against the Japanese, and the longest air battle for Navy or Marine pilots in aviation history (up until WWII). Okinawa remains the unsung battle in the Pacific because it is politically incorrect to write or speak about how its unprecidented bloodbath literally defeated the Japanese.

*Read more about *Goodbye To All That?* and see similarities between my father's and my perspectives at: www.fallintofreedom.com

When in the course of human events, it becomes necessary for one People to dissolve the Political bands which have connected them with another, and to assume among the Powers of the Earth the separate and equal station to which the laws of nature entitle them, a descent respect to the opinions of Mankind requires that they should declare the causes which impel them to the Separation.
– Thomas Jefferson, *Declaration Of Independence*

17
Part I

A Theater For The Ridiculous

August 24, 1987, 6:35 A.M.

The sun had barely peeked above the horizon when I felt the heavenly nature of John's hand caressing my breast. Sexual impulses surged in every part of my body, foreshadowing the promise of raging rapids and jagged rocks. His unrepentant theatrics had forced my back to the wall. Whether I had been right or wrong in loaning my soul to my husband during my period of redemption, my efforts to show him how two souls could be one had failed. Verbalizing Fate as his choice of who *not to kill* at Ed's bar signaled the time for me to take back both my body and my soul. John's rebellion against oneness had established, once and for all, that physiological yearnings for his body had to be sublimated and sex between us put to an end.

Gently, I pushed his hand away and pronounced, "John, I'm setting you free so you can find what makes you happy."

With dazzling speed, he jumped out of bed, hopped to attention, and headed toward the den where I had carefully arranged his birthday presents the night before after helping him to bed. Curious about his direct ascent into the den, I joined him. Apparently, his drinking memory was, as I suspected, opportunistically selective. Demonstrating how he could affect any area of his life simply by making the choice to *act* differently, John walked straight over to the picture I painted of colorful little fish we had seen while snorkeling in Hawaii the previous summer and began raving about every intricate detail.

Next he lifted up my great-grandfather's solid gold pocket watch and read the inscription inside as if the words were gifts from gods, then harkened. "This is very special. Thank you for giving it to me."

Standing speechless, I watched John expedite his maneuvering of the instant return of the *good little housewife*. He opened his desk drawer, reached in, and guess what? Out popped his magic wallet! He peeked in and visually counted the usual wad of large bills. Since this master of the castle earned all the money, he knew our economic inequality placed me in my most vulnerable position. Seldom leaving the house for over a month, all at once it dawned on me that John had been giving me none of those large bills during that time.

Why I fell and how to survive my fall were the battles I had been fighting. By picking myself up from the bottomless pit far enough for me to give John his freedom, I had catalyzed in him a new battle. This battle, darker than all previous battles, lay in a wallet nearly two inches thick with cash. Not one of my acts of contrition diminished the way John worshiped a resource that could neither see, hear, breath, walk, or talk.

Why should he not worship his money? I asked myself. *Our economic inequality assures him that he retains the power to remain my master.*

Just starting to awaken to a reality where *good little housewives* of nearly twenty years held no monetary value in John's real world, I stood staring at a happy man counting one one-hundred-dollar bill after the next. Cherisse's and Tamara's needs came into my thoughts. I shrunk a bit and fell for the prank.

Yielding to the politics of John's tactics by telling him exactly what he wanted to hear, I rendered, "Cherisse and Tamara need money for school clothes."

Looking for power in all the wrong places, John celebrated his success in manipulating his income where it degraded Cherisse, Tamara, and me the most.

"Call them," he ordered.

When they entered the den and saw cash in their father's hand, Cherisse and Tamara flashed wide-eyed hopes, then tried very hard not to show their disappointment or their embarrassment when they heard him boastfully proclaim, "This should be enough for you *girls*," then hand each *girl* sixty-dollars.

Though they were disappointed about the amount of money their father thought was "enough," Cherisse's and Tamara's embarrassment had nothing to do with their father's stinginess. Their shame had its roots in John's delight in judging all women "dumb cunts" who deserved to be treated as if they were *less than human*. His words, "you deserved it," spoken years earlier, he now transfigured into *like mother, like daughter*. Parading in front of his children a wallet full of cash, then giving them what one might tip a waiter at a good restaurant, showcased bitter vengeance toward three "stupid women" who had loved and taken care of him most of his adult life.

As I would learn in the years to come, although most people think of domestic violence as men beating up women (battering), many of John's actions that were not battering (e.g., using money to control family members) were also *domestic violence.* Research shows that 95% of battering *is* men hitting women (versus women hitting men) and *is* a vicious act of violence. Battering is the most frequently committed crime in the United States and the most unreported. Seventy-five-percent of *all* assault cases, usually thought of as all-male street crimes, result from the domestic violence of a man hitting a woman. Taking place every 18 seconds, men hitting women costs five *billion* dollars annually, including expenses such as lost time at work and 25% percent of all emergency room visits. Medical expenses alone total 100 million dollars annually. In a sample studied by the American Psychological Association (APA), over 50% of the American population questioned say they have experienced domestic violence, and it is widely known that there is a huge discrepancy between how many woman submit to being hit and how many report this *worldwide* phenomenon. In fact, all countries studied said their data is similar to the U.S. Uniform Crime Statistics (National Institute of Justice, 1994), report that 95 out of 100 arrests for battering occur because of incidents where men batter their women partners.

As shocking as these statistics are, even more alarming is the fact that battering is neither the only nor the most prevalent form of domestic violence! In 1996 the APA Task Force on Violence and the Family defined domestic violence as: "a pattern of abusive behaviors including a wide range of physical, sexual, and psychological maltreatment used by one person in an intimate relationship against another to gain power unfairly or maintain that person's misuse of power, control, and authority."

None of the following are battering. All are domestic violence. All spell power and control. All are rampant worldwide. All curse the heart, the mind, and the soul: (1) threats: coercion, threatening to leave, to commit suicide, to kill her; all result in making her do things she does not want to do, (2) intimidation: smashing things, abusing pets, displaying weapons; all result in making her afraid, (3) emotional manipulation: name calling, mind games, something is always wrong about her, telling her she is worthless, putting her down; all result in making her feel bad about herself, think she is crazy, or feel guilty, (4) isolation: controlling what she does, where she goes, who she sees and talks to, what she reads, using jealousy to justify actions; all result in separating her from the rest of the world, (5) minimize: denying abuse, blaming her, making light of the abuse, not taking her concerns about it seriously, telling her she caused it; all result in her feeling something is wrong with her, (6) children: making her feel guilty about the children, using children to relay messages, using visitation to harass her, threatening to take the children away, fighting in front of the children, child abuse in any form; all result in making her feel she is a bad mother, (7) male privilege: treating her like a servant, making all the big decisions, acting like the master of the castle, being the one to define man's and women's roles; all result in making her feel inferior and unimportant, (8) economic abuse: withholding money, making her ask for money, giving her an allowance, taking her money, not letting her know about or have access to family income, preventing her from getting or keeping a job, telling her she is too stupid to support herself; all result in making her feel she is incapable in making it in the world without him.

Sexual abuse, the common denominator of violence against women, includes the following: rape, date rape, incest, sex slave, sex guilt, adultery, withholding sex, and whore language etc., etc., etc. Sexual abuse is physical, psychological, and spiritual violence that is an invisible killer of millions of women's psyche. Though there are no physical cuts, bruises, or scars to prove psychologically crippling damage, sexual violence affects the way women think, feel, and behave. It all boils down to dead-woman-walking reality replacing happily-ever-after dreams.

So, why all this violence against women? Darn that Eve for stealing Adam's rib and bringing passion into the world!

Standing firm in not allowing how their father used words as *weapon of mass destruction* to break their spirits, Cherisse and Tamara accepted the money gracefully and expressed their manners. "Thank you, Dad."

Deaf, dumb, and blind to his daughters' understated psychological and spiritual superiority, John seized illusions of economic power he spent years rehearsing and marched forth in his reign of tyranny. "Diana, I want to talk to the *girls* alone."

I could not stop John nor my acute foreboding when he expressed his intentions. Although an intimate conversation between father and daughters never occurred before, John did have the right to talk with his children in private. Cherisse and Tamara appeared cautious but unafraid, so I turned to leave.

Bemused by my conceding to his demand, John escorted me to the door and closed it hard behind me. Left standing in the entrance hall alone, yet refusing to be left in the cold unknowingness, I stepped lightly into the kitchen, turned, and poked my ear around the corner.

John's voice came through the cracks in the doorway loud and clear. "There's too much water under the bridge between your mother and me."

Accustomed to her father's follies, Cherisse would not let him off the hook that easily. "Dad, this whole thing with Fate is ridiculous. It's never going to work. Tamara and I don't understand why you can't see it that way."

Tamara matched her sister. "I think you're acting like a child."

John retorted, sounding bold and viral, "Fate loves me and we are good together."

The foreshadowing of jagged rocks and raging rapids had exceeded expectations. I felt appalled and sick at heart, not only for Cherisse and Tamara, but for John, too. The one occasion he took the time to communicate with his daughters, he told them he had found love outside of his marriage to their mother. His cruel and oppressive *coup d'etat* forced Cherisse and Tamara to hear their father's cowardice and indiscretion as if they should think him the heroic warrior ready to meet the challenge of a younger woman.

Besieged with frustration, two wounded troupers who rose up to defensively confront a man competing with his own children to *win* marched, heads up, out of the den. The cold-blooded massacre told me to stop sympathizing with a man who would ascend from the bottomless abyss to wage war, conquer, and kill his wife and children and face the harsh reality. From here on out, John did not intend to make anything easy for Cherisse, Tamara, or me.

August 26, 1987, 7:45 P.M.

I had chosen not to call Ruth since my fall into fear. Our fifteen-year friendship had been based on me being the strong one. My inner voice kept telling me that calling Ruth in my ongoing agoraphobic crisis would aggravate in her an onslaught of panic attacks. With agoraphobia no longer the ever-present nemesis, the voice changed. Compelled to call my dear friend, I picked up the receiver of the telephone and dialed Ruth's number. She answered on the second ring.

After reciting for her the saga of John's affair, my fear of leaving my bedroom, how I fell in love with him all over again but since had decided our romance was over, Ruth breathed a sigh of relief for my not calling sooner, then with an air of humor, set my memory straight. "If you could only hear yourself a couple of months ago, Diana, telling me how you were going to divorce John. I think you will feel sure of your reaffirmation to divorce if you weigh the positives and negatives of your marriage."

Ruth's words were like music to my ears. She confirmed what John's failed coup with Cherisse and Tamara taught me about my underestimation of jagged rocks and raging rivers. Additionally, Ruth's suggestion to weigh the odds gave me a realistic ground rule on how to manage the emotions bound to cause problems throughout the process of ending a relationship.

The one positive thing I could come up with other than sex, and even then he cheated and lied in the most despicable way, was weighed down by negatives. John had a will of iron. The man simply refused to fall. He worked like a machine to maintain our lifestyle. Yet, his maniacal work schedule left Cherisse, Tamara, and me to enjoy not only the benefits of that lifestyle without him, but the rest of our lives as well. To add insult to injury, most of the time he shared with us he spent getting drunk and criticizing me.

To compound those negatives, John had given his identity over to the material rewards of hard work. Financial success narrowed his already tunneled vision of the family system. Contributing little more to Cherisse's and Tamara's lives than "a roof over their heads and food on the table," John's identification with the lifestyle wealth afforded not only built his ego, he believed greed was an accepted standard of moral behavior. Immoral standards stunted his growth intellectually, psychologically, and spiritually. Greed without conscience made it impossible for John to reap the boundless rewards of family unity. Worse yet, he used the few occasions of family unity to maliciously abuse me, therefore our children.

True, I enjoyed living on our nearly three acres of earth. Also true, the threat of losing the home we built on that marvelous land compounded every fear my husband pounded into my brain for eighteen years. However, wealth in-and-of-itself had never tempted my passions. Being loved by the ones I loved and being free to be myself had always been my happily ever after.

Because John's definition of the family system was a never-ending battle to win, and mine was a never-ending passion for happiness, even without taking into consideration my journey of enlightenment, the scales were heavily tipped in favor of the impossibility of us ever having any workable relationship.

Ruth supported me by asking if I would like her to telephone The Big G and tell John what she thought about his affair; more than curious to know how John would react to a call from Ruth, I exclaimed, "Yes! Please do!"

Ten minutes later, I answered the telephone on the first ring and instantly heard Ruth's comforting voice. "Diana, I told John I think his behavior is ridiculous. I asked him if he thought he might be going through middle-age crisis. I warned him that he might lose you." Then she added with a tone of shock and dismay. "He said he loves Fate."

I felt deeply beholden to a very special person that night. Confrontations were not part of Ruth's natural inclination to be congenial. More significantly, by telephoning John she discarded the possibility of having a panic attack and boldly stood by my side. Braving to go out on a limb for a friend, she confirmed that my marriage was indeed over and perhaps it never really began. That night my friendship with Ruth made the valley I walked a bountiful place to be.

Ruth ended our conversation with a question. "Diana, do you think the renewal of love you felt for John was due to fear?"

Her question about fear urged me, one more time, to piece together a lifetime of shadows my fall unveiled in a number of weeks. Her provoking prodded me to take a long, hard look at the totality of my revelations since my fall. There were still more pieces to be placed on the puzzle. This piece was a precipice that had scared me so horribly, I felt compelled to romanticize an unfaithful husband hell-bent on destroying everything that made my life worth living. A shadow remained on the other side of the curtain so wrathful, it mutated a free-spirited woman into a mental cripple, who for weeks was petrified to leave her bed. This shadow was so demonic it made her believe she was in love with a man who waged war against everything she had ever been and all she could ever be.

For forty years, my way of being contained the power to be strong-willed. The strength of my will to be fearless in facing life's hardships came directly from my belief in happily ever after. It took forty years, but a global belief in "all's fair in love and war," and a husband who spent eighteen years violently justifying "all's fair in love and war," imprisoned my will. A worldwide consciousness that infiltrated my husband's consciousness dropped an atom bomb named Fate on my happily-ever-after consciousness.

With my willpower locked behind prison walls, I lay helpless to stop a holocaust of negative emotions. On D-Day, when the dark night of my soul approached, John awaited, sword in hand, ready to cut my heart into little pieces. When the perfect moment arrived and my happily ever after was turning black, John called Fate to assist in the cutting.

All our grand debates regarding the theory of good and evil had foretold the fate we set up for ourselves. For one moment, John won every debate. For one moment, the art of his war stole my power. In that moment, as I stood on the razor's edge of a worldwide precipice, a fear awakened in me too soulless to fathom. I feared my ordeal in the fiery abyss of lost souls was merely an initiation into a global abyss where John had been a tiny symptom, one infinitesimal characterization of a massive pit of lost souls. The double-edged sword scaring me so horribly was that the collective consciousness Cherisse, Tamara, and I were headed toward was the same consciousness who taught John to worship the kingdom of mammon rather than the kingdom of God.

The demon Ruth prodded me to seek, the one who had been named the Devil and Satan, that wrathful pestilence worshiped by John . . . was the same pestilence worshiped by multitudes. Such a standardized beast would kill my soul a second time to save a dime . . . would wage war against my philosophy in the name of God . . . would justify killing understanding, forgiveness, and compassion by calling it an axis of evil. I feared the river of no return Cherisse, Tamara, and I were about to paddle down was just like John, one humanity indivisible in its choice to kill its own soul for the savior it believed in, the god it trusted. I feared my trial by fire was merely Cherisse's, Tamara's, and my initiation into a planetary consciousness that worshiped an illusion that castles would set them free. . . . I feared that deadly, greed-driven evil force called . . . materialism.

August 27, 1987, 4:45 A.M.

If my trial by fire was the precipice over a global abyss, then my happily-ever-after dream did not imply opening the door to welcome dark forces. The evil lurking around every corner was a signpost that the world Cherisse, Tamara, and I were about to embark upon would be ruled by hellfire and damnation. If the three of us did not learn how to protect ourselves from the evil beneath the mask, we would not survive. Searching beneath John's mask one last time was required before Cherisse, Tamara, and I embarked upon the future long awaiting us.

Since John had chosen the spirit of materialism over Universal

Spirit and his money-paved, carnal-lined highway appeared to be his straight and narrow path, before he left for work that morning, I hounded him one last time. "John, I have appealed to you since Cherisse and Tamara could walk for you to take seriously their ability to play golf. You have a gift you've shared with so many other children. Yet, you have never taken any interest in giving your own children your greatest talent. Why?"

"Diana!" he pushed angrily. "I'm sick of hearing your voice. For once and for all, I didn't take the time because they are *girls!*"

August 27, 1987, noon

One five-letter word spoken with so much disgust, heaved forth the flesh-eating grossness of John's bitter blame for my giving birth to "girls." With one word, all of Cherisse's and Tamara's human wealth had been laid waste. More precious than gold, jewels, or castles, the fruits of his daughters' splendor had been lost to him. Through the tunnel of vaginal caves into the womb that brought the light of Cherisse's and Tamara's lives onto this earth, John experienced only the darkness scripted into those caves hundreds of years before his birth.

No better a way to ruin a boy's life than to teach him to judge that his mother, his wife, and his daughters are less than human because they are not men. How arresting and appropriate that in his mind John should strip Cherisse and Tamara of their souls. The tone in John's voice when he said "girls" mocked at human comedy that characterized tragedy. Eve as evil had stolen from John the glory of experiencing his daughter's lives: the creativity inherent in the incarnation of their souls. The standard of holding males bondage to judgment's dehumanizing effects, the internal violence of judgments that ruin boys' lives no less than it ruins girls' lives, what a better distraction from truth!

John's servitude to fear and ignorance of his divine nature, and dependence on sins of the flesh, had at long last declared the cause of why Cherisse, Tamara, and I had no other choice than to dive off the precipice and start paddling down the river of no return. His "too much water under the bridge" did not nearly state the case of our relationship. The bridge between my husband's and my conscious way of thinking had been washed out.

To survive no-return rivers, Cherisse, Tamara, and I needed money. Without a doubt, John would refuse to give us money while we were in the process of leaving him. Having knowledge of good versus evil, we began our trek by going to the bank where I withdrew $3,000 from our checking account. Then we went to another bank and deposited the money in an account under my name. The sixty-dollars John gave Cherisse and Tamara barely covered the cost of shoes, so we went shopping for school clothes, supplies, etc. Completing our journey by going to my favorite store, I treated myself to a gift: a beautiful oriental screen I had fallen in love with long before I learned my husband was having an affair.

John wore too many masks to guess how he would to react to what we were about to do next. His potential for violence necessitated I pick the safest place possible for our prophetic deed. I chose The Big G. There he had an image to uphold, so he would not show anger.

The sense of doing the right thing stayed with me every mile of our one-and-one-half-hour drive. Just as I turned the steering wheel in the direction of The Big G's parking lot, I looked at Cherisse and Tamara. My vision beheld an astounding strength of character. The three of us were heading to a place where we were going to say goodbye to all our hopes and dreams of happily ever after with John. Yet, on Cherisse's and Tamara's faces I did not see lost dreams anymore than they saw lost dreams as they looked at my face.

We might have chosen to be scared. We were not scared. We might have chosen to be sad. We were not sad. We were happy about what we were going to do. We were beginning our dreams, not ending them.

The beast shall hate the whore; these shall make her desolate and naked,
and shall eat her flesh, and burn her with fire. . . . For all nations have
drunk of the wine of the wrath of her fornication, and the kings of the earth
have committed fornication with her, and the merchants of the earth are
waxed rich through the abundance of her delicacies.
– Revelation 17:16; 18:3, *The Good Samaritan Bible*

17
Part II

The Icepick Incident

August 27, 1987, 1:30 P.M.

I had barely turned the steering wheel of the car in the direction
of the parking lot of The Big G when Tamara spotted an empty parking
space near the front entrance. I pulled the car into the space and then
asked Cherisse and Tamara to wait for me while I went to go find
Daddy, as I had always called John when I was talking to them. I slid
out of the car and walked straight toward the small antiquated golf
shop and through the open double-door entrance. A young man, tall
and slim, with thick, dark hair stood behind the counter watching me
walk toward him.

"Is John around?" I inquired calmly.

"He went to buy a wheelbarrow. He should be back any minute,"
the young man replied with the casual confidence his age and physical
endowments afforded.

He had no idea I was John's wife nor the irony of John buying a
wheelbarrow on that particular day. In the face of incongruence, one
thing was certain. Whatever John's plans were for a new wheelbarrow,
Cherisse, Tamara, and I drove a long way to change them.

Trying to recollect how we came to own that old corroded
wheelbarrow, I turned and walked out of the golf shop. The black tar
pavement of The Big G's parking lot swam in the heat of that August

day. The sun's rays reflecting off car windshields were blinding.

Just as I arrived at the car, Cherisse grimaced her dry humor. "Here comes Dad with a new wheelbarrow in the back of his truck."

Sweat beaded up and rolled down the sides of John's face as he drove past us. A shiny, red wheelbarrow, half assembled, sat in the back of his little yellow truck. He grimaced a menacing glare as he parked and promptly scooted out of his truck.

Pacing toward us as if his family had absolutely no right to be at his place of work, he demanded irately, "What are you doing here?"

"We're here to talk with you," I answered, quietly assured that our reason for being there would mediate his offensive tactics.

Cherisse and Tamara climbed out of the car while I looked for a safe spot to do the deed we came to do. A shady, very public grassy area to the left of The Big G entrance fit our needs perfectly. John walked across the parking lot alongside the three of us. When we arrived, he stepped around us and sat on a large gray rock in the middle of the grassy area. He looked up saying nothing, only glancing sporadically into each of our eyes. I felt an alarmed curiosity within John, then a softening, as if his soul's knowing aided our task. I concentrated on everything about him and the words I planned to say.

Except for the rock, the plush, green grass, the bright blue sky, and my little family, the world around us ceased to exist. A mild breeze cooled John's brow while forming gentle waves in the grass. The light gray rock he sat upon emanated heavenly nature as it supported his weight without judgment. A sense of the harmony and wisdom in the grassy area made me keenly aware that nature's loving vibrations engulfed all four of us equally.

John's powder blue eyes glistened like cool, clear sparkling pools. His unblemished skin flushed pink and the blond highlights in his hair curled at the ends. Angel wings might have sprouted on the back of a man whose face now showed a deep love for what he saw. Cherisse and Tamara stood on either side of me like a fortress, guarding, protecting, and encouraging me onward.

Words carefully formulated and memorized flowed from my lips. "John, you and Fate have been having an affair without a thought for anyone but yourselves. Not your children, not your wife, not Fate's husband, nor anybody in either of your families. Everything I've done to make amends for my past failings you've thrown in my face, including our lovemaking. Every time you made the choice to stay with me, you went back on your word. Cherisse, Tamara, and I have lost trust in anything you say because your words mean nothing."

Mystification seeped profusely onto John's face. He began nervously twisting my grandfather's United States Naval Academy class ring he had been wearing on his wedding finger since I gave it to him on our anniversary.

Like all the happily-ever-after movies I studied while growing up, I wanted my husband to give me a reason to hold him in my arms and tell him I would see him through to everything he needed to do. He just sat on the rock gazing at the three of us as if he were bewildered why we were even there, especially on the day he bought a shiny, new red wheelbarrow.

His silence left me no choice but to finish what Cherisse, Tamara, and I drove all the way to The Big G to do. "John, you have someone else now, a woman you say you love more than me. The two of you are alike. You deserve each other."

Diana? Fate? Diana? Fate? wrote volumes all over John's speechless face, none of which he was about to speak.

The emotional chaos passing through his heart and soul penetrated my heart and soul. I ached for him to stop me, to fight for the three women he vowed to love forever and ever. All my life, every part of me believed a family had to stand together as one or it would surely fall apart.

My thoughts screamed, *Why don't you stand up and cry out that you don't want to lose me, that you don't want to lose Cherisse, that you don't want to lose Tamara? Why do you just sit there saying nothing?*

John's silence was an absolute rejection of our family unit standing as one. I grounded myself in my knowing that the love the four of us shared would never die and on a soul level we would always be one. With my fondest regrets, his silence forced words I vowed eighteen years earlier never to say. "Cherisse and Tamara and I want a divorce. We don't want to be married to you anymore."

John's body reared up. Tamara began to cry. Cherisse stared at her father with the inevitability of his sorrow in her eyes. I heard multitudes of angels. They too were crying.

At last, John broke his silence. "Look at what you're doing to your daughters."

Coming from a man whose affair opposed every decent instinct and repudiated every positive impulse regarding the family system, he had blamed the victim of his unfaithfulness to rescue himself from the tribulations of his fornication. John's defamation of my character because Cherisse, Tamara, and I had asked for a divorce punctuated the razor's-edge precipice upon which three of us were poised. Considering he prayed at the house of materialistic pleasures, that den of robbers had left John blind, deaf, and dumb in our eyes. A hint of apocalypse in the air, by blaming me for Cherisse's and Tamara's sorrow, John had cursed his own soul.

Flying in the face of his witless backlash, Cherisse, Tamara, and I stood as one. My two fortresses remained on either side of me as the three of us turned to leave. By walking away from a man I had made every attempt to love for better or worse, I had signed, sealed, and delivered the contract I made with my heart, mind, and soul and the hearts, minds, and souls of my daughters. The glorious light of our bubble of love walked with us. For better or worse, the future was ours!

As I drove the car out of The Big G parking lot, Tamara spotted her father giving his next golf lesson. He stood on the second story of the driving range scowling down at us. A golf club swung from his right hand.

Tamara explained, "Dad looks like he wants to hit us with his seven iron."

Cherisse nodded in agreement. I thought it was amazing that Tamara knew John held a seven iron.

August 28, 1987, 10:15 A.M.

From the kitchen, I heard John stomp in the front door. He paced around the corner into the kitchen with a can of beer in one hand, a large brown bag in the other, and passed where I stood, still looking as if he wanted to hit someone.

He put the brown bag in the refrigerator, then directed his body toward the den with a summons. "Follow me."

I did not hesitate.

He seated himself at his desk, opened the desk drawer, then cross examined me, "Is everything you said yesterday true?"

"Yes, it's all true," I answered truthfully.

Lifting some papers out of the drawer, he reaffirmed, "I'm happier with Fate. I love her more than I love you. I spent all last night thinking about you and me. I realized we can't make it."

Breathing John's controlled rage in the air, my reply was tempered. "Thank you for being honest."

He wrote something on one of his papers, then filled out a check and handed it to me while coldly disclosing, "Here's half the money from our stock."

The check was made out in my name for $11,000. I read the amount remembering the day he told me it cost five to six thousand dollars a month to afford our house and property. The $11,000 plus the $3,000 I withdrew from our checking account totaled $14,000, less than three months' basic living expenses.

Curious about his shenanigans, I made it clear the check did not appease our oncoming financial dilemma. "Cherisse and Tamara and I have a right to at least half of your income."

Squeezing his down-turned lips together, he grabbed the rest of the papers he had taken out of the drawer, sneered at me, and then with a menacing tone divulged his objective. "See these 1040 tax forms? They say I'm self-employed and earn $42,000 a year. After deductions, you are entitled to $500 a month support and $250 each for Cherisse and Tamara until they are eighteen."

Oh my God, he's trashing Cherisse and Tamara and me like we were garbage. I quickly surmised, sickened and unprepared for his vengeful betrayal.

Each year at tax time, John simply handed me the filled out tax forms and told me to sign them . . . if I knew what was good for us. I knew he earned more money than he claimed because the bills alone were more money than $42,000 a year. But he paid the bills and spent so much time in bars, I had no way of calculating his true income.

Whatever his income, John's offer of spousal and child support relative to how much money it cost to maintain our lifestyle was absurd and horrifying. Considering my inheritance made the down payment on our first house and we would not have had our present lifestyle if it were not for my parents' deaths, his proposition of one-thousand dollars a month would not only force Cherisse, Tamara, and me into unjust poverty, the financial free-fall would be comparable to walking out of the gates of heaven into the depths of hell. He was threatening Cherisse, Tamara, and me with misery.

No longer a hint in the air, an apocalyptic horseman had arrived in the form of a man who was throwing away everything good in his life. Apparently the man who promised Cherisse, Tamara, and me that he would love us "forever and ever" only months before intended to make our miseries his mission in life. Regardless of a divorce, Cherisse and Tamara would always be his children, and I would always be the mother of his children. The psychological and emotional violence of placing more value in money than he placed in the three of us exclaimed and exalted his fatal attraction. John planned on garbaging us for a younger woman who had her heart set *not* on John but on John's money.

Trapped in his personal catch-me-if-you-can con-game, John had fallen for the same trickery he crafted to break my spirit since the day we married. Then again, the domestic violence of paying for sex with a woman other than his wife, while economically screwing his family, had at long last solved the mystery of the sharp two-edged dagger John's words had spoken of since the day he said, "Doesn't your sister look pretty." Forever and ever *the good wife*, until he spelled out those words in dollars and cents, I had absolutely no idea he had been telling me the truth.

The repercussions for Cherisse, Tamara, and me of the terms John had laid on the table that morning resulted from what is called the *politics of poverty.* Impoverished politics morally justified adulterating us, junking us, and keeping our lifestyle all for himself. The politics of poverty, that unruly progeny of *religious fanaticism*, was responsible for the way not only John but much of mankind had learned to view the world. By organizing the universe to keep women economically dependent upon men, thus controlled by men, the garden-of-evil fabrication had signed, sealed, and delivered the pathology of female biology. Seen as immutable, vagina-assassination would be the cause of women's financial slavery to men's fleshy appetites for centuries. Church and state happily wedded, *man-as-good, women-as-evil* robotics rewarded the entire male species the right to systematically financially oppress women. The *political correctness* of pitting men's biology against women's biology could be evidenced in every part of the system.

Biology as destiny? The vagina as whore? Womb as pathological? Guess what those little pieces of fiction generated? Between 1992-2000, the U.S. Bureau of Justice reported that annually women age 12 and older experienced 131,950 completed rapes, 98,970 attempted rapes, and 135,550 sexual assaults. That totals 366,460 men against women acts of sexual violence *a year*! or 2,931,712 acts of sexual violence toward the female gender for that eight-year period. In a post 2000 APA study, 77% of women reported some form of unwanted sexual aggression. In as much as findings that 80% of date-rapes are not reported, and annually there are hundreds of thousands of date rapes, the true incidence of sexual violence against women in America was a catastrophic societal emergency. The stopgap of the emergency? Rape was socially accepted as biologically *normal for men only.*

Rape was not, is not, nor will ever be normal. Another APA study found that women who were victims of childhood sexual abuse (e.g., incest) had a lifetime average of seven D.S.M.-III-R (Diagnostic and Statistical Manual Of Mental Disorders) diagnoses. That is an average of seven mental illnesses! A woman's pathology did not create rape. Rape created a woman's pathology. Rape was, is, and will always be a brutal crime procreated by weak-mindedness and reproduced time after time by habitual sexist robotics, that ignorant dependence on a *politically correct democracy* computerized to *blame victims* of rape. *You've come a long way baby!*

Psychologists have pitched in their fare share of biology as destiny. No theory of personality has ever resulted from research that included women, nor has the soul ever been factored into personality development. Every single personality theorist from Sigmund Freud onward used *male as normative.* The four horsemen of for-men-only *healthy* identity were theorized to be *competitive, powerful, aggressive, and possessing others as objects.* Men are considered successful if they have the ability to use other human beings as a means to an end.

In the end, women as a rule get sexualized. One famous personality theorist, Eric Erikson, replaced the soul as a woman's "inner space" with the three scarlet goddesses of reproduction: uterus, ovaries, and vagina. When all is said and done, what these respected men of letters succeeded in doing to women was reinforce the systematic violence of possessing vaginas as sexual objects.

Without a doubt, there is an *armageddon* of men's biology against women's biology in the *land of the free*. And one does not have to read Revelation to learn that women are losing the great battle in heaven. *God-as-male, female-as-harlot* religious politics has spawned this final conflict between good and evil. The for-men-only four living creatures who thundered in conquering and to conquer have spread abominations across the land.

In *the land of opportunity* there exists an *apocalyptic red-horseman* termed *the wage gap*. Women are media-marketed to believe they have achieved equal opportunity. Men and women as equal is not born out in the labor market. Lacerated by the swift sword of biological economics, women of every color, race, and ethnic background earn less money than White men, Asian men, Native American men, Hispanic men, and Black men. Equal pay for equal work is a romanticized illusion created by mass media marketing. Until the year 2005, when men's average pay dropped five cents due to the escalation of outsourcing of jobs to other countries, a woman earned 76 cents to a man's dollar, two cents more than she did fifty years earlier. This job inequality subjected all women to the gravest mutilation of never having an equal chance to reach for their dream. Initiated by the "all boys club" at the top, by not allowing women to break through the "glass ceiling" to sit on most corporate boards, America leads the rest of the world by example. From the glass ceiling to "the bottom line," women are routinely held to a higher standard than men. The results? A female college graduate earns the same amount of money as a male high school graduate and so on down the line, men routinely securing a higher bottom line.

The *balance* carried by the *apocalyptic black-horseman* is phrased *feminism in poverty*. Keeping women poor is all about keeping men rich. All women are domestic goddesses in the institutional and interpersonal house of economic disparities. *Armageddon politics as usual* takes the form of barriers that are erected in every part of the system. With the help of the medical industry, women's biology—including menstruation and menopause—have been popularized as medical and psychological illnesses that prevent the entire female species from competing equally in systems outside the home. *Women-as-less healthy*, the systematic status quo, women routinely secure a lifestyle below the poverty line.

Being given the key to the shaft leading to the bottomless pit, *rich man, poor women* guarantees this systemic status quo. Owing its existence to the universality of misogyny, androcentrism, and gynophobia among a battalion of psychotic judgments, a woman can expect the abomination of having a 60% chance of being poor in old age. This apocalyptic statistic is the result of women getting the shaft early on. Signed, sealed, and delivered, a woman's biology as pathological is the reason most people who live in poverty in the United States are female and children of single mothers. As demonstrated by the unseen 19.4% poverty stricken single *working* mothers, dropping women down the tunnel into poverty is not enough inequality for status quo. After they become poor, they are excluded from society and treated like worthless trash. Excluding poor women and children from the majority is legitimized by rationalizing the poor as being pathological. As if they were immoral by nature, distancing those who live in poverty from the moral majority has become politically correct.

Out of sight, out of mind is social justice, right? The trouble is this healthy, wealthy, and wise for-men-only system has falsely charged half of the world's population of mind, body, and spirit as being less than human. By dehumanizing half of the human race, the four male living images of success, (competitive, powerful, aggressive, and possessing others as objects) have created the four female living hells of *domestic violence, rape, the wage gap, and feminism in poverty.* This men versus women war has lead the entire human race headlong into the scene of the final battle between the two beasts of Revelation, God and Satan. In other words, there are those who worship the one true God and those who worship false gods. Idol worship of false images, the task master of the moral majority, has fathered that earthshaking condition called *every man for himself.*

Yes, Satan! The deceiver of the whole world is winning the battle between heaven and hell. At the expense of the greater good, the emphasis on *all-for-me* wealth has created a walking, talking *apocalyptic pale-horseman:* the death and hell of America's moral democracy called *greed.* Hades in the land of the *free to be greedy* is the magnitude of economic inequities. The majority tormented by this insatiable ever-expanding beast, dramatic and increasing disparities separating the rich and the poor have raced into crisis proportions.

A 2005 American earning the federally mandated minimum wage of $5.15 an hour, working 8 hours a day, 40 hours a week, for 50 weeks, earns $10,300 annually. That the poverty threshold for a family of four is $19,157 (2004), minimum wage is *working* poor . . . for both ladies and gentlemen. The cost of freedom gets worse. Between 1979 and 1997, the after-tax income of the poorest 20% decreased from $10,900 to $10,800, while the top 1% increased from $263,700 to $677,900. This gap expands as we speak, racing faster and faster toward economic collapse. The oil and the wine has floated to the top. And that's what we love about freedom!

But wait! The cost of freedom still gets worse. Surfacing from greed's bottomless abyss, governing political leaders elected by the majority are given huge amounts of money by the power-ball corporate men's club, and in return are given huge tax credits to throw the cautionary tail of *fossil-fuel-emission-induced-climate-change* to the wind. Those same power elite, CEOs that is, who own the media, indoctrinate the money-hungry collective population to consume, consume, consume.

Out of the mouth of *consumerism* slithers a four-headed dragon ready and willing to *lie, cheat, steal, even kill* to pray at the feet of *oil, coal, cars,* and *utilities.* Victimized by corporate-sponsored commercialism, this four-headed prophet of a better life sadistically sucks the life force out of an unrepentant democracy eager to sell their souls and sacrifice the whole earth for the treasured lifestyles of the rich and famous!

No! Nothing is sacred to those who worship false idols except the bottom line, and because of the bottom line, 17.8% or 13 million (2004) *children* in the U.S. live in poverty (U.S. Census Bureau), a virtual tsunami of poor children abandoned by charitable America.

Compared to the rest of the industrialized world, America's children remain at the bottom. And guess who is with them at the bottom? That's *feminism in poverty*! Synonymous of Mother Earth herself, she rides the four winds in heaven with the voice of thunder . . . churning up the sea of the four living creatures making war with God. . . . She has a bow aimed at the end times of false gods . . . and a crown to go out conquering the glass ceiling and to conquer the beast of greed and to open the seven seals of the one true God . . . this sacrificial lamb of *politics as usual* . . . the *apocalyptic white-horsemen* named The American Way! Those are US moral values! That is what Americans call freedom! Welcome to the new world order!

Was this new world order the secret alternative plan the man I married had been keeping secret from me as I watched him mixing cement in his old corroded wheelbarrow, looking as if he wanted to die? Inoculated with immoral systematic beatings inside the home, had John's father set him up to be beaten into puppetry for a morally bankrupt system outside the home? Were John's economic beatings of Cherisse, Tamara, and me his way of paying it forward? Was the fall of the collective conscience into greed his platform for the gross negligence of responsibility to financially provide for the women who had provided for him?

Choose one of you and kill the other told the tale of Cherisse, Tamara, and me surviving on $12,000 a year. Nonetheless, John's tale of woe, like the *armageddon politics* he puppeteered, got worse. Cherisse had turned 16 years old May 4th, three months earlier. In less than two years when she turned 18, our support would drop to $8,000 a year. In four years, on Tamara's 18th birthday, support would drop to $6,000 a year. The happy birthday John plotted for his *girls*? abject poverty. After adding up our living expenses, plus all the extras I could think of, I was sure he earned over $100,000 a year, maybe even $112,000. That would be $100,000 for him to start his new life and $12,000 for Cherisse, Tamara, and me to start our new lives, a $100,000 difference, that is, for two years! Then it would get worse!

No matter what we settled on, John had made it clear I would need additional income. That would force me to put some of my half of the money from the sale of our house into the bank. After we payed off the mortgage, my half would afford Cherisse, Tamara, and me a small condominium. Plus, recently he had been talking about the tax consequences of selling our house. I understood next to nothing about tax consequences (capitol gains tax), and after asking him for a divorce, he was not about to explain the tax consequences. As unfathomable as it may sound, freedom from John still got worse. Yes, we lived in an expensive house, but we were living above our means, and most of John's income went to bills. After food and household expenses, Cherisse's and Tamara's necessities and extracurricular activities were where I spent money, for which I had to ask John. The lifestyle John painted for his children would not include wardrobes let alone extracurricular activities. And what about college? And cars to get to jobs that would help them pay for college? Defined in real-life terms, abject poverty would be hell on earth.

John knew the shock and awe I could only guess that morning. I was taking art classes at a local community college. Though I had never completed college, studying a profession had not crossed my mind since I married. A housewife taking care of her family for over eighteen years who had never been employed outside the home, most fittingly, I had no job skills above basic typing. The bottom line for Cherisse and Tamara? At forty years old, their mother's worth in the job market added up to minimum wage. The bottom line for John? Dropping us down the shaft to the bottom, this could *not* have been an overnight revelation.

The inhuman treatment of humankind toward humankind: How can we endure it? Why do we treat others that way? "You deserved it" had reached its shining hour. The great day of John's wrath had commenced!

Having been given few tips about my legal rights, I replied to John's economic terrorism by trying to effect change in his attitude. "If those are your intentions, I will fight you in court."

His closed, down-turned lips tightened more intensely as he stood up and laughed in my face, while threatening. "We'll see."

He stomped into the master bedroom, threw back the covers, and lunged into bed. Not a second to waste on another breakdown and in serious need of help, I drove to a pay phone and called an old roommate from my days at University of Southern California who had since become an attorney.

After explaining my situation to Rachael, how John was self-employed and the disparity between how much it cost us to live in our house and how much spousal and child support he said he would give me, she advised, "Make two copies of all the bills, cash receipts, and any other papers that prove how much money it costs to live in your house. Keep one copy in a safe place where John will not find them and one copy with a friend."

While mentally retracing where John kept our records, I recalled someone telling me I could purchase a *Do It Yourself Divorce* packet at the local courthouse. John would be suspicious if I was gone too long, so I drove to the courthouse, paid my ten cents, promptly flipped through the pages, then drove home. John remained in bed sleeping like a baby. I guessed he felt he had a right to our bed. This pressured me to sleep in the den. Repulsed by his hung-over declaration of my financial independence, I felt nauseous at the mere thought of going near him. Superseding my repulsion, however, was my desire for the comfort of my nightgown and my pillow.

Venturing into the dimly lit room, I passed John. He was lying flat on his back with his eyes wide open staring straight up at the ceiling. He actually appeared to be deep in thought.

Without moving his eyes from the ceiling, he professed in a rare moment of honest emotion, "My mind is all fucked up!"

Feeling the need to get out of the darkened room as fast as possible, I sternly interpreted for him the superficial cause of his admission. "John, you fucked up the first time you took down Fate's pants."

Not waiting for one of his farcical responses, I continued toward my closet, stepped in, and lifted my nightgown off the hanger. I circled around through the bathroom, grabbed my pillow, then swiftly exited the room, leaving John to enjoy, all by himself, his fucked-up mind.

Once in the den, I rolled out the sofa-bed and threw on the bed-coverings and my pillow. It looked cozy enough. Cherisse and Tamara tip-toed in, hopped in bed and lay on either side of me. All snuggled up, we chatted quietly. Every so often, we heard John's footsteps pace into the kitchen, open the refrigerator door, pop open a beer, then pace back into the master bedroom. By asking for a divorce, the light of the *DCT* (Diana, Cherisse, Tamara) bubble of love had exposed the dark subconscious sea of John's hate. The oil and wine had floated to the surface to lift Satan's veil and liberate the kingdom of John's truth. The production was about to begin. . . .

Act I: The Armageddon: the final conflict between good and evil.

John's mountainous body suddenly stood in the doorway of the den, a tall shadowy figure with its mouth shouting, "I'm going to kill myself!"

He paced around the entrance hall sounding like some fearsome creature, returned to the same spot, and roared, "Cherisse and Tamara, do you know how bad Diana's mother was? You would get sick if you knew the crazy things Marie did. Someday you're going to find out the truth about Diana. She's just like her mother. Then you'll know how bad she really is!"

Two ancient souls in teenage bodies, disgust and pity scribbled all over the infinite wisdom inscribed on their faces, Cherisse and Tamara had heard it all before, too many times to count. For me, everything changed. That oceanic abyss of ancestral lacerations from the past showing in my daughter's eyes scarred everything the three of us had ever been and everything we had worked so hard to be. The execration of me and my family aimed at Cherisse and Tamara, the devil ascending from the bottomless pit to speak with tongues like a dragon had found my weak spot. My family and I were one-half of our children's genetic heritage. The dehumanizing ordeal of John slashing open old wounds by expressing his hate for my side of their gene pool cut through to the core of my soul.

I began to pray for him to stop the words. The more I prayed, the louder he roared. "Not only was Diana's mother bad, so is her sister, Susan. Diana, do you know how bad your father was?"

I could not believe my ears! In eighteen years, not once had my husband uttered one critical word about my father. He usually joked appreciatively about Daddy's characteristic displays of personality, sometimes even bragging about their close relationship. I believed my husband loved my father. Had John been keeping this secret too? That he hated my father as much as he hated me and the rest of my family!

By the time John came into my life, my father's body had been racked and torn by malignant melanoma, a deadly form of skin cancer. Daddy walked me down the isle as a one-legged man. The other cancer-ridden leg had been amputated at the hip the previous year. John never knew my father as a whole healthy viral man because Daddy was crippled and his health deteriorating when they met. In his humiliating condition, Daddy being a target of John's dragon tongues tugged at how much my will could tolerate. In this fiery test, my finding triumph of endurance over his capacity for cruelty floundered. He had stained the names of every single person in my immediate family and, by doing so, stained Cherisse's and Tamara's names as well. Did my husband hate our children too? My defenses could not assimilate that much hurt all at once. I pushed my fingers against my ears. Every part of me wept.

Cherisse and Tamara started shaking. When I felt their bodies shake, the hurt that had cut through to the core of my soul bolted up as anger. I began writhing with rage. The beast rising from the smokey abyss like a great furnace to make war with angels had teeth of spears and arrows and a tongue of a razor-sharp double-edged sword. Believing there is no greater sin of the flesh than to raise the voice of wrath against one's own children, I ascended from my connectedness with Mother Earth. Those maternal instincts drove me to crush the beastly instincts ruling John. My hands pushed my body up and off the sofa-bed. I lunged toward him and pounded my fists on his chest.

Setting out conquering the fire in my core and to conquer this apocalyptic trial, I heard my voice scream. "I hate you. I hate you. I hate you!"

He pushed me away spewing barren repetitions of "I'm going to kill myself."

As I stumbled back into bed, Tamara declared, "Dad, you're not going to kill yourself."

No, none of us believed John would actually kill himself, least of all John. It was his wrathful ego joyously feeding off the gratification of our miseries for which those lower energies lusted that drove John's impersonation of Satan. Play-acting the devil who could not remember the divinity from which he had fallen, John ended his last chance to save his children from his satanic ruler. He glared and turned to go into the kitchen. I squeezed between Cherisse and Tamara and pulled them close to me. Our ordeal in the chamber of John's shadow was not over. Finding the courage to endure and get past the beast beneath the mask of John's face was about be tested again.

Act II: The Apocalypse: the four-headed horseman

The sound of heavy utensils clanging against one another, then the kitchen drawer slamming closed was followed by the return of John's figure in the doorway. He had an icepick in his hand.

With an upward motion, he lifted and pointed the icepick toward his temple while simultaneously yelling, "I'm going to kill myself. There's nothing to live for if I have to give you all that money."

One more time suspended in disbelief, I mutely questioned the staging of the farce. *This can't all be about money? John can't be serious?*

The *pale horseman* from the lower regions had surfaced to steal the peace from our little heaven. Out of the mouth of death and hell had slithered a dragon with four heads. Each *apocalyptic* head— *adultery, alcohol, icepick, and hateful words*—had the face of John. Surfacing from those subterranean chambers of thickening shadows, the devil's four demons were thundering forth to battle John's most precious jewels. His true wealth, the earthly treasure of his daughters, the dragon felt pleased to sieve down the shaft of poverty in exchange for the material riches of silver and gold.

Cherisse, Tamara, and I huddled three-as-one on the sofa-bed. The hand that held the icepick began to make jerky stabbing motions toward John's right temple. His head moved in-sync with the icepick, but in the opposite direction, making him look like a huge windup doll. The devil had made a hasty decent from the light of his offspring's heavenly love into the darkness of hate's burning hell. The scene's atrocity took a further toll. Cherisse began to cry.

She pleaded, "Please, Dad, don't kill yourself!"

Tamara added, "We love you, Dad. Please stop!"

On this great and terrible day of the unveiling of their father's worst demons, Cherisse and Tamara denied him the reciprocation of the tempest he beat down upon them. Instead, they lovingly endured their part in his ridiculous drama. His daughters' unconditional love had exposed their father's conditional love. Cherisse, Tamara, and I were little more than props for the theater of war being performed on the grand stage of John's inner conflicts. Icepick robotics in the land of unconscionable greed parabled his internal armageddon. He would not stop the jabbing motions.

By this time, Cherisse, Tamara, and I were all crying hysterically. Our crying only served to escalate the jabbing motions. The motions became more erratic. Tragedy characterized by his comedic performance, icepick in hand, John finally had our full emotional attention. And he played upon his audience's emotions with the fervor befitting kings of castles in air.

Cherisse's and Tamara's tearful pleading, "Don't, Dad, don't," reminded me of the girl who lost the bubble that once protected her from real pain and fear.

When John threatened to choose one and kill the other, it never crossed my mind he would choose to cause real pain and fear by attempting to psychologically assassinate our daughters. With *sword, famine, pestilence, and wild beasts*, the dragon was giving Satan power to crush and devour the lamb and then trample under foot whatever was left. Unrepentant of his fallen divinity, the sins of the fathers were crystal clear in John's metaphorical enactment of ones who worship false idols.

The darkness of hell struggling to shut out the light of heaven, John maintained false stabbing motions and kept raving about money and suicide. Although his performance did not convince any of us he would actually shove the icepick through his temple, his play-acting did characterize both the hilarity and heinousness of victimization in the name of greed. A consequence of greed without conscience, John's moment of judgment was at-hand.

I watched the show and tried to guess how long the icepick scene would last. It was John's play, the theatrical production of all his psychological and spiritual conflicts, and no one liked his or her part except the star. However many apocalyptic pathologies plaguing John's psyche, his howdy-doody impersonation of the transgressions of the fathers had sealed his fate.

At last, he lowered his hand and took the icepick back into the kitchen. We listened to him toss his *WMD* into the drawer and breathed a sigh of relief, but not for long. The curtain had been lowered only on the icepick scene. Though his fate had been sealed, the flesh-eating grossness of the downward spin of John's three act play had just concluded its second major climax.

Act III: The Bitter Scroll: salvation or damnation.

The curtain lifted with the sound of the closet door in the master bedroom slamming shut. I knew what the sound meant. No longer trapped on the sofa-bed, I refused to allow my children to endure their father's schoolboy acting-out one more second.

"Cherisse and Tamara, stay here. I'll go talk to Daddy," I insisted, scrambling out of bed.

I hurried to the master bedroom. When I arrived at the closet, I became very still and listened. From behind the door, I heard John sobbing. By huddling together in our refusal to believe his *act*, we had persevered to pass the test of endurance. We survived our ordeal in the chamber of John's central fire, the fiery pit of a lost soul. Not allowing him to break our spirits broke the spirit of the beast. The goodness of our love had prevailed over the evil of his hate to award us our apocalyptic rite of passage from our trial by fire.

Keeping secret from himself his beastly aspects by projecting them into us with unrepentant theatrics, John recoiled the devil and his four demons back through the tunnel into the bottomless abyss from whence they came. To lose the earthly riches of the three souls who survived death and Hades to show him the way, the counter spin of John's cycles of violence spiraled his wrathful rebellion into the subconscious hell chambering ego's bitter scroll: John's cave of dark unknowingness.

Befitting castles in air, financial worth as a measure of human worth, what *was* John's final judgment of his personal worth? Oh, that he should have to suffer the slings and arrows of lost fortune. It must have been awful for him to think he could not keep his mistress plus have his wife's and daughter's money, too.

If anyone worships the beast and its image and receives the mark on his forehead or on his hands, he also shall drink the wine of God's wrath, poured unmixed into the cup of his anger, and he shall be tormented with fire and brimstone in the presence of the holy angels and in the presence of the Lamb. "John?" I beckoned, tapping lightly on the door.

"I have a rifle pointed at my head," cried the wimpish, tear-stained voice of the sacred but lost and grief-stricken child whose eternal beatings he endured only for those same beatings to steal his soul and damn his life.

And there were flashes of lightening, loud noises, peals of thunder, and a great earthquake . . . great hailstones, heavy as a hundred-weight, dropped on men from heaven. A lifetime of punishing wounds had sounded in my husband's tone. In my mind, I visualized his amazing powder blue eyes filled with the most pitiful tears on earth.

The chamber of central fire, those unprocessed feelings of hurt tormenting John since childhood, had turned into a pain beyond his capacity to endure. His mother's and father's abandonment of who he was as a boy stole the man's feelings of inner safety. Petrified of the abandonment of who he was, he never felt safe enough to feel the inner battle between love and fear chambered in his heart. Fearing to extreme the orphaned feelings damning his life, John would slay his wife and children, even himself, to keep those feelings secret. Making it too easy for him to hide from truth, the financial wealth spoon-feeding ego's bitter coil served to abandon his already abandoned feelings. Material riches aided and abetted the loss of the pot of gold John was threatening to kill himself to find.

Having no understanding that the revelation of his divine self awaited the tribulation of his ego self, John chose to assassinate those opportunities rather than feel the great and terrible day of ego death. By making war, conquering, and killing his living soul, the four-headed horseman had won damnation, salvation being the apocalyptic loser. Until John opened his heart to the eventual certainty that in *the end times* of false saviors good would prevail over evil, the man I married would choose *not* freedom from his four fleshy harlots but to be controlled by Satan, the one who would remain his master.

Epilogue: The Last Judgment

That on earth as in heaven there is no chance, only cause and effect, in one short hour John's *apocalyptic choice* of hate over love had effected a *fall from heaven* over a *fall into freedom*. Because the death of his wealth was synonymous with the death of his ego, John denied the opportunity to end the world as he knew it by *ending the time of false gods*. A man who should envy the death of ego rather than the "fucked up" life he had chosen grieved only that he should lose that living hell. Praying that in a different time the man I married might reap another critical opportunity to choose the bow and the crown of Mother Earth . . . and end the time of the four-headed dragon of greed beating her up . . . and pierce the seven seals of the one living God. . . . The only thing left for the lamb to do was to help the lost boy stay alive.

"Please don't, John. You know we love you," I implored.

John said nothing. He did nothing. I waited. I listened for the dreaded shot. I waited . . . I waited . . . I waited. . . .

No, no shot rang out that night. And no, it was not the first time John had gone into his closet and threatened to shoot himself.

I remained on the floor, exhausted, waiting, pondering, *I wonder if John will remember this in the morning?*

*The oligarchy changes into a democracy something in this way: through its
insatiate desire for that which it sets before itself as a good and a duty
to become as rich as possible. . . . That is how democracy is established,
whether by force of arms, or by fear.*

– Plato, *The Republic, Book VIII*

18

Paradise Lost

August 29, 1987, dawn

I do not know what time it was, but I lifted my body up off the
floor, dragged myself to our king-sized bed, and fell into a deep sleep.
When I awoke, I was no longer alone. A large hand, rough and callused
from cement mixture after cement mixture, held mine. The man who
once held all my dreams in the palm of that hand moved his body
next to mine.

"Do you still love me?" he questioned hopefully.

Love?

*And when the fifth seal opened . . . I saw under the altar the souls
of those who had been slain for the word of God and for the witness
they had borne. . . .* Breaking the fifth seal on the voice of my soul,
automatic writing had set into motion my fall from my bubble into
apocalyptic revelations that gave me the *keys to truths held secret
through the ages.* In rebellion, John mimicked the downward spiral
of a tornado blowing into pieces everything in its path. With his
unrepentant insurrection against the understanding, forgiveness, and
compassion my automatic writings were teaching me to live, my
husband's last judgment with his bride had come to pass. On the floor
of a closet with a shotgun pointed at his head, John had lowered the
final curtain on our eighteen year armageddon—me debating good,
John fighting evil—whose real-life epilogue began forty-two days

earlier.

Forty-two days earlier, lifetimes earlier, the tribulation that catalyzed my revelations flooded into my life. Poured unmixed from the cup John's four-headed beast of riches, tormenting me with the fire that burns with the brimstone of the four-headed beast of poverty, Fates voice coursed straight to the core of my being. Telephoning my home to make war, conquer, and kill the spirit of my soul was my husband's other lover. The wrath of my husband and his archetypal twin threw me into the pit, shut the lid, and—believing my soul was dead—sealed the lid over my head. Together consummating the fallen self, the adulterer and his mistress might have succeeded in silencing the spiritual force of a million other women. But this woman was one in a million.

And when the sixth seal opened . . . I looked . . . and behold there was a great earthquake . . . and the sun became black . . . and the stars fell from heaven unto the earth . . . and the sky vanished like a scroll that is rolled up. . . . Abominations of the desolation of his compulsory new world order would be the epilogue written at the end of the book of John's life with Diana, Cherisse, and Tamara. Although my husband and his twin avenger were the tribunal who sentenced me to face my demons of fear, judgment, and unknowingness, surrendering to those purgatorial fires dropped me into a meditation overflowing with truths about *John's new world order of weapons of mass destruction.*

Breaking the sixth seal that had silenced the voice of my soul, *meditation* opened a door to the voice of *ancient secrets* John could not shut. Opening my mind to the secret that because the voice of my husband's soul had been sealed up by church doctrine ordering humanity's fall from the garden right in front of their eyes, his stupefied mind lusted to witness my fall from Paradise.

Canonized as the fourth living creature of the apocalypse, the man I counted on to be my happily ever after had been my inquisition since the day I vowed to love him for better or for worse . . . *cutting up each and every detail of my life like a surgeon with a scalpel . . . cutting away at my family and friends . . . trying to convince me that no one who ever played any meaningful part in my life was worth anything . . . every last word eating up the freedom of my soul to be my driving force. . . .* The man who repeated over and over, *Diana, you're stupid. You'll never be able to do anything in the real world. When I'm done with you, I'm going to send you back to Santa Ana . . .* had been wielding the age-old weapon to entomb my soul as his soul had been entombed. The man I wedded used the *weapon of words*, his *WMD* to indoctrinate thoughts of worthlessness that would, sooner or later, break my spirit, leaving him free to rob me of my youth, take my money, and make merry with younger women.

Unlocking and opening the door between the voice of my conscious mind and the voice of my soul mind, meditation unsealed *ancient mysteries* I knew nothing about. Meditative revelations initiated my mind into the mystery of my husband's weapon of words. As a grain of sand amid multitudes dating back to biblical *Revelation*, John's *WMD*, like *John's* synagogue of Satan, were the words Christian theology authored to forever consecrate the secret of the ages an ancient mystery.

The four living creatures foretold in my revelations were John's insatiable appetite to slay the freedom of my soul *to be*. Because *mankind* had been religiously instructed to have faith that a woman originated sin by partaking of the tree of God's knowledge and then became fruitful and planted the seed of birth, all womens' vaginas mutated into the dark mysterious tunnel through which all men had been born. To gain power over that darkness whether by force of arms or by fear, the church and state as holders of secrets democratized mankind to believe it was a good and a duty *for men only* to become as rich as possible. Like a mind rolled up to create tunnel vision, the uncommon stupidity of John's icepick theatrics depicted a cannon-correct performance he believed would reap the *cash cow* that would give him the sacred *power* to order my soul *not to be*.

Masquerading as a marital system in crisis, *fate* had set the stage for my *initiation*. When I heard Fate's voice on the telephone, holy terror grew roots in my soul, ravaging a lifetime of the free-spirited person I remembered as me. I found myself falling . . . falling . . . falling . . . until I entered the *pit*, the *gap in my heart* created by eighteen years of John's *WMD*. Because I was subconsciously petrified by his secret alternative plan, when I heard the voice of the woman who came to replace me, my fearless bubble burst and I fell into the pit, the gap in my heart where my subconscious fear separated my conscious mind from my soul mind.

That point of separation was where my *initiation* began. Unknowingness blocking all escapes from the pit, I prayed to the depths of my soul for understanding. My prayers were answered by the miracle that takes place in the void, the fusion of material and spiritual consciousness that makes every mystery understandable. Like the unsealing and unrolling of a scroll that opens the mind to wisdom, the void's illuminating land set me free from antiquated falsehoods. As an outpouring of *divine grace*, unblocked were truths held secret through the ages. The void's kingdom of heaven granted me *secret teachings* that were keys to bridging the gap in my heart, the only way out of the pit. Into my consciousness streamed stories of a woman whose mind had been prostituted by tyrannical gender standards spoken by a man whose ego fed off the gratification of sexism's control of women.

When my meditation ended, my initiation into tests of courage to fulfill the obligation of grace began. Awaiting me were severe trials by fire where I was given an unknown period of time in which to empty my heart of tyranny while staying obedient to the grace of secret teachings. The initiation had sentenced my fallen spirit to combat the spirit of materialism. Symbolized by the four living creatures to be purged from my heart was every last judgment, every thought, word, and deed in the book of my life that had not expressed my soul's truth. Every judgment, every thought, word and deed seeded by anything other than the love in my soul was essential for me to seek, find, and eradicate with understanding, forgiveness, and compassion.

I stooped to progress the ordeal of the tunnel mirroring the brainwashing that originated my "stupid" mind, crawling through blind passages; purging, repenting, atoning; seeking and finding more and more indoctrinated shadows, practicing *UFC* by being faithful to the secrets being given to me. These tests of courage and faith in grace *initiated* my conscious mind into the agony and ecstacy of truths that both humbled and exalted my existence.

Then, on D-Day, I hit a wall of falsehoods so fraudulent to truth, my will to live emptied out of my body. The old man of suffering had crushed the baby of wisdom. In that black pit of lost souls, dead was the will to live with a man who chose to emulate a mass consciousness fallen so deeply into the seductions of the flesh. If I chose life, grace would require I leave the bottomless abyss of my husband's tongue and walk heads-up into the global abyss his tongue mirrored. I would be bound to practice *The Philosophy* of my initiation amid chillingly unthinking, uncaring men and mortal enemies of learning and letters who had kept the tradition of oppressive gender standards sacred for thousands of years. Grace would demand I stay virginal to my one-in-a-million journey in . . . *a world where the fruit the soul longed for was gone . . . replaced by the fire and brimstone of the judgment that the great harlot corrupted the earth with her fornication . . . and she shall be burned with fire; for mighty is the Lord God who judges her . . . Hallelujah!*

Infected with the understanding that the *secret harlot* at Armageddon was man's insatiate desire to deliver him from evil by possessing the *riches* of Babylon; wherefore, my conscious mind willed what even the devil had failed to do. I laid down in my coffin, shut the lid, and sealed it over my head. But because my one-in-a-million journey had been graced with the jewels of the *philosopher's stone*, my death could not hold back the dawn. For staying true to *The Philosophy's* string of pearls, I was awarded a rite of passage. Nature connected with my soul in oneness, spiritualized my body, and willed my mind back to life. Pain and fear were magically gone, instantly bridging the gap in my heart. As with automatic writing and meditation, oneness with nature bridged the chasm between my consciousness and universal consciousness. In the twinkling of an eye, my mind took an evolutionary leap from seeking truth in the darkness of unknowing into seeking truth in the light of knowing.

For surviving the ordeal of my awakenings, never again would my human will have the power to hold back my divine will. Written on the book of my life was the absolute certainty of my initiatory journey. Though seeking and finding liberation from judgments laid upon my heart was a ruthless journey, from the vast despair of the crematorial fires that burned up my finite mind came the overpowering elation of the second birth of my infinite mind.

Because John's soul had been strong enough to light the fire of my illuminating purgatory, the prince of deception transfigured into the princely redeemer. God and Satan, the two beasts at the biblical place called Armageddon had caused the same effect. In losing my false identity, I found my true identity. Both the darkness and the light turned out to be liberators of truth. If it were true as experience taught me that only those tried by fire can open the seven seals of the living soul, by partaking of the great and terrible days of my initiation into Eden lost, I gained the fruits of wisdom that cleared my way home to the truth about Eve.

In the beginning (Genesis), God's first words to the male and female blessed them by saying, *Be fruitful.* Then came the serpent who became the catalyst for Eve partaking of the fruit when he said, *For God knows that when you eat of it your eyes will be opened and you will be as gods knowing good and evil. . . . The woman saw that the tree was good for food, and that it was a delight to the eyes, and that the tree was to be desired to make one wise. . . .* Though God blessed Adam and Eve to eat freely of the fruits of God's *knowing,* orthodox Christian theology commands *us* to have complete faith and trust that woman's desire *to be* like God was the *first original sin.*

So, she took of its fruit and ate; and also gave some to her husband, and he ate. . . . Then God said to the serpent, Because you (Adam) have listened to the voice of your wife . . . cursed is the ground because of you. . . . Church doctrine demands an undisputable confession of faith that the voice of Adam's wife cursed the ground upon which he walked. The faithful are bound by God's curse to believe without a doubt that *humankind's fall* from Paradise into suffering was because the mother of the human race chose to free her mind *to be* wise like God, knowing good and evil.

In the end (Revelation), however, an angel reveals the secret of Eve to John, *Why marvel? I will tell you the mystery of the woman. This calls for a mind with wisdom. . . .* The serpent, that old trickster historically known for its wisdom in avoiding danger, by tempting Eve to be like God, sets the stage for liberating truth even before the drama begins. By courageously eating from the tree of life, woman initiates the human experience of being wise like God.

In the end, the two beasts at Armageddon, God and Satan, are as in the beginning. The serpent and God turn out to be two faces of one

God: one face a jealous, judgmental god who creates fear by punishing passion, delight, and wisdom; the other face an understanding, forgiving, and compassionate god who creates love by encouraging passion, delight, and wisdom. The demonic god steals power by demanding submission to a hellish outside ruler. The divine god gives power by liberating the kingdom of a heavenly inner ruler. Who then is the deceiver? Who is the redeemer?

In the end, as in the beginning, human *mind is the builder* of God. The tree of life in the body flows from the mind of God. *To be* fruitful is to use the mind to break open the seven seals that free the soul *to be*. Personally experiencing the seven soul kingdoms within the body is to *know* the wisdom of God. Knowing that God is in each of *us* is the meaning of life, the only happily ever after, the only freedom. What freedom *is*, and how to be free, is the secret of the ages. It is the soul afraid of its fall into sin that never learns to live. Filled with delight and full of passion to be fruitful, what *is* the truth about Eve? Woman initiated the knowledge that the glory of being human is the chance *to be* one with God, co-creating the living soul!

Because I listened to the voice of my husband, I came to believe I was stupid thus worthless in the world. It was the voice of woman who catalyzed my fall into freedom from "stupid" and "worthless." As Eve, by partaking of my soul mind, I initiated the knowledge that liberated me from *evil*, clearing my way home to the *good* about me. In my soul I found no sin, no fall, no evil garden. What I found was the wisdom that was my savior-faire.

Whatsoever good thing any one doeth, the same shall one receiveth . . . whether one be bound or free. . . . That on earth as in heaven we reap what we sow, the effect of our lives is caused by the way we use our minds, be it for good or evil. Be it the deceiver or the redeemer, there is no reason to fear God, for God is *us*. All journeys eventually lead to the river of the water of life. The absolute certainty that by using my mind to build my soul into my life, wherefore my initiatory experience had come to pass.

Then I saw a new heaven and a new earth; for the first heaven and the first earth had passed away. . . . I spent forty-two days conquering fictions that had taken control of my free mind. My courage to travel the excruciating death of my deceived mind, unsealed, opened, and lifted the lid from my coffin. My sarcophagus was empty. A second death would hold no power over my finite mind. Experiencing truths held secret through the ages graced my soul with a second birth. With this new birth came the voice of my *infinite mind co-creating with my finite mind.*

Opened was another book of my life. Written there were feelings that my children needed me. I went to them. When I got there, I saw in their faces what the voice of their father had done to them. When I felt what had been done, through the oneness of our pain and our love we saw the light at the end of the tunnel. *It* was in the opening of the seventh seal that three souls became *free to be one-spirit-indivisible, never-ending, one mind co-creating forever and ever.* After seeking, finding, then losing at-*ONE*-ment with John, the *soul* of the *DCT spirit initiated its* journey into *The Philosophy of UFC+US . . .* by asking John for a divorce!

And when the lamb opened the seventh seal . . . there was silence in heaven for about half an hour . . . then I saw the seven angels . . . and when the forth angel blew his trumpet I beheld three woes. . . . Less of a prince than a butcher, the three acts of John's symbolic war in heaven against the *oneness* before his eyes had played themselves out by milking his sacred cow to the last drop. With all that, his bucket remained empty. The actor's mask John wore neither angered nor excited the *DCT spirit.* The mask's apocryphal dialogue about money and suicide dramatized the man's complete disregard of our needs and emotions. His three testimonial acts stirred not love nor hate nor judgment. Cherisse, Tamara, and I were no more than tearful spectators of a paradise lost to man. The magic mirror he once held in the palm of his hand had lost its mystery.

We had given the devil his due and then asked to be set free. In retaliation for our every effort to lovingly conclude our time with him, John rebelled by pitting his demagogue of separation against our god of unity. He hid in a cave of ignorance by making war with wisdom. That insurrection taught us about the dangers of a man so afraid of his own soul, he would kill *it* rather than understand *it* and take *us* down with him without a second thought.

Forcing *us* to witness the suicide of his soul was decidedly not the husband I created. If the fearless girl who lived in a bubble did not mirror apocalypse now, then why did she fight an eighteen-year armageddon that resulted in forty-two days of apocalyptic revelations, culminating in her husband's last judgement with her two daughters and herself? Awe, but the puzzle was not complete after all! Just when I imagined my old world had been defeated, I was mandated all over again to go back in time and find out why a simple girl who cherished happily ever after would place all her dreams in the palm of the devil's hand.

The first time I laid my eyes on the man who would spend eighteen years testing my love, I looked across a crowded room and saw a glorious, statuesque work of art whose dreams were alive! The figure emitted an inner enthusiasm filled with such courage and beauty, it stood out like a beacon diminishing all else. But what drew me to the figure lay far beneath the glorious exterior and far beneath the inner enthusiasm, even the courage. It was the soul's invitation. *Come share my dreams.*

Four-and-one-half months later, John and I were married and living on the Professional Golf Tour. My new husband's friendly personality, all-American good looks, and smooth golf swing emulated every outward appearance of the ideal PGA Professional.

Nevertheless, signs warning *danger ahead* were posted on every road we traveled. When other PGA Professionals were friendly with me, John became *jealous*. Though I did not understand at the time, jealousy meant he was envious and/or resentful that I was getting the attention, and/or he was projecting his sexual desire for other women onto me, fantasizing that I desired other men. Neither did I think of the attention as anything other than friendliness nor did I desire other men. Nevertheless, John's jealousy made him *angry* at me. As a result of his jealous-anger, he began leaving me in motel rooms everyday of the week except Monday.

In the late sixties and early seventies, Mondays were qualifying days. Every Monday, a hundred or so men went to the golf course to try to qualify for a few available spots in that week's PGA tournament. The qualifiers were nicknamed "rabbits" because they hopped from city to city every week in an effort to be one of the chosen few.

Mondays were full of pressure. On Mondays, I followed John for eighteen holes, watching him handle pressure. After a bad shot, he was unable to calm his emotions for the next one or two swings. One or two poor swings made the difference between qualifying and not qualifying. I felt how not qualifying broke John's heart every week. I avoided feeling how he blamed me for not qualifying every week.

Failing to make a reasonable amount of money after three years on tour ended John's sale-ability to attract sponsors. His PGA touring career ended and he *blamed me.*

"Do you still love me?" took me back to those first few years. In looking past all those signs warning *danger ahead,* I held onto my vision of my husband as my dream. His gloriously fluid golf swing was one of the best in the world. John's problem lay in how inner rage controlled his game. My problem lay in how John's game mirrored his life.

- - - What therefore God hath joined together in marriage, let no man put asunder - - -

The icepick incident brought to life what my revelations taught me about signs warning *danger ahead.* The inner rage controlling John's outer life intensified every year of our marriage. His use of *blame* and *jealousy* as an acceptable excuse for *violence against women* grew into an evil force so deadly, my fearless safety net snapped, and I descended into the abyss of human suffering.

The shadow my husband projected into me since the day we became man and wife dropped me into the world of pain he had lived in all his life. The deep-seeded Garden-of-Eden myth that women were to blame for the fall of man was so ingrained in John's consciousness that he was convinced I caused everything that went wrong with his life. The judgment rooted in "all women are bad" grew into such a compulsion for cruelty that eighteen years of words and fists were not enough external violence to alleviate John's internal rage. Faith that God's judgment and punishment pardoned his breaking my spirit. It also excused breaking Cherisse's and Tamara's spirits.

On July 17, 1987, when John told me he loved Fate but had not had sex with her yet, his *plot* set Cherisse, Tamara, and me up for the punishment he thought we deserved. The emotional manipulation of *who shall I choose, who shall I kill* created feelings in me so excruciating that when my bubble burst, the bubble of love Cherisse, Tamara, and I shared also burst. The pain I suffered behind my closed door had caused my daughters to suffer as much pain at the loss of their mother behind that closed door. The fall of their mother as scripted by their father broke the spirit of yet another generation of women. After eighteen years, John won his biblical eye for an eye, not only with the woman he married, but also with the female babies to which his wife gave birth.

The man of the house had succeeded in paying three women back for ruining his life. An eye for an eye three times over, nonetheless, was not enough retribution for a man with holocausts of unresolved psychological and spiritual conflicts, and fate was on the side of conflict. Because Cherisse's, Tamara's, and my asking for a divorce resulted in John's mind being all fucked-up, we unwittingly offered him a window of opportunity for his apocalypse against evil women.

When John stood in the doorway and used an icepick, threats of suicide, and money to kill inner rage, whatever his drinking memory would conveniently select to remember, he became the worst of the world in which he grew up. Using our love to conspire for us to walk through the valley of the shadow of his death made John, in his mind, a hero.

- - - And the voice of the bridegroom and the bride shall be heard no more - - -

Since the night I spotted John across a crowded room, I looked straight past the ugliness that made him feel secure and felt the beauty of the dreams in his soul. From my natural inclination to connect with the soul of another came my fearlessness to place my dreams in one man's hand. The girl in the bubble walked into fire because of that soul to soul connection. The dreams in the soul, nonetheless, were not the measure of the man. Sign posts of the insidious nature in which violence against women crept into and took control of John's mind I unrelentingly ignored. Ignoring sign posts had opened, not only me but also my daughters to the infectious handiwork of the devil.

Now, his hand holding mine merely reminded me, *John isn't dead. His bullet ridden brains aren't all over the floor waiting to be cleaned up. There are no police running around the house deepening the suffering we've already experienced.*

Answering a question about love was necessary for the man who once held all my dreams in the palm of his hand. However, the morning after a conspiracy of hate in the name of greed, the perils of my fearless inclinations and the cost of ignoring danger signs were as visible as the nose on his face. The icepick incident brought to light shadows cast long in advance. His WMD was indoctrinating Cherisse and Tamara not to use their minds to build their dreams. The weapon of words he had been using to kill my self-worth was killing Cherisse's and Tamara's self-worth. To gain control of their minds and souls, John had been using me to teach his daughters how to be victims of violence, which could literally get them killed.

Irrespective of the obvious, that I had to get Cherisse, Tamara, and myself away from John as soon as realistically possible, his question of the moment demanded an answer. Yet, how could I give an honest answer to a plea for love from a man who was dangerously ill? If I denied my truth for the sake of fear, I would again be inviting Satan. *The Philosophy* now calling the shots, I faced the devil with understanding, forgiveness, and compassion.

I moved my body away and distanced myself further with carefully chosen words. "John, I've always loved you. Regardless, I can no longer live with a man who willfully hurts me and my children."

The icepick man pleaded ignorance. "Diana, I've done nothing to hurt you. I don't know why Fate wants me anyway."

His plea for love turned out to be nothing more than an attempt to lift the curtain on yet another dramatic diversion from truth, just another drama that would end in tragedy. The penitence Cherisse, Tamara, and I paid was invisible to John. Dopamine's drug-like effect still at work on his brain, he looked straight through our "one-for-all, all-for-one" philosophy and saw the reflection of Fate's drug-inducing seduction of his "all-for-me" image.

Refusing for one more second to be the target of the accelerating conflict between John's soul and his ego, I responded to his plea for innocent acquittal by insisting, "John, you need to get counseling."

Surprisingly, he replied humbly, "I want to get counseling, but I have to dry out first."

John's humility belied the chaos in his mind. He did not understand why he was so mixed up. From being around alcohol my entire life, I knew with childlike wisdom that John drank alcohol to ease his pain, the pain caused by years of his parents abandoning his feelings. Every feeling of pain he had ever experienced in his conscious mind had been stored in his subconscious mind. His subconscious pain had great power to torture his conscious thoughts. John did not understand the pain that poured from his subconscious into his consciousness, but he did understand that alcohol eased the pain.

As a result, he began using alcohol to ease the pain as one would a drug. In other words, John drank alcohol to medicate the pain. But since alcohol, like drugs, did not stop but merely eased the pain, he drank more and more often until he became *dependent on his medication.* Alcohol-ism, jealousy-ism, work-ism, blame-ism, affair-ism, hate-ism, rage-ism, greed-ism, all were *dependent-isms* that eased the pain. *Isms* were John's hiding place from his abandoned feelings . . . his world that over the years ran further and further away from mine . . . the ugliness I looked past far too long.

All of John's dependent-isms were *symptoms* of abandoned feelings. Abandonment was the *root cause* of all of John's symptoms. To cure the symptoms, the *roots* had to be understood, and the roots were in his subconscious. Counseling would make his subconscious feelings conscious in a way John could understand. Because he would no longer have to hide from the unknowingness that caused his mental chaos, understanding the pain, getting it up and out was the only way stop the symptoms.

The therapeutic process, however, would take tremendous courage. Feeling and understanding years of stored up pain would be brutal, and *isms* saved John from brutal. Moreover, one *ism* saved him from entering the illuminating purgatory of therapy more than all the rest combined. For who should bear the burden of overcoming the passions of the flesh? Certainly not those who are cock-sure they will be saved by the power of the cash cow. Greed-ism was the number one ugliness that made John feel secure. As long as he had enough money to afford dependent-isms, his ego could run from the forgotten boy no matter what the personal cost to the man.

Naturally, drying out was a good idea. Nevertheless, if he quit drinking, as he had several times before, his rageful pain would show up in another symptom. *Treating the effect would never cure the cause*. No matter how many dependent-isms he hid, he could never run away from the lost little boy. The lost boy had to be found and counseled to heal the man's pain. Counseling had to begin right away, rather than in some magic moment of sobriety. Drying out was John's escape from braving the courage to face his feelings head on.

Diverting further conversation about counseling, he changed the subject. "I haven't had sex with Fate in a week. She's nothing in bed."

Empowered, this time with the *knowledge* that the reason for his humble plea for love was infatuation's brutal withdrawal effects, I assisted his confession. "John, I don't know why you can't understand what Fate sees in you. She's after your money, status, and golfing ability. Do you think she loves you?"

He shook his head back and forth in disparaging agreement. I took the headshake as a cue for me to weed our lives of the true incarnation of the evil garden.

For my weed-eater of choice, I counted on my experience. "Hasn't Fate proved she doesn't care what she has to do or who she has to hurt to break your alliance with your family and get your money? She's got nothing to lose. Can't you see how she's cursed our lives?"

Honesty succeeded in prying open Fate's Pandora's box. Contributing to my advantage, her dirty secrets were about to fly out of John's mouth. "Fate has been taking me over. She's *jealous*. She hides around the corner, watches every move I make, and is always telling me how bad you are." He exclaimed enthusiastically, then continued digging up more dirt, "Fate says she's going to sue you!"

"What!" I blurted out, wondering if there would have ever been an icepick incident if it were not for Fate. "I've never met the woman. She's going to sue me for what?" I asked.

"I told her you knew karate. She says you're going to give her a karate chop," he replied, a chuckle ready to break loose.

I laughed for him. "Because of one semester of karate, Fate fantasizes I'm going to hit her? Karate is a defensive, not offensive, exercise. Anyway, the woman's fantasy is a joke. Why didn't you tell her I don't hit people?"

John did not answer. He could not answer. Fate fabricated my physical violence to *project* her materialistic violence onto me. My arch rival had the same greed disease as my husband, their goofy dramas being the method of controlling the minds of others. Although hilariously juvenile, her delusions about how to get my money explained John's inability to answer my question. Terminally underestimating the power of his subconscious to control his conscious behavior, John had an affair with the qualities he both loved and despised in himself. They captivated then decapitated his emotions.

I tried to release my hand from John's. He held on tighter and tighter. I felt the calluses on his hand. The calluses were full of emotions . . . emotions that built a one-acre corral for Telly, Tamara's horse . . . emotions that cemented the front steps Cherisse and I sat on, crying . . . emotions that cemented the rocks behind the pool I designed . . . emotions that stirred cement mixture after cement mixture in his old corroded wheelbarrow.

All at once, I understood why John wanted to hit Cherisse, Tamara, and me with his golf club after we asked for a divorce. I understood why the icepick in the doorway and why the gun in the closet. The reason for "I'm going to kill myself," and the reason for "Do you still love me?" *It was John's shiny new red wheelbarrow!*

September 1, 1987, 7:30 A.M.

From the den where I slept, I heard John pick up the telephone after the second ring, then respond, "I'll talk to her about it later."

He hung up the phone, joined me in the den, and relayed the message in his typical trickster style. "Fate's going in for the final kill. She had Joe at The Big G call me to say she's having trouble getting money from her ex-husband. Fate calling our house is like kicking a dying animal. I can't wait to end it with her. I can't tell her it's completely over *yet* because she takes telephone appointments for me. She can give my golf lessons to other golf pros. Did you see the pile of bills on my desk? I wish we had sold the house so I could tell her where to go!"

Though distancing myself by sleeping in the den, John's mental instability had me convinced not to even mention divorce until his relationship with Fate had ended completely and he demonstrated some mental stability. But Fate giving away his golf lessons? Joe calling our house? Who had John boxed in? Was Fate John's self-fulfilling prophecy, or were these acts of Fate what John agreed upon to get my money?

"Can't tell her it's completely over yet" made me rethink the drama surrounding the icepick incident and John's acting ability. "In for the final kill" was not in reference to John killing himself. "Kicking a dying animal" was the manner in which herds of animals' stalk, wear down, overpower, then eat their prey---alive---

In the woods is perpetual youth. Within these plantations of God, a decorum and sanctity reign, a perennial festival is dressed. . . . In the woods, we return to reason and faith.

– Ralph Waldo Emerson, *Nature*

19

Moonlight And An Oriental Screen

I looked into John's eyes. They danced with the humor of the game he played. At the very moment a shiny new red wheelbarrow tempted me to imagine a bit of the man's soul might break through, the devilish joy in his voice told me the wheelbarrow was just another mask, another disguise for cruelty. A new wheelbarrow would give John time to kick the life out of a dying animal. With Fate as his ally, John thought he was one step away from the "final kill."

He paced to the side of the sofa-bed, sat down next to me, and played some more. "Now I realize I never loved Fate."

He took my hand and placed it in his. He lifted our hands in the air together and gazed into my palm as if it held the keys to the kingdom of heaven on earth. Slowly, he turned my hand over, squeezed his eyes closed, and pressed the back of my hand against his lips. He appeared to be praying.

When John opened his eyes, I looked into them and saw not the eyes of a killer, but of a soul sick with experiencing a lifelong war with the world. The world that taught John how *not to be* had trapped his soul beneath the apocalypse his heart fought with an evil myth. The light of John's soul lay in silent misery, watching him suffocate the one voice who could set it free.

John did not understand why he both loved and hated me. He only knew that an armageddon of inner conflict caused him to need me. He needed the understanding, forgiveness, and compassion my psychological and spiritual awakenings birthed in me. He needed the feelings his cruelty stirred in me. He needed the unconditional love his affair taught me. He needed the keys to paradise found.

My fall came as a defining moment to change my life forever. It seduced in me feelings that turned out not to be of a dark, evil nature, but the light of blissful truth. The primal fire of feelings burned up the shadows of my past, one by one. As each dark shadow yielded to the light of truth, my feelings quickened. As my feelings quickened, I realized the quickening was leading me closer to my truth, to universal truth. The closer I got to the oneness of all truth, the clearer my dreams became.

Whether I connected with my soul through automatic writing, meditation, communing with nature, or spontaneously, my dreams were always the same. They all spoke of love. They all spoke of divine spiritual nature. They all spoke of happily ever after. They all spoke of freedom.

I felt the power of the love still alive in John's heart. His heart prayed for the keys to open the door to the kingdom within. But my momentary glimpse of John's soul told me his heart did not have a chance of defending itself against "you deserved it." Even as he kissed my hand, we both knew "Santa Ana" would win the battle between John's heart and his ego. His ego would heroically rise up to defend itself against the dark, evil nature the world taught John to believe in: the four horsemen he called---Diana---

John stood up and announced, "I'm going to quit drinking."

He turned around and proudly walked toward the master bedroom. Soon after he disappeared from sight, I heard the shower being turned on. John thought that once he told me he never loved Fate and he was going to quit drinking, everything would go back to the way it used to be. The man thought our time together had just begun, when our time together was all but over.

His voice told my heart that the last kill was not about John killing me. The last kill was about me killing John. His soul knew I found the voice I married the man to find. Threatening suicide was his ego's final attempt to scare me into staying. If I stayed, my understanding, forgiveness, and compassion would protect John's ego. *UFC's* unconditional love would save him from walking through the primal fire that would lead him to the feelings in his soul, the feelings he thought would kill him.

John's tragic drama whose origin and commencement sprung from abandoned feelings had to run its course without the *DCT spirit of love.* I lay on the sofa-bed and let my thoughts drift off. The tranquility of the shower water gently soothed memories of dying animals and final kills. Warbling trickles mesmerized and transported my mind far away from my physical and emotional reality. I entered the void. Light ascended. I was going home. . . .

My meditation had me suspended high above a serene river running tranquilly through a forest of tall slender trees. Here and there small fish jumped out of the placid water, charming me with their gaiety.

My vision expanded. Far down the river, trees dwindled into jagged rocks. Tranquil waters evolved into raging rapids. The flight of the fish through the rapids seemed impossible. I began to feel fear for the fish on their journey ahead. I pitied the ones who would not make it to where the river's mouth opened up to the sea. One hearty fish flew high out of the water and sailed through the air.

The fish looked straight into my eyes, saw my fear and my pity, and spoke:

> *Diana, this world is full of wild adventures. See the fish swimming toward life in happy transport. Some of them will make it to where the river opens up to the sea and some will not. If you let yourself visit the spirit of the fish, you will find that whether or not each fish makes it to the sea, every single fish is having the ride of its life!*

My meditation ended, but the wisdom of the fish remained. The flying fish was showing me that nature is the highest example of divine grace that exists on earth because it demonstrates non-judgment, harmony, and pure joy. When I was able to transcend my reality to that degree of happiness, my life would flow like a river of great adventures and I would be home.

September 4, 1987, 11:05 A.M.

I picked up the telephone's receiver after two rings.

"Did Fate call?" John asked nervously.

I answered questioning, "No. Why?"

He hesitated then spoke, "I was worried she might call you again. I'll call you later."

The phone went dead.

After not calling back by early afternoon, my curiosity peaked. I dialed The Big G.

Fate answered angrily. "Hello."

Calmly, I requested, "May I speak with John?"

The phone went dead again. I dialed The Big G a second time. This time a man answered. I repeated my request.

The male voice replied, "Hold on, I'll call him."

John came on the line in his typical straightforward manner. "This is John."

"John," I uttered adamantly. "I called a minute ago. Fate answered. When she realized it was me calling you, she hung up on me!"

He explained, "I told her it's over. I'm coming home."

September 5, 1987, 1:15 A.M.

The thunder of our solid oak front door slamming shut woke me up. Earlier in the day, Tamara and I had picked up the oriental screen I bought several weeks earlier as a present to myself for asking John for a divorce. It stood next to the wall in the master bedroom looking amazingly beautiful. Hypnotized by its magnificence, I fell asleep in our bed. When I heard the front door slam shut my eyes shot open and I sat up. The master bedroom door flew open. John appeared in the doorway.

Heaving his body through the doorway, he looked straight at the oriental screen as if he were prepared to see something he did not like. His face went white. His down-turned lips squeezed tightly together. The beast had returned. . . .

"What is this piece of shit? How much did it cost?" he yelled, the walls shaking with roaring shrieks that made it sound as if this time he was literally going in for the final kill.

Remembering my last bout with John's fist, I answered in

forthright, sober terms. "Eight hundred dollars."

Through my valley of fear I concluded what I started the day Cherisse, Tamara, and I asked for a divorce. "I paid for the screen with my money, but I also withdrew three-thousand dollars from our checking account. Except for my half of our stock, you haven't given me any money since you told me you loved Fate. John, I've been a housewife for over eighteen years. Being a housewife was the nonverbal contract we agreed upon when I went with you on the PGA Tour. How did you expect Cherisse, Tamara, and I were going to live without any money?"

My words fell upon deaf ears; pacing around the room like a lion stalking its prey, the verbal assault escalated. "You spent all that money on this piece of junk! How could you do this to me? I had to stop three times for beer on the way home . . . because of how bad I felt when I told Fate it was over."

John stalked as if preparing to attack; Fate, the archetypal twin of satanic sex and violence, had her ex-lover bellowing wild, fearsome wails from his lowest animalistic nature. "You have no heart. I'm going to live in the wilderness with just a dog."

After flinging every poisonous dart at the screen I had paid for and thrilled over, he returned to personal attacks in pursuit of one thing, to kick the dying animal long enough for the inevitable to happen.

Words were back, this time to stay. Words eased the conflicting messages that caused the chaos in John's mind. Words eased his confusion. Words told me about what the affair taught my husband. His WMD detailed the future he planned for us. My husband planned a future full of what eased his suffering the most, breaking my spirit.

Words succeeded in breaking my spirit that night, but only for a brief moment. Even as I felt the impact of the spontaneous, narcissistic drama, my heart told me John's words were my past, not my future. I picked up my pillow and walked out the door.

On the way out, I mentally resolved, *I will not finish one more of John's wars for him. The wild adventure we shared will not flow into the river of no return with John thinking he had won the Silver Star by heroically defending himself against an oriental screen.*

Too numb to open the sofa bed, I pulled a blanket out of the closet, went into the living room, and slumped onto the sofa. Lying on my back unable to move, unable to sleep, with my eyes wide open, tears running down the sides of my cheeks, I stared at the night sky outside the living room's large picture windows. Moonbeams effused dreamily down through the windows into the room, then scattered. Scattered beams of light displayed such a spellbinding sight that the entrancing effect cut through my tears. Under the spell of the sight I beheld, criticisms of my beautiful oriental screen gave way to a song from my childhood:

When you wish upon a star, makes no difference who you are, anything your heart desires will come to you. If your heart is in your dream, no request is too extreme, when you wish upon a star as dreamers do. Fate is kind. She brings to those who love the sweet fulfillment of their secret longing. Like a bolt out of the blue, fate steps in and sees you through. . . .

Those words were who I was as a child, I remembered. *Jiminey Cricket and the wisdom of a star were at the heart of my determination to live my happily ever after. I walked through the valley of the shadow of my own death because my heart would not give up on my wish to make my dreams come true.*

Then, all at once, I knew! *I know why a simple girl who cherished happily ever after would walk into apocalypse now by placing all her dreams in the palm of the devil's hand! I know why I fought an eighteen-year armageddon resulting in forty-two days of apocalyptic revelations that culminated in my husband's last judgement with me, Cherisse, and Tamara!*

The night I spotted John across a crowded room, it was not John, but the beacon of *light* that called out to me. —*It* came to me. I did not go to *it.*—Quicker than intuition, that in-the-moment feeling drew me to *it* before one thought entered my mind. *It* was the light of John's soul. His soul had jumped out of his body with an invitation to my soul, *Come share my dreams.* Our souls' arrangement was for me to live at a place called Armageddon until an apocalyptic event forced change in me. Fated to live with the devil until I learned the truth about Eve, John's last judgment sealed for me the end of Eden lost.

The fall that resulted from placing all my dreams in the devil's hand lifted the veil of judgments camouflaging truths held secret through the ages. Eve's fall into evil judgments tyrannized the evolution of the mind of multitudes. The original sin that begat humanity stopped the clock on the evolution of the mind of generations, the first task of an outside savior to kill at birth the wisdom inherent in baby's soul mind. Laying waste humanity's true pot of gold, the carnal pleasures in which the garden story was based turned the soul into sexual passion, setting into motion the fear of God's judgment. Replacing the soul with fallen flesh, fear of God was handed down from generation to generation, lighting the crematory fires of the hell and damnation of the origin of humanity.

As the tree of life in the body flows from the mind of God, Eve bore the sacred fruit for which my soul longed. Just as marrying John set into motion my fall into mindless traditions, falling into the truth about Eve set into motion the freeing of my mind from those traditions. If my fall connected me with the wisdom in my soul, then Eve's fall connected me with the wisdom of my mind. John's gift of mindlessness was my past; Eve's gift of knowingness was my future!

I lay on the sofa celebrating in mental jubilation, *All those women I thought were weak, it was not their fault! Born into judgments that they were less-than-human objects to be used by men for carnal pleasures, by forced choice they became ignorant and dependent on the devil, their souls stolen by mindless traditions. I, too, learned mindlessness, but I didn't learn soullessness. All my life people told me I was different. The difference was that Mother and Daddy never told me not to be me. Because they never buried my soul in tradition, the feelings in my soul guided me all my life. Those feelings were my driving force. When I met John, my feelings told me we were meant to be together. My heart felt my soul's passion with delight! Everything that has happened since the night I spotted John across a crowded room, happened for one reason.*

It was 'Write your book,' not John, who granted the wish upon a star I had made as a child!!! The love all my dreams were made of, the truth my soul sought, has been seeking me all my life! When I heard 'Write your book,' I suddenly knew something I could not possibly have known. My wish had returned to me as a voice wielding absolute authority, as though writing a book was my idea. It was my idea. The voice was my human self witnessing my soul self. My happily-ever-after dream to live a simple life that spoke only of love returned to me as a philosophy of love. Writing about a philosophy to give women, as well as men, back the voice of their souls speaks of my dreams coming true!

Charmed by my waking dreams coming true, I examined moonbeams with unrestrained glee. Moonbeams struck a circular crystal globe on the coffee table. Unstructured light reflected off the crystal onto the table and danced fancifully around the room. My mind danced with the unchambered display of nature's perfect grace.

With the help of an oriental screen, moonbeams found me and lifted me above material reality to my truth. *The abyss was simply my naïve way of wandering outside of myself. I got lost in John's sorrows. My lost self had to fall to find its way home to the real live me.*

Retrieving the real Diana brought back pictures, lots of pictures. I pictured myself as a child. I was climbing trees and wandering in the woods. Trees energized my wandering. I felt most at home with trees. Trees were my garden of paradise. Still, I left my treasured trees and wandered into the lives of other children. Other children were critical of me. Criticisms did not feel like my dreams. Criticisms hurt my feelings. So, I withdrew from children and returned to trees.

Trees made my feelings happy. Trees did not notice that I was not perfect. They gave me no reason to pretend to be perfect or not to be me. Trees kept my heart strong. My strong heart allowed my soul feelings to be alive in my mind. My mind lived my dreams when I wandered among trees. My soul learned how to be free from trees.

By the time I became an adult, my soul's way of being had become as natural as trees, as free spirited as trees, as unobstructed by material imperfections as trees. When I wandered in and out of other people's lives, my being was so deeply connected to trees, it came naturally for me not to allow the way others behaved to cause me to feel sad or to withdraw. Nature's perfect grace had taught my heart to trust what came naturally.

One night I wandered into the dense forest of my future husband's life. My way of being made me naturally inclined to look past the behavior and see the heart of the man and the dreams of his soul. What I learned by paying more attention to John's heart and soul had been told to me by the wisdom of the fish.

Trees were the earthly kingdom of heaven that drove my dreams.

Trees, water, grass, earth, air, stars, sun, even fire, they were all my apocalyptic allies, the horsemen who pulled my soul across a crowded room. My soul's natural way of being in my mind was that one-in-a-million quality John fell in love with, the quality he grew to hate because he could not own it. His hate reflected a jealous god whose judgment fell upon those who desired and delighted in mentally experiencing the soul, a jealous god that did not exist. Living with a jealous man whose fear of a non-existant god cursed the natural way my mind expressed my soul. Marrying John was my soul's burnt offering. His judging my soul to be a carnal curse was the sacrificial lamb burned at the stake for a planet that should light up the universe.

My soul's sacrifice was for me to be mindless until the time was right to use my mind. *Write your book* designated the time had come to seek, find, and climb the ladder of truth. My purpose was to understand the collective carnal shadow and the fear of a god that suppressed the wisdom in the soul, killing humanity's only protection from suffering. If I learned to understand John, I would understand millions who lived "boxed in" the chaos of lost souls. If I *had* learned to use my mind before I met John, I would never have placed all my dreams in the palm of the devil's hand. Nor would I have grown to understand the wisdom of the fish.

Who else could have shown me the predicament of human suffering with more enthusiasm, more excitement, more thrills? Every time John's soul tried to break through his warlike conditioning, I was there. Every time his breakthrough failed and his heart broke, I was there. Every time his down-turned lips said a new battle had begun, I was there. My wild ride down the raging rapids and jagged rocks of the war going on inside John had truly been a great adventure. Living an eighteen-year armageddon that resulted in forty-two days of apocalyptic revelations, culminating in my husband's last judgement, gave me the wisdom to protect the philosopher's stone and the knowledge of who I had to seek to give me the courage to make my dreams come true!

Moonbeams and an oriental screen gave me the gift of *remembering* the girl John met. Her kinship with trees showed her how to love a soul no matter how sad the heart or troubled the mind. Trees had always been the home inside the girl. The moon drifted out of sight, but the enormity of the truth with which I lived my life remained.

As the new day arose behind the rolling hills outside the picture windows, I closed my eyes and let my consciousness merge as I had done so naturally as a child, with the happy nature inside myself. I opened my eyes. On the hilly horizon, there appeared trees. In those trees I saw my life, my death, and my life reborn.

Then, as if another cool breeze blew through my thoughts, I heard my husband crying. The heart of the lost little boy in the next room flowed through me.

The boy's heart asked longingly, *My suffering has taught you so much. Please come and fix my broken wing so my dreams can fly like yours.*

Knowing told me I would go into our bedroom. Knowing told me I would not stay. John would conveniently forget screaming at me. I would try to help him fly on his own. Knowing he could only fix his broken wing from one voice, the voice within himself, I would fail. Someday his heart would be healed, and the tremendous light I saw in his soul would arise. He would courageously take off the mask and begin his journey home to his dreams. When he went home, my soul would be there to greet his soul.

September 5, 1987, just after dawn

The sun rose above the horizon behind our picture windows in the living room. Streams of morning sunlight abounded through soft, billowy clouds onto the countryside below.

I stared at the immense bounty before my eyes and remembered, *A man is lying not far from an oriental screen waiting just for me.*

As usual, John slept like a baby. I lay down beside him and stroked his head. I felt no fear, no pity, no regret. I felt only compassionate love.

The broken heart of the lost little boy in John waited to be treasured for who he was so his soul could be free. His closed eyes squeezed together and took my hand. Each of his fingers interlocked with each of mine. A grateful smile came over his face.

John opened his eyes and released his disappointment. "Fate just wanted to use me to help her with her golf career. She wants to go on the Ladies' Professional Golf Tour."

"Is she good enough?" I asked.

"I'm not sure if she has the ability. She'd have to spend a lot of time practicing and get a lot stronger. She doesn't have much of a body. Not like yours."

September 7, 1987, early A.M.

My eyes popped open in the middle of a vivid dream. In my dream, a hot air balloon floated in the sky with a basket hanging beneath it. The balloon burst, and the basket fell quickly to the ground. In the fallen basket stood John. He was looking down at his palm. He had the saddest look on his face. I could not stop myself from crying.

I thought and thought about my dream. *It is as if a small treasured object was lying dead in John's palm. What is that treasured object? What does John treasure more than anything else in the world?*

By using Fate as a tool to break my spirit, John had won our eighteen-year war. In the process, he lost what I had given him the night we met. He lost the girl who allowed him to hold all her dreams in the palm of his hand.

Again, John's palm appeared in my vision. I looked carefully at his palm for some object. His palm was empty. John's greatest treasure had flown away. She had been lifted into the divine flight he helped her win. The prize was hers, not his. Diana's dreams flew away to return to her beloved children, the spirit of the fish, her treasured trees, and *Write your book.*

He who arms himself with love wins every fortune.

– Michelangelo

20

Summer Vacation Ends

Since they were born, Cherisse and Tamara were my best friends. They, as no other, shared my inner life and the way my inner life painted the portrait of my outer life. Any doubt the three of us were meant to be together never entered my mind. Though as a child I knew beyond a shadow of a doubt I wanted two children, not until after Cherisse and Tamara were born did I begin to feel the fate we would share, a fate destined to set us apart from collective negativity, that pool of fear into which their father's new world order added volumes.

As we floated around in our protective love bubble, the world around us sped toward the twenty-first century, a century in which this new world order was misconstrued to be nuclear rather than vernacular. Weapons of mass destruction were mistaken to be WMDs that would kill the body rather than words that would kill the soul. The twenty-first century was looking to be an underworld of nuclear proliferation rooted in the all-for-me consciousness indefensible to the *DCT* one-for-all, all-for-one consciousness.

Then, seemingly, from out of nowhere, the mother who had been there from the moment they were born to meet her children's every need with a happy heart and iron will disappeared. Since my capture by their father's unilateral seizure, most of the time Cherisse and Tamara spent with their mother, I was either stricken with fear and panic or filled with miraculous revelations and determinations.

Shut in my room, Cherisse and Tamara thought I was taking a nap, which I did regularly. I always told them not to disturb me when I napped, so they were scared to knock on my door and wake me up. As time passed and they realized I was not opening my door, confused and distraught, they too, became paralyzed with fear and panic.

Cherisse would later recall, "The minutes felt like hours. I knew something was terribly wrong. I sat by your door with my ear to it, listening in anguish of what to do . . . feeling helpless to do anything. Afraid for myself, for what I would see, I was in a constant state of fear and panic. With no prior experience, I couldn't believe this was my life. I didn't want to believe it. My stomach and heart ached with so much pain. I was more afraid to open the door than to stay waiting outside."

When finally I opened my door, called out their names, and recounted my revelations in detail, Cherisse and Tamara had nearly identical reactions, Tamara remembering, "It all made perfect sense. It was wonderful, finding and understanding the truth of why we are here. I understood the psychology of everything. I didn't have any anger at Dad . . . only in how he treated you. I thought the best thing to do was for him to leave . . . though instinctively I saw Dad for who he was . . . very lost and not willing to grow and change. I wanted you to be happy no matter what . . . even if that included Dad. I believed in miracles."

Cherisse recollected, "Your revelations and automatic writings 'felt right' . . . more real than anything existing in life. They were not a surprise to me at all. They gave me peace in my heart and helped me understand what was happening in our family. Though I knew there was a higher reason for these events, I also knew Dad was lost and would not change. I wanted him to leave. "

When Cherisse's and Tamara's prophecy about their father not changing came true, even worse, he was using his affair to control my every emotion, they were horrified. Tamara thought my tortured feelings were the scariest place anyone could go. Being older and more familiar with his abandonment than Tamara, Cherisse was angry at her father, calling his actions despicable. Because every single day of their lives Cherisse, Tamara, and I shared a bubble of love, when my bubble burst, they felt my fallen feelings as their own.

Their father had caused Cherisse and Tamara to lose their mother, the mother who had been the strongest person they had ever known. "Mom" was their leader, their life, and they were waiting for their life to come back, scared to death it was not coming back. For a long time it did not come back. It got worse, much worse. Mom hit bottom. On D-Day when I told Cherisse and Tamara I wanted to die, they too wanted to die.

Then, beneath a star-filled night sky, my premonition fated to foretell our destiny, forever would our little triangle of love be illuminated. Nature connected with me, mind, body, and soul. Nature told me my children wanted Mom back so they could live again. I rushed to them, and in the tunnel birthed by our loss of our innocence, the agony of what we lost proclaimed the ecstasy of what we gained. Through our tears light marched forth. Spiritually elevated by our experience in the valley of the shadow of my death, multitudes of angels were singing, *One love born of three souls is our light at the end of the tunnel.*

Light did shine to show us the way. *It* came as the voice of inspiration saying, *Write your book!* When I told Cherisse and Tamara about that prophetic voice, for them the agony and ecstasy we were experiencing fell into place. *Write your book* solved the mystery of why our bubble burst. Telling our story gave our lives a new direction, a clear purpose. Just like I felt when I was a child, Cherisse and Tamara felt different than other children. Being different explained the reason for writing. Writing explained the reason for being different.

We were different because when everyone else's bubbles blew away, ours remained floating above the condition of human suffering. Because for so long we had experienced life without suffering, we knew bubbles were possible. At first, when our bubble burst and fell to the ground and we felt the feelings of pain others suffered, we did not understand. Mom's writing a book about our bubble and our fall gave our suffering meaning. Three small words, *Write your book*, had sealed our destiny. Confusion metamorphosed into clarity. It was all worth it!

More than the uncertainly of hope, we had the certainty of experience. Understanding the bigger, harder, grander meaning of life, our purpose was to give what we were learning to the world. There was a passageway between the mind and the soul. Mom had found *it,* and *it* had healed her. Before her bubble burst she lived *it* without knowing it. Being of like mind, so did Cherisse and Tamara. Now, Mom had found a way for everyone to have *it.*

If the three of us as a team, the *DCT spirit team,* could teach enough people how to heal their minds with understanding, forgiveness, and compassion, and bridge the gap in their hearts by connecting their minds and souls in oneness, then like the ripple effect, the loving oneness of the *living soul* could be expanded exponentially. Given time, original sin (fear) would be replaced by original soul (love), so more love would flow into the subconscious mind from the conscious mind than fear. If enough love radiated into the collective consciousness, we would be helping to spiritualize life on earth. Someday the planet could be brought to a state of love rather than conflict. *It* was an absolute certainty. *The Philosophy* of *UFC+US* was the *DCT spirit team's* mission in life!

True, Cherisse and Tamara experienced the agony and ecstasy on their summer vacation 1987. But what they would remember would be a miracle. Not the miracle of their father changing, for he did not change. Far grander, the miracle of learning the meaning of life and purpose of their lives. Meanwhile, the real-world jungles of their father's WMDs awaited. Directly outside our door awaited an ordered world we had only just begun to experience. Only when Cherisse, Tamara, and I could paint a portrait of the bigger picture as true to life as our little picture would *Write your book* have enough knowledge of good and evil to build bridges. Only when *The Philosophy* of the *DCT bubble of love* could help build a rainbow bridge between the mind and soul of a critical mass would the summer of 1987 be a miracle.

September 8, 1987, 7:15 A.M.

A monumental event was about to take place, and I was determined to play my part. It was the first day of high school for Tamara and the first day of Cherisse's junior year. My daughters were about to tackle the high school experience together, and they were sure to be headed for a wild ride. Sending them on their way with a happy heart was my number one priority, my way of showing them their Mom was back in their lives to stay.

Voices in the kitchen told me Cherisse and Tamara were dressed and ready for school. John did not come home the previous night. The undue discomfort of the sofa-bed had me grateful to be sleeping in my bed. Eager to see Cherisse and Tamara in the new school clothes we had paid such a heavy price to buy, I jumped out of bed, threw on my bathrobe, and scurried to the kitchen. When I got there, what I saw was striking!

Two little women who stood casually eating cereal emitted a combination of intelligent posture and youthful glow that surpassed my wildest imagination.

"You both look beautiful!" I exclaimed, then hugged and kissed each daughter good morning.

Elated that both Cherisse and Tamara emanated such glowing health, I showered my exhilaration on Tamara. "Are you excited about your first day of high school?"

"Kind of," she replied with an anxious smile.

Cherisse prodded her sister. "At least you don't have to take the bus like I did my freshman year."

In spite of the fact my children were on their way to a place where they were not going to be talking about summer vacation like their friends, rewriting the summer of 1987 would not be necessary. The outer beauty I saw standing before me diminished in the light of the inner beauty I felt. Because of summer 1987, two sweet girls blossomed into captivating women. The wisdom Cherisse and Tamara gained in one unforgettable summer produced an intelligent, youthful radiance I found striking.

Basking in their glow, I walked with two astonishing individuals out the front door. The countryside looked almost as breathtaking as the humanity gifting my morning. Under a big blue sky, sunlit greens and browns of the hills and valleys enveloped us. Dew drops sprayed over tall leafy trees along both sides of the driveway twinkled like a billion glittering stars. The groundcover below seemed to glide like a colorful magic carpet. Telly whinnied as he peeked over his pasture fence, delighted in the knowledge breakfast was forthcoming. Mickey and Suki danced four-footed prances, celebrating the totality of the occasion.

Cherisse's car sat on the driveway, waiting to carry her and her sister to an environment where creating interpersonal bonds with peers would be more important than anything else in the world. Greater first-hand pressure would be placed on them to conform to social norms and female gender roles than ever before or ever again. To maintain the morality, integrity, and individuality that defined the glowing health I saw standing in the kitchen that morning, their identities were required to be written in stone.

For Cherisse and Tamara, one life-altering challenge was being followed by a second life-altering challenge. Well aware of the magnitude of the razor's edge upon which each daughter stood poised, I felt my emotions well up inside of me. With the crystal-clear understanding that they were walking into a wilderness of conformist peer pressure that would put their selfhoods at risk, tears filled my eyes. I could do nothing more to save my grown-up babies from a reality overwrought with raging rivers and jagged rocks than hug and kiss them goodbye, wish them good luck, stand as I had always stood before the summer of 1987 blew away our bubble, and watch them drive away.

Just before Cherisse's midget car putt-putted a left turn at the bottom of the long, bumpy driveway and vanished behind the tree-lined street, Cherisse and Tamara turned their heads backwards and looked at me. They both knew from a lifetime of experience that their mother would be standing there, smiling, and waving goodbye.

I heard several honks as Cherisse and Tamara waved and smiled the biggest smiles. Mickey chased the putt-putting noise around the corner, barking loud and clear and then turned around and pranced back up the driveway where Suki greeted him.

My heart beamed at the vision of my children's smiling faces and my soul spoke to me. *Cherisse's and Tamara's identities are written in stone, a stone built from seeds of love sown long before castles crumbled into grains of sand. Smiling faces tell the tale of their lives. The deep-rooted selfhood that created two valiant troopers is impossible to destroy. The history they shared with their mother before summer 1987 was built on something richer than castles, more powerful than teflon fathers, mightier than peer pressure. Their identities were built upon a lifetime of their mother . . . always being there for them . . . with pure love.*

September 15, 1987, 3:30 P.M.

It was only Tamara's second week of high school and her fourteenth birthday was speeding into the present. Too soon after the school year started for her to have made enough close friends to plan a party, I drove to school so that the minute school let out she would see me waiting.

Typically, Tamara spotted me before I spotted her. By the time she caught my eye, she was walking straight toward the car, her feet landing firmly on the ground. The closer she came to the car, the more I noticed the seriousness underlying her high-spirited demeanor. With a pile of books in one hand, Tamara opened the car door with the other hand then wedged into the front seat. Suddenly grim-faced, she set the stack of books on the floor and fastened her seatbelt.

The prophecy the summer of 1987 foreshadowed had come to pass. Both Tamara and Cherisse were becoming familiar with high school as backpacks full of real-world jungles. Before summer vacation blew away our safe little world, Mom being there with pure love had protected their growing minds and tender hearts from a civilization falling into material values. Before they were above it. Now they were in it. And being in it hurt.

A masterful dichotomy, Tamara and Cherisse falling into enlightenment translated into Tamara not relating to new friends any more than Cherisse related to established friends. Not that their friends were not "nice girls"; their friends were absolutely nice girls, nice accounting for the dichotomy. Fallen prey to commercialized materialism, nice girls were unaware that the sameness of their states of mind was accelerating the double standard in the direction of the new century. Buying into the movies, television, magazines, and music that marketed girls to compete for boys by comparing themselves to super-models and mass-media barbie-dolls, no girl felt secure in her own body.

Commercialized to think the impossible, that freedom from self-image insecurities could be purchased, girl-glitter masked the devastation caused by the variety of womanly shapes that came with puberty. Obsessions with weight, clothes, makeup, and hair developed from the hopelessness of looking like the commercialized ideal body: a very tall prepubescent girl with breasts. The specter of commercialism was everywhere. Advertisements fed addictions to purchasing the products that saturated the mass market.

Shopping compulsions snowballed. Obsessions and compulsions *inhibited* rather than freed the thinking *mind*, feeding into the goliath of superficiality. Superficial values engendered an epidemic of petty gossip. Everybody looking how every body was advertised to look consumed girl-talk. Gossip took the form of judgments consistent with media-madness. Judgmental words were the catharsis that eased the pain of self-image insecurity. Words were nice girls' WMD aimed toward other nice girls.

Verbal war games made trivialities monstrosities that threatened, *If you don't fall into line, this will happen to you again and again and again.*

Confirming *insecurity* as a *mind-altering substance*, no torso escaped gossip's tragic drama. Seized preemptively into sameness by conformist peer pressure, no girl was left behind. No girl was safe from the fear of body differences. No girl escaped the loss of homeland security, the security of feeling comfortable with her own body in her own bed. All girls sunk into a manic-depressive, media-crazed commercialized hell that was turning them into petty thieves. They stole the dreams in their soul by superimposing girl-glitter over their minds. The more they tried to mask the underlying pain, the more they *forgot how to think for themselves.* The result of being scared into suffocating their dreams was a mind-body-soul pathology . . . a crisis of identity . . . a psychological and spiritual crisis.

The ideal body that serviced the rape of the inspiration born of a free mind also served to widen the gender gap. Selling a downward spiral of morality, media-mania's two-fold path magnified the differences in how boys and girls used their minds to think. Boys were marketed to concentrate on having sex with girls and getting rich. Girls were marketed to compete with each other for boys by the way they looked. While boys were learning to love their penises, girls were learning to hate their bodies. This positive/negative gender gap instigated and accelerated sexual war games.

The battle between the sexes upped the anti on tragic drama. The primal need that could not be suppressed but was forced to be suppressed by girls' minds, sex sold tickets to the show. Everyone bought into sex shows. But the voice of girlhood was forced into silence by peer law that demanded a double standard. Silence resulted in vagina dismemberment by denunciation. Denunciation of the vagina, the voiceless killer of dreams inspired by mind-body-soul freedom, vaginas were everywhere beaten up by the gender-gap-whipping-boy. Every girl was pressured into controlling what she could not control. Hear no evil, see no evil, and speak no evil would become the institutionalized beast, the cave in which the silent majority of the next generation of voting women would inhabit. Commercialism raising the bar, peer pressure the controlling force, superficiality was spinning the future women of America out of control in the direction of a new millennium.

Mortified by high school as a civilization standing on the precipice of self-destruction, Cherisse and Tamara were bearing witness to the same game-playing in high school they found ridiculous in their father. Petty dramas that resulted from sameness were the real-world jungle my daughters were experiencing. Far more introspective than their classmates, Cherisse's and Tamara's deep-rooted selfhood made them different but in a different way than they were before summer vacation.

No, enlightenment did not stop the pain of living among the unenlightened. Very unlike the enlightenment envisioned by the unenlightened, the wisdom gained from one summer served to enhance the dark side of truth. No less trapped by being different, than their friends were trapped by being the same, Cherisse and Tamara had no escape from the loneliness of not finding one friend to talk with on a deeper level. Written, printed, and published on Tamara's grim face was the morality, integrity, and individuality upon which she and her sister stood . . . alone.

"Let's go home and celebrate your birthday!" I suggested to Tamara tenderly, trying to cheer her up.

Though Tamara was disappointed by school, the instant we entered the family room and saw the birthday goodies I had meticulously arranged on the table, her face lit up . . . but only for a few minutes. A table full of presents Cherisse and I watched her open did little to diminish Tamara's discontent, the look on Cherisse's face showing how much she related to her sister's predicament.

When our tiny celebration concluded, I picked up the ice cream, which turned out to be a flavor Tamara did not like, and carried it into the kitchen; as I walked toward the freezer, Tamara advised me, "Don't worry; the ice cream will not go to waste."

In Tamara's no-nonsense way of tackling life, she had told me an important lesson she had learned on her summer vacation. Tamara's birthday displayed for Cherisse and me that not being able to rise above the human condition she had fallen into caused her heart to ache. Despite heartache, every inch of Tamara's demeanor spoke of how she planned to conquer the aloneness of being different. What she suffered would "not go to waste."

After Tamara arranged her presents the way she preferred, the three of us were settling on the sofa preparing to watch one of Tamara's favorite movies when the telephone rang. I stood up, walked over, and picked up the receiver. John's voice rang out.

I visualized his barroom swagger as I heard him say, "I can't make it home tonight. I'm going to stay in a motel."

I did not ask John if he knew or cared how Tamara felt about her father not being home on her birthday. Nor did I question if he even remembered it was his daughter's birthday.

After listening to what he had to say, I signed off with, "Thanks for calling," hung up the phone, turned to Tamara, and relayed her father's message. "Daddy's not going to make it home tonight."

Tamara and Cherisse gave out a sigh of relief, in unity exclaiming, "Good."

It was unanimous. We were all happy.

September 24, 1987, 12:30 A.M.

Discovering Fate wanted him for his money deepened John's depression. "Drying out" lasted a few short days, followed by drinking binges. Due to the discomfort of the sofa-bed, and John coming home randomly, I slept in the master bedroom whenever possible.

In the middle of the night, John waltzed into the master bedroom and woke me up as if I should be delighted about his ensuing news. "My ex-wife came to see me today. She's divorcing her fifth husband. Why do you think she wanted to see me?"

He paused, biting-at-the-bit for a reply I did not intend to give.

"I was her best husband and she knows it!" he bragged, saluting new heights of egotism.

If John was her best husband, I can't imagine what her worst husband could have been like, I silently counseled myself, witnessing by forced choice my husband's orgy of personal profit at my expense.

"Did she say you were the best?" I asked with a touch of sarcasm.

"There are hundreds of girls at work who want me," he boasted, relentlessly setting the bar for every red-neck wannabe, "hundreds" being the cue for me to collect my things and sleep in the den.

September 24, 1987, 6:30 A.M.

From the den, I heard tapping on the master bedroom door.

"Come in," John answered.

"Dad, the backyard is flooded," Cherisse warned her father in barely audible tones.

"What did you do?" he shouted out his rush to judgment.

I sat up and leaped off the sofa-bed in time to see John zipping up his cement-encrusted jeans. He stomped outside, his down-turned lips frozen shut. Cherisse and I scurried behind, keeping a safe distance.

Hopping in and out of ankle-deep water, John catastrophized, "There used to be a lake here. It's coming up! Now we'll never be able to sell our house. Diana, you're going to lose everything!"

Considering the enormous amount of grading and soil compaction done on the lot, a rising underground lake seemed inconceivable. Since the major share of our money had been spent buying the property and building the house, however, if the land did vanish under a rising lake, nearly every penny we had in the world would be lost. When I was almost convinced that our house was sinking into never-never land, John spotted a neighbor's sprinkler system draining water down onto our yard.

Exonerated from her father's blame, Cherisse gave a knowing nod and went into the house to finish getting ready for school.

I remained, patiently observing the epilogue of the underground rising lake drama. Once more, John had succeeded in using others to perpetuate awe-inspiring illusions about himself. Dancing his ritual victory dance, while chanting his ritual war chant, he celebrated the delusion that he had conquered impending doom. The spectacle that once made me fly, I now perceived as empty pageantry, as mountainous insecurity, and as lacking humor.

The flimflam man concluded his no-fear backyard con-game while I mused, *I've got to find a way to get myself and my children out of this man's war.*

September 24, 1987, 5:30 P.M.

While sitting on the front porch chatting, Cherisse, Tamara, and I watched John drive his little yellow truck up the driveway and park it at the bottom of the steps directly below us.

He eased out, looked dagger-eyed at our cozy threesome, and resumed the morning's charade. "Why didn't you girls wash the car? Diana, I told you to make them wash the car and pick weeds. Why aren't they picking weeds?"

Unrelenting in his refusal to break hateful chains of ignorance, judgment, and cruelty and use love to build bridges between himself and his daughters, John had passed the crossroads with them. Blowing up all bridges of love with hate had caused in John an emotional deficiency disease. Cherisse, Tamara, and I knew the sick could be healed, but the sick had to want healing, desire healing, delight in the possibility of partaking from the fruits of healing. The burden of unhealed sorrows wore heavy on John's heart. His mind lay buried beneath his personal rubble of washed-out rainbow bridges.

Brown bag in hand, the unbending warrior marched up the steps, passed by us staunch-lipped, and proceeded into the house. I searched Cherisse's and Tamara's eyes for emotion.

Enraged by what I saw, I stood up and chased John into the house demanding to be heard before one gulp of beer was downed. "John, did you notice how shocked and frightened Cherisse and Tamara looked after you yelled at them? First of all, you didn't ask me to tell them to wash the car or pick weeds. Secondly, picking two acres of weeds in a guarded-gate community is unconscionable! And third, Cherisse and Tamara are already overwhelmed by everything expected of them at school. This is Tamara's freshmen year in high school, remember? What are you trying to do to them?"

Strong, assertive language prevailed in getting a pathetic response.

"Diana, I'm not strong like you. I can't stop drinking. I'm going to die."

The squandered mountain of strength staring back at me had spewed the sum total of everything I no longer wanted in a man. John testing my courage by intimidating my children and then blaming it on personal weakness, there is no greater tragedy than a man who is his own worst enemy.

Slogging in the black tide of mud, the man wanted me to help him feel weak, so I did. "John, I want you to move out of the house before New Year's Eve."

Out of the brown bag flew a beer. The celebration had begun! The pop-top popped and congratulations for a war well fought were in order.

"Everyone has deserted me," claimed the hero.

September 25, 1987, 7:30 P.M.

Tamara and I had just arrived at the stadium where the first football game of the season would soon begin. Cherisse had left the house earlier to meet friends. Tamara slid out of the car and scoured the area for someone she knew. She spotted a group of giggling girls, smiled a brave smile, and then quickly waved me a cheerful goodbye. As the flashing headlights of cars scrambling for parking places dashed by, I watched Tamara stride, posture perfect into the distance, grateful she had found friends with whom to have some fun.

As images from my high school days flashed through my thoughts, the scene before me permeated good vibrations. The night air smelled like the football field, popcorn, hot dogs, and the breath of the people. Stadium lights, high in the sky, aimed down onto the field, told a tale about the action and the glory of football players, coaches, cheerleaders, students, teachers, and small town families.

Cozy togetherness infused the night air. Banners waved, cheerleaders cheered, and fans were yelling for the junior varsity game being played in preparation for the "big" varsity game. I felt so much of an affinity with the scene that I wanted to dash out of the car and run straight into the middle of the action. Reverence cried out for me to play my part in the consummate pomp and circumstance. More than any amount of glory, more than life itself, I wanted to stay and support

Cherisse and Tamara, be there with a strong heart and iron will to share the heaven and the hell of all their new experiences.

A horn honked for me to move my car out of the way. I eased down the pedal clearing the space and then turned the steering wheel out of the parking lot toward home. From the garage where I parked the car, I opened the door to the house. Down the long dark hall, a dim light emanating from the television in the master bedroom meant one thing. John was home.

I tackled the hall and then the bedroom entrance. The flickering grays the television screen gave off contrasted sharply with the bright lights of the football stadium. John had called me from work several times during the week to tell me how sick he felt.

Neither sympathetic nor surprised, I surmised, *Working all day and binging all night, how could he not feel sick?*

Wearing boxer shorts and drinking a beer, he now sat in bed pleased as punch. My entrance did not draw his eyes away from the television screen. The series *Dallas* claimed his full attention.

The voice of the character J.R. bragged, "Daddy always said I had the devil in me. I love it. I'm never going to change."

John sat straight up with invigorated zeal, chugged down more beer, and proclaimed, "I'm just like J.R., big, tough and strong. I'm not going to change. Why should I?"

Why indeed should he not give up being ruled by the devil, I reckoned. Like JR he is. Like JR he will stay, maintaining his world according to rich men's materialistic model with no imagination that his model kills his very reason for living.

Responsible for John's escalating manic-depressive syndrom was the greed, pride, lust, and violence of the constant bombardment by the mass media on the culture that had seized control of his mind. Media-mania, controlled by the political dream-team of corporate imperialism, religious fanaticism, and profiteering governments, the socialization of the verbal war games that afflicted their father's selfhood mirrored not only the plight of Cherisse's and Tamara's peers but also the widespread desperation consistent with WMD mind-body-soul politics.

The media-madness that had learned how to program the mind at earlier and earlier ages was liable for civilization's growing addiction to world wars, religious wars, sex wars, and domestic wars. This violence against individual selfhood pathologized inspiration. Inspiration the corpse of war, it was as if from *spirit we come, to spirit we shall return* had been lost in translation. Stepping to the tune of history, the seeds of WWII had been sewn at the end of WWI with the Treaty of Versalles, and the seeds of all future wars had been sewn at the end of WWII with Hiroshima and Nagasaki. These seeds reflected the thoughts and attitudes of a civilization frightened into the false belief that freedom could be purchased by winning a war. Beastly traditions revealed, as one war ended, the next war had already been signed, sealed, and delivered. A study of history shows us peace treaties were war pacts that insured the high and mighty they would stay high and mighty.

Ignoring all signs that his devilish belief system mimicked a civilization standing at a crossroads between destruction or enlightenment, John would put a gun to his head rather than lose the devil's ransom. Unbeknownst to John, his pledge to use sex and money to wage war with his wife and children profited only a few very rich men, and indeed, made him very poor.

I collected my nightgown, said goodnight, and left John to get his kicks from JR. As I prepared the sofa-bed, laid down, and looked out the window, my thoughts returned to Cherisse and Tamara. The same star-filled September night sky my children thrilled beneath just a few miles away twinkled outside the window across from where I lay.

By way of twinkling stars, I felt the fun Cherisse and Tamara were having. I felt the thrills and the glory of high school football games, flood lights, cheerleaders, and the loving togetherness of small town people. I felt it all as if I were there.

Next time, I will be there. I told the stars. *I will experience the ecstasy and the agony of life lived to the fullest. I will live it and love it, all of it.*

Yes! Summer vacation had ended.

Once you were ashamed of your sins. Now you do not show
any shame at all! You have exhibited your ugliness to the
world and your stench has risen to the heavens.

– Girolamo Savonarola

21

Playing Hardball

September 26, 1987, 4:55 A.M.

While leaving for work, John stopped by the den, stood in the doorway, and said warmly, "I love you."

I looked into his eyes. They were looking into my eyes, waiting. I said nothing, denying him the safety of the love I had given him for eighteen years. He turned and walked down our long hall toward the garage.

Listening to footsteps walking away from the tremendous love I felt but could never again express caused my thoughts to return to Cherisse and Tamara. *My daughters lost their mother because she got lost in their father's kill-or-be-killed world. I will let my husband walk back into his illusions of a noble wilderness. If he stays, he will teach Cherisse and Tamara the culture of materialism that unforgivingly teaches his soul not to be. I will not allow their souls to be captured and imprisoned by animalistic standards. I survived the abyss of my fall into fear by discovering my soul is my everlasting reality. Learning to live that truth in my ever-changing material reality gave me back my life. The spiritual nature that illuminates my human nature returned me to my children and made our three souls one. As the DCT spirit team, we will tread the abysmal tunnel of the winner-take-all world before us. In unity we will journey the shadow of a mass consciousness crucified by fear. The oneness of our love will overcome and transcend the overwhelming odds ahead, and our souls' nature will survive to shine the light at the end of the tunnel upon our new world order: the We Speak of Love ideal of our UFC + US philosophy. Someday we will once again float around in our happily-ever-after bubble. But when that time comes, we will know we are home.*

The curtain was falling on the adventure John and I lived as man and wife. I loved it falling. The curtain was rising on the adventure of team Diana, Cherisse, and Tamara. I loved it rising. Psychological and spiritual transformation had enlightened our consciousness about a philosophy where the goals were the same for all people. Passion to live and write about what our *new standard of enlightenment* was teaching us was expanding my driving force of love.

After hearing the sound of John's truck drive away, I grabbed my pillow, pitter-pattered into the master bedroom, and jumped in bed, my wonderful comfortable king-sized bed! My mirthful mood, intuition-a-calling, propelled me right back out of bed and into the master bathroom.

The morning sun set the room ablaze. Intense perpendicular rays darted through the four large tinted windows, streaked inside our glass-encircled double-shower, then bounced off the clear blue ceramic tiles. The scene was mystical, too irresistible for me not to take advantage. I stepped into and fused with the warmth of the rays. Fusion with the golden rays elated me. Effortlessly, my emotions became one with the perfection encapsulating me.

Outside the windows, a large bird of paradise swayed in a soft early morning breeze. The sound of the huge leaves brushing against the windows added music to mystical elation. Energy radiated out of nature's harmonious diversity, filling my cup to overflowing. The rapture in and around my body lifted me to heaven, solving the mystery of nature. Nature, the living expression of the everlasting light of the creator, was the universe's secret garden of indescribable grace that was no secret at all.

Standing in and connecting with the reverent aura of the interdependent evolving process of nature transported my consciousness into the void, that higher plane of energy vibration that had become wonderfully familiar. Every cell in my body meditated with nature's perfect harmony. My mind operated on two levels of consciousness simultaneously. Soaring with the universal flow of energy reaffirmed the unchangeability of ancient wisdom: the higher the level of spiritual awareness, the higher the level of human happiness.

In that moment of bliss, I felt a presence. An energy force materialized into the essence of a spiritual figure. Radiating a brilliant white unearthly light, the figure did not walk. It floated above ground toward me, stopping at my right shoulder, slightly behind me. The presence felt like the same essence that came to me once before when I was on my knees praying to God to stop the pain. This time *it* had more form. Seen from my mind more than my eyes, the light-being lifted its left arm and laid its hand softly on my right shoulder. Out of the hand poured power, kindness, and intelligence. Though the form seemed masculine, the angelic outpouring felt both masculine and feminine. Like the ebb and flow of the tide, beams radiating love filled every hole in the circle of my life.

I stood not moving, feeling that the higher plane upon which the figure stood was only a frequency lighter than mine, but immortal, perhaps the way my soul would appear when I shed the mortal coil of my human body. My fusion with the sun's golden rays combined with the partaking of the birds of paradise had raised my energy vibration enough to bridge the frequency gap for me to see this figure of light. We were side by side in my universe and a higher universe simultaneously, parallel universes overlapping and interpenetrating.

This feeling had to be similar to how it felt to experience the light at the end of the tunnel. I had taken a giant step in the progressive awakening of my mind into total awareness of my soul, another quantum leap in my initiatory journey. Pieces to the puzzle had turned into cycles of enlightenment. As the essence and I stood sharing earth's garden, telepathically confirming my silent revelations about energy vibrations, the pure goodness of being spoke:

> *My child, love humankind.*
> *Teach them to love one another.*

Humbled by the confidence placed in me, exalted by the demands put upon me, *words* left me awe-inspired. The ocean of nature's infinite light had lifted my already mirthful mood into rapture. Rapture connected me with a being from a higher, more expansive universe. The boundless beingness protectively guiding the upward spiral of my spiritual development had clarified that *love* was the *nature of my search* in my quest to write only truth. Soundless words made me feel my love for, and contribution to, humankind was the greatest gift I could ever receive. The gifts of power and wisdom were to be mine if I promised to give them to the world . . . *I promised.*

October 28, 1987

My journey to give Cherisse and Tamara back the mother they lost had taken flight. Just like before my fall, I made use of every available opportunity to make them feel loved. Encouraging everything my children wanted to try felt like playtime. Cherisse's and Tamara's enlightenment was the glorious gift of my enlightenment, and as always, I glorified in watching each daughter lead her own parade. I listened, participated, and contributed suggestions. They talked, participated, and made their own choices.

The driving force of my soul to be fully alive went everywhere I went. I resumed swimming, working out on my weight bench, riding my bike, and taking walks with Mickey. I began sumi-e', an oriental brush painting class at the local community college. I read, prayed, meditated, wrote in my journal, and did my automatic writing every day. I returned to the football stadium and more. I attended every Friday night game, met Cherisse's and Tamara's friends, and helped prepare for the most heralded event of the year: Homecoming!

As the excitement of Homecoming week reved into full gear, I took turns chaperoning Cherisse's and Tamara's float-decorating parties. With pleasure, I worked alongside each daughter and her classmates in the slow process of making paper flowers.

Each day as I watched my daughters, they watched me. Every move they made breathed life into the word dignity. Neither Cherisse nor Tamara dwelled in heartache. Both daughters moved forward with their lives without hesitation or complaint. They journeyed into a challenging new world gallantly, hesitating for only one thing: making sure Mom was there.

October 29, 1987, 10:15 A.M.

    I heard the door of John's little yellow truck slam shut outside the back room by the driveway where I was lifting weights. Following another three-day binge, the man of the house had sounded his presence. I opened the door and watched him ascend the driveway. In a controlled swagger, he made his way past me without a glance. His eyes were glued to the red Mexican tile floor. As he passed, the odor of raw onion breath eaten to cover up the smell of alcohol, combined with the appearance of sweat-soaked, smoke-satiated, slept-in clothes, insulted a pleasant autumn day.

    Head bent down, eyes focused on the floor, John shrugged into the hall bemoaning, "I woke up at a rest stop next to some trash cans and saw all these lonely faces of people walking around with nowhere to go. I'm not going to drink anymore."

    John made slow headway across two-thousand square feet of Mexican tiles, aiming his downtrodden demeanor toward the master bedroom and our bed. I contemplated the tiles my husband had just stepped upon. Like most of the architectural details of our house, because I wanted those particular tiles, John laid them. He had counted on me to handle the creative work of building our dream home while I counted on him to handle the physical work. Five years of John's blood, sweat, and tears, however, did not change one important truth. I was not going to get to sleep in my bed that night.

    Around 2:00 in the afternoon, John arose from bed, drove away in his truck, returned half-drunk, twelve-pack in hand, lamenting, "I don't care if I die. I can't stop drinking. My whole life has been wasted. Please drink with me."

    John's depression had grown too serious for me to just ignore his request. After John had the experience of waking up beneath trash cans, drinking alone would deepen the loneliness of "nowhere to go." If I did not at least pretend to drink with him after he admitted his newest crisis, worse than blaming me for his lonely feelings, he might once again become suicidal.

    Refusing to put my children or myself in harm's way needlessly, I chose the lesser of two evils. I walked over to the refrigerator and lifted out a beer. By drinking beer, I knew what I was getting myself into. What I was getting into did not matter, nor did it take long.

John's humor improved so much, so fast, the acidity of a new persona jumped into his body and spoke through it. "If you fight me for more money than I told you I was going to give you, you'd better believe I'm going to play hardball!"

There it was, John's definitive word. "Hardball" lifted the curtain on the path of darkness my husband chose to divorce his wife and children. "Hardball" was the game he planned to play with Cherisse, Tamara, and me. His explosive WMD sought to divide and conquer. The art of this war painted our financial devastation. War as the extension of greed, peace as the extension of God, the *flesh eating: temptations of the flesh* had won out over the *spiritual building of lead us not into temptation*. Tempted by dark hopes, John had chosen extreme measures as his awful task, the devil's last stand on closing a man's mind to the light of his soul. The beast was staking his very soul on the values of a culture fallen into the ideology that freedom could be *stolen*. Hardball verbally pronounced John's bondage to all that glitters. A slave to the fear of losing his money, John had sold his soul in hopes that financial wealth could buy freedom, and selling his soul had gradually imprisoned his mind. Fear's hellish dungeon was the wilderness of human waste he had met in his youth.

Yes, the evolution of John's soul falling into a deep sleep had been a long time in the making. Rooted in *heartbreak*, the dictatorship of his upbringing stole his soul's freedom to be. Parading as an emissary of justice, his father saw within his power the chance to make his boys slaves to his control. He fed them the same beatings everyday until they marched in-step with his tune. Internal rivalry the necessary evil, the key to obedience was infecting their young minds with his kill-or-be-killed nature. There was no possible way to better destroy his boy's freedom to think original thoughts than to break his heart, the passageway to his soul.

While John still lived under his father's roof, the grave ruins of his heart led him into the world of golf. In those days, golf was strictly for the rich and famous, and John was neither. At the golf course, lofty thoughts of a better life began to lead John's search for freedom from his broken heart. To pay for golf lessons, he began to caddy. Hope for freedom born of huge tips, John was able to carry two golf bags, one on each shoulder, for thirty-six holes. The financial rewards that sprung from tip money stole his obedience to his father's injustice.

At seventeen, after graduating from high school, he took his money and ran as far as he could from his father. He sewed his wild oats for one summer at the dog races in Florida then joined the Navy. For two-years he played golf for the Navy, winning the Navy a golf title and then was shipped to Vietnam. His participation in that gut-wrenching war, experiencing death, the Viet Cong, and the stink of poverty deepened his heartbreak, dashing his hopes for freedom. The "spoils" of war upped the anti on heartbreak, enriching his obedience to wealth.

Fluctuating between hope and despair, John returned to the good old U.S.A. where survival of the richest was rapidly becoming the new American dream. The masses were falling hard and fast into economic injustice as modern social policy. Hope for freedom was again stilled, this time by a war-weary civilization that had become a shadow of what it was before Vietnam. John had run from familial injustice into the injustice of war and then back home to societal injustice where he wandered aimlessly among the collective darkness of greedy hearts, his eyes wild for the spoils of golf to return hope for freedom.

When at long last John found hope, he found it not in golf's golden rewards but in a girl with a heart of gold. Very soon he learned he could not beg, borrow, or steal the freedom born of an unbroken heart. Once again hope died. This time, the death of hope translated into jealousy and envy. Manifesting from his obedience to internal rivalry, jealousy and envy spent their days and nights passionate to steal the freedom of one whose heart was pure. In the end, John's renewed hope for freedom was what jealousy and envy killed.

Along with the potential for grace and genius, John had been given at birth a severe fiery trial. His soul was to be tested with a broken heart. Heartbreak offered the most important decision the man could make. In the great crises of life, *to be or not to be* is the test one must pass to enter the initiation. In choosing hardball's noble wilderness, the man remained uninitiated, squandering the baby's incarnated divinity. By turning flowers into worms, he failed the test of life. To heal his heart so that he could co-create with his soul, he had to purify his shadow.

But John's ego refused the task. He flunked the rite of passage out of darkness into enlightenment. The music of his hopeful soul had been beaten into silence. A pure heart being the only way to the unknown self, the dark corridor of his mind finally chose to shut off that guiding light. Imprisoned in the tunnel of unknowingness by his own doing, John sacrificed his soul's power *to be*. His soul stilled by heartbreak, *not to be* was John's freedom from fear and ignorance. Dead was the purity of innocence. Rather than eternal springs of everlasting life, the tempest of mortal shadows followed him wherever he went. Cast out of heaven by the art of his own war, John had sold his soul to identify with the devil.

> *All the shows o' the world are frail and vain to weep a loss*
> *That turns their lights to shade . . . the web of human things,*
> *Birth and the grave, that are not as they were.*
> — Percy Bysshe Shelley

The oratory about the mighty game of hardball gushed forth and continued gushing as if John had struck oil. The longer I gave audience, the louder the lion roared. What capped off a most successful afternoon on behalf of the art of John's war, however, turned out to be his final remark.

"I love myself first!"

October 30, 1987, Homecoming!

Four class floats were to be the highlight of the evening's festivities. Cherisse's and Tamara's high school was famous in the area for its outstanding floats. Homecoming day was big! During halftime of the football game, the floats were to parade around the field. Escorted by their fathers, four senior-class beauties would step off freshman, sophomore, junior, and senior class floats. Fathers would proudly parade their daughters across the field where their beauties would step onto a stage in the center of the field and the queen would be crowned. Crowning was followed by the main event.

The entire high school anticipated the announcement of the first-and-second-place floats. The senior float almost always won first place. The freshmen float had never won first or second place. Float completion had wavered in the final hours. All of the participants worried their float would not be finished in time. As tradition would have it, all four floats were finished in the nick-of-time and all turned out more gorgeous than the year before.

Cherisse and Tamara spent weeks working on their class floats. I knew how much the evening meant to them, so I told John I thought he should be there for them. He said he wanted to go. He even dressed. Nevertheless, not long before the time came to leave, he passed out on the sofa.

Undaunted by their father's routine, Cherisse and Tamara rushed to get dressed after a long day of float assembly. With high hopes, Cherisse, Tamara, and I embarked upon Homecoming.

Just like old times, three girls reveled in soaking up every available ounce of fun. Being in the middle of the action and the glory of the small town event with my children embodied wishes coming true. Every person there thrilled to the same sights and sounds we thrilled to. Small town people cheered, the homecoming queen was beautiful, and the popcorn was tasty.

Cherisse's junior class float was awarded a rare first-place! Tamara's freshman class float came in a miraculous second! And me? Under the very same stars, in the very same stadium, I sat with my daughters by my side in front row seats!

After the festivities concluded, the three of us walked with an entire stadium of people straight through the center of the football field. About halfway across the field, Cherisse and Tamara kissed me goodbye and sped off with their friends to go to the Homecoming dance.

"Have a good time," I hollered, watching them frolic in and out of the crowd, getting smaller and smaller.

I continued across the field, concentrating on the atmosphere, listening to the air. I felt happy. This happiness had a different meaning than before my fall. This happiness included an appreciation for the intricacies of life I did not notice before. I breathed in the gift of appreciation and continued walking. I took pleasure in the atmosphere and delighted in the chilly night air.

From a distance, I heard voices, familiar voices, laughing voices. The laughter made me happier than any other sound in my big wonderful new world. No, no other sound could have made me happier than hearing the familiar voices . . . the laughing voices . . . of my two *girls*!

November 2, 1987, 11:05 A.M.

I picked up the receiver of the ringing telephone. Following a repeated string of calls telling me how sick he felt, I guessed it might be John. I guessed right.

Binge after binge would make anyone sick, I thought, wondering why John had not come to that simple conclusion.

After relaying his bad news, John asked with timid curiosity, "What did you do on Halloween?"

Although he did not ask, I added his children to my answer. "Cherisse and Tamara dressed in costumes they designed themselves and went to Halloween parties with friends. I handed out candy to trick-or-treaters and then I went to the country club with your nephew."

Without my asking, John recited his Halloween as if the night touched him deeply. "I stayed in a motel. A movie was on television about a man who lived in a cave with a rabbit and constantly quoted from the bible."

Instead of putting into words exactly what moved him about the movie, he had interpreted its personal meaning. "I have to figure out what I want to do with my life, Diana. I have nothing against you. I'm just going through some kind of a crisis. I feel like I'm nothing. I want you to be with me."

Sinking tones told me John was drowning in a drama he felt incapable of ending. Every ounce of compassion churned in me, but I was unwilling to reach out to John. Compassion's wisdom knew that saving John from his crisis would help him just enough to service the speed of his hardball.

Rather than nurture John's crisis, I attempted to help him interpret his Halloween revelations. "John, you owe Cherisse and Tamara an apology for flaunting your affair in front of them. If you were more personally involved with their lives, perhaps you would not have to figure out what to do with the rest of your life."

He replied, "Hmm," and then announced, "I'll be home early."

I said, "Goodbye."

November 2, 1987, 4:45 P.M.

The first thing John did when he got home was drink a beer and declare coldly, "I don't want to be married anymore."

Rather than ask if not wanting to be married had any relationship to my advice that he should try to be a real father, I suggested, "Let's sit on the patio and talk about it."

He agreed to my proposal, grabbed another beer, and followed me outside.

The sunset flashed brilliant shades of orange through billowy gray clouds, setting off a turquoise sky beyond. As night approached, the pool water began to mirror a romantic crescent moon.

Reflected moonbeams frolicked around John's face as he repeated, "I'm nothing. My whole life has been wasted."

Five years of hard work on our house passed through my thoughts. *This sick and tired man has given so much of himself to his material world, yet he has given so little of himself to his inner world. He doesn't have a clue who he is.*

Sensing the profound defeat inside the man I had slept in the same bed with for more than eighteen years, I spoke about my relenting compassion. "John, you are important and your accomplishments have been many. Look at the beauty all around you. Think how much of it you built with your own hands."

Confirming his stance on my compassion, John used my kindness to unleash his favorite weapon. "Diana, I'm unhappy and you are to blame. You were the reason I didn't make it on the golf tour. Let me tell you how bad you are, you snake in the grass. . . ."

"No thanks," I interrupted standing up to leave.

Boisterous shouts I knew the neighbors could hear stopped me cold. "I can't stand the sound of your voice. You have used me for eighteen years as your meal ticket. You fucking women don't know anything. All you do is sit on your ass all day. I hate you. I hate all women. Diana, you don't deserve to be on this planet. If you don't give me what I want, I'll take you to court. You better get ready to play hardball."

Never failing to squander his most precious possession, the chance to live a soulful life, John had thrown a hardball that promised protection from the sorrowful creature he had become. Still, on that moonlit night I did not fully understand the art of his *steal*. It took me nearly seventeen years to unravel the circumference of John's hardball and seventeen years I needed to emotionally withstand the story I am about to tell.

On May 8, 1971, four days after giving birth to Cherisse, as Daddy lay dying of cancer at the Navel Hospital in Long Beach, California, John and Mother had picked Cherisse and me up from Hoag Hospital in Newport Beach, California and was driving all of us home. John became hungry, so we stopped at a fast food restaurant and he went in. I mentioned to Mother that my husband of one-year and nine-months was acting strange.

She made sense of his displeasure. "John is jealous of Cherisse. He's used to getting all your attention."

Overwhelmed with joy at the miracle of my gorgeous healthy baby, I forgot the incident thinking he would get over jealously as soon as he grew to love our precious offspring as much as I. I had been home for six weeks on doctor's orders not to travel at the end of my pregnancy. He insisted that a normal recovery from childbirth would take another six weeks. Having not traveled with John for six weeks, he returned to the PGA tour to be alone for another six weeks.

After that second six-week period, just before he flew home, the doctors at the Naval Hospital told Mother that Daddy had only three weeks to live. When John returned, he volunteered to help Mother get her estate in order. She was so happy and grateful. She loved him deeply for making her feel safe.

Regardless of the fact that in three weeks my father would be dead, John told me we could not afford to fly home for his funeral, telling me he had spent all of our money on round-trip tickets to pick Cherisse and me up. Raised to believe my place was with my husband, I made the decision to go back on the PGA tour knowing I would never see my father again. I felt comfortable with the knowledge that I had spent three months running errands for Mother and taking her to and from the hospital to visit Daddy. Plus, she had the opportunity to spend six weeks getting to know "the most beautiful baby" she had ever seen. With that, I said my loving goodbyes to Daddy and left for the PGA tour with my husband and my baby.

As we toured from city to city, John failing to qualify for one tournament after Cherisse was born, he insistently repeated that we did not have a spare dime, even for one long distance telephone call to my mother. Believing I married an honest man, I took his words for truth and obeyed.

Hence, on July 6th, three weeks after I waved goodbye to my mother as she stood on the front lawn waving back, John said I could call home. Mother answered, saying she was so happy to hear my voice because Daddy had just died. Feeling sad for her, I asked if she was okay and if she wanted me to fly home. She told me she was okay and not to spend the money. True to John's persistent orders, I did not call home again until July 20th. We were at the Westchester Open in New York. John and I sat together in a motel room, and I made the call.

Instantly irritated when one of Susan's friends answered Mother's telephone, misspending my long-distance minutes, I firmly requested, "May I please speak with my mother."

Susan came on the line, blurting out, "Mother's dead."

I slammed down the phone and fell to the floor where I sat crying hysterically. John simply sat in his chair staring down at me with a quizzical expression on his face. With both of my parents dead in eleven days, we flew home.

Cherisse had just thrown up forty minutes of breast feeding on the bus on the way to pick up the car when John confessed, "It's just like I won the golf tournament!"

Not until 2004, nearly thirty-three years after my parents died, almost seventeen years after John threatened hardball, would his confession "won the tournament" reach its final day of reckoning.

When John helped Mother prepare her estate, he learned exactly how much money I would inherit when she died. My inheritance turned out to be the approximate amount of money he would have received if he had won the Westchester Open, hence "won the tournament."

But that betrayal did not come close to the questions I am about to propose. Before we married, John found out that Daddy and Mother had a suicide pack, and Mother had saved enough Seconal pills to kill herself after Daddy died. John knew that I was eternally faithful to his word. He also knew that when we were touring, I would obey him and not telephone Mother. My personal day of reckoning, too, would come when I realized that my not calling Mother made her lonely, and loneliness had to be one of the reasons she felt she could no longer go on living. That woeful truth, nonetheless, did not come close to the horrifyingly grotesque implications of that quizzical expression on John's face when I told him my mother was dead. In my mind . . . still . . . that look on John's face bids these unanswered questions.

Did John script my not calling my grieving mother knowing she and Daddy had a suicide pact? Was hardball the game he married me to play, the theatrical performance that began before we married? Had the man to whom I gave my heart planned to cause the suicide of a harmless woman with a heart of gold? And after using up my inheritance to get rich, did he hedge his bets on "like mother, like daughter" (suicide) so he could run off with a younger woman and her future inheritance?

No, John did not learn to play the mighty game of hardball that moonlit November 1987 evening as we sat on the patio. The theater of his thievery had cast him out of heaven long before he met me. The evolution of "follow the evil" that began with heartbreak stemmed from a cultural ideology that made the American dream an instrument of a greedy kind of soul murder.

Spiritual freedom to think for himself had been seized by his father's Reich and cemented by the American Reich. John's fiery trial was the progression of lost hope defined by his solitude. Heartbreak, the root cause of his psychic suffering, hardball his obedience, John truly believed greed was good. The cultural platform of *survival of the richest* fed from his father's *survival of the fittest* translated the economic injustice born of John's duty to the fatherland. Failing the test of life with his rebellion against my family, John had infected the entire universe by remaining obedient to temptations of the flesh.

Unwilling to witness the collective shadow John both fed from and added to, I let him relieve himself of a few more hardballs, walked into the house, collected my car keys and a book, and left. Feelings of peace consumed me as I directed my car up one of the rolling hills within our community. At the top of the hill, I parked in a cul-de-sac where there were no houses. What appeared to be the entire incredible universe lay before my eyes. In the center of a star-filled universe, the same crescent moon my husband threw hardballs under just a few blocks away shone romantically for me.

I sat in silence and listened for the crescent moon's romantic song. I wanted to hear romantic words. I wanted to feel romantic feelings. I wanted to know if love would find me again.

Romance rang out for all the universe to hear. *Let John throw all the hardballs he wants, Diana. Nothing on earth can take away your determination to seize every moment of your life and eat it up!*

The hardball John threw, he threw at his own face. He might easily have found life's meaning through his children, in the glory of what he should have taught them, in the glory of the love he should have given them, in the glory of seeing all he could ever be in their eyes. I gazed at the night sky. Stars twinkled. The crescent moon winked. The song of love being sung to me felt more wonderful than. . . .

Ultimately we and the tree are one and the same.
Everything is interconnected and will teach you something
you did not know about yourself.

– Plato

22
Part I

Love Yourself: Therein Lies Happiness

November 10, 1987, 3:30 P.M

The countryside looked magnificent! Hills and valleys covered with luscious green trees, plants, and grass paid tribute to the earth in its neverending bounty. While standing on the front porch waiting for my sister, Susan, to arrive, I praised the earth and thanked the universe for my being alive and able to participate on such a planet. Each leaf, each bud, each blossom, every mountain, river, lake, and ocean blessed my existence in the garden called earth. Trees born of the water of life, bright as crystal, flowing from the throne of the devine pattern within mother nature made me feel part of the wonderful flow of the universe. Every aspect of the nature before my eyes was a particle of the paradise flowing through me.

How could anyone believe a divine creator resides in some far off heaven when kingdom of heaven is right here? I counseled myself. The tree of life inherent in nature could heal the world if each person learned to connect with its divine energy, I concluded, delighted with my simple idea. *Soaking up the light of the sun everything beneath it is my path of sanity. Bathing in the nourishment earth gives freely is where I find perfect healing. When I wandered in the woods and climbed trees as a child, I felt closest to my deepest meaning. Wild places taught me how to be me, freed me to be who I am. In unaltered nature I found out how to stay connected to my inborn world. In nature my body hears the way my soul sounds and feels the way my soul feels. Those feelings saved my life as the morning dawned after my darkest night. Even the dark night of my soul could not stop the dawn. The sacred power of the reverent world outside my window fused with my soul and reminded me that it is my inborn nature to be happy. That reminder raised me from the dead by giving me the good news that the meaning of my life is learning and living the happiness of knowing the kingdom that lies within myself!*

A joyous spiritual awareness filled every atom of my being as I stood on the front porch honoring mother earth with a wide-awake countryside meditation. This mind, body, and soul oneness with nature made me feel as if I were standing on the edge of eternity. Earth heaven moved the very matter of my body as pearls on a thread arranged in an upward spiral, awakening every physiological cell to a greater awareness of the world of eternal light. From head to toe, I could feel the everlasting river of light flowing from divine forces into me. Each time I had one of these wide-awake meditations with nature, every aspect of my body evolved toward the timeless source of all that existed. Each and every time I jumped into this flow with nature, a seed was planted that germinated in an upward movement toward my soul's oneness with everlasting life. Seed by seed, that spiritualizing process was enLIGHTening my very DNA!

In the years to come I would learn that the mind-body-soul enlightening process I experienced is scientific fact biologically, psychologically, and spiritually. The following is my simplified version of how the science of enlightenment works:

The *science of physics* has shown that every gland, every cell, every neuron, the very strands of human DNA that carry genetic information in the body are all made of *atoms*. Not only is the body and everything in it composed of atoms, everything inside the universe is composed of atoms, including all substances (e.g., air/water) and material objects (e.g., trees/animals). Atoms are the smallest unit of energy, irreducible to a smaller unit. Every atom is an exact replica of every other atom, consisting of a *positively* charged nucleus surrounded by *negatively* charged electrons. That atoms in the universe and atoms in the body are identical, every body is interconnected with every other body by atoms, and all bodies are interconnected with the universe by atoms, one gigantic interconnecting network, a worldwide matrix, one indivisible interactive universal force of atomic energy!

In every teeny-tiny invisible atom is recorded a complete holographic library, not only of every thought, word, and deed of every person who has ever lived, but also all the information in the universe, past, present, and future, a virtual eternal memory bank. Because atoms in the body replicate atoms in the universe, in the body lies all the knowledge, mysteries, and powers of the universe, the very fabric of creation. This is called *natural law*. Wherein the natural law of the universe is epitomized in the body, every single body is a miniature universe!

The *science of biology* has shown that this miniature universe of the body is also one interactive atomic system within itself, the chemical properties of which are composed in seven major glands. Starting at the base of the spine upward to the brain, the glands are as follows: 1) gonads, 2) laden, 3) adrenal, 4) thymus, 5) thyroid, 6) pituitary, 7) pineal.

Atoms in the brain form brain cells. Brain cells send messages to receptor cells in the seven glands. These messages are sent with a specialized cell in neurons called neurotransmitter proteins. Neurotransmitter proteins transmit nerve impulses, nerve to nerve, from the brain straight down the spinal chord. Nerve impulses cause the cells in the glandular system to replicate the cells in the brain. In other words, the brain systematically transforms the cells in the seven glands to be identical to the cells in the brain.

As a result, the brain and the seven glands are one unit, an indivisible interactive matrix in which *mind is the builder* of cellular structure in the body. Mind the cause, body the effect, this *cellular oneness* is called the *mind/body connection*. Every piece of information the intellect learns, the glands learn. Every feeling the intellect feels, the glands feel. Everything learned and felt is stored in the mind and the seven glands. Mind literally has the power to transform strands of DNA, change human genetics by way of this glandular system. The science of the mind/body connection makes it a biological certainty that what the mind thinks and feels the body will become!

Every thought and emotion in the mind, including every thought, word, and deed stored in the subconscious mind is replicated in glandular cells by nerve impulses. Positive and negative thoughts and feelings in the brain are replicated by glandular cells in positive and negative ways. Consequently, the body is changed in positive and negative ways. In addition, nerve impulses can be increased or decreased with use or non-use of the brain at any time in life, which is one reason why two people of the same age can have very different intellects and very different physical attributes.

Neither intelligence nor physicality is fixed, ever! As long as the brain functions normally, both the science of physics and the science of biology tell us that everybody will become everything s/he thinks and feels. Intellectually and figuratively, the mind transforms the body. If the mind is sick, nothing can heal the body. Conversely, with exceptions, nothing can make the body sick if the mind is healthy. What the body looks like, inside and out, is a direct result of the mind.

The *science of spirituality* has shown that the body is not only physiological walking, talking mind; the body is also spiritual walking, talking mind. Corresponding to the seven biological glands are seven spiritual centers. These centers are where the soul enters and operates in the body. *She enters, ascending to the highest mind and evolves her own essence for her own reasons.* Starting at the base of the spine upward to the top of the head, the soul centers are as follows: 1) root, 2) prostate, 3) solar plexus, 4) heart, 5) throat, 6) brow, 7) crown.

These *seven spiritual centers are counter-clockwise interconnecting spiral-shaped* frequencies of energy that look like an upside-down tornado. Therefore, the spiritual centers are energy centers, and just like the seven glandular cells replicate brain cells by nerve impulses, the seven energy centers replicate the energy frequency of brain cells in accordance with positive and negative thoughts and feelings of the mind. Translated by energy frequency, this process is a spiritual *mind/body connection.*

Thoughts and feelings cause the spiral-shaped energy centers to spin like wheels. The "wheels" spin at faster or slower speeds dependent upon the energy of thoughts and feelings. The frequency of the spin expressed in the body's seven soul centers is faster (positive) or slower (negative) to the degree the frequence is in-tune with the soul, spiritualizing the body more or less respectively, the more spiritualized the more enlightened.

These seven corresponding biological glands and spiritual centers make up the three great *psychological chambers* in the body: the lower chamber, middle chamber, and upper chamber. These psychological chambers show how the mind builds the life of the body in positive and negative ways. The three lower frequency centers are the chamber of the lower mind. They are as follows: 1) survival (greed/generosity), 2) sex (lust/love), 3) power (violence/creativity). The middle center is as follows: 4) heart (hate/love). The three higher frequency centers are the chamber of the higher mind. They are as follows: 5) expressing (anger/wisdom), 6) eternity (fear/love), 7) soul (death/divinity or everlasting life).

The chart on the next page shows where the biological glands and spiritual centers correspond, how they are divided up into three psychological chambers, and what is the affect of positive (of the soul) thoughts and negative (of the soul) thoughts and feelings as related to individual behavior.

To reiderate, atoms in the body, mind, and soul contain a holographic history of everything that has ever been and all that will ever be, including all the knowledge, mysteries, and powers of the universe, a scientific fact called *natural law*. Seemingly contrary to the nature of the *visible* material world, the natural law of atoms is *invisible*, hence, hidden or kept secret from the mind. Invisible nature, however, is not contrary to what is visible. In fact, it is complimentary. Making the invisible visible is understanding and living natural law. Making the knowledge, mysteries, and powers of the universe visible to the conscious mind is experiencing the *meaning of life* (e.g., the kingdom that lies within, enlightenment, etc).

Enlightenment takes place by spiritualizing the three great chambers of the body. The process of spiritualizing the body connects the mind/body (by way of the mind and the body connection) with the soul in oneness. This process systematically raises the energy frequency, transforming the body so that it is more and more in-tune with the soul. The mind/soul connection is how the mind and the soul co-create life. Mind and soul co-creating life is called the living soul, meaning the soul is fully alive in the body. The glory of being human

BIOLOGICAL   *PSYCHOLOGICAL*   *SPIRITUAL*

The seven corresponding areas in the human body/mind/soul.

	LOWER MIND ↓	HIGHER MIND ↓	
7. pineal	soul death	soul divinity	crown
6. pituitary	eternity fear	eternity love	brow
5. thyroid	expressing anger	expressing wisdom	throat

UPPER CHAMBER

4. thymus	hate ♥	love	heart

MIDDLE CHAMBER

3. adrenal	power violence	power creativity	solar plexis
2. laden	sex lust	sex love	prostate
1. gonads	survival greed	survival generosity	root

LOWER CHAMBER

lower mind ↓   higher mind ↓

psychological involution   psychological evolution

is the chance to co-create with the soul, for the soul is spirit, which is the divine energy of the creator. The process of learning how to co-create is called the initiation. Only those tried by the fire of the initiation can open the seven seals of the living soul.

Δ *The Initiation* Δ

The *initiation* is the *initiate* (individual) journeying the meaning of life. In other words, the mind learns to co-create with the soul by spiritualizing the body. The initiatory journey makes visible to the conscious mind truths that have been invisible. By atoning, purifying, transforming, thus spiritualizing the seven centers which have been sealed closed by energy not in-tune with the soul, the initiate increases the energy frequency of the center, breaking open the seals. Spiritualizing is the process of making the mind/body more and more in-tune with the soul. Spiritualizing the seven spiritual centers opens seven secret doors to seven sacred schools. In these schools the initiate solves the mystery of self and the mystery of ancient wisdom.

The body is not the individual. Body is the house for the soul who fashioned it. By spiritualizing (e.g., enlightening/raising the consciousness) the mind/body, the initiate makes the house a home for the soul. As helical strands of DNA are analogous to coiling forms found throughout *nature*, the initiation is an upward spiraling movement through the seven spiritual centers that purifies negative energy in the cells of the body. Through the tunnel of dark matter, in progressive stages, the light of the soul ascends from the base to the crown. As *the light of truth* gets brighter, the darkness of ignorance must yield to truth's power to quicken energy. Quickening purifies darkness, opening the seven sealed mysteries. This seven-fold journey unseals the *ancient wisdom* contained in the three great chambers of the human body.

Because the soul in *us* is capable of teaching the meaning and purpose of life by exciting the energy in the body with images of the pure intelligence and unconditional love underlying all creation, *the initiation is a journey of soul development in the body*. On the deepest level, the initiated mind attains eternal oneness with the infinite multitude of being.

The *first stage* of the initiation is *candidacy*. The candidate is required to *solve the mystery of the chamber of the lower mind* or procreative system. A baby is born with the conscious mind unified with the soul mind, or subconscious mind. At birth, the soul voice is conscious *mind's driving force*. Wisdom, eternity, and divine energy frequency *co-creating naturally* with conscious mind is how a baby first understands and feels the meaning and purpose of life. This first experience of the world is why babies are blissfully happy. Following birth, the material world is so powerful, it is easy for the voices and behaviors of those in the environment to teach a baby to think and feel that material possessions and physical desires are the meaning and purpose of life and will therefore bring happiness. Material possessions and physical desires fill the conscious mind with thoughts and feelings related to money, sex, and power. This materialistic conditioning turns the extraordinary into the ordinary, which turns divine energy into dense energy, wisdom into ignorance, eternity into death and dying. This process diminishes the voice of the soul.

Since there is too much environmental information to hold in consciousness, everything that is learned is stored in the subconscious mind, which becomes separated from the conscious mind. The soul voice is gradually pushed into the far reaches of the subconscious mind. Materialistic understandings and feelings conditioned into the conscious and subconscious mind are the new way the growing individual experiences the world. *Mind's driving force* becomes a win/lose battle for money, sex, and power until death does one part. This is the chamber of the lower mind.

Because materialistic possessions and physical desires part at death, they fail to bring the lasting happiness promised. Whereas the soul is immortal and the body is mortal, losing money, sex, and power creates the fear of death, which is energy negative to soul energy. Morbidity and materialism are the keys to the bottomless pit of fear. In the pit of fear lives the bestial instincts and false reason of greed, lust, and power to which the individual grows up to be a slave.

The candidate is required to find the key that liberates the mind from slavery to the beast. Any meaning and purpose other than the meaning and purpose of the soul are the veils of illusion that must be dropped. To crush the beast and liberate the mind from slavery, thoughts and feelings that create energy negative to soul energy must be purified. This requires meditation and a psychological examination.

The *psychological examination* is journeying the candidate's *shadow*. The shadow is the accumulation of negative thoughts and feelings stored in the subconscious since birth, and for the most part, subconscious thoughts and feelings drive consciousness. From birth forward, material possessions and physical desires are the way the individual learns to experience life. Enslaved in various degrees by greed, lust, and fear of death, individual unhappiness is the everlasting reoccurring plague. The deepest materialism being the furthest from the soul, what results from thoughts and feelings negative to the soul is a *broken heart*. The first cause of a broken heart, *hurt* feelings, evolves into *pain*, then *hate*, then *anger,* and then that reoccurring plague of *fear*. But because the voice of the soul lingers in the far reaches of the mind as the true self, the mind denies the understandings and feelings of the false self. To stay in *denial*, the cause of hurt, pain, anger, hate, and fear is *projected* onto others.

Projection is the fine art of teaching the next generation to live in prisons of hurt, pain, anger, hate, and fear built by negative thoughts and feelings of the former generation and the simple art of placing the cause of personal negative feelings onto someone else. Projected thoughts and feelings are conditioned into the subconscious. The ordeal in the chamber of the shadow is making conscious hurt, pain, anger, and fear. Processing and purifying those shadowy parts of the subconscious takes time because purification quickens spiritual energies and the nervous system cannot tolerate quickening at too fast a pace.

The candidate not only must endure the tunnel of shadowy thoughts and feelings, s/he also is required to *atone* for projection of those thoughts and feelings as well. For breaking the heart of someone else because the candidates heart was broken, for every hurt the candidate caused another, every inflicted pain, every angry word, every deed that resulted in another feeling fear, the candidate is required to understand, feel, and atone. These severe trials that test the heart and try the mind are only for the brave at heart. Nevertheless, as each triumph of endurance purifies negative energy a little more, the mind opens a little more to the energy frequency of the soul where meaning and purpose are found.

A *general study of the psychology of human behavior* goes hand in hand with a personal psychological investigation. Because faded illusions of happiness have broken the heart and stupefied the mind, the candidate is required to understand the roots of beastly thoughts, feelings, and behaviors and then practice the understandings s/he has learned. With *no understanding* of the psychological reason for the diversity of human behavior, there can be *no forgiveness*. With no forgiveness there can be *no compassion*. Without down-to-earth, heart-felt, day-by-day practice, there can be no happy, healthy, loving relationships. The key to happiness is spiritualizing relationships with self, others, and the world through the psychological process of *understanding, forgiveness, and compassion.*

Meditation is conscious mind directly connecting with soul mind, a short cut to the soul that serves the psychological examination. Candidacy requires personal experience of the wisdom, eternity, and energy frequency of the divine self. Without experiencing the happiness in the soul, the candidate will fail to endure the severe trials of the ordeal in the chamber of the shadow. The courage to continue purifying and atoning demands the healing powers of meditation.

On earth as in heaven, natural law, universal law, and soul law being one in the same, meditating with *nature* is a natural way to directly connect with the voice of the soul, a special wide-awake meditation. When thoughts and feelings are silenced and atoms in the air are breathed in, the thoughts and feelings of the soul mind become audibly visible to conscious mind. Because nature is divine, meditating with nature opens a window to the voice of the soul, which is the purpose of all meditation. Each time a window is opened, mind/body awakens to a fuller awareness of the many prisons of bestial nature and the many mansions of divine nature.

Meditation and a psychological investigation are equally inescapable to maintain life-balance. Without both, life will go out of balance. *Imbalance causes* mental chaos and confusion, which in turn *effects* psychological and spiritual *conflict*. Traveling one and not the other will throw a spike in the upward spiral of the initiation process, forestalling rites of passage. If candidate fails both, s/he returns to the bestial sphere of fear's bottomless pit. Though passing the psychological test is a triumph of endurance, slaying the illusions of materiality de-stupifies the mind and heals the heart. Solving the mystery in the chamber of the lower mind prepares the candidate for initiatory rites.

The *second stage* of the initiation is for the candidate to become an *initiate*. The initiate is required to *solve the mystery in the chamber of the higher mind* or enlightened mind. In the higher mind are all the secrets hidden from the lower mind, the wisdom, eternity, and divine consciousness that are the *soul's driving force*. Though as a candidate, the initiate connected with the soul in meditation, s/he does not fully understand the meaning and purpose of the soul. The three highest spiritual centers, the throat, brow, and crown, are the great pyramid of the soul, the tree of life flowing from the mind of Universal Spirit. By journeying the pyramid of the higher mind, the initiate reunifies conscious mind with soul mind where meaning and purpose are found. This is the second birth of the voice of the soul.

Because the heart is the passageway between the lower and higher mind, the initiate begins in the pit of the heart. The pit is where the candidate understands, feels, and atones for thoughts and feelings rooted in heartbreak. Solving the mysteries of the lower mind bridges the chasm in the heart opening up the passageway. Opening the heart channels the wisdom, eternal life, and divine power of the higher centers into the greed, lust, and violence of the lower centers, transforming them into generosity, love and creativity, and expands intelligence and love in all seven spiritual centers. From here on out, for every thought, word, or deed rooted in thoughts or feelings other than *understanding, forgiveness, and compassion*, the initiate pays dearly.

While the initiate is beginning to understand a conditioned multitude enslaved by the greed, lust, and power held in the hands of an elite few, s/he is awakening to the *ancient truths* held secret by generational and societal conditioning. Truths transmitted into the seven spiritual centers in the body deeply and profoundly transform the initiate. The mind shifts from identifying with the physical self to identifying with spiritual self. Each shift adds vitality to the seven energy centers. Soul energy amplifies radiance in the body, quickening energy frequency, speeding the upward spin of the spirals, firing up nerve impulses in the glands, and cleansing the cells at an ever-increasing pace. Surprisingly, each time divine consciousness penetrates human consciousness at a deeper level, the tests get harder.

With expanding enlightenment comes intense surges of purifying energy. With each surge of light, dark energies become more clearly defined. With each expansion of intelligence and love, the physical self is required to grow more virtuous and moral. Hence, a heavier price is to be paid for falling back into bestial habits. To serve purification, trials by fire ensue. Residue of dark thoughts and feelings must suffer a new lesson with the dawning of each new day. Still, each triumph of endurance awards the initiate a closer inspection of meaning and purpose.

Understanding the true self to be a divine, eternal being tests the courage of the initiate to live daily life by the higher standard given in *The Philosophy* of *understanding, forgiveness, and compassion*. As the higher mind patiently studies the intricacies of the riddle of life and practices *UFC+US* (understanding, forgiveness, compassion + meditation with the soul/Universal Spirit), with each victory of wisdom over ignorance, love over fear, everlasting life over death, flows a little more of the initiate's holy grail, his or her *purpose in life*. As the *tomb* of the lower mind is consistently exchanged for the *temple* of the higher mind, the initiate becomes a little more the *living image of his or her personal divine plan*. All the mysteries of the universe are not known nor are they meant to be known because the nature of life is the riddle to be solved. With every trial by fire the initiate passes comes a rite of passage more deeply into the *ancient wisdom*.

The *third stage* of the initiation is to be *initiated*. To be initiated is graduation from the initiation. To graduate, the initiate is required to *solve the mystery in the chamber of the heart*, or divine illumination. Since the heart is the passageway between the mind and the soul, when the heart is divinely illuminated conscious mind *co-creates naturally* with soul mind. Even the higher mind, that ancient builder of the house for the soul, must solve the mystery of the heart. Even the enlightened mind questions, *In a world filled with war and destruction, how do I live free from fear?* Even the ancient wisdom encoded on the language of enlightenment begs, *On a planet of death and dying, how can I be a living example of everlasting life?* After the initiate has journeyed the heights and depths to bridge heaven and earth, the superfluous excellency of the higher mind practically walking on water to solve the mysteries, one question remains, *In a world where gold rules, how do I live in happy obedience to the golden rule?*

Yes, to be free from fear, to be an example of *the living soul*, to *co-create naturally*, even the highest mind is required to ask itself, *What is my driving force?* No matter what the level of enlightenment, the initiate is required to peer-amid the pyramid to find the answer to the final question. For in the middle of the three spiritual centers burns the divine flame. Though it is the quality of thinking that defines the success of being human, it is the quality of love that defines the success of being divine. Even after the initiate has solved the *secret of the ages*, it is still the understandings and feelings in the heart that drive the mind to direct that *ancient wisdom* toward good or evil. If the heart is not purified, if the flames of heartbreak still burn, beastly understandings and feelings will be the highest mind's driving force. Even after enlightenment, the beast begs, *Please save me.*

Only when *she in herself* enters the heart will the heart risk all to drive the mind, *to be or not to be.* Whether the initiated's holy grail is to sing the greatest song, paint the greatest portrait, find the greatest love, or simply nurture a tiny garden, *the heart is the mind's driving force.* The heart is the tree of life that drinks from the rivers of *divine illumination.* Only when the heart is driven by the love in the soul is the mind saved.

For in the chamber of the heart lies the most holy mystery: the genus of the soul is the unity of beings. Only through the passageway of a heart that is no longer broken does the voice of the soul confer the life, the light, and the love that sets the mind free *to be.* In the end, as in the beginning, before the question was asked, the baby knew the *secret of secrets. It is love* that transforms the ordinary back into the extraordinary. Love alone fears no evil. Love alone crushes the beast. Even Jiminy Cricket knew the simple truth. "Like a bolt out of the blue, if your heart is in your dreams, *your dreams* will come true. . . ."

Δ

November 10, 1987, 10:45 P.M

Meditating with nature had become the rainbow-bridge to my heart. Nature connected every cell in my body to my ideal of understanding, forgiveness, and compassion. With every breath I took as I stood on the front porch waiting for my sister Susan, every intricate detail of the countryside before my eyes enlightened me, heart, mind, body, and soul. My very beingness became one with its perfect poetry. Nature's flawless spirit caressed me, elated me. A perfect copy of all the love and knowledge in the universe, nature and its glorious spell made me a perfect example of everything I ever wanted to be. In nature, I ate from the fruit of spirit and drank from the divine inspiration of the wisdom written on the wind!

If there's a promised land, this is it! Life here is precious, I reasoned, captivated by the splendor before my eyes. *It's hard to believe the years Susan and I have spent not sharing this magnificent land. What did we waste those years for?*

Though as children Susan and I were very close, as adults we evolved in opposite directions. As one feels in the heart, so one behaves in the mind. A pure heart lead my mind. Heartbreak lead Susan's mind. As John's broken heart resulted in him being jealous of my inner happiness, Susan's heartbreak resulted in her being jealous of my happy heart. Behaviors that resulted from my sister's thoughts and feelings propelled me to walk out of her life the same way I was about to walk out on John's life.

Susan and I had seen one another only a few times since Daddy and Mother died. Seven years had passed in our most recent separation, yet one telephone call on the day of my first automatic writing caused each of us to give the one gift necessary to tear down the walls separating our hearts: forgiveness.

I wanted to run to the green car coming up the driveway. The love I felt for my only sibling bathed my heart in pure joy. The car stopped at the foot of the cement steps between John's latest project, two gray stone pillars. I rushed down the steps to hug Susan as she stepped out of her car.

Stunned by her appearance, I exclaimed, "You look like Mother with your hair blond!"

Deep sentiment consumed Susan's face and tears flooded her eyes as she spoke. "I knew you were going to say that."

We hugged and kissed and talked more about how each of us appeared to the other. Susan and I were together after another long absence. I felt our growth as human beings had guided us back to each other and hoped nothing on earth would have the power to separate our hearts again.

I helped Susan carry her things into the den and gave her a tour of our home. The tour ended in the kitchen where she began telling stories about her numerous escapades around the world. To my surprise, John joined us, dressed to kill. Susan greeted him, scooted up and sat on the kitchen counter top, and then picked up her fables where she left off.

Since our last meeting, my sister had chosen a radical life, experimenting with sex, drugs, and rock-n-roll. As she detailed her adventures, John's attention riveted on her every word. Although on his face I could see judgmental disgust, he was visibly aroused and impassioned by Susan's provocative stories. Never had John in my presence responded to another woman with such frenzied arousal.

True to form, however, he verbally expressed his double standard of morality. "Susan, women shouldn't act like that."

Susan fought back. "I act the way I choose. Men don't tell me how to behave."

Her defensive battle stirred John's competitive and lusty passions even more, and Susan's every bodily movement told me she knew exactly what she was doing. The power of the ego, John's and Susan's ultimate aphrodisiac, they both had acquired the bittersweet habit of concentrating on the sexual and forgetting the spiritual.

Inflamed animation caressed John's scantily veiled correlation between my sister and myself. "Diana ruined my career and my life." Then, as if I were oblivious to his sexual overtones, my husband stood three feet from me and expressed the foul dust that floated on the wake of his dreams. "Susan, come and go for a ride with me. I'll show you the community."

Rather than respond to John's proposition, instead she waited to see what was going to happen next.

To nip their fiery exchange at the bud, I suggested, "Susan, let's go into the den so you can unpack."

Comprehending exactly my underlying meaning, Susan gave John a piercing stare and stated firmly, "John, Diana and I have many things we need to talk over privately. Do you mind?"

Grateful for my sister's explicit way of getting rid of my husband,

I took her arm and we walked side by side into the den.

Just before I closed the door, she stated with humble sincerity, "Your house is gorgeous."

Together we opened the rollout sofa, then put on the bedding. Susan opened her duffel bag and handed me lovely gifts from a clothing store she would soon open. Then, we settled down to talk.

In Susan's voice, I heard an angry hunger for love and support. On her body I saw the latent genetics of the immutable and absolute equality of universal law. With no escape from the law of cause and effect, what she had sown, so she had reaped. Sixteen years of repressed guilt had taken their toll. The years that transpired since her vengeful deed were sketched in the lines etched on her once beautiful face. The dark side of heartbreak expressed itself directly in the weight she carried on her body. Both the poison and the perfume of her inner being were inscribed on her outer being, her body communicating its perfect witness to her mind. Mind forever the builder of good and evil, desperation to release the inner monster had come and gone, leaving stains of bitterness.

No matter what Susan was about to tell me, I felt the occasion presented me an opportunity to help her seize the monstrous pain. The only way for my sister to awaken her mind to her soul would be to embrace and purify the painful shadows in her heart with a search for truth. I hoped my love and support would spark that perennial quest. My hopeful wish was to help Susan initiate her search for the truths that had separated our hearts, truths herein that ripped us apart. . . .

Sixteen years earlier, the weekend of July 17th, 1971, eleven days after Daddy's death, Susan had stayed with Mother. When I telephoned home from Westchester, New York, on July 20th and heard Susan say "Mother's dead," I slammed down the receiver, struck down by the damnation of my mother's untimely death. In anguish, I called back and summoned Susan to tell me how Mother died. Again Susan was abrupt and short, alleging Mother committed suicide on July 17th .

Far too consumed with Mother's death to question my husband about how we suddenly had enough money for plane tickets, John and I and our two-and-one-half month old baby, Cherisse, flew home. Inundated with the abhorrence that my mother was stolen from me in the blink of an eye, I was propelled with thoughts of going home to see her for the last time and find out the circumstances of her death.

When John, Cherisse, and I arrived at the house, I was shocked that Susan was not there. After all, she knew what time we were coming. Shocked again when John unexpectedly became hungry and sped off to buy something to eat, I felt strangely alone, though not really alone. With my baby in my arms, I opened the front door and walked into the living room of my parent's house, the house in which I had lived for ten years. When I left they were both alive. Now, they were both dead. Even so, the moment I entered, a nostalgic omnipresence surged through me, giving me a heady sensation. Everywhere was the essence of two people whose lives, though at times crazy, had been for me an amazingly loving adventure. I felt their spirits everywhere, consuming both the room and my very beingness in the most mystic of ways, the actual energy of their souls alive and loving me just as always.

On the tables were bouquets of fresh flowers. Not flowers Susan bought for mother after her death, these flowers were from Daddy's funeral, flowers Mother cared for with a lamb's touch. They were still as beautiful and alive as my parents were in me. My body was telling me that even after her death, Mother watched over the flowers so they would be pretty for me when I came home!

While standing on the new plush green shag carpet Mother bought before Daddy died (trying as hard as she could to emotionally prepare for life without her companion of nearly thirty years), I looked out the window and watched Susan drive up in an open convertible, her head covered by a bright silk scarf. Looking as if she were playing a part in an old Hollywood movie, she appeared light-hearted and gay, happier than I had seen her for years.

The inappropriateness of the scene broke the sentiment that had me under its spell and added insult to injury when almost immediately after greeting me, Susan insisted, "Let's divide up Mother's and Daddy's things," her words snapping me back to the reality that my parents were never coming home.

It was then, for the first time, the word inheritance crossed my mind; while adjusting to the idea of choosing among my parents' possessions, which I was not emotionally prepared to do, I asked

Susan, "Where is Mother? I want to see her now!"

"I had her cremated," Susan professed, with the force of one who did not want to be cross-examined.

"What!" I struck out, feeling my mother had been stolen from me a second time. "Why did you do that?"

"That's what Mother wanted. Anyway, by the time we found her on the 20th, her body had already begun to get stiff. She had to be cremated," she rebutted forcefully.

My heart cringed. I could not believe my mother had been dead almost three days before Susan knew it! Prior to going back out on the golf tour with John, I requested that Susan stay with Mother for two weeks after Daddy died. *What happened? It had been only eleven days between the sixth and the seventeenth?* When I spoke with Mother on the telephone on the day Daddy died, she told me she kissed him goodbye for the last time as he lay in the casket. I wanted to kiss my mother goodbye. Tortured by Susan's story, I felt an anger that infused what was left of my ability to remain calm.

I demanded harshly, "What about a funeral?"

Again she defended herself, this time with an answer I did not believe, "Mother didn't want a funeral."

Though I felt Mother would have wanted some kind of memorial, it was too late, so I pushed for more information. "How did Mother die?"

Susan acquiesced. "I found her lying in bed wearing her purple velvet caftan. The bed was made up as elegantly as Mother. A note was on the table next to her bed."

"Show me the note." I ordered, zealous to get as close to my mother's mind-set as possible.

"Follow me," Susan replyed.

I walked down the hall behind my sister and into Mother's and Daddy's bedroom. Mother owned two jewelry boxes, a fabric jewelry box and a metal jewelry box, both she kept in her top drawer. Susan opened the drawer with familiarity; then with the same familiarity, she opened the fabric box containing a tiny piece of paper. On the paper was perfect script handwriting. Oh the stories Mommy told about how her teachers made her practice penmanship over and over until every letter of the alphabet looked exactly like the exemplar.

I picked up the paper, my eyes searching the jewelry box for

Mother's treasure: the real pearl neckless her father gave her at her high school graduation. It was not so much that I wanted the pearls for my own. At that moment, I solely wanted to hold a part of my mother that she held dear to her heart. The pearls were gone. I asked Susan where they were. She asserted that she did not know. With that, I read the words Mother chose to say her last goodbye:

To my beautiful daughters,
  I leave you both my jewels. Please do to each accordingly. With all my heart and soul.
  Your loving Mommy

There were other things missing in the house that July day in 1971. In 1987 when Susan came to visit, it had been sixteen years since I read Mother's note. In the intervening years, I would see Susan's daughter, my niece, who was seven when Mother and Daddy died, wearing the pearls Susan confessed she knew nothing about. I reasoned that if Susan wanted them enough not to "share and share alike," she could keep the pearls. Important to me was Mommy's note, which did not appear important to Susan, for when I asked if I could have it, she gave me the note freely without a sign of sentimentality.

Susan chose the fabric jewelry box right then and there. The fabric box was prettier and probably more valuable than the metal box, but it held little importance to me either. I could keep the note! Since that day, I saved the tiny goodbye message in Mother's metal jewelry box. I also asked Susan if I could have Mother's caftan, which seemed to come as a relief to Susan.

Susan could not have known how special the caftan was to me. Years earlier while I lived at home, Daddy had given Mother some money to buy something pretty to wear around the house. Because of Mother's nervous condition, she had quit driving, so Daddy asked me to take her shopping. Mother had been drinking that day. For some reason she was especially happy, and because her happiness made me happy, I did not care how she behaved or what anyone thought.

I drove her to Buffums, her favorite store. Buffums was small and more intimate than the bigger stores like Bullocks, and it had quality clothing. The sales lady treated Mother with delicacy and respect, for which I was grateful. After Mother described what she had in mind, the sales lady took her straight to the caftan. Mother loved it instantly! I felt relieved she had found something she liked that much so quickly. She took the caftan home and wore it for Daddy right away. He, too, was happy that Mother was happy.

Every day of the sixteen years since Mother's death, I envisioned my stunningly beautiful Mother lying on her bed, wearing her purple velvet caftan. My sister had allowed sixteen years to pass, and now she was about to tell me a different story.

As if the truth she held secret inside for more than a third of her life was being forced from her gut, each word strained from Susan's lips. "Mother had been drinking and carrying on all weekend. My friends and I got tired of it, so we left and went out. When we returned, I found Mother on the bathroom floor leaning over the toilet, passed out. I decided to leave and let Mother choose whether she wanted to live or die."

Infamous in my experience for her ill-planned contradictions, Susan had told me two entirely different stories. As with my questions about my husband's part in my mother's death, it would take me until early 2004, almost thirty-three years, to find the courage to feel the emotions of re-experiencing the circumstances surrounding my mother's suicide. Nearly thirty-three years were required for me to begin my investigation of Susan's conflicting stories. Still, after analyzing every detail I could remember, my investigation left the following unanswered questions:

What was Susan thinking that day in 1971 when she drove up to Daddy's and Mother's house in an open convertible looking so light-hearted and gay? Why did she insist upon dividing up their belongings so soon after I got home? And why did she take Mother's pearls when she knew they were the one piece of Mother's jewelry I treasured? Most of all, why did Mother pass out over the toilet?

Susan knew from living with her for eighteen years that alcohol kept Mother awake. Mother could stay up for days if the festivities called for it. To pass out, she had to have taken the Seconal pills she had saved. Susan was well-aware of the pills and of Mother's and Daddy's suicide pact. *What could Mother have possibly been doing with her head over the toilet if she had not taken the pills, had a change of heart, and was attempting to throw up the pills?* Life or death was not a choice Mother could make after passing out, which the autopsy confirmed. To live, Mother had to be saved.

That day in 1987, sixteen years after Susan's original story, four months after my emotional collapse, and four months into my spiritual enlightenment, I had no desire to deliberate events I have since found necessary in my search for truth. In 1987, I only knew that every word she relieved herself of groaned brutally for forgiveness. My sister had made a life-altering choice that she was never going to be able to take back, and her soul carried the burden of her choice every step she had taken since.

The defensive quality of her tone told me she was not asking for judgment, and I had no desire to judge my sister. One automatic writing ended my right to judge, whether the truths I found in my search appeared to be good or evil. Every step I had taken in my initiation into truth confirmed that I had no right to judge another soul; I could only bless that soul with the healing power of understanding, forgiveness, and compassion. Life is a spiritual event for the development of the soul. In every choice each of us makes, be it good or evil, a lesson is to be learned. Hopefully that lesson will lead us from evil.

I, too, made choices sixteen years earlier I had to live with, and my actions were the only ones I had a right to judge. My prayer was that I could bless my own soul with the healing power of understanding, forgiveness, and compassion. I did not know the day of Susan's 1987 visit if she had learned any lessons from her decision to "let Mother choose whether she wanted to live or die." I did know that no matter how far Susan ran from her deeds, nothing could hold back the dawn. Sooner or later she would be required to face the inner truths written on her outer countenance. That day, I wanted nothing more than to smile upon a seriously troubled human being.

So, I spoke the words I had spoken to my sister a thousand times when we were growing up. "Susan, everything is going to be okay."

If it had been in my power to take it all back, for my sister, for myself, and for the grandmother our daughters would never know, I would have. The impossibility of my changing the past hung heavily on Susan's face. Words that healed the child did not meet the needs of the adult.

Thus, I gave my one treasured sibling the unconditional love springing forth from my heart and soul. "Susan, to find peace with the way Mother died, you must understand why she died. Mother died because you chose not to forgive her. To understand why you were unable to forgive, you must understand yourself and understand your relationship with Mother. Yes, Mother hurt you many times while you were growing up, but she hurt you because she was hurting. Although her broken heart broke your heart, your broken heart broke her heart in return. Ending the cycle of retribution with understanding is learning to forgive. Only when you seek to forgive both mother and yourself will you find the compassion that will release both of your souls from shame. To heal your broken heart, you must mentally return to your childhood and feel all over again every time Mother hurt your feelings. Then you must remember every time you hurt her feelings. Hurt feelings must be revealed to be healed. Getting the pain up is the way to get it out. Peace will only come into your heart when you forgive. To love Mother, to love the world, you must love yourself enough to take that step."

The instant I finished speaking, Susan's face softened and her eyes gazed at me lovingly. She knew my words meant I had truly forgiven her for her part in Mother's death and that my wish was for her to move forward and heal. My unconditional forgiveness eased the pain her decision caused me; nonetheless, my forgiveness would not relieve Susan of the responsibility to walk through the tunnel of truths surrounding Mother's death. In my absolute certainty that she would continue to reap what she had sewn either by personal choice or by forced choice, by human justice or divine justice, I hoped my forgiveness would ease her pain enough for her to choose the path of healing.

We talked all night. In the morning, we watched the sun rise up across Telly's pasture, behind the rolling hills. Light began filtering through tall emerald trees, making my sister's eyes shine. She was getting a glimpse of a patch of nature I had grown to love.

Later, we dressed and went to the country club where we toasted two sisters reunited in oneness. Together we sat gazing out the window at the golf course and watched the day come to a close. Swans on the course's lake flapped their wings, spiriting water into the air. The setting sun reflected angels in each droplet telling Susan and me we were in paradise.

The next morning we waved goodbye with tears in our eyes and sunshine in our hearts. Whatever either of us had to overcome in the future, my prayer was that we had each other to count on.

Infinite space forever and ever in all directions is filled with consciousness.
One single indivisible being infinitely present everywhere. And that is
what we are. There isn't anything else.

– Eyvind Earle

22

Part II

Rites of Passage

November 12, 1987, 11:00 A.M.

I remained on the front porch with my eyes glued to Susan's green car until it faded from sight. Our reuniting left me bursting with good feelings. At last, my sister spoke the truth about our mother's death out loud. The courage it took to endure the feelings of telling her sister her truth was a giant step in changing her life.

I felt Susan's journey toward the light of her soul began at that moment. She had stepped into the arduous task of peeling off layer after layer of painful shadows, many created for her, many she created. Someday, my sister might understand the unresolved anger that led her to the point where she would decide not to save our mother's life. The speed with which Susan walked through her valley and purified her shadow was solely between her and her *desire* to admit, feel, and atone for each negative thought and emotion she faced. To seize and destroy her need for beastly reciprocity, Susan would need to be relentless in having an attitude of *willingness*. An imperishable desire to pursue trials by fire would be the key to her soul's development. Her initiation into the mysteries of the unknown self had to begin in the pit of her heart where dark shadows had manifested. I hoped my heart had given her heart the courage to slay the demons arising from the fallibilities of human reason and feed her hungry soul with the divine reason of *UFC*.

For my part, Susan's truth turned out to be a prophecy. Destiny urged my feelings to go to the one place they did not want to go in my quest to know my whole truth. Inescapably intertwined were the roots of Mother's suicide and my suicide attempt. My job as a human being desiring full spiritual enlightenment was to investigate how those roots were connected.

Like a fragile little sparrow, Mother's heart was innocent and tender, sensitive and vulnerable. Unhappily, her unyielding sentimental heart was burdened with shame.

In one of Mother's nostalgic moods, after a long, hard night of drinking, followed by a long crying spell in the morning over her deceased parents she missed so much, she would recite incidents from her childhood. "My father used to whip me with his razor strap. Once I fell against the toilet and killed my front tooth. That's why it's discolored. The color has always bothered me. Both of my parents drank to the point of passing out every night. On the day of the only birthday party my mother and I ever planned for me, she decorated the house and made a birthday cake. After school when I walked through the door with my friends, she sat passed out on the chair in the living room. I was so ashamed, I told everyone to go home."

Though Mother's photographic memory gained her a 4.0 grade point average in high school and a college scholarship, she was never able to psychologically overcome the shame inevitable when a child has two parents addicted to alcohol. The emotional abandonment of physical whippings and two collapsing parents caused Mother to be too insecure to pursue a career. She married my father during her first year in college and grew to be so dependent upon him, she felt incapable of living without him. At forty-seven years old, eleven days after Daddy died of cancer, Mother decided to fulfill their suicide pact and join him.

Growing up, I watched Mother with the same loving eyes that watched Daddy. Beneath her sweet way of nurturing me lay the breath of sadness. When she cried, my heart cried for her sorrow. When she drank, my soul drank from her wounded heart. To stop my heart and soul from feeling Mother's every wound, I adopted Daddy's "live-

and-let-live" character and emulated his capacity to "live life to the fullest."

Prior to my fall, I spent a lifetime denying how immeasurably Mother's life affected my life. My revelations taught me how adopting Daddy's strengths caused me to judge Mother's wounded heart as weakness and how judgment caused me to abandon my mother in myself. By repressing my mother's wounded heart and storing it in my subconscious, my judgment of weakness turned into a fear of which I was in conscious denial. Denial of my fear of my mother in myself stunted my capacity for understanding, not only for the psychology of the behaviors of others but also for the psychology of my own behaviors.

Being confronted with the manner in which Mother died called into account the extensive roots of her suicide in me. Locked away in my subconscious, beyond conscious reach, remained the indelible connection between my mother and myself. I needed help in opening a window of understanding, and I knew exactly where to seek and find that open window. With automatic writing, I could silence the activity in my mind and effortlessly receive and record information from my soul's oneness with Universal Spirit. The information I sought flowed directly into and spoke through my hands. I walked into the master bedroom, sat on my bed, picked up my pencil, asked my question, and then made a direct connection with the source of my life:

Diana, as a child you wanted to mend the wounds in your mother's sad eyes. To do this, you waited until you grew up and then married her suffering. You became the victim of a violent, emotionally abusive, control-obsessed man like your mother's father. Experiencing your mother's abandonment through your husband was the way you chose to learn how her wounded heart felt. You went so far as to experience your own emotional death in order to feel the emptiness that led to your mother's tragic end. You learned that the abyss results from feelings of being left alone, not from a sentimental heart, and that your mother's suicide left an empty space in your heart where a loving life should have been.

I stopped my pencil and remembered how John's menacing degradation, *you're just like your mother*, repeatedly raped my denial of my fear of my mother in myself, finally blowing a hole in the life force of my soul. When my driving force broke down, denial fled and my subconscious judgments landslided into my consciousness. What remained was a personal experience of my mother's wounded heart. Just like my mother, the empty space my husband left in my heart that should have been filled with love killed my will to live.

Nevertheless, outside my windows lived trees and the nature of a child named Diana. Trees, the clearest mirror of the child's soul, spoke to the woman. Glimpsing my true nature imparted miraculous healing. My original nature arose from the dead to fill the holes of loneliness in my heart with love. Nature was reborn in the woman and woke her up to the wisdom of her experience: Twas love that killed the beast of loneliness. My thoughts stopped, so I let my pencil continue:

> *You learned that emptiness did not kill the way John wounded your heart any more than death killed your mother's wounded heart. Unlike your mother, you stood tall, walked through the tunnel of lonely feelings, and then began detaching from the emotional hold your husband had on your life. By answering the call of divine grace, you learned why life is the greatest gift and suicide the greatest tragedy. Suicide steals the opportunity to learn the lessons necessary to fill every lonely hole with love. Diana, you can fill the empty spaces of your mother's unfinished life for her and mend her wounded soul. With the divine grace alive in you, blow life back into the mother you killed in yourself. When you love your mother in yourself fully and unconditionally, you will have released her from bondage to an unfinished life and fill every lonely hole in her soul with love. US*

I looked up from my automatic writing. I found it incredible how my husband and my mother were so inescapably interconnected in my subconscious. Not once did I have a conscious thought that I spent eighteen years living in an abusive relationship to take the sadness out of my mother's eyes. Nor did I know that miracle was possible! Exhaustively, my conscious mind underestimated the degree to which my mother's and my life were intertwined. After Mother's life was cut short, whatever the sacrifice, my subconscious would have pushed me to the ends of the earth to give my mother back her life.

By staying with John for so long after Mother died, I walked into hell for a heavenly cause. Yes, I experienced my mother's wounded heart and wanted to die. But wanting to die taught me the humility necessary to stop judging my mother's sad eyes as weakness and see them for what they were: the window into a human being whose feelings had been abandoned. My suffering gave me the understanding I needed to ease my mother's suffering out of me and fill the empty spaces of her unfinished life with love.

John knew Mother's wounded heart as well as he knew my trusting heart, that *like Mother like daughter* our hearts were intertwined in vulnerability and innocence. Sadly, he hedged his bets that if he wounded my trust, I would not want to live *just like my mother*. His bets, however, contained a tragic error. Alive in me was my iron will to live life to the fullest *just like my father*.

The courage of my iron will to fall offered me the opportunity to truly live life to the fullest. For it was in falling that I learned to pick myself up and stand tall. In sacrificing my innocence, against all odds, I broke the cycle of violence in my home. My fall had turned worms into flowers. For me, *like Mother like daughter,* abandoned feelings would be no longer. And for my daughters, *just like your mother* would be living life to the fullest!

A picture of Mother and Daddy on the table next to my bed drew my attention away from my thoughts. I looked into their eyes and felt the boundless love in their eyes looking back at me.

Daddy's voice blew through the spell of matter and blasted out in my mind. *Diana, remember who you are! Aren't you a chip off the old block?*

As tears of love welled up in my eyes, my heart cried, *Yes, Daddy!*

Then, something he loved asking me changed my tears into laughter, *What's the most important thing about the bullfights?*

The answer had always been the same.

The tickets! my heart cried out.

My father's sprit called me to live my truth. *Always remember, Diana, you are a product of your father and your mother. Knowing who you are and loving who you are is your ticket to be.*

Able to hear Daddy's pearls of wisdom and feel their truth, I felt his spirit in the room with me living life to the fullest. My experience with the light-being in the bathroom had demonstrated how my parents were only a vibration away, alive and well, living in a parallel universe, overlapping and interpenetrating my universe. Learning to connect with Universal Spirit by way of automatic writing had given me the ability, as well, to hear and feel the spirits of my beloved parents, Charley and Marie, when they were around. In truth, they were nearer to me than before they died. Nearer than my head was to my pillow, Mother, Father, and child, we were truly one!

With divine grace alive in me, I answered Daddy's call to arms. I released the shadows of fear of my mother in myself and blew life back into her. I sat in bed loving my mother unconditionally. Feeling the fullness of her life being reborn in me, I felt unconditional love filling the empty spaces of the mother I abandoned in myself. I could feel the glory of the life she had lived, the beauty of all she had sacrificed to make my life a heavenly place to be. Far and above anything she could have ever done to give me a wonderful life was my mother's inexorably sentimental heart.

With my mother's spirit living happily in me, my soul rejoiced! Mother's spirit appeared iridescent in its light. It radiated from my eyes as brightly as my father's spirit always had. With joy I felt the wholeness of my mother and my father in myself. The circle of my life with my parents complete, I closed my eyes and finished my automatic writing:

Behold, Diana, the purity of your love for your mother and your father! Your love has always been pure. You simply needed to fall to realize pure love is the way to your true nature, which is divine. Divine spiritual nature flows through all souls. It is the rainbow-bridge that connects every soul. By feeling the abandoned feelings of your mother, your husband, your sister, and your children, you have experienced the oneness of all of humanity. Being one with those you love

*has spread love throughout the entire universe. Feeling
nothing but love for all you know is your ticket to be.*
Love, US

"To be" was the ticket I held in the palm of my hand before my fall.
Unchained by temptations of my flesh, I desired nothing other than to
be free to be me. My mission to love all that I knew unconditionally
was *my driving force*. One with my soul everywhere I wandered, I
never knew real pain or fear. My *soul* chose to give up freedom and
forced me to suffer mental beatings and abandoned feelings. *It*
challenged me to overcome death in order to practice prior lessons at
ever-deepening levels.

Surviving the fall convinced me that my life had some purpose
other than the one I was following. When I heard the voice "write
your book," the reason for my fall began to answer itself in three
required tasks. *First*: I was required to experience the schoolhouse of
multitudes beaten and abandoned. My experiential investigation with
the condition of human suffering would give me the *keys* to
psychological healing. Understanding, forgiveness, and compassion
would bridge the gap in my broken heart, the only way for me to get
out of the pit. *Second*: My mind was required to connect with the voice
of my soul. The knowledge gained from my soul's oneness with
Universal Spirit would give me *keys* to *spiritual healing*. Once I had
been given the keys to psychological and spiritual healing, I was
required to the give them freely to whomever I met. *Third:* If I could
accomplish the first and second task, I would have sought, found, and
been a living example of *The Philosophy*. Only when that *ancient
wisdom* was mine to have, hold, and give to the world could I complete
a book that answered the question in my mind. . . .

Learning understanding, forgiveness, and compassion for the
darkness as well as the light in myself was the *key* to learning
unconditional love for the darkness as well as the light. Having
knowledge of, and love for, both good and evil resulted from being
initiated into the secret teaching that it did not matter how many forks
in the road, all soul journeys lead to the same rainbow's-end of oneness
with Universal Spirit. My initiatory journey taught me that by seeking,
finding, and learning how to be a living example of *The Philosophy*

of *UFC+US,* I had discovered the rainbow-bridge out of spiritual darkness into the light of wisdom. If I had not sought, found, and was learning to live my truth, how else could I have known those *keys to happiness* were what I was seeking?

Whereas my revelations initiated me into the upward spiral of the seven-fold path to my divine spiritual nature, experiencing the enlightenment of the three great chambers of my body taught me that the arch sin of religion is that it forestalls experience. Dogma rules out the kingdom of heaven because it rules out the paradise only to be found within.

Because a rainbow-bridge has been discovered for humanity to return to heaven, to be sounded are the bells that tole for the doom of hell. The theological tower of confusion and chaos built of the false doctrine that has made a million mysteries out of the one great truth shall either be lifted into the fiery trials of the initiation into heaven or be lowered into the hell that burns with the fire and brimstone dogma itself created.

By knowing who I was seeking, I learned that this final armageddon between the lower and higher mind shall end in the destruction of those million mysteries. Cast into a sea of hellfire and damnation will be the false profit of the soul's evil nature. These fires will awaken severe trials in the name of humanity's purification and transformation. In this last win/lose battle between flesh and spirit, the last judgment shall vanquish the secret of the ages, wherein the book of life will be opened to the weighting of all souls according to *its* works. Out of the ashes of the collective shadow of lifeless creeds shall rise a global initiation into humanity's spiritual nature, *freedom* from death to life!

From the schoolhouse of my fall into freedom, I learned that no one ever need be sick in the mind, body, or soul. Heartbreak will end for those who study their higher mind to understand that the meaning of life is to co-create with universal laws, for those natural laws are epitomized in the human mind. *The liberation of the ancient wisdom that every single soul is an irreplaceable aspect of a flawless universe can heal the world and bring peace on earth.* When each of us simply remembers the who that *I AM,* that each of us is the creator that created ourselves, divine, eternal, patterned after the supreme being, happiness

THE PHILOSOPHY

The Philosophy of *UFC (Understanding, Forgiveness, and Compassion)* +*US (Universal Spirit)* is a psycho-spiritual model of enlightenment. *UFC* is the psychological process of enlightening the mind/body. *US* (meditation with *Universal Spirit*) is the spiritual process of enlightening the mind/body. *UFC+US* work as one to enlighten the mind, as exemplified in *Fall Into Freedom.*

UFC PYRAMID: *The Three Keys To Happiness*

UNDERSTANDING: The Key to Forgiveness
1) The root cause of unhappiness begins as hurt feelings, then turns into pain, then anger, then hate, and finally fear.
2) To free oneself from fear, hurt feelings (the root cause of fear) must be understood to be healed.
3) One must take responsibility and be accountable for healing hurt feelings.

FORGIVENESS: The Key to Compassion
1) Completes the process of healing of hurt feelings.
2) Healing hurt feelings frees oneself from fear.
3) Freeing oneself from fear ends unhappiness.

COMPASSION: The Key to Oneness
1) Opens the heart, the passageway between mind and soul.
2) Opening the passageway allows mind and soul to co-create life as one (enlightenment).
3) Oneness of mind and soul effects unconditional love for all souls; oneness is *the living soul, i.e., happiness.*

UFC+US

Meditation is the mind directly connecting with the soul, which is spirit. The soul, now and forever, is one with all souls, i.e., *Universal Spirit (US).* Oneness with *US* is practiced daily for ourselves, for others, and for nature with the three keys to happiness *(UFC)!*

THREE KEYS TO HAPPINESS

UNDERSTANDING

PURIFY

Hurt - Pain - Anger
Hate - Fear

SPIRITUALIZE

Mind - Body

FORGIVENESS   *COMPASSION*

UFC: *The Way to Manifest*
The Living Soul!

will live in our hearts forever and ever!

Given the wisdom and the power to enlighten the cellular structure of the body by making a mental shift from physical to spiritual, the high mountain of the mind can quicken the energy pattern of the seven spiritual centers in the body and build the divine kingdom into the human kingdom. To fulfill our destiny from human to divine, we must purify our hearts so we can give to the whole world the three keys to happiness (see pages 328-329), the understanding, forgiveness, and compassion that will create the unconditional love that will return to *us* in-kind.

> *I will give you the keys to the kingdom of heaven,*
> *and whatever you bind on earth shall be bound in heaven,*
> *and whatever you loose on earth shall be loosed in heaven.*
> – Matt, 16:19

Given the rite of passage to the highest peak in the pyramid of Diana's mind were the three golden keys to the seven sacred wonders of the soul sanctified inside the temple of her body. The golden keys of *The Philosophy* of *UFC+US* are the rainbow-bridge to conscious immortality. By uniting itself with its own spiritual source, Diana found that with the power of the mind, one by one we can drop the veil of matter, purify and transform our bodies, and build a ground swell into an enlightened multitude who can initiate the *second coming of the soul on earth, the living soul!* A global initiation will make possible an enlightened age to arise from the bottomless pit of the unenlightened. After the storm, a rainbow! Arisen into union with the soul, the illuminated heart and understanding mind of an awakened multitude will establish a new heaven and a new earth, initiating planetary *I AM THAT I AM*, that imperishable spark of the inner kingdom of life everlasting! The light, the life, the truth of the destiny of the human race is that in the end times of false doctrine, there shall be a joyous world without end for each and every *ONE!*

The greatest thing you will ever learn is just
to love and be loved in return.
— Eden Ahbez (born Alexander Aberle), *Nature Boy*

23
Bubble Of Love

November 19, 1987, 4:00 P.M.

Gaiety pervaded our home. Flames from the fire in the fireplace dividing the family room and the kitchen nook bounced cheerfully. A winter rain had washed every cloud from the sky leaving an afternoon sun to light millions of flawlessly placed raindrops. Trees cast jarring contrasts between lights and shadows outside every window. Waterstars on blades of grass added even more sparkle to the countryside panorama dazzling my eyes.

After spending the day preparing her costume for the high school play, *Dracula*, Cherisse strolled buoyantly into the kitchen where I moved from place to place making dinner.

"Are you nervous about the play tonight?" I asked.

"A little, I have only a couple of lines and I have them memorized," she replied as she handed me two tickets, explaining, "You're in the second row."

"Perfect," I cheered, taking into consideration my nearsightedness.

Tamara joined us, savoring the aroma of the Italian spices in my hot, freshly cooked spaghetti sauce.

"Dinner smells good," she whiffed enthusiastically.

We lifted our plates off the kitchen counter, covered them with pasta, sauce, and garlic bread, then sat down on nook chairs to the joy of eating!

Cherisse eagerly described her part in the play. "I'm mostly in the group scenes. It's going to be hilarious because so many of my friends are in the same scenes. We all wear wild costumes and even wilder make-up. Most of the time we just crawl around moaning ghoulish sounds."

Tamara chuckled, started to tease her sister when John hobbled in from the direction of the garage. Our cheerful small-talk came to a speedy halt as we stared at a crooked man in obvious pain. His body was bent to the left at the hip and a bottle of Korbel Extra Dry swung back and forth from his right hand.

Sneering at our cozy little dinner, he groaned, "I just stood up and my hip popped out. It hurt all last night and all day today."

Cherisse, Tamara, and I glanced at each other. Happy talk, now curious silence, we all had the same, *What the heck?* formed on our faces. Rounding the kitchen counter, John tugged the champagne cork while concocting his besotted announcement.

"This is to celebrate our anniversary," he said, not a trace of celebration in his *I've already had a few* tone.

Without the slightest effort to diagnose the crooked man's diagnosable behavior, I stated plain truth. "Our anniversary was three months ago. Tonight is Cherisse's winter play."

I looked at Cherisse.

Her expression made clear her *I don't want Dad to go to the play in that condition* feelings.

I did not mention the play to John again.

Under tall, randomly strewn eucalyptus trees, the enchanting high school theater was in a separate building from the main campus. It stood alone at the end of a short, curving, blacktop road. Inside, the quaint drama room arranged like a miniature theater felt instantly intimate and snug. After Tamara and I located the two chairs in the second row that matched the numbers on our tickets, she considerately kept me company by sitting in her father's empty chair.

Mothers, fathers, brothers, and sisters of cast members positioned in chairs surrounding us made the room hum with rhythmic chatter. Attempting not to appear too conspicuous, I snatched a glimpse of as many faces as my position allowed. The intensity of the loving energy radiating from faces of supportive families inspired my warm gratitude. With one daughter by my side, the other ready to entertain us, the night paid tribute to the lack of emotional separation that had divinely graced our passage into the sweetness of this charmed evening.

At intermission Tamara requested, "Would it be okay if I watched the rest of the play with my friends?"

"Yes, I want you to," I answered enthusiastically, sure she would have a better time with her classmates.

Dracula entertained throughout, crawling ghouls and all, making me sure every person in the miniature playhouse had as much fun as I. After the last bow, Tamara rejoined me and we mingled for a while, complimenting each actor, especially Cherisse, on how exceptionally well all the actors had performed their roles. After congratulations were given and the evening was drawing to a close, Tamara and I wished Cherisse a good time at the cast party, then hugged and kissed her goodbye. All-in-all the evening a smashing success, we drove home in high spirits.

Ahead of me, Tamara opened the door to the house from the garage. Mickey barked, noisily protecting his territory. After petting Mickey and Suki, we went straight to the kitchen where we spotted a very empty bottle of Korbel on the counter, the culprit nowhere to be seen. As we gazed at each other breathing a sigh of relief at his absence, the phone rang.

His singular style of grabbing my attention sounded on the other end of the line. "Come to the country club. There's someone here who wants to meet you."

Dressed and ready to go, how could I resist?

Practically every stool along the glamourously lit clubhouse bar stood empty. Against the stool nearest the front entrance leaned John, mentally critiquing the totality of my appearance the second I stepped through the door. A stylishly dressed man with a sophisticated demeanor, whom I guessed to be in his early-fifties, sat easily on the stool next to John. The man stood the moment he saw me.

Like John, but in a sensitive and far less obtrusive manner, the stranger also analyzed my appearance. When I got close enough, he discreetly introduced himself, then studied John's eyes as if beseeching him for help. When the help did not arrive, the man shook his head.

A discouraged depth of knowing engendered his speech. "John, this is not the woman you described to me. I'm truly disappointed. All this time I've spent with you, listening to everything you had to say. I believed what you told me."

He paused and waited for an explanation. I did not attempt to guess the words John had used to describe me to a stranger. Certain to have vilified not venerated my feminine qualities, whatever lengthy accusations his primitive style could embellish, John remained leaning against his stool watching the two of us as if we were entertainment, offering nothing more than a knowing smile.

Realizing he spoke to deaf ears, the gentleman whose name I cannot remember appeared to be tortured by what he wanted to say next.

He lowered his voice, this time demanding audience, and pronounced his words in harsh, serious tones. "John, I think you better reevaluate your situation."

The gentleman, small in stature, huge in integrity, turned toward me and stared through my eyes as if into my soul. A pure, giving energy emanated from his being into mine. From his eyes flowed a lifetime of lessons learned. Compassion for my predicament prayed mercifully to be shared, knowing it would not be shared.

I wished the man knew I read in his eyes the billion heartbeats it took to become the giant he showed himself to be. I stood silent, allowing the man who would always remain a stranger a gentleman's exit.

His farewell heralded gentleness. "You are a beautiful woman. It has been my pleasure meeting you."

Having given me the remindful gift of demonstrating that my husband's dragon-path diversions from truth hurt anyone they touched, an extraordinary human being left, still shaking his head. The clubhouse door had not completely closed when the amusing observations on John's face transmuted into lethal weapons.

As if he wanted nothing less than to rip my face off, a different but no less divisive dragon emerging to give tongues to his inebriated condition. "See, Diana! Nobody likes you. You have made my life miserable."

I opted to respond calmly yet firmly. "I'll drive you home. We can get your truck in the morning."

He counted the cash on the bar, tossed the bartender a tip, scrunched up the rest of the wad, shoved it into his pocket, and then blurted out how fear unforgivingly turns lights into shadows. "It would be easy for me just to end up on skid row and die."

Exactly when John's middle-age crisis began I did not know. But all those days I had the feeling that he wanted to die as I watched him mix cement in the front yard, what I actually sensed was that, on top of everything else, he had begun to fight an inner war with his death. His heart wounded by the crucifiction of his infinite self, the symptom of his fear of his finite self was the divine comedy of falling into love's ring of fire with a younger woman. But even the empowering flames of capturing a younger woman could not burn up his belief in life's one absolute. The certainty of death had so much power over his mind that fear had him trapped in a cave with death.

After begrudgingly walking with me to the car, the entire drive on the curved, two-lane road home, John treated me to his singular manner of capturing my attention. "I hate you, Diana. I want to die. I'm going to kill myself!"

November 26, 1987, Thanksgiving

"Everybody knows a turkey and some mistletoe help to make the season bright." I sang out loud as I reached to open the oven door.

Our twenty-two pound turkey had cooked to a soft golden brown while simmering in its own bubbling juices. The old boy was ready to be covered up so he would be just the right shade for carving. Every inch of our house thrilled to the fragrance of Thanksgiving turkey.

Cherisse, Tamara, and I arose early to make sure all the preparations were completed before company arrived. All morning they stood by my side, chopping, peeling, stuffing, table setting, and, keeping with family tradition, playing Christmas carols!

Both Ruth and Darlene called during those early hours to send Thanksgiving cheer our way. New friends, Bill and Adele, were coming over for eggnog and hors d'oeuvres, and John's brother Bob and his new wife were arriving later to share in the partaking of the feast. Neither Cherisse nor Tamara commented on their father not being home that morning.

Bright eyes sauntered in around 9:00 in the morning wearing a new red button-down sweater, very similar to the one he wore the night we met.

I welcomed him with, "Happy Thanksgiving," as he passed, checking out the totality of the scene.

He replied with what sounded like, "Hmm," then headed straight for the refrigerator and a beer.

In the early afternoon, Bill and Adele arrived with a splendid offering of Bill's homemade pasta. After giving them the traditional home tour, the girls and boys separated for girl-talk and boy-talk. Later we all gathered around the kitchen counter where hors d'oeuvres were ready to tantalize Thanksgiving appetites.

We all chatted in animated, high-spirited tones. After engaging in the finer moments of the group's exchange of thoughts, Cherisse and Tamara politely excused themselves. The conversation had gravitated between Bill, who was older than John's father, and John.

Resonating in dramatically lower tones, a vehement distaste for what he was about to say led Bill's absence of pretense about his viewpoint. "John, all you do is talk about how bad your wife has been for eighteen years. You say she deserves your hate, yet you haven't explained what is so bad about Diana. Take a look around at your home, your daughters, your wife, and their preparations for this day of Thanksgiving. What do you see?"

John's eyes inspected the kitchen, then the nook, and then the family room. Finally, he riveted his attention on the enormous wood beam spanning the length of the thirty-foot ceiling in the family room. I recalled his narrative on how our construction crew needed his help to guide the gigantic beam into place. He had not uttered one word to validate or invalidate Bill's point of view. Arrogant pride filled his eyes.

Adele moved closer to support her aging husband from being hurt by John's speechless arrogance.

Bill held his wife's hand and sacrificed not one syllable of his sagacity. "Adele and I believe God's law. This hate of yours, John, will someday return to you."

John laughed defiantly and then accentuated his philosophical schizophrenia. "God is in me. People and things around me are what make me know I'm standing here. If other people weren't around me, how would I know I'm alive? Everything Diana and I have, I did it all. Diana did nothing. I don't intend to forgive her!"

Exposed in the contest of conversation was the conflict between John's inner and outer convictions. Bill, the wise father John never had, had pursued the offender only to show him the way home. He had tried with all his heart to tell John how he separated himself from the love of his wife and children by caving himself in hate. In return, John showed the sage how a closed mind blocks the way home. The sum-total of his Thanksgiving wishes for two dear souls was to do battle. His tempest no deeper than ignorance of truth, John had used hate-crimes to war the honesty of Bill's words.

Bill and Adele waited patiently for John to complete his repetitive oratory and then abruptly announced their departure. I escorted them to the front steps and thanked them warmly for blessing our family with their companionship and gifting us with Bill's special pasta.

Once we were out of John's earshot, my angelic friends spoke in quiet, concerned tones. "John is interested only in remaining unforgiving and mean and in hating you. His selfishness is intolerable. He's determined not to change. We're concerned for your and your daughters' safety, Diana. The three of you deserve happiness."

Feeling every ounce of the love Bill and Adele gave so freely, I reciprocated by attempting to ease their struggle. "I appreciate your concern and agree with every word you said today. I wanted John to spend the holidays in the house we built, but he's going to move out before New Year's Eve. Please don't worry about Cherisse, Tamara, or me. We'll be all right."

In unison, the couple turned toward the countryside. Hand in hand they ascended the steps, concern not leaving either of their faces. I waved goodbye as their car circled the driveway, grateful we had a few moments of enjoyment before one person had the chance to spoil it for everyone else. As their car passed behind the driveway's dirt center, I pictured the tree John told me he wanted to plant there.

Just as true friends were departing, John's brother and his wife drove up. I invited them into the house. We entered the family room in the nick of time to witness John disintegrate into drunkenness. When the moment arrived for the turkey carving ceremony, he sat passed out on the sofa, head leaning backward, snoring a freight train concerto.

After Cherisse and Tamara rejoined us, I requested from Bob that he have the honor of carving the turkey. He graciously accepted and then rapidly proceeded to chop the old boy into large chunks. Excluding John, we all took our places at the Thanksgiving table, not one ill word spoken about the host's absence. Keeping with one of my favorite traditions, I requested that each person at the table bestow personal thanks for what s/he was most thankful for in the past year. Following an array of thanks, we all ravaged our food.

When our Thanksgiving feast had been consumed down to the last piece of pumpkin pie and everyone had adjourned from the table, my sister-in-law took me aside. Having been married numerous times, with concern for me in her voice she volunteered some gracious advice about divorce lawyers she had known. I listened in confidential agreement that while she supported me, she did not want her husband to know.

With no one to talk to except the dogs, Bob strolled aimlessly around the house for a while, meandered into the family room, and suggested to his wife that they leave. Cherisse, Tamara, and I waved goodbye to our last guests, after which an urge to call my sister came over me. Heeding that inner call, I strolled into the master bedroom and dialed Susan's telephone number.

She answered, sounding grateful to hear my voice. "Diana, my life has been much better since my visit with you."

Our short conversation reaffirmed my feelings of peace between us. I placed the receiver on the hook and sat thinking about Thanksgiving and how many reasons one day had brought me to be thankful.

Cherisse and Tamara had elevated my soul with towering flames of loving companionship. Ruth and Darlene had brightened my day with Thanksgiving wishes from afar. Bill and Adele were the embodiment of angels of mercy. Bob and his wife had lightened my burden by taking my mind off the fact that my husband passed out before anyone sat down to the dinner I had spent weeks planning and preparing. A table of caring and sharing was set before me all day. I had much for which to be thankful.

December 14, 1987, 12:45 P.M.

"Santa's on his way. He's filled his sleigh with things, pretty things for you and for me." Frank Sinatra's fabulous voice rang out.

"Should we get our tree at the Christmas Tree Farm again this year?" Cherisse requested, as she, Tamara, and I gathered together in the kitchen, prepared for our search for the perfect tree.

I returned her question with a question. "Of course! How many feet do you think will look best in the family room?"

"At least eight feet," Tamara demanded, with studied assurance.

I responded to my younger daughter's decree by asking for her advice. "Do you think Santa will fit down the chimney? Wait! Which of our three chimneys is he going to come down?"

We all laughed.

"It's that time of year when the world falls in love. Every song you hear, seems to say, Merry Christmas. May your every New Year's dream come true." Old Blue Eyes drew to a close the Jules Styne-Sammy Cahn masterpiece, *The Christmas Waltz*.

Francis Albert Sinatra was helping us celebrate our Christmas season with his unparalleled phrasing and tones that reached out from the core of his soul. His music had been a part of every Christmas of Cherisse's and Tamara's lives and, because of Charley Weitzel, all of mine before they were born. We had that in common, Cherisse, Tamara and I, as we had so much in common. We were a team again that Christmas of 1987.

We had begun our journey into maturity in true oneness, an all-for-one, one-for-all attitude the three of us understood on the deepest level. Because my heart had been willing to go the distance, my mind's connection to my soul had broken the cycle of violence in my home. My children would not marry into domestic violence and pass it down to another generation. One love born of three souls would include all souls born to my children and my children's children.

Future bubbles would not be forced to burst because of heartbreak. The meaning and purpose of future generations of children would be safeguarded and nurtured so body, mind, heart, and soul could function as one. In sacrificing our innocence, we had lit an inner flame no one could extinguish. Cherisse, Tamara, and I were going to begin a new world in our own home, a golden age where bubbles of love had sovereign power. Wherever we were in our initiatory journey, we had begun a new cycle of learning the lessons we needed to reach our destiny. And for now those lessons included guess who!

I alerted my children. "I'll have to go and get money for the tree from Daddy."

To avert a confrontation with her father, Cherisse announced her aversive position. "I'll wait here."

"I'll go with you," Tamara volunteered bravely.

At 6:00 that morning, John woke me up to provoke me into signing several inconsequential papers and then ambulated outside to butcher our overgrown silver dollar trees running along the right side of the driveway. Amassing evidence in support of advancing stages of developmental arrest, at 9:30 A.M. he left trimmed tree branches strewn all over the ground, started drinking, and then slipped into his little yellow truck and drove away. I knew where Tamara and I could find him.

Stinger's barstools were full of cowboys, the kind of cowboys who work until noon and then hang out at *last chance saloon* to spin a wintry tale or two. Tamara stood guard at the front door while I took my chances with her father. Winter in southern California seemed to be a friendly season for cowboys. Each buckaroo sat straight up on his barstool gaping at me as if I were a Christmas surprise! I could have sworn I spotted a twinkle in one cowboy's eye.

I offered good tidings to the group with a neighborly, "Hi," and promptly fixed my attention on John. "John, Tamara and I came to get money for our Christmas tree."

John riveted his head toward the doorway to assure himself that I was telling the truth.

"Hi, Tamara," he reluctantly allowed his daughter.

The cowboy second from my right befriended my predicament. "Give her the money, man. Your daughter needs a Christmas tree."

John motioned toward the pile of large bills that lay on the bar close to his drink.

"Take what you want," he slurred.

I retrieved enough money for a nice sized tree and turned to leave when a different cowboy signaled me over. I stepped a few paces toward his stool.

"Take him with you. He's been at the rodeo too long," he cautioned.

"I'm sorry I can't get him out of your way," I apologized, feeling his irritation. Acknowledging that John would not willingly go with me, I explained. "He must decide when he wants to go home himself."

Mission accomplished, Tamara and I left and drove home to pick up Cherisse.

December 14, 1987, 2:15 P.M.

The Christmas Tree Farm smelled like heaven. Trees grew in all shapes and sizes. Cherisse, Tamara, and I reveled in our search for the perfect tree, measuring height, contemplating fullness and shape, and visualizing it in the family room. We worked at choosing our tree until we were completely satisfied with our final selection.

Tamara proudly designated the symbolic task hers. "I'll cut down the tree."

Cherisse and I steadied the centerpiece of our holiday season while Tamara sawed. Gleefully, all three of us carried our Noble Pine to a young man who measured its footage. Tamara was truly a prophet! Our choice had grown exactly eight feet tall!

Like three peas in a pod, we sang Christmas carols in-sync with the car radio the whole way home. Our whimsical visions pictured lights, ornaments, decorations, and presents abounding. Old St. Nick was a kind old soul who lit our hearts with song. If it is true that your parents' words make you feel most at home, and if it is also true that the amount of your soul that is expressed in your life is shown in your children's lives, then the song Cherisse and Tamara sang was the most magical mirror I had ever looked into! Our bubble of love, a divine kingdom, three souls were alive and well that December day, making peace, harmony, and joy in this heaven called earth. Three as one, our evolution toward unity epitomized my every heart's desire.

Mickey and Suki stood guard by the Christmas tree stand as they watched us carry our prize tree through the back door that led straight into the family room. With concentrated effort, it took the strength of six hands to maneuver our celebrated tree in the upright position, after which we stood marveling over the majesty before us. For the next three weeks, the handpicked centerpiece of our holiday season would remind us that the inherent forces of nature were unsurpassed.

I turned on Christmas carols. Tamara untangled the lights. Cherisse answered the ringing telephone.

She handed me the receiver saying, "A strange-sounding man asked to speak to John's wife."

I put the receiver to my ear and listened. "I'm the man you met at Stingers. Will you please come and take your husband home. He's in bad shape."

No one had ever telephoned me from a bar regarding John's drunkenness.

Hearing honest distress in the man's voice, I replied, "Yes, I'll leave right now."

December 14, 1987, 4:45 P.M.

The man who had telephoned signaled me over as soon as I stepped through the entrance of Stingers. He stood up and escorted me to where John sat slouched, his head bent forward.

The cowboy shook him awake while insisting, "Go home with your wife."

Surprisingly, John attempted to stand up, but his motor coordination barely functioned. The man stabilized his body as it slipped sideways off his barstool. John pushed his arm away and staggered out the door. He made it to the car, opened the door, and plopped into the front seat, body parts spread in various, awkward positions. The two-mile drive up the curved road home was enough to torture the most stouthearted.

Unable to sit straight or hold his head upright, John's spat-sputtered garble babbled in tune with his desolate monologue. "Get your divorce papers in order and send in the life insurance money. I'm going to die."

At home, Cherisse and Tamara avoided their father's entry by hiding out behind closed bedroom doors. John shuffled past his daughters' rooms like someone on a chain gang, halting in the kitchen long enough to maneuver a beer out of the refrigerator. He completed his trek to the master bedroom by turning on the television and sliding his body down the end of the bed where it plummeted upon the floor.

Feebly trying to hold himself erect, he sat bobbing to the side. By allowing the foot of the bed to support his upper body, an exceedingly intoxicated man avoided falling over. I went into the kitchen and prepared a plate of food in hopes of soaking up some of the liquor. Then I went back into the master bedroom and placed the hot dinner on his lap.

"What's this piece of shit food," he gurgled, his mouth stuffed with mashed potatoes. "You don't care about me. No one cares about me."

Slobber and chunks of food dripped back onto his plate as he shoved huge globs into his mouth. It appeared as if he swallowed his food whole. Witnessing this eating style felt repulsive. I left the sight, stepped lightly into the family room, and turned on the television.

Cherisse and Tamara ventured out of their rooms and sat with me on the sofa where we watched James Stewart and Donna Reed in Frank Capra's *It's A Wonderful Life*. Our Christmas tree stood nearby waiting to be decorated the next day. We breathed in the tree's earthy fragrance, discussed its beauty, and congratulated ourselves for choosing such an exceptional specimen.

After the movie ended, I cleaned up the kitchen while Cherisse and Tamara dressed for bed. Following a tradition I began as soon as they could talk, I spent time with each daughter in her bedroom. The topic of conversation was each child's personal choice, her special time alone with me. Not only did this special time show my love and respect for them as individuals, it also developed the habit of constant and open communication, mother/daughter relationships of sharing ideas and emotions that would last a lifetime.

"Sweet dreams," was my night-night wish for two extraordinarily thought-out women, who it seemed only yesterday were my precious little girls.

After saying I love you, I shut their doors and bravely marched down the hall toward the master bedroom in quest of my nightgown. When I arrived, John remained on the floor propped up against the foot of the bed, head bent to the side, passed out. My entrance woke him up. He began to crawl toward the bathroom, drooling and garbling mumbo-jumbo. When he arrived, he stuck his head in the toilet, threw up, and passed out again. I left him on the floor at the foot of the toilet, thinking he might need to throw up again.

December 15, 1987, 1:00 A.M.

Concerned for John's safety, I had decided to sleep in the master bedroom. The next thing I knew a hand was shaking me out of sleep. Somehow, he had managed to lift himself up off the bathroom floor and make it to the bed.

"I called Fate two days ago. She told me I ruined her life," he groaned, self-loathing and long-suffering underscoring every syllable.

Sounding dismembered, he cried, "I'm not a man anymore. I haven't been able to get a hard-on for a month. No one will help me. I asked them all, Fate, my ex-wife. . . ."

Panic had hit John like a storm. He could not understand why he was in crisis when he had lived his life exactly how he had been taught, sooner or later reducing every experience to money or sex. Finally, all his material possessions and physical desires had backfired in a fate worse than death. The wall of tradition he believed was his holy grail had crippled his ability to get a *hard on*.

The incarnation of disrespect for all women, John treated me as if Diana was the whore leading the parade by pleading "Please have sex with me."

"No, John, I can't," I pleaded in return, defending myself from my husband's lust to dismember my emotions.

Echoing my state of mind just a few months earlier, decimated whimpers dangled from a man sinking in the quicksand of fear and panic. Whimpers told the story of the ravaged soul of a man fallen into the *no-penis abyss*. A man who had been given so many chances to light up the universe heaved forth the deepest poverty, poverty of the soul.

My soul recognized a life teetering in the balance of a man's miseries. Misery's deathly shrieks darted straight to the heart of my own experience. Fear and panic's echoes played their tune in my memory. The genocide of my husband's soul penetrated the genocidal chord he had sounded in me. This was obviously not the goal my husband had planned for Christmastime when we were supposed to "begin again." Whatever his plan when he jumped starry-eyed into his little yellow truck and drove away abandoning me, now five-months later the abyss oozed from my husband as he had caused it to ooze from me.

Hours passed with John repeating the same "Please have sex with me" WMD over and over and over.

My familiarity with the knowledge that his nuclear armament held for me the keys to death and hades, I repeated, "No, John, no" over and over and over.

That all the burning questions in life have nothing to do with sex or money, my husband had made it impossible for me to pour a deeper truth into a mind that was closed. Yet, if he remained in panic's ring of fire, he might burn alive. And witnessing cremation a second time my heart could not tolerate. So, although I repeatedly said "no," the tone of John's voice warned me not to leave his side.

December 15, 1987, 4:05 A.M.

After enduring hours of John's pleading, I implored wearily, "John, please let me sleep."

He refused.

"You have to help me get a hard-on or my life is over," he uttered, in eerily grave monotones.

From the same wounded heart I had worked so hard to fix in my mother, from my husband my heart heard, "Please help me, Diana."

Like Mother, John did not have the courage to walk through the valley I survived. Just as my mother's wounded heart had reached into my heart, my husband was begging my heart to save his life. My initiation had taught me that the same divine force flowed through John as flowed through me. It also taught me that a rite of passage from this cataclysmic experience required I find the courage to live divine truth. John's derision from his soul had flowed to his penis, simple as that. *The Philosophy the elixir*, my soul guided my connectedness with my husband's soul to end the blackness of his putrification.

Because I prayed his dreams might rise up when the new book of his life opened, my choice to save John's life was no choice. And because two hearts lay in the balance of my choice, by choosing to save his life, I saved my own life. My soul poured love into my heart as I reached over and gently placed a band-aid over my husband's wounded heart. I caressed the velvety penile skin I had denied myself for months. Almost immediately, its flaccid condition hardened.

Not surprised about the miracle true love supplied, I congratulated John for my soul's efforts, "I guess you can get a hard-on."

Because of my sacrifice, the no-penis abyss was not to become John's tragic end. Once again he could proudly wear his fig-leaf without a clue it protected the human democracy that cast out the promise of divine democracy.

December 15, 1987, 4:20 A.M.

I had barely dozed off when, again, I felt a hand shaking me out of sleep. The man was not satisfied.

"Please masturbate me," he pressed, desperation returning to his voice.

Every attempt to tell John "no" wasted more of the little energy I had left for the day ahead. Irrespective of my day, the word *no* caused John to feel punished. Just as John would not take *no* for punishment at three years old when he ran miles away from home in the snow, he would not take *no* for punishment from me. Regardless, that severely punished boy was so much alive in the man, he had no control over how *no* felt. Whimpers returned, tragic comedy driven by the helplessness of its rebellion against both of our souls.

Rebelling against the helplessness my husband once caused me, I refused to return to the servitude of the gender standard now enslaving him. Though I knew it was going to hurt, I had learned something from allowing my heart to be wounded to save my mother's wounded heart. I was required to risk an emotional holocaust to save my husband's wounded heart. Two souls hanging in the balance of my decision, I massaged John's penis until my hands were too tired to go on. Unable to ejaculate, he urged me to continue.

Barely able to enunciate the words, I appealed, "John, I'm tired. You have your hard-on. You're going to be fine. Please let me sleep."

December 15, 1987, 4:50 A.M.

Bill's and Adele's warning of danger ahead reared its prophetic head.

"I'll pay you to have sex with me. I can't live this way," he threatened.

The man whose children I had birthed kept me awake most of the night to proposition my body. As the new day was about to dawn, this time prostitution was the worm-hole John chose to try to kill the love in my soul. His soul now unrecognizable, the glory of sex being the sacred earthly union of the female/male principle, John's proposition had the intent of dividing the spirit of the female and male race into separate universes.

"I don't want your money to have sex, John," I petitioned, foggy and depleted.

The lack of compassion for the brutality of what he asked had reached its crowning point. Mind, body, heart, and soul, I starved for the comfort of sex, the closeness of sex, the touch of sex, and the release of sex. Mounting hunger for what I had denied myself for months, nonetheless, did not compare to the hideousness of John's request. My husband was asking if I wanted money to be raped. If I risked rape to save his soul, however, that selfless act would bring me closer to true virginity, the secret symbol of purity. Thus, my resolve to have intercourse was an act of pure giving.

John's body felt warm and sensual as I allowed him to lay it upon mine. His maleness did not take long to express itself, even with the condom he had conveniently ready after I insisted upon it. Orgasm and ejaculation completed, John rose, showered, and dressed for work. Upon leaving, he passed by the bed with a change of clothes draped over his arm. Arisen from the dead, he stood tall, ready to engage in the festivities of a man reborn.

As he passed by my bedside, with a snicker he gave me his regards, "I left some money for you on the bathroom sink."

After I heard his little yellow truck go bumpity-bump down the driveway, I got out of bed and walked into the bathroom. On the sink lay the backwater of his snickering, a folded twenty-dollar bill. . . .

No! I told myself. *This time death will not capture me. The flames in my soul refuse to ever be snuffed out again!*

My sacrifice gave a gift John might never understand, the gift of understanding, forgiveness, and compassion. Nevertheless, when he had slept away the intoxication of his poisoned chalice, he would welcome the rising sun of truth. By permitting my body to be used, I gave the greatest gift I had ever given anyone: life.

The dark tunnel pervading the act of rape was being consumed by a giant, powerful, spiritual emotion. The emotion came from divine grace. My divinity arose during one of the great trials of my life and demonstrated a *love* capable of overcoming an emotional holocaust. Feeling my soul in my physical senses empowered divine truth to flow through me: In spiritual reality our souls would eternally be one. That flood of spiritual light elevated my mind above the act of the rape of my body. The miracle of the wisdom inherent in my soul, no man could kill.

The flames of wisdom grew higher and higher. I hungered for life and love without John. I hungered to live free. I looked past the gray haze of my rape, toward the blackness of my crucifixion, across the valley of the shadow of my death, through the tunnel of my resurrection, and saw the light of Diana's truth. It was in the giving that I received the womb of mysteries. My soul had been forever uplifted by the life my body conceived. The gateway to eternal life, the vast colors of my spirit had been no illusion!

I turned my head toward four tall bathroom windows. Outside, the bird of paradise stood aflame in reds, oranges, yellows, greens, blues, and violets. White light emanated outwardly from within paradise to shine its perfection upon the world. I visualized my colors in the light of a new day: beautiful and strong, giving and receiving, child and adult, simple and wise, human and spirit.

My soul danced to the agony and ecstasy of my rape. My mind sang to the music heartbreak played. My love for my truth expanded with my song and dance. Outside the windows, past the bird of paradise, across Telly's pasture, and behind the rolling hills, a glorious, rising sun spoke.

Diana, today is your birthday. Today you are free!

God became human in order that we could become God.

– St. Athanasuis, ca. 296-373

24

We Speak Of Love

– US

December 15, 1987, 11:20 A.M.

I turned my car right and rounded the corner. The incomparable Pacific Ocean flooded my eyes. Light mirroring off the massive expanse of water captivated me with its imposing beauty. Nothing on earth had the power to steal the quickening I received from the harmonic ebb and flow of such a formidable intelligence. The waves off the southern coast of California that I had treasured all the days of my life revealed my savior.

Go to the places in nature you love. Face the sun. Sing of love and be happy, an automatic writing had seraphically reminded me of what in life made me feel whole.

Universal Spirit, the multitudes with whom I had connected in oneness nearly six months earlier, knew my heaven was a present reality in the Pacific Ocean. The living dynamic of those waters reveled in my flight of freedom from my husband, roared with delight, and reminded me that my life, life itself, moves in cycles of endless ebbing and flowing. Embedded in that harmonious equilibrium lay the extraordinary wisdom of my fall into freedom.

Naïve intuition transformed into enlightened thought, my initiatory passage from infinite mind into finite mind, then finite mind back into infinite mind, destined me to remove the shroud of obscurity keeping secret ancient truths. John and Diana were mere symbols of the well preserved myth of feminine and masculine being polar opposites. The popularization of *the gender gap* in modern society had served to progressively polarize *us* from each other, more importantly, from one-half of our own *androgynous soul*, the feminine half. Destined to raise her from the darkness of the dark ages of inequality into the light of the golden age of equality, I had found the deeper meaning of John's and my marriage. The light of the golden age would be found by bridging the gender gap and becoming *whole*, each within our own soul.

As discussed, all matter in the universe, seen and unseen, is reducible to atoms that contain a positively charged nucleus surrounded by negatively charge electrons. Contrary to being opposing forces, negative and positive *energies* in atoms complement each other, i.e., *negative*: darkness, yielding, concrete, receptive, unifying; *i.e., positive*: light, flowing, driving, initiating, dividing. Working as one, positive and negative energies are one whole and complete force (e.g., darkness and light, night and day, heaven and earth), as inseparably interdependent and interactive as ocean waves.

Nature had been my lifetime key to avoiding the shadow of the false teachings that stigmatized the gender gap as an unsolvable mystery. As one example of nature, the ebb and flow of ocean waves had always illustrated to me the obvious contradiction of the two genders being opposites, or even opposing forces. The beauty and wisdom of the female and male body synonymous with the ebb and flow of ocean waves are symbols of positive and negative atomic energy. Perpetually annulling the mystery and exposing the demonic untruth of gender gaps, the deeper meaning of female and male goes no deeper than the simple science of atoms.

No matter how sacred, no mystery can defy the natural law of atoms. Though the visible human body is compositioned as a division between female and male, the invisible body replicates atoms. Atoms are compositioned as the fusion of positive (masculine) and negative (feminine) energy that beautifully and wisely ebbs and flows in an eternal search for balance and harmony, which physicists have found to be *light*.

In their evolution toward *light*/en*light*enment, atoms *never die*.

They simply change configuration, and the *configuration* of photons or quantum of *light* in electrons is *infinite*. Enlightenment infinitely evolves in this way: Photons reconfigure themselves until they reach a point of balance and harmony where understanding of knowledge is found. Each point of *understanding* creates more *light*. That all light in the universe exists as waves, as each wave of *understanding* reaches its crowning point or peak, a reconfiguration of photons begins anew, eternally seeking a new peak of en*light*enment.

What began as miraculous, but later became no more complex than ocean waves, my *initiation* mirrored the science of light. Like the peak of a wave, each purification effected a rite of passage into greater understanding. Each understanding began a new wave in my evolution toward enlightenment. When I was initiated into enlightenment, I was initiated into the science of atoms: the equality of the feminine and masculine principle within my soul, complimentary energies I found to be ageless, timeless, limitless forces eternally seeking more light.

Less miraculous than humourous, a wave of my initiatory search for truth lead me to *The Egyptian Book of the Dead* translated by E. A. Wallis Budge. Budge interprets the hieroglyphics written on the papyrus of Ani, which date from B.C. 1500 to 1400. He explains that those Egyptian texts express the religious views of people who more than three-thousand years ago proclaimed the resurrection of a spiritual body and the immortality of the soul.

Three thousand or three million, when my soul inspired my hand to sketch a pyramid on a piece of paper, I discovered that I needed to search no further than the present to corroborate my initiatory journey. I learned that the great pyramid of Giza symbolizes the deeper meaning of life. Inscribed on the inner walls of the monument is the initiation. Temple walls lure the initiatory quest for truth. Through passageways of crisis, revelation, suffering, death, and resurrection into eternal life, hieroglyphics journey the ordeals of the awakening: *how the candidate is initiated into the oneness of forever.*

The initiation, natural law, modern physics, and ancient Egyptians agree that all matter (e.g., the human body), which is 99.99% empty space, can be converted into energy. Matter, a mask (e.g., illusion), is in reality a quantum field of energy full of creativity. Science, math, art, music, philosophy, the wonders of wisdom, and the beauty of imagination as expressions of individual purpose are all birthed from a unified consciousness that, on the deepest level is *one consciousness*. Thus, every thought, word, and deed of the individual effects the one consciousness, and the one consciousness effects the individual.

Philosophy, the science of divine-human, cause-effect relationships between the "one" and the "all" is what the initiation is all about. The Mother and Father of truth, philosophy serves to show that inspiration i.e., in spirit, is the origin of creativity. Light energy is spirit within matter. Thus all of *us* are initiated within our souls. For all life is light traveling in endless cycles of the regeneration and renewal so beautifully evidenced in ocean waves: the ebb and flow of those waves harbors the glorious simplicity of creation.

The androgynous fusion of positive and negative energies is what the human mind seeks and finds through the marriage of feminine and masculine forces in the soul. *To be* in search of two as one flesh is *to be* in search of the *whole living soul in the self*. The circle of life is the opportunity to free the self from the illusion that our inner being is separated into female and male so that the complete *wo/man* may forever partake of *soul paradise*, the meaning and purpose of life. To live in the world without seeking to understand meaning and purpose defies life itself, for the soul alone opens the door to the personal experience of eternal life.

Lost, then found, the second birth of my whole soul brought forth natural magic. Twice born, the second coming from the womb of solved mysteries, my soul shone its light on the divine fe/male I found all humanity to be heir. Twice inheritor of the garden before the fall, I understood the magic of Merlin. Though magical, I learned that second birth could not be made. It had to be earned. Light revealed her magic to those tried and initiated who earned the right to lift the shroud from the divine feminine so she could step up and stand face to face with the divine masculine!

The four horsemen of my initiation—fire, water, air, and trees— rose from *earth* to give me the energy to survive. The three kingdoms of my initiation—sun, moon, and stars—fell from *heaven* to give me the light of enlightenment. Though I fell from an infinite being into a finite being, the heaven and earth that drove my initiation shed light upon *The Philosophy*, turning finite back into infinite. Ever-present in my initiation was the ebb and flow of both paradise lost and paradise found.

When enlightenment brought her latent divinity out of her cave to fuse with him, balanced and harmonized were the polar opposites within myself, freeing me from the man whose polarized self had him trapped in the dark ages. That neither man nor woman can be enlightened without the androgynous fusion of the *fe/male*, birthed from that alchemical magic, the wholeness of my soul co-creating with my mind turned out to be the elixir of life, the banquet to which everyone is invited.

The cup overflowing with the soul's inexhaustible fountain of creativity, life's holy grail is sought and found in the marriage between the divine feminine and the divine masculine. Transparent golden sands are eternal streams of spiritual light in which the initiate passes on life's path toward that divine flame. Celebrated in a blaze of beauty and glory, the festival of the living soul was the true pot of gold that defined my fall into freedom!

December 15, 1987, 2:00 P.M.

Darlene rushed through the entrance of the ocean front restaurant, where I sat waiting. She placed an adorably wrapped present on my lap and burst out, "Happy Birthday, Diana!"

It was not the utterly incomprehensible explanation for being two-and-one-half hours late that tickled something inside of me about Darlene. It was her talent for telling a story. Darlene's account made being late sound mythologically courageous. The irresistible hypothetical involved her surprise companion, Dick.

She introduced him with stupendous speed and then changed the subject. "Have anything you want to eat, Diana. I have Don's credit card!"

Written all over Darlene and Dick was the sex they were keeping secret. Don had hit the bull's eye when he told me about his wife's affair and the fact she enjoyed the ride courtesy of his good credit.

Darlene, Dick, and I followed the waitress into the dining room. Crystal wine glasses scattered on Christmasy tables applauded the merry-making of the holiday season. Typically, Darlene talked nonstop.

With all her bemusing, her pretense about what she and Dick were doing during the time I waited could not diminish the love I felt for my treasured friend. My love, nonetheless, made looking at Dick a menacing experience.

Rather than talk about the recent events of my life of which I had not told Darlene, each time we were alone, I attempted to reach beneath her awkwardly naïve entanglement. "Darlene, the problems in your marriage you must work out with your husband. The wedding vows that you took in my home pledged your love and faithfulness to one man. The two of you are no more twain but one flesh, remember? By continuing this relationship with Dick, you dishonor your word. Think about the pain you are causing Don by all this time you're spending with Dick. Can't you see Dick is using your husband's money and your body to fill his selfish desires?"

Darlene discarded my sentiment mischievously. "Dick and I are just having a good time. Anyway, you don't know how Don treats me when we're alone. Don't *worry* Diana, Jesus is still my *savior*. He's still my *lord* and *master*."

In very few words, Darlene had *denied* her affair, *blamed* her adultery on her husband, and *used* lord and master as if words saved her from deeds. Applying her religion to anesthetize the spider web she wove magnified how dramatically six months of searching for truth had transformed my way of thinking. The psychological and spiritual shift in my intellect had opened my eyes to the reasons for my friend's woeful flight from her husband.

My search, which included direct and scholarly study of parts of the bible, convinced me that Jesus's mission was not to save Christians from reaping what they had sewn, but to be a living example of *the way* to God in the self. Jesus challenged people to think for themselves by preaching, *Is it not written in your law, I said,* **Ye are Gods***?* (John 10:34); *Seek and ye shall find* (Matt 7:7-8); *God is not the God of the dead, but of the* **living** (Matt 22:32).

A nearly perfect model of the catastrophe of biblical translations changing divine revelation into human exploitation, Darlene used a savior other than "ye" to pierce her heart and decimate her soul. At the expense of her divine self, not to mention her integrity, Darlene's *lord and master saved* her from the responsibility to seek reasons for her behavior, accountability for those reasons, and searching for an inner master rather than the outer master controlling her life. Blind faith never leading to the balance and harmony that comes with understanding, rather blind faith leads to the ignorance that sooner or later is paid for heavily. The crucifixion chained around Darlene's neck demonstrated how every time a great teacher of truth goes public, people stop worshiping God and begin worshiping the teacher, soon saying *he* is the only living God, which is scientifically and spiritually impossible.

In seeking I found truths clearly visible in Darlene's bible that were clearly invisible in her conduct. Defying the messenger, Darlene had forgotten the message; *Thou shall not commit adultery* (Matt 6:10); *. . . as ye did it not to the least of these, ye did it not to me* (Matt 26:45); *. . . by thy words thou shalt be justified, and by thy words thou shalt be condemned* (Matt 13:37).

With the intention of controlling the Christian mind, biblical translators invented Jesus's miracles to alienate the intelligent and impress the ignorant. Jesus-magic had succeeded in dumbing down Darlene's mind, stripping my longtime friend of the *free will to reason.* Juvenile interpretations created *no-reason legend* that maintained guardianship of her intellect by elevating faith above reason. Her mind completely in the control of religious dogma, she was a living example of the church's missionary to exploit Christians by crucifying the divine revelations of the kingdom within. The catastrophe for Darlene was that she had lost the ability and the desire to seek within to reason truth.

Because her mind had been closed before she learned to think for herself, her intellect was not open to historical accounts that describe how saviors unlimited had died for the sins of the many by the hands of the few. Divine-man perpetually slaughtered by animal-man, Christ's crucifixion symbolized all initiate/philosophers who were tried for heresy if they went public with the knowledge that latent divinity is in every *one, i.e., I AM the one.* These enlightened individuals taught that *Christos* was God imprisoned in every *body.* To be *christened,* i.e., to "resurrect" the eternal *one* was the first duty of the initiate. The "resurrection" of the imprisoned Christ, i.e., the soul, was the true meaning of *saved*. To the initiated/philosophers, the only hope for salvation was liberation from the imprisoned self by seeking and finding union with the immortal self. Union of the mortal self with the immortal self constituted immortality. Immortality signified the second coming of Christ, meaning the twice initiated soul.

Despite all the efforts of the philosophic elite to inform humanity that mortal-human received *deification* when s/he had found *at-one-ment* with the soul, their sacrifices were an assault on church wealth, i.e., power to control the mind of the masses. By killing the initiated/ philosophers, the church killed hope for salvation and continued the killings until almost all the initiated ones went into hiding by writing either under a pseudonym or in symbols (e.g., *The Holy Bible*) to disguise truth. Inevitably, the number of initiate/philosophers shrunk rather than grew, future multitudes paying the ultimate price.

The church's persecution of the immortal principle of every *one* with the agony of the mortality of every *body* blasphemed the course of civilization. When individual revelation was replaced by church doctrine, lost was the personal search for truth, closing the door to noble thoughts. The savior principle became the mental crutch for the many. *En-masse*, the price of separation from the soul was the condition of human suffering: fear.

For Darlene there would be no initiation, no enlightenment, no philosopher's stone. No magic Merlin would guide Darlene to develop the potential abilities latent in her soul. Exemplar of the church's need for collective suffering, instead of the pure gold of individual wisdom, the church succeeded in using Jesus to create medals of ignorance for Darlene. Saved from the ordeals of the awakening, a longtime friend had shrunken into the shadowy mind of infantilism for his namesake.

If the noblest quest is growing in the understanding and the living of truth, what Darlene learned from the church's misuse of power was that one man died so that the sins of all "mankind" should be magically forgiven. The church's lie hypnotized Darlene into believing she was safe from paying the price for the corruption of her flesh. Faith's supremacy over the supremacy of the soul had exchanged the gold of natural magic for church gold. Because the higher mind counts on the heart to determine the fate of the soul, though she had a well intended heart, Darlene's worship of an outside lord and master left her lower mind in control of her life.

Let no man worship any man nor give God aspects of man, for the kingdom of God is within. . . . Thy kingdom come thy will be done on earth as in heaven. . . .

Because the soul's savior is free will to reason an understanding of truth, Darlene's and Dick's savior magic would disappear as magically as it appeared. Dependence on an outer power rather than an inner power had left Darlene with no defense against her *follow the evil* flight from Don. Because her mind was closed off to the noble quest, my treasured friend did not know how to rise above the lower nature, her baser instincts driving her flight from freedom.

No, Darlene's husband was not to *blame* for the affair she *denied.* To blame for that "something missing" in her life was meaning and purpose. Her free will impoverished, Darlene was on the brink of moral bankruptcy. The biological, psychological, and spiritual violence of being dependent on words she believed saved her from deeds had Darlene standing on the precipice of the big black hole of blind faith.

Though lighting the candle of my soul voice had cast a giant shadow upon a dear friend, getting between her and her savior would break the bond we shared. The collapsing attempts I made to rescue the marriage of two close friends turned out to be far more meaningful for me than Darlene's unfaithful song and dance. From my capacity to triumph over my return to Armageddon while simultaneously striving to be there for another came a feeling of tremendous inner glory.

I took one final glance at the glorious Pacific Ocean and turned my car left toward the freeway. With all emotion suspended in holiday mirth, my car lead the way home. The closer to home my car drove, the more mirthful my visions became. This year, Cherisse, Tamara, and I had decided to decorate our Christmas tree on my birthday. I envisioned my precious daughters waiting just for me with boxes of ornaments ready to be hung, Frank Sinatra singing Christmas carols, and, naturally, smiling faces.

I honked twice as my car pulled between two completed gray stone pillars at the bottom of the front steps. Out of the house ran the two miracles born unto me. Each miracle grabbed a hand and led me into the nook. On the table lay birthday presents, decorations, and a birthday cake.

Cherisse burst out with pride, "Mom, I made the cake myself!"

My heart leapt, my joy unsurpassed. It was the most beautiful birthday cake I had ever seen!

December 25, 1987, Christmas

Every Christmas of Cherisse's and Tamara's lives had been spent with John's family. As far as I knew, no one in his family knew anything about his affair or my breakdown. Knowing nothing was the way I wanted John's family to remain when I invited them to our house for Christmas 1987.

The holiday brought the opportunity for Cherisse and Tamara to have what intuition told me would be their last holiday celebration with the relatives they grew up knowing. Cherisse's, Tamara's, and my mutual aspiration to give the world *The Philosophy* as a *model of psychological and spiritual enlightenment* would not fit comfortably with John's family's Catholic beliefs.

John's family was a reflection of a part of me that initiatory fires had burned at the stake. They wore the uninitiated mask of the patriarchal hierarchy. John's father ruled the family, and from day-one "the old man," as John called his father, was full of judgment for what Diana symbolized in the Catholic Inquisition.

More than five-hundred years after Jesus's crucifixion, the Catholic Inquisition converted the world from matriarchal paganism to patriarchal Christianity. The Inquisition translated *Goddess Diana*, the symbol of the divine feminine, into a courtesan, commonly called whore. Waging a campaign of propaganda to demonize the sacred female, the Inquisition obliterated the goddess from modern religion. For three-hundred years the world was indoctrinated about the evils of free-thinking, free-spirited women.

To assure male dominance, church elite taught the clergy how to capture, torture, and murder female scholars, nature lovers, and herb gatherers. You name it; five million women deemed suspiciously attuned to the nature of their souls were burned at the stake. Midwives, for example, were killed for the heretical practice of applying their medicinal knowledge to ease the pain of childbirth, a suffering the church claimed was God's rightful punishment for Eve's original sin of partaking of the fruit of knowledge.

The divine feminine and the divine masculine that were celebrated by pagans as the two halves of the whole (self) necessary for enlightenment had been cut in half. One-half of the whole was banished from the world. The church remodeled sexual union between the body of man and the body of women to be shameful, making the seductions of the female body the work of the devil. By design, the con-game decimated half of the souls necessary for planetary enlightenment. The contrived misuse of knowledge was so dark, to this day the sacred feminine is vanquished from the earth, killing the latent divinity of almost every wo/man on the planet.

The father's mind controlling the son's mind long before the son's wife entered the picture, the old man raged to kill John's wife's free-spirited nature. The father's killing took the form of blaming courtesan Diana for John's not making it on the PGA tour. Handed down from father to son was the inquisition of blame instilled in John's mind that Diana ruined his career. John failed to be successful because after he hit a bad shot he choked, just like his father choked the free spirit out of the son.

What was the simple truth of who killed our marriage? The death of two as one flesh was the polarity between my father's voiced love for the sacred in me and my husband's father's silent hate for the sacred in me.

With all that, it would have been improbable for John's family's imagination to ponder that Cherisse, Tamara, and their mother had become enlightened women with a oneness of purpose.

A *DCT trinity* with a collective consciousness based upon Diana's revelations and inspirations undoubtedly would be considered heresy to a family spoon-fed by patriarchal standards. Integral to the immeasurable work ahead, it would be mandatory for Cherisse, Tamara, and me to keep *The Philosophy* secret until the book was published. Though we understood the road ahead would be no less steep, thorny, and beset with perils of every kind than the road behind, we had gained the wisdom to know that our perilous journey would lead to the very soul of humanity. Wisdom would give *us* the courage to stay the course. Secrecy would safeguard our

Philosopher's stone.

Notwithstanding Cherisse's and Tamara's last Christmas with their father's family, John needed his family's support beyond measure. He had put so much hard work into our home and property, I felt his family's appreciation and encouragement might help him through one of the most critical periods of his life: mid-life crisis. My hope was that his family would appreciate, support, and encourage his achievements.

A happy heart arose with me early Christmas morning. Already taking pleasure in the giving I would partake of all day, I became curious about what my automatic writing might say. I picked up my pencil and wrote. What came through into my hands was a direct, unimpeded transfer of thoughts, clearer than ever before. The lucidity of this particular writing got me thinking about Universal Spirit, the authors of words that forever changed my life. Had I not connected with the self-described multitudes who were also me one month before my breakdown, I would not have fallen into the enlightenment that set me free from fear. But what was *Universal Spirit?* Who exactly was the miracle of *US?*

When I emptied my consciousness, instantaneously entered into me was a supremely loving, all-knowing consciousness. From *one* voice with no shadowy side, every message I wrote had a happily-ever-after plan prepared just for me. After my first automatic writing, any place, any time I wanted, I could allow the finite nature of my mind to evaporate into the infinite nature of my mind and bridge the separation between my consciousness and a consciousness filled with timeless, ageless, infinite wisdom.

It was not until years after my first automatic writing I learned that all atoms, including those in the human body, are made of *light* and light is *infinite* and has *unlimited energy.* Later I learned that light is *the only reality in the universe* and is *aware of* and *communicates with* its surroundings. This meant that light is *consciousness.* Not only that, the discovery that light, which operates outside of time and space, can travel anywhere in the universe backward or forward in time *faster than the speed of light.* Not only does light *never age,* astonishingly it seems to have a plan, *a divine plan!* Timeless, ageless, tireless, infinite, ever-expanding in all directions, light was the *one* consciousness that filled the whole universe, a *supreme being.* A light-being that could be anywhere instantaneously, exactly like my automatic writings!

A ten-cent book I had forgotten buying, that somehow found its way under my bed, guided me to the rainbow-bridge between my consciousness and universal consciousness. Mind, body, heart, and soul, I had learned *to be one* with the *one consciousness* that filled the whole universe. The ability to directly connect with the collective voice of the multitude of consciousness had been given to me. I had broken through to the other side! Two worlds, one visible, one invisible, met in oneness to show me *the way* to come out of the shadow of illusive reality into the light of true reality.

Even more astonishing, scientifically the separation I broke through did not exist. Since light was the *only* reality in the universe, separation was not possible! Matter, 99.99% empty space, was really an illusion! Like an actor's mask worn for creative purposes, the body was a mask for the creative purpose of the soul who designed it.

This, of course, confirmed there was no separate "God as a father" who lived in some far off kingdom. The source of humankind as *one* consciousness with a *divine plan* proved a "God" separate from "light" was scientifically and spiritually impossible. Separation an illusion, a separate "god" impossible, there was here and here was there. The "other side" was right here on earth!

This, too, proved the first original sin causing the fall of humanity was fiction! Mythological stories interpreted by man to be the one and only *word* of God were designed to create separation, which created the fear of God i.e., the soul. From personally bridging that separation, I had gained the knowledge of good and evil. *Good* was that the *one* consciousness, or the one and only *word* of God, was right here in us, mind, body, heart, and soul. And since the conditioning of separation created fear, separation was the one and only sin, the epitome of *evil.* Lie becoming truth and truth becoming lie, the "mask" of matter became a world stage for the darkness of separation rather than a world stage for the light of *one* consciousness.

Still, the world has more than hope for a global shift from material to spiritual because in the body lies all the treasures of the divine plan.

Just as the one consciousness that fills the universe had sought me by-way of a tiny book, the higher consciousness forever seeks expression in the lower consciousness. According to the *divine plan* of human evolution, the last judgment is for each *one* of *us* to break through matter. To be revealed to all humanity is the truth that mind, body, heart, and soul, we are all divinely endowed with the power of God, for God is light. In the *end of time* we will be transformed by alchemical magic into the *kingdom of enlightenment*, the *light* that *reigns supreme*.

When the higher vibration of spirit becomes integrated with the lower vibration of matter, miracles happen. With the *second coming of the living soul* of humankind, we will become *one-spirit-indivisible*. As *one consciousness*, each *one* of *us* will have the power of good over evil. The *evil* that showed the way to fear will be magically transformed into the *good* that shows the way to life everlasting.

When I broke through matter, I broke through to the *one living God* who is also *us*. When the door opened to wisdom, eternity, and divinity, the festival of the living soul unfolded in full splendor. Divine oneness transformed the ordinary back into the extraordinary in the unrelenting sun of understanding, forgiveness, and compassion. I had found my rainbow-bridge to the multitudes who were also me.

Automatic writing confirmed my belief as a child. Earth has always been and still is the Garden of Eden. For as it was in the beginning of time, *one* consciousness incarnated souls into individual bodies, sinless, ageless, timeless, infinite strands of light glorified in a garden of Paradise. The kingdom of radiance destined to be revealed on earth in *the end times, one is all and all is one*. The sovereignty of the eternal over the temporal will be revealed in every *one*, for we are the kingdom without end.

So, who is *Universal Spirit?* Only an energy frequency away, *US* is *us* . . . the *one* consciousness that fills the universe . . . the *one* light . . . the *one* voice . . . the *I AM that has always been and forever shall be*. . . .

I looked down and read my automatic writing. Overjoyed, the Christmas message was not just for me. The *words* were for everyone! Feeling like one of Santa's elves, I typed the good tidings on a sheet of green paper and taped it on the dolphin-shaped mirror above the wet-bar in the family room. My 1987 Christmas message from *Universal Spirit* was as follows:

> *Merry Christmas, May your blessings be the ones that fill your hearts with the gladness that brings the soul upward into the shining light of the universe's bountiful love. You are powerhouses of love. You can do anything with your power of love. Your love can heal. Your love can destroy. Love is meant to do all good things for all people. Love used to destroy will destroy the soul of the user. God's powerful universal energy source used for good can produce everything imaginable. But the greatest thing it can produce is healing. Love someone and you will heal that person of their loneliness and pain. Love someone and you can alter that person's life and the way s/he feels about herself or himself forever. Love humanity as a whole and you can change the world and bring peace on earth. Forgive yourselves and you will walk on the white sands with us in paradise. Once you forgive yourselves, you forgive humankind. You are all one. True love comes from true forgiveness of self and what you see as the errors of others. When you let your problems and guilts go, you also let those of others go. Then you will find the beautiful purity of love that warms the heart until there is so much happiness and joy you will know you are meant to take those steps into paradise! Pray for world peace, world love, and have a wonderful Christmas.*
>
> – US

The message went unmentioned by everyone except John's younger sister Karen, who remarked, "The writing on the mirror is nice."

If anyone else read my automatic writing, I was not aware of it, for no one said a word. Still, the conspiracy of silence ruling John's family represented not only what was missing but also what was present. Though the unspoken caves of the Inquisition had sovereign power over John's family, underlying the fear of God they suffered for the sake of their faith lay the same divine force that flowed through me and my children. And though the words of appreciation for John I hoped for never came, I understood that his family expressed their love and support by simply being there. After all, being there was one dance of divine benevolence.

December 26, 1987, 10:05 A.M.

John's family had packed and were ready to leave. In those final minutes before they departed, I took John's mother's hand, led her into the den, and closed the door.

I spoke in quiet, respectful tones. "John and I are going to get a divorce. He's moving out before the New Year."

Her eyes glazed over and took on a far away look filled with wonder; from a place deep inside, a place John's mother had not revealed to me in more than eighteen years, she spoke her truth. "John was the apple of my eye. He was so good looking."

As John's mother voiced the passion for her son she had kept secret, the flushed pink on her cheeks and the dream-like wonder in her eyes became unexpectedly familiar. It was the same glistening pink and dream-like gaze I saw on her son's face, but not the day he told me he loved Fate. The roots of this look penetrated far deeper than infatuation. It dug down to the depths of his soul. The look I remembered was the one that radiated from John's face the day he married me.

I listened to his mother's heart, the intelligence of my heart questioning, *Didn't you know that John was the apple of my eye too?*

My mother-in-law naïvely continued, "You and John were never meant for each other."

Neither John's father nor his mother chose to be there the day their son married me. So she could not have seen the look on her son's face when he gazed at his bride with wonder. Following our wedding, she never allowed herself to accept that I might have been the apple of her son's eye or the depth of my love for him. She never grew to understand the reasons John and I were meant for each other. Experience had not taught her that because people change, the reasons they are meant to be together at one time might be the very reasons they are not meant to be together another time. Even though my mother-in-law waited eighteen years to tell me her truth, I believed in her soul she knew John and I were meant for each other.

I stood on the front porch until every person in John's family waved his and her last goodbye, and then I walked back into the house. I spotted John in the master bedroom zipping up his cement-encrusted jeans. As he sped past me toward the garage to get his shiny new red wheelbarrow, I stopped him, "John, I told your mother we're going to get a divorce."

He charged in retaliation. "Diana, you haven't done anything for eighteen years."

Plato wrote of men who confined their entire lives to a dark cave, their eyesight only revealing the shadows cast from a fire on cave walls, while Socrates spoke of the justice, beauty, and good in the world dimly visible to the senses.

The happiest man on earth would look into the mirror and see himself exactly as his is, his every heart's desire come true. Driven mad by the sadness of not knowing the man in the mirror, John could think of nothing more than to project his shadow onto me. Though there was no magic in John's mirror, written on the sands of time the love we shared would live on forever. Did I believe this man in his soul wanted to hurt me? Never! His soul rose me up to light the flame in the middle of the pyramid of the *The Philosophy!*

The sound of a door blown shut by a sudden breeze diffused any hurt feelings that may have arisen from the injustice of *words*. I turned my head, looked out the kitchen window, and saw the stillness of a beautiful southern California day. In my view stood a tree. A leaf detached itself from a branch, floated gently in the air, quietly twisted and turned, finally rested upon the earth.

The tree reminded me of who I was. *Diana, let me sing you my song and you will never be alone.*

Δ

Once upon a time, in my childhood, I felt free to dream. I dreamed of growing up and being happy. I did not understand why all people did not dream of being happy. I went into the forest and wandered among trees. I loved trees. They taught me that happiness lies in being free. Their gift of truth gave me a reason to live. No matter where I went as I grew up, trees were everywhere. Together, trees and I united in a bubble of happiness.

When I grew up, I did not understand why the man I married criticized, ostracized, and tried endlessly to burst my bubble. I fortified the greatest gift of my life with two little bubbles. I called them Cherisse and Tamara. Together the three of us united as one in a bubble of love. Still, my husband pierced relentlessly at our bubble as if it were his enemy. I did not understand why anyone would want to kill freedom.

Until I fell, I did not understand . . . that the question in my mind . . . was my answer . . . *to be or not to be.* . . .

My fall was required. When dark forces transgressed my light-filled bubble, my freedom was silenced. In the silence, the multitudes within my soul arose to tell me why the multitudes on earth did not dream of being free.

When I fell, I became one with the loneliness and fear that resulted from the pain oozing from wounded hearts. I found myself trapped in a world where men and women created a stage on which they played out illusionary dramas. Their mythological *Garden of Evil* dramas metaphorically imitated the violent abandonment they were attempting to escape, the violence created by worldwide corporate powers who idolized money, despised love, and produced win/lose wars for the purpose of controlling, shaming, and weakening the soul of the "less fortunate" multitudes.

While my wounded heart imprisoned my freedom, I came to understand the evil I experienced at the hands of my husband and his lover. Twin Satans in male and female form were tiny icons of a powerful elite whose greed and lust modeled the loss of morality, integrity, responsibility, and spirituality. That high echelon of political and religious Satans celebrated a material savior who saved the multitudes from reaping what they had sown. Satan's materialistic standard demanded the separation between the self and the soul. Materialism dropped humanity into a world chained by the loneliness of separation and the fear of reaping what it had sown. Imprisoned by the shadows of loneliness and fear, humanity lost its freedom.

Yes, my fall was required. Until I understood evil as the desperate cry of multitudes crucified by ignorance of their soul and fear of their deeds, I did not know why John wanted to burst my bubble and kill freedom. Until I fell, I did not understand why the multitudes lost their dream of being free. Until I learned *not to be* . . . my bubble had no voice.

Δ

And it came to pass a child was born December 15, 1946. She was born on her mother Marie's birthday, and her mother named her Diana Marie. Diana Marie was not unlike other children. She had a light-filled bubble encircling her. As other children grew up and their bubbles burst and grounded in matter, Diana's bubble miraculously remained floating. It encircled her like a protective rainbow of colorful lights.

When my bubble burst and grounded in matter, I knew I needed to seek myself before fear wounded my heart. I sought my youngest self and found a child of pure love. I remembered how good it felt for my heart to find love in all things.

Then, I heard the voice. At first, I did not recognize the voice. It felt beautiful, beyond my wildest imagination. The voice loved me more, understood me better, and felt more powerful than anything I had ever known.

At first, the voice seemed like a miracle. As time passed, the voice became more and more familiar. Then one day, I understood who the voice was. The voice was the wisdom and power who guided me to trees, who told me it was my natural-born right to live free, who encircled me like a bubble, who led me to psychological and spiritual truths, who had always been the light at the end of the tunnel.

Wisdom and power was the silent inner voice who had been waiting . . . waiting for fate . . . fate who would come like an angelic force . . . to open a window . . . to clear my way home . . . home to my feelings . . . home to my destiny . . . home to my soul . . . home to divine spiritual nature . . . home to the multitudes. . . .

Find yourself and you will find humanity, spoke my awakened voice.

Find your soul and you will find divinity, spoke my awakened voice.

Find divinity in yourself and you will find divinity in humanity, spoke my awakened voice.

At last, I knew who the voice was! What was once the silent voice of a protective bubble that encircled me like a rainbow of colorful lights became the awakened voice of my soul speaking to me of my truth. My truth spoke of my love for the freedom to have a dream.

You see, a bubble that encapsulates a person is the soul manifesting love in all things. And when an individual gets separated from his or her soul, freedom becomes a lost dream. But when one soul awakens to shine its light upon humanity, that is when one voice gets . . . *TO BE.*

The voice of my soul was my answer, *I AM.*

Δ

December 31, 1987, 8:00 New Year's Eve!

Lights were strung up everywhere at Stingers. New Year's hope charmed the air. Hats, noisemakers, and confetti lay on each table and across the bar. My eyes dazzled when I peeked in the door, glimpsed the festive atmosphere, and spotted one empty barstool at the far end of the bar waiting just for me.

As I crossed the crowded room, I beheld the glowing faces I passed. Each face glowed brighter than the face before. I eased onto my barstool, taking in the energy of spirits so high, it made friends out of a room full of strangers.

A young man on the barstool to my right greeted me with, "Happy New Year."

We started talking, and as the evening approached midnight, I felt I had been placed in that exact spot for a specific purpose.

Hopelessness filled almost every corner of the young man's voice. "Since I was a little boy I wanted to be a photographer, but I wasted my youth. Now, I'm twenty-eight and find myself working all day long and barely earn enough money to pay my bills. Breaking into the photography industry requires a history of successes. I have nothing to show for all the years of my life."

My New Year's Eve companion's self-reproach touched my heart. His vision of himself at such a young age had narrowed to the degree he believed his dreams had passed him by. The thought had never entered his mind that his dreams had already come true.

"You are the luckiest of men," I offered earnestly. "Your dreams have mental shape, form, and substance. The gift of knowing your passion was given to you in your youth. Learning to live those dreams is your holy grail. All you have to do is risk the first step. The second, third, and forth steps will appear before your eyes. Perhaps all the steps you take will be risks, but those risks will lead you to your very heart's desire!"

"What do you mean?" he asked, the intelligence of his heart surfacing to his throat.

"Save every little bit of money you can afford," I answered. "Buy an inexpensive second-hand camera. The big expensive equipment will come when you have earned it. Take pictures of everything that interests you. Don't worry about what anyone thinks. Seeking your individual voice will lead you to success. Don't be afraid of finding your truth. It is your ticket to freedom. And always remember, realizing your dream is a process, not a sudden event."

After I spoke, I realized the loving support I offered freely and fearlessly came from my heart, my mind, and my soul. Suddenly the young man seemed to be filled with enthusiasm. He talked and talked about how he had always loved photography. I continued to listen with an open mind, trusting heart, and loving soul.

When I felt it was the right time to speak, my response had been well thought out. "Every time you have a free minute, go alone into the world. See outside of yourself with curious, sensitive eyes. The feelings behind your eyes will discover a world of marvelous diversity. Study the wonders of diversity and learn the way your vision interprets it. Actualizing one individual vision is a learned, practiced, evolving skill. Day by day your individual style will grow in shape, form, substance, and depth. Your growth as a human being will be the key to freeing your dreams because your pictures will be you, the mirror of who you are. Begin right away. Start by building a history of pictures. Chronicle your pictures in a portfolio and watch them mature in quality, depth, spirit, and. . . ."

Noisemakers interrupted my words of wisdom. I gazed around the room.

Everyone was yelling, "Happy New Year!"

Hats had been placed on heads, horns were blowing, and confetti turned the air into a shower of colorful snowflakes. People were kissing and hugging, roaming around the room, and kissing and hugging some more.

Surprised, I turned my head back toward my companion. Four hours felt like a few minutes. The stranger who had become a friend stared at me unconcerned that 1987 had turned into 1988. I saw and felt a powerful force of light steaming from his face and head. The light contained amazing currents of energy. The nearly electric energy was directed straight into my eyes.

He explained the change in him. "As far back as I can remember, no one cared enough to talk with me the way you have tonight. You don't know how much I have to thank you for. You don't know what you've done for me." Then the young man of fond heart repeated over and over, "Thank you, thank you, thank you!"

He paused and remained staring at me as if he felt sure I held the keys to a magic kingdom.

Stardust lighting up the feelings in his eyes, he spoke. "You're an angel! You must be an angel!"

Voices around us rang out in unison. "Should old acquaintance be forgot and never brought to mind? Should old acquaintance be forgot in days of Auld Lang Syne? For Auld Lang Syne, my dear, for Auld Lang Syne. . . ."

Sparkles of New Year present surrounded me, consummately satisfying my every breath. The simple act of opening a door had made me one with the passing parade of life. All the experiences of my life flowed into that one moment, the moment when another human being told me I had given him back his dream.

Sitting on a barstool at Stingers, I looked around at all the singing people and wondered, *What do angels do?*

I thought about Mother and Daddy and *how they had been there for me with unconditional love.* I thought about Ruth, Kassy, and Dutch, and the *small miracles* of their advice. I thought about Darren and Gina and *tearing down walls.* Then I thought about Darlene and Don, even Dick, and *the way each of our behaviors affects the whole universe.* I thought about Bill's *wisdom,* Adele's *warmth,* and a stranger's *gentle nature.* I thought about Susan and *cheered our sisterhood.*

Happily, I guessed, *I'll bet I know what Cherisse and Tamara are doing right this second. They're singing Auld Lang Syne, kissing and hugging, roaming around a crowded room, and kissing and hugging some more.*

Then I thought about John, and wondered, *What did he do with that old corroded wheelbarrow?*

I looked again at all the singing people. I concentrated on the atmosphere. I listened to the air.

The multitudes were singing, *We'll sip a cup of kindness yet for Auld Lang Syne.*

And the answer came. . . .

It is love!

All humanity is governed by one law, the law of
cause and effect in moral, mental, and spiritual affairs.
— William Fix, *Lake of Memory Rising*

To order books, schedule television appearances,
radio/magazine interviews, and speaking engagements with
Diana Marie Weitzel,
contact:

WSOL Publishing
P.O. Box 1121
Cardiff by the Sea, CA 92007-1802

Phone toll-free: (888) 360-2617

info@fallintofreedom.com
www.fallintofreedom.com